American History from a Global Perspective

American History from a Global Perspective

An Interpretation

DAVID J. RUSSO

Jon L. Wakelyn, Advisory Editor

PRAEGER

Westport, Connecticut
London

Library of Congress Cataloging-in-Publication Data

Russo, David J.
American history from a global perspective : an interpretation / David J. Russo.
p. cm.
Includes bibliographical references and index.
ISBN 0–275–96896–0 (alk. paper)
1. United States—History. 2. United States—Historiography. 3. National characteristics, American. 4. United States—History—Cross-cultural studies. I. Title.
E179.R97 2000
973'.07'2—dc21 99–054650

British Library Cataloguing in Publication Data is available.

Library of Congress Catalog Card Number: 99–054650
ISBN: 0–275–96896–0

First published in 2000

Praeger Publishers, 88 Post Road West, Westport, CT 06881
An imprint of Greenwood Publishing Group, Inc.
www.praeger.com

Printed in the United States of America

The paper used in this book complies with the Permanent Paper Standard issued by the National Information Standards Organization (Z39.48–1984).

10 9 8 7 6 5 4 3 2 1

For My Mentor,
RICHARD H. BROWN

Contents

Preface

I have written an "interpretive text." By "interpretive," I mean that in this book I have presented compressed analyses of the major aspects of the lives of those who have identified themselves as "Americans." The "parts" and chapters that this book is divided into can be read separately, as independent chapters. But, they are also fully interrelated, and, in their totality, I offer them as a systematic examination of the ways we can investigate the Americans through historic time. This topical approach fragments our view of the history of Americans, and I repeatedly retrace a four century-long time frame or chronology in my investigation of each dimension of their lives. By "text," I mean that this book offers a comprehensive, if not encyclopedic coverage of its subject and does so, in the time-honored manner of history textbook authors everywhere, without the apparatus of notes and references.

The contents of this book are synthesis of the scholarship of a large number of academic historians, as well as political scientists, economists, sociologists, anthropologists, and geographers. I would like to express my gratitude to these largely unnamed scholars whose writings I have drawn on in various ways over many years, first as ingredients and sources for my courses in U.S. history at McMaster University for the past thirty-five years, and, since the 1980s, as the basis for a new conceptualization and interpretation of U.S. history that, after many drafts and reconfigurations, has emerged as this book. I would also like to thank those colleagues in many of the humanities and social science departments at McMaster who shared with me their insights into the nature of the scholarship in their disciplines. Finally, I gladly take this opportunity to say how much the support of Jon L. Wakelyn, Advisory Editor at Greenwood, has meant to me. This is the third time that Jon has shown his faith in my efforts to reconceptualize and reinterpret U.S. history, the most written about of all the historical "fields of study." I am deeply grateful for that support.

Introduction

What follows is a thorough reimagining of an historical field of study, a full-scale reinterpretation of the most written about of all historical fields. My account is based on three and a half decades of teaching a survey course in U.S. history from outside of the United States, in neighboring Canada. The outside perspective that Canada offers has been of crucial importance to my long and growing desire to recast the mold of U.S. history, to see it anew from afar. My proclivity to want to observe the American past in larger contexts derives directly from my location outside of the nation. Born an American, I have nonetheless shared the perspective of those not Americans. Outsiders are more apt to discount claims of distinctiveness, to critically evaluate national myths and apologias.

The influence of the outsider's perspective has commingled in me with a desire to synthesize, to generalize, to find new meanings in the work of the huge number of academic historians whose field is U.S. history, a number that dwarfs all other groups attached to historical fields. *Families and Communities* (1974), *Keepers of Our Past* (1988), and *Clio Confused* (1995) are all efforts to examine anew the scholarship of those who have written academic or amateur accounts of aspects of the American past.

The account that follows is my own effort to reconfigure the American past in the light of the perceived shortcomings of previous synthesizers, that is, textbook authors. Textual accounts are quite detailed and highly descriptive; the presumption is that college and university students must be introduced to the field through the presentation of specific information that occasionally leads to analytical points. I have "flipped" this process and have presented an account that is highly analytical and interpretive and have proceeded with the presumption that readers are already aware of the events and personalities and developments that are so typically at the heart of texts.

The reason is that I want to appeal directly to fellow historians, more advanced students, and high school teachers, as well as to anyone who wants to extend his or her analytical or interpretive reach in an effort to understand the American past. I believe that if the old mold, fixed for so long in text after text, is to be broken, someone should point the way, and the most effective way is to appeal directly to those who are in a position to assess what I attempt to do here and possibly to offer their own alternative ways of presenting U.S. history.

Therefore, each part of the text that follows should be read as a brief analytical, interpretive overview of its subject, and not a fully detailed presentation. It is important to keep this in mind, because I regularly presume at least some prior familiarity with the subject at hand. In various "parts," I have presented syntheses of particular subjects in order to get at their essence. In this way, I hope I have clearly presented my own compressed assessment of the history of Americans and America, especially as that history appears from a global perspective.

The units that follow are without notes, in the usual manner of synthesizers, surveyors, and textbook authors. Like them, I have sought common ground, not historiographical battlefields. Keenly aware of the always-jagged edge of academic inquiry, I have nonetheless attempted to let my text reflect my ongoing assessment of what constitutes an accurate consensus of that which scholars collectively know, can agree upon knowing. I have tried to synthesize and to assess that knowledge, to bring together the burgeoning scholarship on an ever-greater number of historical subjects crowded across the nonpolitical dimensions of human life, and, to do so in what I believe is a novel way.

This study is based upon my overall assessment of the scholarship written since the 1960s from an American perspective, but more particularly on recent writings that deal with America from a translational perspective, scholarship produced both by historians and by social scientists—geographers, anthropologists, economists, sociologists, political scientists—who have also written from a translational or even a global perspective. The value of this study lies in the fresh ways I interpret the past as a result of examining the work of many scholars from many disciplines. The writings of these scholars have been my "evidence," and I hope that I have presented their insights in an accurate and truthful manner.

In order to do this effectively, I have given equal emphasis and attribute equal importance to all the major aspects of the lives of those people we identify as Americans. I examine all the ways "America" has been defined historically: politically, most obviously, but also economically, socially, culturally, and geographically. The political definition is the most basic or fundamental in that, without it, there would be no "America" or "Americans." Like other national political groups, Americans created a nation and occupied a national territory. But, once again, like other national political groups, Americans have believed that they have created an "American" economy, society, culture, geography.

However, because the nonpolitical aspects of American life have differing shapes and sizes, I have not confined my treatment of them to the territory of the United States. In fact, I have shown that in the nonpolitical aspects of their lives Americans either shared patterns that cover larger areas than their own nation, or were divided into regional and local patterns. In order to do this, I have had to develop an awareness of historical developments beyond the nation, in other parts of the globe, in Middle and South America, Asia, Africa, Europe. I have had to place life in America in wider and narrower contexts, all the way from localities and regions to continents, hemispheres, and the globe itself.

My text is in the form of units dealing with each of the significant historical meanings of "America" and "Americans," units that are in turn subdivided into various topics. This "topical" approach is analytical in the fullest sense—my overall subject has been shredded apart and examined from many different angles. I have therefore avoided a chronological treatment, going over the same chronological time frame in each unit. To treat a subject with as many dimensions as this one chronologically is especially difficult in any case, more difficult than textbook authors of American history have acknowledged, in the sense that each aspect of a people's life does not change in lockstep fashion with all the others. A cataclysm in politics may not seriously affect economic, social, or cultural life. Conversely, important developments of an economic, social, or cultural kind may not be reflected in significant political change.

This means that periodization that makes sense in one dimension of life doesn't work for another. American political developments divide into periods extending through the colonial period, through the Revolution and the making of the Constitution, through the Civil War, through the Great Depression, through the present. I have referred to these events in many of the units. But, economic life is best periodized with breaks that mark the onset of industrialization (1815), the coming into prominence of corporations with continental dimensions (1890), and the loss of America's post–World War II economic preeminence (1970). Still another time scheme best fits the evolution of American society, with one period ending with the emergence of "egalitarianism" for white men as the dominant social value (1830), and another period beginning in 1920, with the progressive application of that value to white women, native tribesmen, and black men and women. Similarly, American culture can best be periodized with breaks at 1830, with the broadening of high culture to include the middle class, and at 1920, with the onset of technology as the conduit for cultural activity of all kinds.

* * *

From their beginning, Americans have always believed that the United States has been a special, favored nation. This belief has fostered a parochial, inward-looking mentality. Americans have been unusually unaware of the rest of the world. Of all the political entities that have attained dominance over large parts of the world, the United States is the only one that has never had a significant empire. With minor exceptions, Americans have lacked the experience of governing others, of administering subservient political dominions, unless the western territories across the North American continent be counted as "empire." This lack of colonies partially explains their parochialism. Without a wider political frame of reference, Americans have not had a compelling reason to project their awareness of others outward, beyond their nation, as have other politically defined groups who have attained positions of dominance.

Not even the large American-based business community with international dimensions that has grown throughout the twentieth century, or the large numbers of American military personnel in bases that circled the globe in the decades after World War II, or even the hordes of American tourists who have visited locations everywhere in the world since air travel became a common means of movement—not even these groups have significantly diminished the pervasive parochialism of the population as a whole.

Americans, of all the influential, politically defined groups in history, have been the only one without ethnic purity. In contrast to such groups as the Greeks, the Romans, the Egyptians, the British, the French, the Germans, the Russians, the Chinese, the Indians (in Asia), or the Japanese, Americans have retained a dual identity, partially "American," partially the composite of their European or African or South/Middle American or Asian ethnic and racial origins. Without a secure sense of ethnic or racial identity, Americans have ironically invested a greater, but more anxiously derived reliance on their "American-ness," ignoring the rest of the world in the process.

This overpowering sense of American exceptionalism, uniqueness, distinctiveness, and its accompanying nationalist fervor has infected the historians, humanists, social scientists, and journalists whose specialty is the United States. Such groups have likewise exhibited an unusual indifference toward the rest of the world. Social scientists, humanists, and journalists of all types who write on the economic, social, or cultural/intellectual aspects of contemporary life in America routinely confine their analyses or observations or news reports to the United States itself, presuming that there is an identifiable American way or that it is valid to obtain information on only the United States, and not on any wider context.

As a result of America's sprawling system of several thousand public and private colleges and universities, there is a veritable army of "American historians," and their scholarship dwarfs that of any other "field" of historical study. This scholarship reveals a parochialism as notable as that of the general population: virtually all studies contain local, state, regional, or national dimensions, but almost never a supranational one. Even in the arrangements of their teaching, in the courses offered their students, historians in the United States reveal an all-encompassing national perspective. They offer courses in Latin American, Asian, African, and European history (as do others), but almost never in North American history or in the history of the Americas.

But, Americans are not the only group to have acted in this manner. As the European-based nation-state system spread around the globe, typically in the wake of the collapse of globe-girdling European empires, other groups became similarly nationalistic and developed a perception of the past similar to that of the well-established nations of Europe and Asia. The equation of one's political identity with one's historical identity, the linkage of past politics and history, has produced a popular perception of the human past as having consisted of the stories of distinct nations (or of other political entities). Everywhere in the world where there are established nation-states children learn that history is what happens within one's nation, and adults typically equate their past with their nation's past.

But, this nationalistically induced view has seriously distorted historical reality. If we try to imagine the world as a series of overlapping maps, it is easy to picture a solid and precisely territorial political map with one set of boundaries. But, once we try to depict the other aspects of human life, boundaries shift and blur. Geographical formations can be precisely depicted, but are strikingly different from political ones. Linguistic and religious and ethnic and racial "territories" take on their own configurations: sometimes each can be depicted as distinct and separate; sometimes each must be represented as a commingling of various languages, religions, ethnic, and racial groups sharing the same places. There are many other aspects of human life that could be (but rarely are) cartographically displayed: sports, art forms, philosophical and economic systems—all with the same combinations of distinctive and commingling territorial configurations. Only political and geographical boundaries have precision, but what all of these mappings share is that each *differs* from all the others.

The fact is that no government and no politically organized population has ever been able to organize its life in a distinctive way within its territory. Civilized human life from its earliest time has been too porous, too much a matter of the intermingling of various groups to have produced civilizations totally isolated from one another. That is why the perception held by both ordinary people and historians alike that the past should be viewed through one's political identity so fundamentally distorts historical reality. Political activity—by its nature—is not more fundamental, is not a greater determinant of the way people have lived, than is economic, social, or cultural activity. The history of humanity has been a mixture of these elements, all interacting and evolving in complicated patterns. To organize that history on the basis of political entities like nation-states is to oversimplify and to skew what is richly varied and, to those who attempt to understand it, quite confusing.

To reduce one's historical identity to one's political affiliation is to ignore a long list of other forms of identity that humans all share, but in infinitely varied combinations. Each of these forms of identity is important, and each links us to groups of varying size and place. We all belong to a family with its own genealogy, are in a particular age group, are of a certain gender and sexuality, have an occupation (or several, over time), belong to a class or caste (however difficult to determine), have a racial and ethnic identity (or are a mixture), affiliate with a religion (or belief system of some kind, or at least have some nominal affiliation), speak and write in a particular language (or several, if learned), and live at any point in time in a given place and community (whether a rural neighborhood, town, or city; a province or state; a nation; and, in the past, often within empires—all with political but also other forms of definition).

What follows is a critique of the American historical experience as it has been perceived by both ordinary people and historians. Instead of examining all aspects of what Americans have believed is "American" in a national context, that is, in the United States, I have tried to show how the political, economic, social, cultural, and geographical aspects of American life have looked in a global context. Only then can we begin to see what in reality has been distinctively American. Only then can we try to discern what has been either part of a larger pattern of life with transnational dimensions or a smaller phenomenon of subnational proportions. In short, I try to point out the limitations of using America, and, by implication, any political entity, as the basis for viewing our collective past.

PROLOGUE: THE AMERICANS

Humans have always migrated. Throughout human history, groups have moved from one area to another, usually encountering others who have already settled there. This continuous movement of people has meant that it has been rare for any human group to live in isolation, unaware of how others live, or without being influenced by the ways of newcomers in their midst. The history of any group is complicated by these infusions of new blood, by the alterations in life patterns that result from sporadic immigration and later meldings. In this basic sense, we are all immigrants, all the product of families whose progenitors have been in geographical flux through the generations.

The groups who have come to think of themselves as Americans are as subject to these conditions as any other human groups. Americans originate in all the other major continents of the earth and represent a great ingathering of people from Asia, Europe, Africa, and South America, but lack so far the distinctive physiognomies of well-inbred ethnic groups that exist in Europe, Asia, and Africa. There are no "ethnic Americans," as there are English, French, Dutch, Germans, Spaniards, Italians, Greeks, Russians, Chinese, Japanese, (Asian) Indians, or Bantu. The tribal inbreeding that produced such physically recognizable modern ethnic groups occurred over many generations. But, the global ingathering that produced the modern American is too recent in origin for this process to have resulted in a physically recognizable American type of person.

Large-scale white European, black African, and Oriental and brown Asian immigration has been too recent for there to have been the long-term intermixing that has produced an ethnic identity like those mentioned above. The native tribes, the white Europeans, the black Africans, the oriental and brown Asians, and the Hispanics—and their progeny—have all intermingled among themselves, and to some extent with each other, but Americans are still far from constituting a physically recognizable type.

* * *

From a global perspective, the Americas provided the setting from the sixteenth through the eighteenth centuries for a coming together in the "new world" of three quite distinctive races, all from the "old world": the natives, originally from Asia; the blacks, from Africa; and the whites, from Europe. In the Western Hemisphere, the white Europeans dominated those other races, just as in the Eastern Hemisphere, they dominated Africans and Asians in their homelands. European expansion was global in scope, and Europeans dominated others, whether they were at home or were migrants to a new land.

From the dominant English colonists' perspective, what emerged along the Atlantic Coast during the seventeenth and eighteenth centuries was a colonial society that differed from *both* the European heartland *and* native American as well as black African societies. The white migrants and their descendants developed a way of life that was influenced *both* by their European origins as well as continued European domination *and* by their contacts with alien native Americans and black slaves and a huge new continent.

1

The Native Tribes

The first Americans were Asian immigrants. The aboriginal population of the Western Hemisphere migrated from Siberia after the last ice age, spreading over both continents and creating a racially unified human society over the entire landmass. But that society was enormously varied in its patterns of life and in the size and complexity of its groupings: everything from nomadic hunters and gatherers to peripatetic agriculturalists to stationary town and city dwellers. Aboriginals organized themselves into bands (extended kinship groupings) and tribes and sometimes into confederations or empires.

The native groups with the most sophisticated and complex culture were located in Middle and South America—the Aztecs and the Mayas (in modern Mexico and Guatemala) and the Incas (in modern Peru and Bolivia). These centers of civilization were comparable in complexity to the ancient civilizations of Eurasia and Africa. Either singly or in common, they produced large-scale human organizations and physical constructions; had a large class of priests who were dedicated to the study of both religion and science; developed the ideograph from the pictograph, and, thus, a kind of writing; applied mathematical skills to astronomy, predicting eclipses and preparing accurate calendars; built huge temples and large cities; excelled in the development of agricultural techniques, with systems of drainage, terracing, and irrigation; devised elaborate systems of government; subjugated other groups; established empires or divided into city-states.

They influenced other, far less sophisticated aboriginal groups, both to the south and to the north, either as traders or as colonizers, introducing others to their agricultural techniques or religious practices. The tribes that were later to think of themselves as Americans were either nomadic hunters and gatherers or semisettled or townsdwelling agriculturalists. Except for the rather rare townsdwellers, most agricultural tribes created "seasonal villages"—summer settlements that lasted only as long as the growing season, followed by winter quarters situated near fishing and hunting grounds.

The native population of the Americas was markedly different—in all aspects of its life—from the white European colonists who invaded and settled on its land. The initial contact and subsequent coexistence of the two groups constituted one of those rare experiences in human history in which one group utterly dominated the other, in this case, decimating its civilization, shredding apart its cohesive way of life, reducing its members to wanderers in a cultural twilight zone, neither white nor recognizably precontact aboriginal. Seldom has one race and civilization so overwhelmed another race and civilization, as invaders, conquerors from afar.

The Europeans were like earlier conquerors in their desire to dominate those they invaded. What was distinctive was the unevenness of the contact, the extent to which the invaders decimated the pattern of life of those they invaded. Far more typical was a blending, a mixing of elements from both conquerors and conquered. This had been the case with respect to invasions by nomadic tribes of the ancient civilizations of Mesopotamia, Egypt, Persia, India, China, Greece, and Rome.

The white European colonists, in their ethnocentricity, couldn't see the native population as civilized human beings. Only Christianized Europeans were civilized. From the very beginning, the European colonists perceived the aboriginals in a schizophrenic manner, as savages—but as either noble or ignoble savages. The colonists emphasized the positive (or noble) or the negative (ignoble) side of the natives' savagery, depending on whether their experiences with the natives were essentially benign or threatening, or whether the whites lived near the native population or were at a comfortable distance from them.

Directly connected to European ethnocentrism was the colonists' will to dominate—both the land and its inhabitants. Convinced of their own superiority, the European migrants to the Americas sought to prevail over both the natural setting and the "inferior" race of humans who already lived on it. During the three centuries following 1500 A.D., the pattern of their overwhelmingly successful domination of both became increasingly evident. The ethnocentricity of the European settlers made it impossible for them to understand that the natives had a society, culture, religion, economy, and polity—just as the Europeans had, all different, but just as real or authentic. Europeans could not believe that they were witnessing a valid, alternate form of living. Native ways seemed odd, freakish, bizarre, savage, not the ways of a civilized people.

But Europeans shared with many other conquerors an ethnocentric sense of superiority over "barbarians," a notion that had a deep and resonant history among earlier groups who also had thought of themselves as civilized, for example, the Greeks, Romans, Egyptians, and Chinese. What animated the Europeans was a certitude based on race and religion, on the innate superiority of their white, Christian civilization. But, the Arabs had earlier (after A.D. 600) spread their Islamic civilization to northern and eastern and (through Berber nomadic tribesmen) western Africa without culturally decimating the black African populations they contacted. Like the Europeans, the Arabs were convinced of their racial and religious superiority, but how differently they dominated the host populations! Arabs did not conquer, but blended, convincing the black African natives that Islamic ways were acceptable, could coexist with black African life.

The Europeans reversed the ancient practice of nomadic tribes invading centers of civilization. Beginning with the ancient Romans and their domination of lands around the Mediterranean basin, the Europeans developed a civilization that greatly enlarged its territory by becoming conquerors of less civilized, more primitive people who, except for the Siberians, were not contiguous, were in fact oceans away.

The most devastating aspect of the European invasion of the Western Hemisphere was at the level of disease-carrying microbes. The native American population lacked immunity to various viruses and bacteria that impervious white immigrants carried with them. So, the initial contacts between the two races led to huge epidemics among the natives, killing high percentages of those tribes in close contact with the white settlers, who, unable to understand how disease was transmitted, believed the epidemics among the natives were a punishment from God.

In North America, the Dutch, the French, and the English settlers all persuaded the native tribesmen to trap furs to supply a growing European and colonial demand for fur products. The metal goods and alcoholic beverages that the native population received in exchange resulted in the neglect of their own neolithic crafts and made them ever more dependent on the trade with the white colonists.

In Middle and South America, the economic relationship between the Spanish and Portuguese colonists and the native population developed very differently. There, the white settlers sought a reliable labor force to mine gold and silver and to grow and harvest sugar and coffee, early staple crops with world markets. The Spanish and Portuguese monarchs responded by permitting planters and miners to use natives as laborers as long as they promised to Christianize, civilize, defend, and protect them. For the Spanish colonists, however, the exploitation of the natives as a labor force took priority over royal commands to Europeanize the natives entrusted to their care. As the native population declined, the Spanish settlers in the mining and agricultural areas of the interior of Middle and South America were allowed to move to another labor system: that of contract wage labor, which turned into a debt peonage system when the landowners made loans, to be repaid out of wages so low that the debt was never erased.

Politically, in North America, particular colonial governments—whether English or French—made alliances with particular tribes and confederacies by which natives became subordinates to the English or the French in a wider setting of imperial diplomacy and wars. It was in this context that the colonists introduced the natives to firearms weaponry.

The English colonists also made treaties with various tribes for the legal transference of their land to the migrants for settlement, a procedure that often had a divisive and disruptive effect on tribal life. Both alliances and treaties existed in the midst of both cooperation and much anxiety and fear on each side. A variety of incidents triggered sporadic warfare between particular tribes and confederacies and the English colonists, warfare that became different in important ways from the prevailing mode of European warfare. Instead of meeting on an open field, away from the civilian population, and fighting according to agreed-upon rules of battle, as European armies usually did, the colonists and the native Americans developed a type of warfare that involved ambush, hit-and-run attacks, and massacres of civilians. The white colonists typically prevailed, given their superior firepower.

In Middle and South America, Spain and Portugal did not make alliances with native tribes: they conquered them, easily so. The Spaniards had superior military strength, using gunpowder and horses, and took advantage of tribal divisions and enmities to lay claim to native lands. The Spaniards developed a series of legal devices for acquiring aboriginal land, all of which had the effect of confusing the natives. The *congregacion* concentrated particular tribes in villages, opening land for seizure; the *denuncia* required the natives to show legal claim and title to their property, which they could not do, and which opened their land for seizure; and the *composicion* was a means of claiming land through legal surveys, a procedure that natives did not understand. Once Spanish and Portuguese territorial sovereignty was proclaimed, there was no need for alliances and treaties, and the Spaniards and the Portuguese did not order their colonists to declare war on French or English colonies whenever warfare in Europe involved those powers.

The colonists throughout the hemisphere created and supported Christian missionary organizations to convert the heathen natives, to educate them, to make them, if possible, into civilized beings. In Catholic New France, the Jesuits established missions, outposts from which they sought to convert the native population. The Spanish and Portuguese went much further, herding the scattered, nomadic tribes into *reducciones* (in Spanish America) and *aldeias* (in Portuguese America), specially constructed villages managed by clergy, where tribesmen learned all the major aspects of European civilization, but especially its Catholic Christian religious faith. In Spain and Portugal, church and state were closely intertwined, with the monarchs appointing bishops and priests and with government officials often church prelates. From the beginning, Spanish and Portuguese monarchs insisted that their colonists Christianize and civilize the native population.

By contrast, English efforts to convert the natives were more varied and diffuse, far less centralized, with each Protestant denomination contributing to the enterprise, though the Church of England's Society for the Propagation for the

Spread of the Gospel was the most prominent missionary organization across the colonies.

Whether through devastating epidemics, religious conversion, or political or economic subordination, native civilization throughout the Americas disintegrated under the impact of European colonial domination, a process far advanced by the late eighteenth century.

2

The English Colonists

Of all the groups who have immigrated to North America and who have come to think of themselves as Americans, the white Europeans have been so overwhelmingly dominant that they have defined what it means to be an American. White European domination was immediate, but was a part of a much larger process by which Europeans came to dominate the entire world. The subjugation of the native populations of the Americas, from primitive to sophisticated in their cultural makeup, was only one aspect of a global domination that involved the most mature civilizations of Asia and Africa as well. What gave the Europeans their distinctive drive and energy was the rapid development of an economic system that thrived on enlargement, an ever-deepening racism, an abiding sense of religious superiority, and a heightened form of ethnocentrism.

The penetration and subjugation of the inhabitants of other parts of the world occurred over the course of five centuries and ended late in the twentieth century. That process involved lone adventurers, religious missions, trading posts, ports, garrisons, and full-fledged settlements. Colonization represented the process at its maturest level, with formalized government, territorial boundaries, and significant numbers of settlers from the European homelands.

Europeans achieved political, religious, economic, and social/racial domination over the indigenous populations of most of the non-European world during these centuries. The Western Hemisphere was just one region of the world in which Europeans were active. European explorers made contact by land and by sea with the Americas, Africa, and Asia, all at about the same time, during the late fifteenth and sixteenth centuries, and Europe's subsequent domination of the native populations who inhabited all the other continents of the world was also something that occurred concurrently, but with varying degrees of intensity and fullness and rapidity.

So, the English experience of colonizing North America fitted within a larger pattern of European colonization. In its Western Hemispheric form, British, French, Dutch, Spanish, and Portuguese migrants all had to relate to a startlingly different native population; all had to interact with a physical setting whose climate, soil, geographical configurations, and usable resources differed in varying degrees from what they had experienced in Europe; and all had to relate to each other as transplanted Europeans who mirrored in their relations the political and cultural divisions of their erstwhile homelands.

But, what these migrants shared as transplanted Europeans was more basic than what divided them. As the frontiersmen of a dynamic, expansionist civilization, they were practically all Christians, most of whom sought to own property and accumulate wealth and who maintained a hierarchical social structure, which developed a distinctively Western Hemispheric slave caste and, with the exception of high Spanish and Portuguese officials, lacked the ongoing presence of a nobility.

All the colonies were peripheral to a civilization whose centers lay in the capitals of imperialist European powers—in London, Paris, Madrid, Lisbon, Amsterdam, and Moscow. All the colonists developed a colonial mentality, a sense of inferiority to what they perceived as European models—namely, the society, culture, economy, and politics filtered through their respective European monarchies and aristocracies. At the same time, individual migrants regarded the opportunity to begin a new life as evidence that, for aspiring individuals like themselves, their new land was a better place to live than Europe had been.

European colonists lived with these contradictory perceptions. Once the new land was sufficiently explored, migrants believed that Europe's new frontiers contained material resources superior to Europe's, making possible lives of greater material comfort. But they also believed the native population was uncivilized savages who needed to be Christianized and whose land needed to be secured for the use of themselves, the transplanted Europeans. The imperial governments of England, Spain, Portugal, France, the Netherlands, and Russia—in common—perceived colonization as a means to extend their territory through the founding and maintaining of colonies whose loyal inhabitants would defend the empire from intruders and would provide trade materials needed or wanted within the confines of largely self-contained imperial trading units.

Viewed globally, what the Europeans created in their domination of others was an intensely *competitive* system in which the native populations were expected to play a subservient role in larger worlds whose creators and masters were the expansive white populations of Europe. These Europeans largely succeeded in gaining the acquiescence of those native populations for significantly long periods of time, and in so doing, brought European ways to the entire globe. But the Europeans did so as a result of an intermittent struggle for supremacy in all the areas of the world that they expanded into: in the Americas, in Africa, and in Asia. The only exception was the Russians, who were never challenged by the Chinese or Muslims during their expansion into Siberia.

Among the seaborne empire builders, the Portuguese gave way to the Dutch and French, who in turn gave way to the English, depending on the relative strength of their navies. But, domination was never total: there were always Portuguese, Dutch, and French colonies, even with occasional defeats on sea or land. In the Americas, however, there was only one aggressor, only one power who sought to extend its domain over the territories of other powers: the English, whose expansionist propensity would be later inherited by their progeny, the Americans.

The Europeans, though highly competitive, were sufficiently alike to create a system of domination that contained large common elements, elements that were applied differently at various times in particular areas of the world, but that were recognizably common and European nonetheless.

European land exploration began in the 1550s, when the Russians began to move into Siberia. Sea exploration of other continents began even earlier, in the 1470s, and involved Africa and Asia as well as the Americas. It is important to view the movement of Europeans *westward* across the Atlantic Ocean as having been contemporaneous with their movement *eastward*, over land through Siberia and over sea around Africa and over the Indian Ocean to what is now India and across the Pacific coast to Southeast Asia and China. In the late fifteenth and early to midsixteenth centuries, the Portuguese were in Africa and Asia as well as in America (Brazil) during the same years the Spanish were moving through Middle and South America and finding the Philippines. Along both of these sea lanes of expansionism, the Dutch, the French, and the English all followed by the early seventeenth century.

In Africa and Asia, the Europeans typically established trading stations and forts. With two exceptions they did not seek outlets for European emigrants. Those exceptions involved the Russians, whose government encouraged migration to the more temperate parts of southern Siberia, and the Dutch in the temperate zone of the southern tip of Africa, where settlers were allowed to remain, beginning in the 1650s. On a sliding scale from imperious domination (the Portuguese in Africa) to peaceful agreements with native authorities (the Dutch, French, and British in India and the East Indies), to obsequious tribute (the Dutch, the Portuguese, and the English in China), Europeans thus distinguished between the ancient civilizations of India and China and what they considered to be primitive tribal societies, but, in either case, developed relations with "native" populations in many parts of Africa and Asia at the same time they were similarly engaged in dealing with the aboriginal tribes of the Americas. With the exceptions of Siberia and South Africa, only in the Americas did the Europeans attempt in a significant way to go beyond the establishment of coastal trading facilities and fortifications to sponsor the migration of large numbers of settlers from Europe itself.

To avoid the expense of the exploration, exploitation, and possible settlement of Africa, Asia, and the Americas, all of the emerging European imperial governments at first allowed others to supervise conquests or make territorial claims, and then to sponsor whatever economic activity or settlement and colonization followed. The most favored device was to charter trading companies, which were given monopolies over a certain kind of trade within a certain territory, or over the production and sale of a certain kind of product, or over the conquest or staking out and settlement of a particular territory. But, other arrangements were made with particular individuals who these governments felt could be entrusted with enterprises that would further the home country's interests.

In Siberia, colonizers such as the Stroganovs were given tax-exempt status with their pledge to train and equip a frontier guard, and to develop craft and agricultural activity, prospect for ore and mineral deposits, and mine whatever found. The Portuguese monarchs distributed Brazil to 12 donataries who were given broad authority in return for colonizing the newly discovered American territory and went on to establish monopolistic trading companies in 1649, 1678, 1755, and 1759. The Spanish monarchy made contracts, or *capitulacion*, with aspiring conquistadors, who were given the title of *adelantado* and who invested their own money in the enterprise of conquering, claiming, and settling, a process that involved much of Middle and South America during the half century after Columbus' voyages in the 1490s. By the early seventeenth century, the Dutch government sanctioned the creation of trading companies to sponsor their imperial expansion in New Amsterdam and in the East Indies. During the seventeenth century, the French monarch also created trading companies in India and in New France, which supervised the development of French expansionism in its early phases. The English chartered trading companies that were granted monopolies over the trade with various parts of Europe between 1558 and 1603. In 1600, Elizabeth I chose the by-then-well-tried device of establishing trading companies, the London Company and the Virginia Company and the East India Company, to supervise the earliest phases of its explorations and territorial claims in North America and Asia. But, then James I, Charles I, and Charles II tried something different, a variant of the kind of arrangements the Portuguese and Spanish monarchs had made a century and more before. They allowed friends of the royal family to found colonies as sole or small groups of "proprietors."

For over a century, from 1607 until 1713, there was a succession of individually founded English colonies along the Atlantic Coast of North America. Trading companies founded the Virginia (1607), Plymouth (1620), and Massachusetts Bay colonies (1630). Migrants from Massachusetts founded other chartered colonies in Connecticut (1637) and Rhode Island (1644). Several English monarchs granted authority to various proprietors to found the colonies of New Hampshire and Maine (an association, originally in 1622), Maryland (Lord Calvert, in 1634), Barbados (1637), the Carolinas (another association, in 1663), New York (Duke of York, in 1664), New Jersey (Sir George Carteret and Lord John Berkeley, in 1664), Pennsylvania (William Penn, in 1681), Delaware (also William Penn, in 1682), and Georgia (trustees, in 1713).

The European powers who expanded into the Western Hemisphere after the

1490s did not arrive as newcomers to the task of establishing their domination over others. The Spanish clearly drew on their experience of successfully clearing the Iberian peninsula of the Moors (or Muslims) when creating organizational mechanisms for the new world. And, later, the English just as clearly expanded upon their relationship with the Irish. As in Ireland, the English displaced the native population and attempted to produce whole settlements of transplanted Englishmen abroad.

There was no grand plan or deeply embedded policy to this effect, and there were for a long time parts of the English territories in North America that were sparsely settled, the setting for lone adventurers, failed projects, unknown or shunned landscapes. But it is also the case that the pioneers in most of the mainland colonies were eager promoters and produced an ample promotional literature extolling the benefits of resourceful lands and a temperate climate, much like Europe's. And the English responded. There was nothing in all of the history of Europe's expansion around the world to match the outpouring of white Europeans who emigrated to the part of North America that became the United States.

It was a European migration almost from the beginning because the English consistently retained an open, lenient emigration policy. This policy permitted migrants from other parts of Europe who sought a refuge from religious, political, or economic calamity to enter the English colonies. Alone among the Europeans, the English allowed a multiethnic colonial society to grow in their part of the American frontier, welcoming immigrants from the Germanic states and incorporating Swedish and, by nonviolent conquest, Dutch settlers, even allowing such non-English elements in the colonial population to become naturalized subjects by the 1740s.

Both the Dutch and the French also tried to stimulate the growth of colonial settlements in North America, before the English conquered New Amsterdam and New France. But, by resorting to neofeudal schemes to accomplish their aim, both the Dutch and the French lagged far behind the English in the stimulation of settlement and never envisioned their colonies as havens for other Europeans. The only remotely comparable influx of white Europeans anywhere in the world before the nineteenth century were those of the Dutch settlers to the Cape Colony at the southern tip of Africa and the Russian settlements in southern Siberia, both of which, like much of British America, were also in temperate climate zones.

When interpreted from a global perspective, the British mainland North American colonies, and, later, the United States have been one of several white settler-dominated societies created by European colonists as Europeans, from the sixteenth to the twentieth centuries, spread their people and their ways around the world, emerging as the dominant and preeminent civilization on earth. European domination took many forms: political, economic, social, religious, intellectual, and cultural. But the establishment of white settler-dominated societies, replicas of the sponsoring national group in Europe, were the exception, not the rule. The modern nations of Asian Russia, Canada, Australia, New Zealand, and South Africa share such origins with the United States. All these nations are in temperate zones climatically, similar to northern Europe's. South America's temperate zone, in northern Argentina and southern Brazil, was the last to become a white settler society as large numbers of European immigrants arrived there during the late nineteenth century.

The far more typical way for Europeans to expand, especially in the tropical and semitropical areas of the globe, was to export a tiny elite of white traders and missionaries and settler/occupiers who made various arrangements with preexisting native populations, but did not attempt to displace them with large-scale transplantations of European society. The anomaly in this context was South and Middle America. Though few Spaniards or Portuguese cared to emigrate there, the Spanish and Portuguese governments nonetheless moved quickly to establish administrative authority over this vast land. The European domination of other nontemperate areas of the globe came much later or was much more gradual—in India, in China, in Southeast and Southwest Asia, most spectacularly in Africa. Such elites either remained separate from the native populations (as in Asia and Africa) or intermingled with them (as in South and Middle America).

3

The Black African Slaves

Slavery was a phenomenon of hemispheric proportions, as the Spanish and Portuguese and English and French colonists all developed a slave labor system. In North America, the very availability of land and the wealth that could be garnered from its resources led those who developed agriculture on the largest scale—the "planters," the producers of "staple" crops—to enlist a large, hopefully dependable labor force, and as indentured forms of labor from Europe failed to keep pace with their demands for it, the planters sought forced black migrants from Africa and succeeded in developing a system of "chattel" slavery, which, in the English colonies especially, became the most comprehensive system of slavery in the history of humanity.

Slavery developed in response to the perceived labor needs of large-scale agriculturists and was thus a form of economic domination. But, the chattel system was also a result of the engrained racism of transplanted Englishmen who were, as were all the European colonists who fanned out through the Western Hemisphere in these centuries, enveloped by an ethnocentric view of humanity. Whites believed nonwhites were innately inferior, either as noble or ignoble savage Indians or as bestial black Africans. The Spanish, Portuguese, and English colonists took over the native populations' land, traded and fought with them, tried to convert them to Christianity, and all the while removed them from colonial society. By contrast, these same colonists enslaved the black Africans and forced them to share their land, to labor on it to produce the staples, the most important commodities British North Americans provided the world during the seventeenth and eighteenth centuries.

Throughout the semitropical/tropical areas of North and South America, white settlers sought to find others to labor for them, sought to find "staple" products that could be produced in large quantities by such laborers and sold in wider markets for large profits. This led to the development of a plantation system of huge, largely self-contained enterprises where African slaves were bought from European slave traders as the native population declined in South and Middle America and as white indentured servants became insufficient in North America.

In an even broader context, slavery in the Americas was part of a larger world of unfree labor that included the serfs of eastern Europe, where peasants were progressively enslaved by being customarily and then legally immobilized on the estates of the Russian nobility during the same centuries that slavery matured in the Western Hemisphere. A web of feudal-like duties and obligations bound nobility and serf. The forced labor of the serfs produced either rents for the nobility or shared agricultural products, part of which were sold in urban markets. Both slavery and serfdom were quasi-capitalistic, quasi-feudalistic systems. Both were focused on profits derived by masters from the forced labor of others who were perceived as a lower order of humans. But both also involved reciprocal duties and lacked the impersonal character of the modern industrial corporation.

The black slaves in the Americas were already enslaved as a result of tribal warfare in western Africa and were sold to European slave traders, who in turn sold them to the white colonists of southern North America and of Middle and South America. So, almost contemporaneously with the arrival of Europeans to the Americas came a large influx of involuntary immigrants from Africa. But because these African migrants came from a tropical climate, they easily adjusted to their new setting, or were even already familiar with a lot of the tasks their white masters required of them. The black slaves labored on coffee, sugar, rice, or tobacco plantations, on the cattle ranches, in the mines, or on the docks. They mastered European crafts and even served in military units (at least in the Spanish colonies).

Most of these involuntary black immigrants were from an area of western Africa whose society was as complex and sophisticated as the most advanced native tribes of the Americas in Middle and South America. There had been a succession of large-scale federated states in the rain forest and savannah by the time of the slave trade, states whose ruling elites had come under the influence of Islamic migrants with respect to their law, religion, language, and culture. This Islamized veneer overlay a traditional African tribal culture where family, kin, and village all sustained a communally oriented, agriculturally based life. The slaves of this area were usually war captives, who became members of particular families.

The shock of being sold and shipped to the Western Hemisphere and shifted from communal farming to the gang labor of plantations was immense, and black slaves in the new world resisted their enslavement, whether by running away or rebelling or causing more minor disruptions of the slave labor system. This enslavement produced the same kind of cultural emasculation as occurred among the native population. Under slavery, African ways and tribal and linguistic identities became obliterated or altered as the transplanted Europeans kept these black migrants from freely participating in North American life outside of their duties as slaves.

With respect to slavery, the southern English colonies had more in common with parts of the Spanish and Portuguese colonies than they did with the more northerly English colonies: they were part of a socioeconomic system that embraced a significant portion of the new world, cutting across parts of South and Middle and North America. In one significant sense, the southern English colonies differed from the Spanish and Portuguese colonies, however.

In the Iberian colonies, there was racial mixing from the arrival of the first white settlers, most of whom were male, a mixing that involved the European migrants and both the natives and then the black slaves. What soon emerged was a society of a racially mixed population, with social status determined by the degree of whiteness, redness, or blackness. In the southern English colonies, racial mixing occurred, but it was far rarer than to the south and was not sanctioned. Mulattos were social outcasts. The English settlers retained their sense of racial superiority long after the Spanish and Portuguese settlers were forced by circumstances to lose theirs.

The English colonists, of all the colonial groups in the Western Hemisphere, developed the most intimate relations with small numbers of black slaves on the tobacco farms, the only staple that didn't require the scale of a plantation. Yet it was the English colonists, who in Europe had been farthest removed from slavery as an institution, who also enacted slave codes that created the most comprehensive system of enslavement ever known. Slaves were rarely able to earn their freedom; manumission by slaveowners was infrequent. During the course of the seventeenth and eighteenth centuries, slavery was made a permanent, inherited status for African forced migrants, who were defined simply as chattels, human property. Masters were given, under law, wide freedom to deal with their slaves as they wished.

In South and Middle America, by contrast, slaves fitted into the new world society of Iberian immigrants in the sense that the Iberians had already enslaved Moors (Muslims). Spanish and Portuguese legal codes endowed the slave with a legal personality, as someone with duties and rights. The slave was not simply a chattel (human property), but could marry, could buy his freedom, could testify in court, with rights enforceable in court. Black slaves were converted to Catholicism, were equal before God, and were treated as moral beings. Cruelty was against the law, killing was murder, and manumission was frequent.

4

The Other Americans

White Europeans streamed onto the mainland of North America from the seventeenth century onward. In a global context, these peripatetic Europeans were part of a great migration that started around 1500 and has not yet ended, a migration that was a part of the larger process by which Europe attained a dominant position throughout the world. What the British imperial government allowed, its successor American national government did not try to stop. Over the centuries, from the seventeenth to the twentieth, migrants came from all parts of Europe, from various regions at various times for various reasons. By far the largest number went to the United States, 35 million of the 50 million who left Europe in the peak period between 1820 and 1920. Siberia was a distant second, attracting 7 million Russians in roughly the same period.

Most were from the middling ranks of European society; others were too poor or too rich to leave. Those who did leave were adversely affected by economic change, by the onset of commercialized agriculture or of industrialization. They chose to leave; many others in similar circumstances chose not to. Some of these European migrants also left in search of religious freedom and political asylum or in avoidance of economic calamity. All believed their lives would in some way improve. Many stayed; but others returned to their European homeland.

If North America is perceived as part of a larger transatlantic world, then these migrants can be viewed as individuals and groups who have moved from one home to another, often within particular political entities in Europe, but sometimes across the western "trunkline" of the Atlantic Ocean, following "spurlines" to the white settler societies of the Americas, with more distant voyages to South Africa and Australia or New Zealand. The only eastern movement was overland, to Siberia. The open emigration policy of the British and then American governments meant that the English colonies, and, later, the United States, was the destination of the largest number of the westward-moving transatlantic European migrants, who were attracted by the unequaled variety of material resources and economic opportunity and by a land that served both as a political and religious asylum and as the basis for greater political and social freedom.

Migrants from Europe to the Americas and to other continents as well came in sailing ships on an arduous voyage lasting for several weeks, a form of movement that didn't basically change until the 1870s. There were outbreaks of contagious disease on board these ships, resulting in the deaths of many migrants. Various governments established quarantine procedures for passenger ships. Most who migrated before the 1870s settled in their own colonies, founding white settler societies either overland, in Siberia, or across the seas. Only the English colonies and, after independence, the United States contained a significant number of settlers from outside the founding country. The two most significant "outsider" groups were migrants from various German states and from Ireland, politically joined to Britain in 1800. Both the Germans and Irish migrants arrived at various times, from the late seventeenth to the midnineteenth centuries, for a variety of reasons: to escape political and religious persecution, to embrace economic opportunity, to flee from economic calamity. Their presence created the basis for the first multiethnic society on Europe's frontier. But, it is important to note that, prior to 1870, most who lived in all the white settler societies on three different continents were, ethnically, descendants of the founding groups.

With the loss of the North and South American European colonies between the 1770s and the 1820s, further European migrations to colonized areas outside of the newly independent republics of the Americas involved continued overland migration from Russia to southern Siberia and new overseas emigration to the new British colonies in Australia and New Zealand, to the newly conquered British colony in South Africa (in 1795 and again in 1806, from the Dutch), and to the remnant of the British Empire in North America (named British North America and, later, Canada).

Within a reconfigured British Empire, a generation of English colonial reformers tried to reinvigorate and plan colonial emigration. In the 1780s, the Australia colony began as a place of exile for criminals (thus continuing a practice introduced in connection with the North American colonies during the eighteenth century). Subsequently, various missionary and colonization groups tried to systematize emigration, to control egress in such a way that British society would be replicated by design (*except* for paupers and criminals), by setting up colonization schemes in Australia and New Zealand that were carefully managed. Similarly, the government itself, through its Colonial Land and Emigration Commissioners, sponsored group migration to South Africa.

This kind of planned, idealistic, conservative management of British migration did not become the standard way that Britons migrated during these decades, however. "Gold rushes" provided a far greater incentive, as migrants swarmed to both Australia (in the 1850s) and South Africa (in the 1880s) as a result of discoveries of the most precious of metals. Others left on their own initiative, seeking farmland. White settlers in both Australia and New Zealand rigidly confined migration to a British-only policy until after World War II, and in this they held onto what had been the standard practice in all the white settler societies, with the partial exception of the United States, until 1870.

The whole character of the European migrations changed rather dramatically after 1870, when a truly ethnically mixed mass migration involving not only the United States, but Canada, Argentina, and Brazil erupted, lasting until World War I. Siberia, the sole European land frontier, was confined to one source of immigrants, the Russians. Similarly, Australia, New Zealand, and South Africa continued to favor immigration from Britain. Various factors produced in this period the largest of all the overseas migrations of Europeans. Steam-powered transportation (ships and trains), which greatly lowered the cost and increased the safety and healthiness of migration; an absence of legal constraints as governments on both sides of the Atlantic favored migration; continued agricultural development along the American frontiers; mass industrialization and its creation of wage labor; the support of related, earlier migrants; and the actual sponsorship of governments and corporations—all converged to produce the migration of masses of Europeans across the Atlantic.

Economic factors were central: many moved because they had become economically marginalized with the enormous enlargement of industrialization and of the commercialization and mechanization of agriculture and the effects these processes had on those who lived in the already marginal rural areas of Europe. Many Europeans in a politically united Germany and Italy as well as in Britain and Scandinavia and the Low Countries and the eastern empires of Austro-Hungary and Russia moved to port cities along the coasts of Europe and migrated across the Atlantic, not only to the United States, but to Canada and to Argentina and Brazil. (Russian emigrants now flowed both eastward, overland, to Siberia, and westward, by sea, to North America.)

Many wanted to move permanently and to continue farming along the frontiers of the Americas. But, as these frontiers ceased to absorb homesteaders because farming had become increasingly mechanized and commercialized there, as in Europe, many other migrants went in search of work, the kind of work generated by industrialization, and if they thought their prospects were better across the Atlantic than within Europe, they made a crossing. Work-generated migrations sometimes involved short-term moves, with individuals in fairly frequent transit to the other side of the Atlantic, a kind of extension of seasonal work migrations within Europe itself.

British, Irish, Scandinavian, Dutch, German, Italian, Polish, and Russian migrants went not only to the temperate part of the United States in various mixtures, but also to Canada and to the temperate areas of South America: to northern Argentina and southern Brazil. Long-term farm settlement moved, with the encouragement of national governments, onto the prairies of the United States and Canada, the pampas of Argentina, and the coastal areas of southern Brazil. The Brazilian government actually sponsored farm-colonization schemes with German and Italian migrants. But, most migrants became tenants or sharecroppers on the big landed estates where wheat, cattle, and coffee were grown. The Argentinian and Brazilian governments were dominated by these landowners and were thus unable to devise a land policy that would have opened up staple-crop production to homesteaders.

By contrast, the Canadian and American governments introduced land policies that favored homesteading, whether by German, Scandinavian, or Ukrainian migrants. But, the commercialization and the mechanization of agriculture in the United States developed to the point that, after the disastrous droughts of the late 1880s, there weren't significant numbers of long-term homesteading migrants, whereas, in Canada, the prairies remained open to homesteading until the depression of 1930.

Other migrants moved in search of work in the urban and industrial areas of Argentina, Brazil, Canada, and the United States. Buenos Aires became flooded with foreign-born Italians and Spaniards, as did, to a lesser extent Brazil, in São Paulo and Rio de Janeiro. The newcomers in the urbanized areas of Argentina and Brazil became socially and economically mobile and dominated the commercialization and industrialization that began there at the turn of the century. This was in contrast to the eastern and southern Europeans who migrated to the United States for work: they tended to fill unskilled employment created by industrialization and urbanization already managed by native-born Americans.

Whatever the ethnic variety, the mass migrations of the 1870–1914 period produced ethnically mixed white settler societies throughout the Americas. After World War II, Australia and New Zealand and South Africa became the last white settler societies to attract migrants of a multiethnic white European kind. The Americans became less distinctive as a result of shifts in the destinations of those from many parts of Europe who chose to migrate across the Atlantic and beyond during the years after 1870. Americans could no longer maintain that they alone, by welcoming migrants from many parts of Europe, were the only multiethnic white settler society. All white settler societies became multiethnic.

* * *

As a result of the varied character of the European migrants to North America, the white Europeans who came to identify themselves as Americans, after political independence in the 1780s, became a European composite, and not simply transplanted Englishmen. Alone of all the white settler societies that accompanied European expansion, the Americans were more than an attempted replication of any particular European group. This was not the case with Spanish and Portuguese America (with their hierarchical racial mixtures), Dutch and

British South Africa, British North America (with its French and English duality), and Australia/New Zealand. In all these instances, there was a clear ethnic norm or model (or a dual one), even *after* the multiethnic migrations of the late nineteenth and early twentieth centuries. Only in the United States did the varied ethnic makeup of the population lead some old-stock Americans to perceive their nation as an asylum for Europe's oppressed, as a land of opportunity for white Europeans in general. This perception of what the United States should be with respect to migration was counterbalanced by nativism, by the kind of support for ethnic purity that was prevalent in all the other white settler societies. Supporters of America the "asylum" looked toward the growth of a new kind of multiethnic society, whereas nativists wanted to keep America Protestant, not Catholic, and British, not ethnically or racially mixed.

During the course of the nineteenth century, those of English origin, or at least of northern European sources—the "Nordic race"—looked with favor on a further refinement of the racism that the Europeans in general had subscribed to as they came into contact with nonwhite races after 1500. This new, more refined form of racism was "Anglo-Saxon racism," the view that northern and western Protestant Europeans were superior to southern and eastern Europeans and Catholic Europeans everywhere. This view prevailed among British settlers in Canada, Australia, New Zealand, and South Africa. But, Canada and South Africa were characterized by a dual ethnicity—French and English in Canada; Dutch and English in South Africa—and the British could not obliterate the fact that there was a major "other" ethnic group in both Canada and South Africa who were established long before British settlement began, a group that also claimed a prominent position in society.

In its American formulation, Anglo-Saxon racism was the view that some European immigrants were more "American" than others. The still-dominant English minority sought to establish a white European ethnic hierarchy of the sort the South and Middle Americans had established on a racial basis. What resulted was a shared sense that the older one's family was in its residence in North America and the more purely English it was, the more truly American it was. By contrast, the newer one's family was and the greater the distance from England of its European source, the less American one's family was. This form of nativism was an effort to sustain a tight sense of identity of just who a true American was. Since white Americans lacked the ethnic purity of the other settler societies, the original remnant was quite steadfast in its attempts to make new immigrants from non-Nordic areas of Europe to become aware of an American identity that did not fully extend to them.

And they succeeded: the immigrants from Ireland (long subjugated by the British) during the midnineteenth century and from southern and eastern Europe during the late nineteenth and early twentieth centuries continued for several generations to think of themselves as hyphenated Americans, as Irish-, Italian-, or Polish-, or Russian-Americans, not as simply Americans.

Developments within Europe also raised questions about the relationship between ethnicity and political identity. The political unification of Germany and Italy during the 1860s and 1870s gave political identity to "peoples" who had been politically fragmented. After the collapse of the central and eastern European empires—the Austro-Hungarian and the Ottoman Turk—during World War I, various geographically concentrated ethnic groups sought and some succeeded in gaining political independence. With the collapse of the Soviet Union in 1991, the search of ethnic groups for a political identity resumed, not only within the formerly multiethnic Russian imperial state, but in such ethnically plural states as Czechoslovakia and Yugoslavia. Even in the politically stable areas of western and northern Europe, there have been ethnic minorities: the English with their Scots and Welsh, the Spanish with their Basques and Catalanians, the Belgians with their Walloons, and the Swedes with their Norwegians—groups that have sporadically sought some form of political identity.

In other words, in Europe, there is much evidence that ethnic groups have struggled to create their own states. By contrast, in the United States, only a racial group, black Americans, have spawned nationalist movements, though only a rather small minority of American blacks have ever supported such schemes. Marcus Garvey organized the United Negro Improvement Association in 1916 as a black nationalist organization, and in the 1960s, the Black Muslim movement once again emphasized black separatism. In contrast to Europe, the white ethnic groups who became immigrants to North America did not flock to particular geographical locations that they exclusively occupied. Each ethnic group, though it favored particular neighborhoods in cities or towns in the countryside, lived next to other ethnic groups: there were no exclusively Irish or German or Scandinavian or Italian or Polish or Russian territories in the United States, as there were in Europe. In North America, unlike Europe, this varied ethnic mixture existed within an unusually stable political system (with the exception of the Civil War). Certainly, there were not ethnic nationalist movements whose participants sought political independence. The United States contained an obvious and distinctive ethnic and racial variety within its political borders, but, with the large influx of immigrants from southern and eastern Europe during the late nineteenth and early twentieth centuries, American nationalists nonetheless defined as "American" a model citizen who was male and white, Protestant, and British in origin, and not someone who was black or native or southern or eastern European or a Catholic or a Jew.

So, nationalism as it related to ethnicity in both Europe and North America took on increasingly similar forms: that is, there developed a shared belief that there should be an "ethnic core" that provided nations with their distinctive identity. This was the case, even though America continued to contain an ethnic and racial variety generally absent within European nation-states, both in the case of the established states of western and central Europe and, after 1918, in the newly created ones of eastern Europe as well.

During the nineteenth and first half of the twentieth centuries, white Americans as a whole continued to be racist, to dominate blacks (even after slavery, through segregation and ghettoization) and natives (even after all their land had been taken, through concentration in reservations and continued "civilization" programs), and to discriminate in various ways against oriental Asians. Both the federal and state levels of government responded to such racism. The federal government prohibited further immigration by the Chinese in a series of "exclusion" acts, beginning in 1882. State governments enacted segregation laws, separating blacks and whites, laws that were upheld by federal courts. Beyond racism was a growing sentiment among white Americans that their nation should not be overwhelmed by immigrants from Europe who were not "Nordic" or Protestant. Once again, government responded when the federal government enacted immigration legislation in the early 1920s that established quota systems favoring the further immigration of northern Europeans. Alone among the European migrants spread around the world during the modern age, the dominant white Americans created a dual system based upon *both* racial and ethnic superiority as to who could be properly identified as an American.

5

Multiethnic, Multiracial Americans

Since World War II, both kinds of domination have declined. Social scientists have denounced racism as having been based upon erroneous notions that there are superior and inferior rather than different or, at most, primitive and complex cultures. Protest movements of blacks, natives, Orientals, Latinos or Hispanics, and liberal white sympathizers have denounced white racism and advocated racial equality. The federal government—both judicially and legislatively—responded with favorable judicial interpretations during the 1950s and far-reaching civil rights legislation during the 1960s. Growing numbers of the descendants of immigrants from southern and eastern Europe no longer perceive themselves as simply hyphenated Americans, and families of early, northern European origin are becoming so intermixed with those descended from migrants out of other European homelands that there is increasingly less genealogical purity of the kind that earlier sustained Anglo-Saxon racism. Immigration legislation in 1965 ended the quota system.

Neighboring Latino or Hispanic Americans have migrated in large numbers, both legally and illegally, for work and settlement, that is, for both short-and long-term migratory purposes. The incidence of Oriental and brown Asian migration has also greatly increased, with both freedom from political oppression and economic opportunity as motivating factors. Americans now trace their ancestry to all the continents of the world.

So, who now is an American? Presumably all who live in a multiethnic and multiracial society, a society increasingly less distinctive as governments in many other parts of the world have sanctioned immigration of the kind that produced the varied groups who have come to identify themselves as Americans. The growing belief that all who live in the United States are equally American requires considerable historical amnesia on the part of the blacks, natives, Orientals, and non-British whites who have come to insist upon their equal "American-ness." But the fact that Americans of all kinds are looking beyond a hierarchical ethnic and racist past and proclaiming the United States as the first great multiethnic, multiracial all-equal society itself becomes, with the passage of time, part of the historical record.

Still, Americans are far from having created an unambiguous racial/ethnic identity; they are many generations short of the kind of inbreeding that has produced the modern English themselves. And so, though those resident in the United States have come to think of themselves as Americans, they still are comprised of disparate groups, a situation that allows them to perceive themselves as *both* American and Afro-American, American and native, American and Asian-American, American and European. Americans, in short, are still multiethnic and multiracial, but, in the late twentieth century, have come to think of themselves as having a dual identity, both American and something else, something *before* they became American. Even old-stock white families are concerned in their genealogical investigations to trace their roots back to Europe, to England.

Many other Americans have been so interbred that their pre-American ethnic affiliation is too attenuated to have much meaning. African tribal identities got rather quickly lost when black migrants entered slavery. European ethnic origins became blurred as a result of the varied marital patterns the assimilated progeny of European migrants followed. Most Latino or Hispanic immigrants were already racially mixed.

American identity is therefore still more ambiguous, more complicated than it is for those who are members of well-established ethnic groups around the globe.

6

Conclusion

So, in a global context, how distinctive are those who have come to identify themselves as Americans over the last four centuries? The answer is: somewhat distinctive, for a relatively short period of time. The dominant white Americans were the first multiethnic European group to establish their own nation-state outside of Europe. During the late eighteenth and early and midnineteenth centuries no where else in the world did well-established European ethnic groups live commingled within a particular polity. So, white Americans constituted the world's first mixed European state. But, it was also the case that the majority of Americans before 1870 were of British origin. Within the United States as a whole, there were only a relatively few ethnic minorities: Dutch and Swedes and French (incorporated by the British in colonial times) and, more significantly, Irish and Germans. To the extent that these ethnic minorities stood out as being different from the Anglo majority, they evoked considerable hostility.

It is only after 1870 that whites in the United States contained a truly multiethnic population, with significant numbers of European ethnic groups from all parts of Europe. It is only then that white Americans could claim to be a significantly mixed European population; however, there continued to be considerable hostility expressed toward the recent immigrants from destinations far from Britain. But, by then, the United States was not the only nation so constituted: Canada, southern Brazil, and northern Argentina were also destinations of a variety of European immigrants after 1870, and Australia, New Zealand, and South Africa became so after World War II.

So, white Americans have been the largest and the first of the multiethnic European-derived national populations in areas outside of Europe. But, their distinctiveness was short-lived. As the white American population became truly multiethnic, other white settler societies overseas followed its lead. Black Americans, enslaved as a separate caste and then segregated after emancipation, also represented a mixing of African tribes, thus producing their own multiethnic black population. But, this was not a phenomenon unique to the United States either, as enslaved Africans everywhere in the Americas became ethnic mixtures of antecedent African tribes. Only native Americans tended to keep their ethnic or tribal purity, physically separated into tribal reservations as they have been, at least until the 1930s.

More recent brown and Oriental Asian immigrants have largely retained their ethnic purity, remaining Chinese, Japanese, Indian, Vietnamese, or Filipino. Hispanic or Latino immigrants from Middle and South America have been either racially mixed or of white ethnic European or of purely native origins. During the twentieth century, America became the site of an ingathering of people of all races and racial mixtures and of many ethnic groups, from Middle and South America and Asia, as well as from Europe. Once again, it seemed as though the American population would constitute something distinctive and new. But, once again, other parts of the world have become the settings for similar ingatherings, similar racial and ethnic interminglings, most notably Europe itself, as former colonial peoples have migrated to erstwhile imperial homelands and as nearby poorer Europeans and north Africans and western Asians have migrated to the economically better-off parts of Europe. European nations will themselves eventually become multiethnic and multiracial, becoming another version of the ancient tribal mixtures that produced the ingrown ethnic populations of modern Europe!

Perhaps global migrations will continue so steadily that there will be ethnically and racially mixed populations organized into states everywhere in the world. Perhaps the ethnically or racially pure state will be difficult to sustain, even where geographically cohesive ethnic and racial groups want to maintain their own states. Even the presence of an ethnic or racial "core" in a growing number of multiethnic or multiracial states may be hard to maintain, if the American experience is repeated elsewhere. In short, Americans have served more as a harbinger of things to come than as a population with a long-term distinctiveness.

And, indeed, in another sense, the dominant white Americans have shared with other groups of Europeans outside of Europe the lack of a clear-cut ethnic identity. Americans remained aware of their European ethnic origins, long after their families' arrival in North America. Even after massive ethnic mixing, one's ethnic identity remained European in nature, however varied in its combination. White Americans have always lacked an American ethnic identity. What they experienced was the severance of one's ethnic identity from one's political identity. To be an American was to be in a population defined by citizenship. Ethnic identity referred to one's ancestral bloodlines back to Europe. Similarly, Canadians and Australians and New Zealanders and South Africans thought of themselves as Britishers in new political contexts as long as immigration remained largely British in origin, just as Afrikaners long retained their Dutch identity.

By contrast, enslaved and segregated black Americans were denied both citizenship and an ethnic, tribal identity until well into the twentieth century. But, once again, as multiethnic and multiracial states become more common, distinctions between one's ethnicity and race and one's citizenship will also become more common.

In sum, while it is important to trace the development of each of the groups who have come to identify themselves as Americans, it is also important to place that process in a wider context, to examine the Americans from the perspective of the much wider migrations that involved the movement and settlement of Europeans onto other lands around the world. Only then can we see Americans in an historical setting that fully reveals who they were—and are.

PART I

THE AMERICAN POLITY

Human government had its origins in the need groups felt for protection from outsiders, for the maintenance of law and order, and for the furtherance of their common welfare. Tribal societies, such as those that the black African slaves and the native Americans came from, had governments, but they did not develop ongoing states, that is, formal political institutions that enacted and administered laws, punished lawbreakers, provided military defense, and undertook public works. The bases on which the chiefs and councils of tribal societies were chosen were varied: physical prowess, wisdom, character, family reputation, rarely simply as a matter of heredity. By contrast, the traditional societies that emerged in Asia, Europe, Africa, and the Americans commonly had monarchs and a nobility, elites with inherited status, elites that governed, often with a claimed divine sanction.

The dominant English colonists were part of a traditional European society, politically hierarchical in the way that empires had always been, with levels of government—within the English political world—that extended from the monarch to the aristocracy (in the House of Lords) to the people's representatives (in the House of Commons) to the central bureaucracy (in London) to the various colonial governments (from Maine to Georgia) to several forms of local government (county, municipal, township, borough). This hierarchy or federation had been the standard form for large states since the time of the ancient empires of Asia and Europe, and the more recent empires of Africa and the Americas.

Most citizens' political awareness was usually confined to their local jurisdictions, except for the activities of officials who represented wider political districts. Access to prevailing modes of long-distance transportation and communication was crucial to the authority of far-away elites. Large segments of humanity were for many centuries enfolded within huge polities, with many levels of government dividing political authority.

When the Americans gained their political independence from Britain as a result of a revolutionary war from 1775 to 1781, the nation they created by 1789 was traditional in that it was a federated state, but modern in that it was the first large republic without a monarchy or an aristocracy. The French became a republic during their revolution from 1789 to 1795, but their republic was as short-lived as the English experience with republicanism under Cromwell during the 1650s had been. When the Spanish colonists similarly rebelled against Spain during the 1810s and 1820s, they emulated the erstwhile British colonists and created many republics without monarchies and aristocracies as well.

But, there was a crucial distinction between the South and Middle American republics and the North American republic. In the former, *caudillos* established military dictatorships, keeping the republican name for states with autocratic governments. In the latter, Americans added another modern feature to their polity as they gradually created a political democracy, by establishing the first mass political parties in the world (by 1800), then by enlarging the electorate through the inclusion of all adult white males, not just property owners (by the 1840s), then adult white females (1920), then adult native tribesmen (1924), and then adult male and female blacks (1965).

At the same time, some Europeans gradually created political democracies by progressively limiting the political authority of monarchs and aristocracies while similarly broadening their electorate. Though initiated by the Americans, democracy became a defining feature of European-style polities, more than whether or nor a state had a place for a monarch or a nobility. But, by the twentieth century, other Europeans, like the South and Middle Americans, developed new forms of autocratic governments, even while abruptly abolishing monarchies and aristocracies.

Germany (as well as Italy and Spain) became fascist, and Russia became communist, each adding satellite nations along its borderlands during expansionist phases in the 1930s and the 1940s. But, both the fascist and communist states lost to the more democratic nations of the Western world: the fascists as a result of World War II and the communists as a result of the Cold War. By the 1990s, political democracy became the norm for all of the Europeanized areas of the world.

So, the American nation was quite distinctive as a political offshoot of Europe, as Americans forged the world's first large republic without the governance of a monarch or an aristocracy, that is, elites with inherited status. Americans then went on to lead the way in the creation of political democracy, but were held back by the continued existence of racial castes, both enslaved and segregated and ghettoized blacks as well as displaced natives.

In another context, American government has not been at all unusual, however. What governments actually *did*, the kinds of activities they engaged in, at whatever level within federated systems, didn't differ very much from one polity to another, from one part of Europe to another, from one empire to another, from the European homeland to the peripheries in the Americas, Australia, New Zealand, South Africa. Because of its size, the

United States had a more decentralized federal system than much of Europe had, at least until the twentieth century, when enlargements in the scale of organization for economic, social, and cultural activity, prompted by the speeding up of the means of transportation and communication, led to an enlargement of scale in the American governmental system as well.

But, whether notable for their decentralized or centralized character, polities in the Europeanized world have sporadically but greatly augmented their tasks since the time of the American and French Revolutions of the late eighteenth century, so that by the late twentieth century, virtually every sphere of human activity is affected by governmental regulation, assistance, protection, and restriction. The welfare capitalist state that has emerged since the late nineteenth century has become a protective shield against poverty, illness, ignorance, joblessness, crime, pollution. The state tries to assure steady economic growth, social harmony, cultural vitality.

This enlargement of the ambit of government has accompanied the enlargement in the scale by which people organize their lives and has occurred in every developed or Europeanized nation, whether democratic, fascist, or communist in orientation. To this process, the American political system has certainly not been an exception.

Nor have the white settler societies on the periphery of European civilization. The founding groups of these frontier societies brought with them only a fragment of the political outlook of a more varied and complex Europe. The American polity was liberal in its origins and has remained steadfastly so. Without direct experience of a feudal or communistic or monarchical or aristocratic system, Americans have been naturally liberal, just as the Spanish and Portuguese Americans and the French Canadians and the Dutch South Africans have been more conservative and the Australians and the New Zealanders have been more radical. But whether conservative, liberal, or radical, these nations have not had governments whose functions and activities have been notably out of line with Europe's.

As the first modern nation to come out of the dismemberment of an empire, the United States, the product of the successful American rebellion against the British, was long regarded as a model for political independence movements elsewhere, certainly in South and Middle America during the 1810s and 1820s, but elsewhere as well during the nineteenth century. But, by the twentieth century, there were Communist-led rebellions in Asia and Africa, and the American model was ignored as irrelevant, having led to the creation of a bastion of capitalism, imperialism, and white racism. But in either case, modern political independence movements from the Americans' onward have been led by local political leaders who were trained by the very imperialists whose rule they sought to end. By this means, the nation-state, incubated in Europe, was spread round the world, as significant a European export as capitalism, democracy, or Christianity, and more nearly universal than any of them.

Whether accepted as a model or not, the American government has in one sense been true to its own origins. It has usually favored political independence for parts of fallen empires. This has been the case with the ending of the Spanish empire in America and Asia (though the Americans held on to its final bits as colonies for awhile); of the Ottoman and Austro-Hungarian and most recently Soviet empires in Europe and Asia; of the short-lived Japanese empire in Asia; and of the long-lived Dutch, French, and British empires in both Asia and Africa. There has been both consistency and integrity in this position as long as the manner by which the American nation itself expanded is not defined as imperialistic.

The American government has never perceived itself as an imperial government presiding over an empire, and yet it was territorially expansionist for a 50-year period and annexed huge amounts of contiguous land on the North American continent, not unlike the way Russia expanded. In both cases, the expansionist population spilled over into the newly acquired territories. In both cases, those territories became states in a union of states. In both cases, diplomacy and war were the means by which the nation expanded, sometimes involving the conquest of native populations. And yet, American officials never thought of their nation as constituting an empire, as the Russians clearly did.

With respect to foreign relations in general, the Americans have been notably distinctive. Unlike Europe, indeed unlike any other expansionist nation in the modern world, the American nation became preeminent in the entire Western Hemisphere without any rival nation to contain its spreading power and influence. No other power has achieved its hegemonic position in its sphere with such a puny military force, relying heavily on diplomatic craft and (in the case of the native tribes and the nearby Mexicans) small, decisive warfare. Only when the Americans sought to become a transoceanic world power did they require a huge military apparatus, a defense establishment that proceeded to develop a weaponry so destructive that, in effect, it couldn't be used. When a stalemated cold war between two superpowers ended with the collapse of Soviet Communism, the United States was left as the world's only remaining superpower, having belatedly experienced on a global scale Europe's and Asia's long-time tradition of political power being contained by rival states in particular geopolitical spheres.

Since the end of the Cold War, the United States is the only superpower in a world of nation-states. There have been indications that this world is not a stable basis for the exercise of political sovereignty. Some of the pressure to reduce the authority of national governments has come from within nations. Ethnic nationalism is a strong force in both eastern (in the former Soviet Union and in Yugoslavia, for example) and western (the Scots and Welsh in Britain and the Basques in Spain, for instance) Europe and in North America (Quebec in Canada) and in Africa (tribal secessionist movements) and in Asia (East Timor in Indonesia)—on every continent. Some national governments have begun to devolve power to state or provincial governments. Other pressure on national authority comes from beyond nations. The United Nations and such international organizations as the World Bank, and the International Monetary Fund, and the World Trade Organization have sometimes directly influenced the operations of national governments. Regional organizations such as military alliances or economic leagues—NATO, the Organization of American States, the Organization for African Unity, for example—sometimes call upon national governments to agree to certain positions taken on behalf of a number of nations. The most dramatic infringement on national sovereignty has come from the European Union, in the very heartland of the nation-state, in western Europe itself.

As empires have vanished, new forms of supranational political arrangements have emerged, just as ethnic groups within established nations as well as lower levels of government within those nations have sometimes clamored either for independence or for more authority. The supremacy of a globe-girdling system of sovereign nation-states may turn out to be, in historical terms, a short one. If so, those who have come to identify themselves as Americans may have to widen their already spacious political identity—local, county, state, national—to embrace a global level as well.

7

Colonial Politics

In western Africa and throughout North America, the tribal societies that black African slaves and the native North American population came out of were led by chiefs, who were counseled by advisers of various kinds. Tribes made agreements with other tribes over the use of hunting or fishing or farming territories, and their warriors fought wars when disagreements among the tribes were not settled by peaceful means. In special circumstances, some tribes decided to unite into confederacies.

European polities during the sixteenth, seventeenth, and eighteenth centuries contained a spectrum of political systems, all the way from the decentralized, constitutional, republican confederation of Switzerland to the autocracies of the Russian and Ottoman Empires and the Papal states. There were republics in Venice, Holland, and Poland; constitutional monarchies at times in England, Scotland, and Sweden; and absolutist monarchies in France, Spain, and the Austrian Empire. Other states constituted mixtures of these arrangements, and there were important variations everywhere over time. The prevailing ideal was absolutism, that is, control by a central authority, which was at least partly the result of a reaction to the extreme localisms of the medieval period. Few states actually approached this ideal in practice, since the basic federate character of political life continued unabated. But, all of the European governments that developed empires during these centuries to some extent replicated in their colonies whatever was distinctive in their particular political systems.

The British Empire in its political aspects was similar to those of the Spanish, Portuguese, Dutch, and French in fundamental ways. There were common elements in the process by which these disparate groups of Europeans managed to bring their migrants to the Western Hemisphere within imperial governmental structures. Whether the Dutch, French, and English were aware of earlier Spanish and Portuguese methods or learned from each other or simply developed procedures devised by home ministries is not clear. Certainly, all of the European central governments sought to rationalize and unify their colonial possessions after initially allowing special groups and individuals to sponsor exploration, settlement, and exploitation. In the case of the English, a system of royal colonies was established by Charles II after the restoration of the monarchy in 1660.

The English imperial government did not proclaim law codes that were applicable throughout the empire the way the Portuguese and Spanish monarchs did, but several English kings issued royal charters that forbade founders of colonies from enacting any laws that contravened the rights of Englishmen. Unique among the Europeans, the English in North America allowed representative assemblies to become a feature of colonial government, starting with the early trading company settlements, where migrants refused to be governed by autocratic, absentee shareholders. Later proprietary colonies also instituted assemblies, on both the mainland and in the island colonies. This royal allowance of representative government was the beginning of a crucial distinction between the English and all the other European colonies in the Americas.

Like the Spanish and Portuguese councils and later ministries, the English had a central bureaucracy (at Whitehall) in London, with its Boards and then Secretaries. Similar to the Portuguese and Spanish two-tiered system of Viceroys and Captaincies (political appointees from Spain and Portugal), the English bureaucracy was linked directly to a one-tiered system of Royal Governors (political appointees from Britain), chosen by the monarch and responsible to him—and not to the remainder of the uniquely English provincial governments of which the Governors were the executive part. However, the Spanish *audencia* and the Portuguese *relacao* served as consultative councils, just as the English instituted appointed councils to advise their royal governors.

One large difference between the English and the other European powers in the operations of government was the manner in which law was made. The other European monarchs and the Dutch Stadtholder proclaimed the rules that Viceroys and Captains were supposed to enforce. But, in the English colonies, the assemblies enacted legislation on their own. The English monarch could veto legislation enacted by any provincial government, but this happened fairly rarely.

Like the Viceroys and Captains, the royal governors kept the imperial bureaucracy informed about colonial affairs and tried to maintain influence with the legislatures through the appointed councils and by means of political friendships among assemblymen. However, the English colonial assemblies went further: they appointed agents to look after their interests at the imperial capital, so that information flowed both ways. Furthermore, the Governors lacked the King's appointive power, the colonial assemblies having abrogated much of that power to themselves. With the House of Commons as their model, the assemblies also assumed the power to tax and to appropriate funds for the functioning of the colonial governments, including the royal governors' salaries.

The result was that the provincial governments did not function as smoothly as the British government after whom they were ostensibly modeled. Structurally, unlike the Spanish and Portuguese, whose governmental bodies typically blurred distinctions between the executive, judicial, and legislative functions of government, the provincial governments mirrored the tripartite division into legislative, executive, and judicial parts of the British imperial government: the royal governor was to the monarch what the colonial assemblies were to Parliament and what the colonial judiciary was to the British judicial system. But, though structurally similar to the imperial government in its overall outline or form of government, the colonial level of government contained features that made it quite different from its British model.

The aspect of English political life the least altered by their colonists across the Atlantic was the adjudication and enforcement of the laws. The judicial system in the colonies was a direct transplant of the English original, with judges usually appointed for life on good behavior and judicial decisions usually based upon English precedents. As for the enforcement of the laws, as in England and elsewhere in Europe, crime was not punished through incarceration; criminals were hopefully rehabilitated through the humiliation or pain of stocks and whipping or were publicly hanged as a means of deterring others from committing major criminal acts.

But, there were many other features of government that on the surface the English and their colonists appeared to share, but were in fact significantly distinguishable and led directly to what was truly distinctive in the political system that successfully rebellious colonists later created for an independent United States. Government in the colonies actually functioned as if frozen, stuck in a time warp. The features of the English political system that matured during the Tudor period, before the seventeenth century, were retained in the colonies even as, during the seventeenth and eighteenth centuries, the political system in England significantly evolved. What had been quite distinctive and separate executive, legislative, and judicial organs of government during the Tudor period developed during the Stuart and Hanoverian periods into the modern Parliamentary system in which the executive governs through a ministry selected from sitting members of Parliament and thus located in the legislature—but not in the colonies.

Both the British and the colonial electorates were confined to adult white males with a certain level of wealth or property, based on the widely shared belief that only those with a "stake in society" should be able to vote. But, though this practice produced a small voting list in British ridings, the relative ease with which adult white male colonists satisfied the property-holding qualification meant that the electorate was far larger in the colonies than it ever was in Britain itself, so large that after political independence Americans soon ended the property-holding requirement for that segment of the population and created the first mass electorate of the Western world.

Both the British and the colonial political systems were based upon fundamental rules or constitutions. But, the British constitutional order was "unwritten," or at least not contained in a single document, whereas the colonists became used to living under royal charters, which provided a basis for their governmental arrangements, so much so that when political independence was declared the colonists moved directly to contain new "frames of government" in written constitutions.

Both the British and the colonists divided executive and legislative authority. But in Britain, the King governed through his ministry who were sitting members *in* the House of Commons, in the legislature, whereas in the colonies, the Royal Governors were royally appointed officials, executives fully separate from the assemblies or legislatures, so that, with political independence, the Americans created a presidency, or chief executive, whose advisors of heads of executive departments were not elected members of Congress, but officials appointed by the President with the Senate's concurrence.

Nor was colonial government, with its popularly elected assemblies, confined to a resident Chief and a predetermined council of advisers, as was the case with the native American population and had been the case while still in Africa with the black slaves.

However, colonial governments did not legislate in ways that deeply affected the lives of ordinary colonists. Their chief law-making function, at least in the mainland colonies, was to develop land policy, which was of great importance, but lacked—by itself—the range and depth of the activities performed by local governments within the colonies. In this, the English were like the Spanish and the Portuguese, who allowed representative government only at the local level, in their *cabildos* and *senado da camara*, but even at that level, the monarchs appointed officials to such local councils in areas where they thought it important to have a more direct control. These municipal councils, when elected, were elected by property-holding electorates, and performed a wide variety of tasks for the inhabitants of usually large townships.

In the English colonies, officials elected within villages, towns, cities, and counties supervised and regulated a vast array of daily activities and constituted without question the most important level of government operating within the empire. Local and county government licensed public activity of many kinds and, in the licensing, regulated the way these activities could legally be practiced. These same governments maintained or supervised public things, whether fences, roadways, commons, forests, waterways, buildings. By contrast, the colonial and imperial governments rarely affected, in consequential ways, the ongoing lives of those who settled in British North America.

Only in matters of trade and defense—clearly matters of an imperial reach and scope—did the "central" government in London act in ways that directly shaped the lives of the colonists. Trade regulations governed the production, movement, and sale of products for that relatively small element of the population involved in commerce or the market economy. Defense policy could at times involve all able-bodied men who, as militiamen, could be commanded to aid the British professional army at times of war with England's enemies, though only as ancillary troops.

The trade regulations, to the extent that they fostered the development of colonial-made products within a large and sufficiently profitable empirewide market, were beneficial to the colonists involved in the market economy and, with few exceptions, were supported by those colonists. By contrast, the defense regulations sometimes provoked resistance. The imperial government worked out an elaborate quota system under which each mainland colony was supposed to send a designated number of troops and supplies to aid the British regular army during the colonial wars that occurred fairly frequently throughout the colonial period. These protracted periods of warfare disrupted and distorted the development of economic life in the colonies, causing inflation because of scarcities and interrupting the civilian lives of significant numbers of young men. The governments of those colonies that weren't directly threatened by the military actions between the British and their new world antagonists tended to delay or dilute their military obligations under the quota system.

England created as the political dimension of its empire a vast, sprawling, highly decentralized governmental system, all of whose taxes, most of whose expenditures, and, with the two notable exceptions of trade and defense, all of whose powers were of a local and provincial character. England's imperial system, in its governmental aspects, thus veered away from those of Spain, Portugal, Holland, and France. Although the overall form of government was similar in all of the European empires, the actual functioning of government in the English empire was notably more decentralized than was the case in the empires of its European rivals.

But, it is also important to stress that, even though the Spaniards, Portuguese, Dutch, and French tried to impose a centralized system on their colonists, the actual manner in which royal and statdholder edicts were carried out depended a lot on the local officials responsible for applying those edicts. Such officials varied considerably in their interpretation of imperial decrees as they applied those decrees to the actual functioning of government in the other European colonial empires. *All* the new empires in the Americas shared the same oceanic spatial separation from the centers of European political authority.

Individual English colonists identified with and were loyal to a hierarchy of political communities, inverted in the strength of their attachment—local, provincial, and imperial—just as those communities were inverted in the extent of their power. The structure and, though not to such an extent, the functioning of government were similar at every level in England and in its colonies, as was the practice of a deferentially minded adult male, propertied electorate selecting prominent individuals as representatives and officials, though only in England did the monarchy and aristocracy bring to political life a hereditary element.

The colonists were generally satisfied with this political system, though the sporadic existence of "vigilante" movements and rebellions suggests that, when the formal instrumentalities of government were not responsive to the perceived needs of frontiersmen or disgruntled inhabitants in any area, at least some colonists were willing to create their own forms of government or tried to stop the existing government from functioning. There was at all levels—local, provincial, imperial—suspicion among some colonists that those in office shared a propensity to abuse power, but this suspicion didn't indicate widespread dissatisfaction with the existing political system.

But this system evolved only in those colonies within the empire that were English in origin, and not in the two colonies conquered from France (Quebec) and Spain (Florida) in the last great war of the colonial era.

8

The Revolution

There is overwhelming evidence that the colonists were satisfied with their status within the British Empire, which, with the conquest of New France during the Seven Years' War (1755–1761), rivaled Spain's in its territorial extent and in its economic resources. Though the Empire had developed in piecemeal fashion and was significantly less centralized in its management than the empires of any of Britain's rivals, nonetheless, all the colonists shared major components of a British way of life—a common language, legal system, and form of government. The colonists identified with and were loyal to a political entity—an empire—that was far greater in extent than their localities and particular colonies, with which they also identified and to which they were also loyal. Individuals in British North America ordinarily did not feel much stress and strain living within such a hierarchy of identification and loyalty.

Colonial society was thoroughly imbued with the reality of imposed hierarchies of various kinds. Militiamen called to serve as auxiliary forces sometimes became concerned about the differences between themselves and the English provincial troops stationed abroad. Colonial auxiliaries could feel the inferior status inculcated by the British forces and recoil from perceived British arrogance and notions of superiority. Colonial merchants and planters could resent Parliamentary restrictions that channeled or confined many forms of trade within the Empire. But, before the Seven Years' War, particular colonial governments sometimes ignored imperial requisitions for troops and supplies, thus diminishing provincial involvement in the wars of the Empire. And, the Navigation Acts did not, in most cases, have the effect of suppressing economic development in the colonies. Indeed, in the instance of tobacco, the single most important commodity of trade, the British mercantile community financed, shipped, stored, marketed, and sold the drug.

The Seven Years' War was the event that changed fundamentally the political perception the British and their North American colonists had of one another. Under William Pitt's leadership, the British turned what had usually been the colonial "sideshow" war into the main theater. Pitt hired mercenaries to fight for the British in Europe against France, made his major goal the defeat of the French Empire in North America and India, appointed able young commanders, and actually reimbursed the colonists for their auxiliary troops and their supplies. When the British forces defeated the French, Britain ended the war as the unchallenged imperial power of North America, but was without allies in Europe and heavily in debt.

Pitt's successors were determined to tighten up the administration of the Empire and to make the colonists contribute financially to its defense. But, the British were not alone among the imperial powers in the Americas to seek more effective means of administering their empire. In the very years that the English ministries worked toward that end, the Spanish monarch instituted the intendency system throughout Spanish America. Between 1764 and 1790, the King appointed intendents to all of their colonies, royal officials of Spanish birth who were given extensive administrative, judicial, and financial authority. The intendents reported directly to the monarch on financial matters, though in religious, judicial, and administrative matters, they were subject to the Viceroy. In the 1760s, the Spanish monarch also created a colonial militia with creole officers under the Viceroy's command in order to shift at least some of the burden of defending the empire.

As for the British, a succession of ministries (1) closed off the trans-Appalachian West to further settlement in order to maintain peace with the native tribes there, (2) extended the French-style government of Quebec down to the Mississippi River in order to provide a government for much of the trans-Appalachian West, (3) set up a Board of Customs Commissioners in Halifax and established rules for the confiscation of illegally traded commodities in Vice-Admiralty Courts, (4) established procedures for the quartering of British professional troops stationed in the colonies in peacetime for defensive purposes, and (5) established a series of revenue acts so that the colonists would contribute directly to the expense of maintaining and defending the Empire.

All of these policies were adapted by the British political leadership as sound measures, as appropriate means to the end of creating an efficiently administered transoceanic empire. The British government, after a century and a half of experience in colonization, rather suddenly determined that there were circumstances that compelled it to exercise a greater degree of centralized administration, something the Spanish were doing at the same time. No one in the British political world doubted that the King and Parliament had the authority to act in this manner. Parliament "virtually" represented the Empire, British observers and commentators argued, and thus had power to act as an imperial legislature.

The political divisions that occurred in the years after the Seven Years' War were caused by divergent opinions on the expediency or wisdom of pursuing such important policy initiatives, especially concerning taxation. When some of the colonists openly resisted the British revenue acts of 1765 and 1767, the economic boycotts launched against the British created enough pressure for new ministries that emerged from the unstable coalitional politics that marked Parliament's life in the 1760s to repeal those acts. When, in 1770, the North ministry brought relative stability to its Parliamentary majority, George III reacted with greater decisiveness and confidence in response to the further colonial resistance to British policy that occurred with the enactment of additional trade regulations (particularly the Tea Act of 1773).

By this time, the King and his ministry were willing to believe the reports of conspiracy (that certain colonial politicians were plotting to become politically independent) transmitted by royal governors. Whenever there was a time of political strain, ministries had so reacted, at least since the time of Walpole's ministries during the 1720s and 1730s. The King's response was to have his ministry get Parliamentary approval for a set of Coercive Acts (1774), which in their totality greatly affected the functioning of the colonial and local governments of an offending colony—Massachusetts Bay, where some colonists openly defied the operation of the Tea Act. As resistance to such imperial intervention spread throughout the colonies, the King became determined to suppress this illegal response. Legitimate authority must, he believed, be upheld.

From the British perspective, the legislation enacted after the Seven Years' War was within Parliament's authority and was, to many, appropriate in the circumstances. To some, these policies were ill-timed and unwise, while to others, they were necessary as a response to growing evidence of conspiracies and plots. Everyone agreed that colonial resistance was illegal, though to some it was understandable. Most concluded, with the King, that the rebellion that broke out in 1775 should be crushed.

But, from the colonial perspective, British policy from 1765 to 1774 seemed increasingly authoritarian, to some, and tyrannical, to others. Those who led the colonial resistance believed that the postwar legislation revealed a tyrannical design on the part of the ministers who designed it. The resisters could find no other explanation.

The Quebec Act placed much of the "backcountry" under a colonial government that, because of Britain's prior failure to replace a French-style administration with their own, was without an assembly, which the English colonists regarded as the foundation of representative, limited government. The claimants of all commodities examined by the imperial customs service as contraband were to have their case put before a juryless Vice-Admiralty court and thus were to be denied a trial by their peers. The Quartering Act allowed a professional army to be quartered among the civilian population in peacetime, something that constituted a direct threat to the liberty of the population. Above all, the colonists were being taxed without any representation in the legislature through which the revenue acts were passed and were thus ordered to give up a portion of their property without their having taken part in the decision. The Tea Act gave a monopolistic, favored position to one company, the East India Company, and was thus highly arbitrary and unfair. And finally, the Coercive Acts changed the settled functioning of the provincial level of government (in Massachusetts Bay colony) and baldly revealed how arbitrary and dictatorial the imperial government had become.

The resisters rejected the argument that the British Parliament "virtually" represented them, insisting that it was impractical for them to have transoceanic representatives in any case, came in time to disregard Parliamentary supremacy, and finally—though reluctantly—refused their allegiance to the Crown, pledging themselves to support a rightful revolution as an appropriate reaction to such sustained and systematic tyranny. Appropriate too, in their view, was the form of resistance chosen as a response to each incursion on their liberty. Mob action, economic boycott, intercolonial assemblies—all were illegal, but all were justifiable means of forcing the imperial government to end its tyranny.

Such responses provoked the desired result in the case of the Revenue Acts of 1765 and 1767: repeal. But, an unrepentant King and Parliament refused to react in the desired manner to colonial petitions that the Tea Act and the Coercive Acts be similarly treated. In their Declaration of Independence, the colonial resisters presented a lawyer's brief, an exaggeratedly itemized account of all the ways that the imperial government, and particularly the King, had abused its authority. When any government infringes on the liberties of the people it was formed to protect, then revolution is justifiable, argued those who led portions of the colonial population into open rebellion.

But the rebels misunderstood British policymakers. Those charged with the responsibility for the colonies did not develop a grand scheme for tyranny, as those who resisted the policy innovations after 1763 argued. British officials also misunderstood the nature of the opposition in the colonies. The resisters were not conspirators: they were not secretly plotting to gain their political independence by any means. The rebel leaders of 1775–1776 were reluctant revolutionaries, who chose independence only after every available means to bring about the end of an era of arbitrary and tyrannical policymaking had inevitably failed. Each side misunderstood the purposes and motives of the other. An obstinate King whose ministry had a safe Parliamentary majority presiding over a geographically far-flung empire with a strong tradition of decentralization and containing a population of great political sophistication—all at a time when, from the imperial perspective, there was an obvious need for greater centralization, efficiency, and shared costs—such were the elements that led to a political explosion.

In the war that followed, Britain's presumed superiority was undermined in many ways. The British had to keep a "home defense" force at the channel to protect itself from France, which later combined with Spain in a war that enveloped the colonial war for independence. A league of neutrals isolated Britain in Europe. When France found opportunities to assist in the division of the

British Empire and diminish British power, it sided with the rebels, secretly at first and then in open alliance, significantly augmenting rebel power during the conflict. The British experienced colossal logistical problems when they sent troops and supplies across the Atlantic Ocean. Britain's professional troops fought in faraway, strange settings that local rebel militia units knew well. The British forces never felt they could completely trust or rely on those who proclaimed their loyalty, and, as a consequence, loyalist units, while useful in the later stages of the fighting, were only slowly organized. The British high command lacked imagination and daring. The Gages were hesitant about how vigorously to prosecute the war, as long as it remained unclear whether either side might seek conciliation. Later, Clinton failed to develop strategy and campaigns that he rigorously pursued.

Overall, the British—somewhat like the Union during the Civil War and the United States in the Vietnam War—sought to blockade the rebellious colonies, occupy their coastal cities, and strike inland cutting off and surrounding whole sections of the rebellious areas, pulverizing the resistance. The British failed because they lacked needed brilliance in their field commanders; because the resistance was too scattered and localized ever to be subdued in a vast, sprawling, often unfamiliar territory; because Washington and his Continental Army, which became adept at the warfare of maneuverability, were never completely defeated on the field of battle; and because of French supplies, ships, and troops.

In the peace treaty of 1783, the British—in protracted negotiations—were hampered by an unstable political situation and shifting ministries, by a war-weary population, and by American negotiators willing to overlook treaty provisions with the French that they not make a separate peace with the British, willing as well to take full advantage of the British negotiators' distractions. The result was a settlement highly favorable to the rebellious colonists: recognition of American independence and the relinquishment of all British territory west of the Appalachians and south of the Great Lakes.

The civilian population's life was sporadically disrupted by the war—along the Atlantic Coast, by the British blockade; inland, by whatever campaigns were being fought; everywhere, by disrupted trade and by inflation caused by the shortage of products of many kinds. A lot of colonists tried to remain neutral or aloof or uninvolved—unmoved by either the rebel or the loyalist positions. Others became associated with the rebel cause through war contracts, supplying the Continental Army and enhancing their economic status thereby. Whether an individual became an active rebel or loyalist or remained uncommitted was a position taken under the influence of many factors—material (or economic), intellectual, psychological, emotional in character—and indeed was sometimes reassessed sporadically throughout the war.

Minorities—newer, non-English immigrants, native Americans, runaway slaves, small religious sects—*tended* to remain loyal, as did those in the upper strata of the colonial population whose position was created or sustained by imperial connections (officials, Anglican clergy). Those who were on the rise economically, socially, or politically *tended* to become rebels. Risk takers were more apt to opt for revolution, whereas those who craved security and the status quo were not. In some areas, rebel committees demanded oaths of allegiance to the rebel cause and branded (or tarred and feathered) as loyalist all who would not give such an oath.

The new state governments enacted legislation that seriously compromised the liberty of professed loyalists. Those who publicly remained loyal in particular colonies/states in varied combinations: (1) were banned from certain occupations, (2) had their property confiscated, (3) were banished or forced into exile (thousands fled during and at the end of the war), and (4) if convicted of openly aiding British forces, were put to death. The rebels were not bothered by the inconsistency of taking away the liberty of fellow colonists in a revolution whose aim was to assure liberty and end tyranny. Since the loyalists opposed their cause, the rebels believed that various restrictions placed on the liberty of such misguided individuals were justified; nothing must be allowed to jeopardize the revolutionary movement. The result was deeply divided, antagonistic groups who existed in the midst of an even wider and indifferent populace, a keenly felt civil war in the midst of a war for independence.

The revolution was political in nature: the rebels succeeded in establishing their political independence in the first successful colonial revolt in modern history. But, the war for independence was just that: it did not produce immediate major political, economic, social, or cultural-intellectual change for the civilian population involved. The Continental Congress, a body of delegates from each of the rebelling colonies, kept on sitting throughout the war, serving as a new central government, delegating authority to committees, hoping—vainly—to win the approval of the new state governments for a constitution that sanctified what it was already doing, which was to wage war, negotiate a peace treaty, regulate postal communications—the very powers that the imperial government had exercised before the revolt. The only major difference between the two governments was that Congress did not have the power to tax. Unlike the British Parliament, which had presumed that it had the authority to tax the provinces even though they were not represented in it, Congress carefully avoided taxing the former colonists, who had not elected Congress' members.

Drawing on their experiences with written royal charters as frames of government, the new state governments drew up and approved constitutions during the war years. The forms of government thus sanctioned evolved out of the colonial experience. Royal governors became state governors, who, like their predecessors, were administrators and executives separate from the new state legislatures, which, in turn, were separate from the judiciary. The only major distinction between colonial and state governments was that the locus of power shifted downward, skewed toward the lower houses of the legislature, which were to be frequently elected and thus more emphatically and directly accountable to the people than had been the case previously. The electorate still consisted of propertied white adult males, which—however—continued to be proportionately larger than in Europe because of the relative ease with which the property-holding qualification could be met. There was, in sum, no politically revolutionary change within the colonies themselves as a result of the revolution. Continuity was far more basic than change.

However, the departure of the loyalists meant that the "Americans" lost the most articulate advocates of the prevailing political and social conservatism of that time. In the revolution, rebelling Americans believed that they had advanced the cause of liberalism, but, without the loyalists, the former colonists' spectrum of beliefs on the proper character of government and society was suddenly truncated. Since the revolution, except for some proslavery defenders during the antebellum period, Americans have lacked that brand of conservatism whose greatest proponent was Edmund Burke: the belief that society and government properly change slowly, organically; that rebellion and revolution disrupt the traditions and order and legitimacy of an ongoing society and must not be allowed to succeed, as they give credibility to illegal and illegitimate and violent change. A society should change peacefully, gradually, without great upheavals.

The nature and direction of the erstwhile colonists' economic activity were not changed as a consequence of the war—disrupted, even temporarily deranged, but not basically altered. The Americans were still oriented toward the acquisition and accumulation of wealth, an orientation that continued to receive both religious and secular sanction. Most people continued to be farmers and craftsmen. The land continued to provide materials for an unusual abundance of largely handcrafted products. Socially, the class and caste system of colonial times continued largely unaltered: no new group rose up and seized control from a planter-merchant–dominated elite. Slavery did not end. The native population continued to move ever westward, and their relationships with the white migrants and their progeny remained unaltered. Thought and culture—previously largely derivative of European modes—were not profoundly affected by the revolution, even though there were individuals who advocated that American independence and uniqueness ought to extend across all dimensions of life, not just the political. In sum, the revolution was restricted in its definition to being a political war of independence.

And yet, the republican political ideology that the revolution greatly stimulated, an ideology that guided the constitution making of the 1770s and 1780s, had a profound influence on the way Americans later perceived society. A republican outlook rejected a society based upon inherited, fixed rank and status, a society of patriarchy, patronage, and dependency. In its place, a republican government would govern independent, property-owning citizens who were capable themselves of discerning what the public interest was through the exercise of public virtue. Such citizens would elect a natural elite who would govern in a disinterested fashion in the public interest. Such a society and such a polity would be profoundly different from those that prevailed while Americans were colonists.

But, in a geographical sense, the American Revolution was limited as well.

Even though the English had long called their North American colonists "Americans" and their mainland colonies "America," it was not all the continental colonies that contained resistance movements or that openly rebelled and fought a war for independence. Even in the colonies that revolted, the population was deeply divided. The fragment of the British Empire that gained its independence was geographically contiguous, but not continental in scope.

Quebeckers, most of whom were descendants of French migrants, remained neutral, in spite of appeals from a rebel force that temporarily captured Montreal in 1775. Though there was some expression of support among the minority English-speaking groups, most French-speaking settlers thought of rebellion as something dividing the English world and not of much meaning and usefulness to them. Nova Scotians, many of them immigrants from New England, were heavily dependent on the imperial government for services and security at Halifax and did not wish to jeopardize this arrangement. Similarly, the settlers of (formerly Spanish) Florida hovered around forts. In the West Indies, the small white elite who were elected to the island assemblies sent petitions to Parliament in support of the continental rebels' positions, but the West Indians, like the Nova Scotians and the Floridians, were heavily dependent upon the presence of the British navy, and resistance movements did not develop in Barbados and (formerly Spanish) Jamaica.

* * *

The revolution was also unique and differed substantially from other major civil wars and revolutions that sporadically punctuated the history of European civilization, such eruptions as the English Civil War of the 1640s, the French Revolution of the 1790s, and the Russian Revolution of the 1910s. Although these other conflicts shared a common sequence—moderate to radical to conservative phases, in the case of the British colonial revolt of 1775–1781, the moderate colonial leadership of the 1765–1775 decade of discontent and resistance remained in control throughout the war for independence and in the years that followed. The only substantial change that came as a result of the American Revolution was the replacement of the British imperial government by a confederacy whose central government, not directly elected, lacked what had been widely regarded as the offensive power to tax.

The successful American revolt occurred in an era of revolutionary movements that exploded across Europe and its colonies from the 1770s to the 1820s. What the American rebels *did* share with their revolutionary counterparts elsewhere was a "liberal" philosophy and objective. All of these movements stressed the importance of there being a state whose government was pledged to protect the civil liberties of its subjects or citizens.

The Middle and South Americans who revolted from Spain during the 1810s and 1820s tried to emulate their American republican neighbor, copying its form of government and libertarian creed, creating their own republics. Educated

Spanish and Portuguese colonists were aware of the liberal political philosophy that had been used to justify the American and French revolutions. When Napoleon entered Spain and Portugal and displaced the reigning Iberian monarchs, factions of the native-born elites (or creoles and *mestizos*) came, over time, to support independence from European rule, just as factions of the British colonial elites had done several generations before.

And, just as in the British colonies, the violent independence movements in Middle and South America were in fact civil wars, as all segments of the colonial populations were divided between those loyal to Spain and those favoring political freedom. National liberation armies under such commanders as Bolivar and Martin led successful revolts against Spain, just as Washington's Continental Army had earlier brought the British North American colonial revolt to a successful conclusion several decades earlier. As in North America, so later in Middle and South America, the same elite governed before, during, and after the revolts themselves. In both cases, these nativeborn or creole elites simply went on governing and dominating the society and the economy. In both continents, revolution did not lead to basic economic, social, or cultural change. In all these ways, the North American and South American revolts were alike.

Only the Portuguese colony of Brazil remained a European-style kingdom, as the Portuguese monarch, King John VI, fled to the Americas when Napoleon's armies invaded the Iberian peninsula in 1808. John VI's descendants, Pedro I and Pedro II, as Emperors, added a European-style state to the many republics of the Western Hemisphere.

And yet, the American rebels were distinctive in creating a nation-state whose essence was both libertarian and republican. Neither the Middle nor South Americans nor, later, the Asian and African "creoles" who became involved in colonial revolutions were able to replicate the American achievement because these areas of the globe had experienced a form of colonization in which small elites ruled autocratically over native masses who remained poor even as transplanted Europeans garnered great wealth, property, and products from the extensive lands and seas that they colonized around the world. In sharp contrast to the English colonists in North America, in Middle and South America, the former Spanish colonists had no experience with representative government, as Spain had never allowed its colonists to establish elected government at the colonial level.

Only the Americans, and among the Americans, only those who lived in the temperate zone from the Chesapeake Bay to the Bay of Fundy, had been able to recreate the middle-class society of northern and western Europe, and, particularly, of England, and thus place themselves in a position to extend Europe's liberal political culture beyond the motherland, first in the form of colonial assemblies and later in the shape of independent state and national governments.

Southern planters such as Thomas Jefferson and James Madison were among the chief apostles of republicanism and were in an anomalous position. Members of a tiny elite who dominated the southern English colonies in every sense, the planters nonetheless provided the rebellion and its republican-oriented state makers with its most inspired leadership. And yet, the planters governed a socioeconomic, semitropical climatic zone that had far more in common with Spanish and Portuguese America than it did with the rest of British America. But, in an important sense the southern English colonies differed from those of the Spanish and Portuguese: white settlers poured into the colonial south, where small farms could coexist with plantations, as the leading staple crop, tobacco, could be produced profitably in settings of varying size.

However, planters such as Jefferson and Madison came out of a political system that was republican in everything but name. The way that they made sense out of a such a political system overlayering a socioeconomic system that was alien to the rest of the English colonists was to base their engrained republicanism on race. Theirs was a republic of a majority white population whose economy was also deeply involved with black slave labor. What southern republicanism did was to make the black population invisible socially and politically. The caste of race made such a republican world possible, workable. Such planters joined with resisters elsewhere to argue and fight for independence and the imposition of a new republican order that would cover a continental nation, fatefully divided as it was into two socioeconomic zones.

But, the peculiarities of the British colonial experience created a nonreplicable revolt. The British effort to transplant, to recreate "little Englands" elsewhere led directly to the growth of a sizable white population that tried to duplicate English society in North America, displacing the native population and enslaving forced African emigrants. It was a portion of this colonial society (with its middle-class orientation) that rejected policies that appeared to be tyrannical in character and fought a war of independence with the objective of creating a liberally oriented society, something that has not occurred in those areas of the world where a society of tiny white elites and a massive poor native population have existed. Though rebel movements in Middle and South America, Africa, and Asia have proclaimed a European-derived liberal rhetoric, they have usually been unable to establish liberal nation-states.

* * *

The Revolution as a historical event has had a great impact on the minds of Americans, even though it did not significantly change the way they have lived afterwards. The Declaration of Independence has been revered as a form of secular scripture, the very source of the American nation, worthy of being viewed under glass in a shrinelike room of the National Archives (since the 1940s), its anniversary—July 4—justifiably celebrated (since the 1820s) as the nation's birthday. This one document, Americans have believed, instantaneously created a nation-state, one dedicated to liberty, a large republic in a world then dominated by monarchical and aristocratic dynastic kingdoms.

America did not evolve: it exploded into being. It was unique, special, worthy of intense national loyalty. Since the revolution, the philosophy that various reform and protest groups have perceived in the Declaration has been used to justify a great range of political, economic, and social ameliorative change. Woman's rights groups, abolitionists, civil rights movements, labor unions—all have at one time or another appealed to the Declaration as justification for their cause. Only the socialists have looked beyond this expression of libertarian thought to European sources that have stressed equality as much as liberty.

In the nineteenth century, Americans supported revolution elsewhere (Middle and South American in the 1810s and the 1890s, European in the 1840s) and pointed to their own Declaration as a proper sanction. But, in the twentieth century, communist-led revolts were not popular among Americans, basically because of the revolts' antiliberal character. However, from the late nineteenth century to the late twentieth century, the United States was not a revolutionary model for Latin America, Asia, and Africa in any case. With an expansionist industrial, capitalistic economy, the nonelite population of these continents often favored political movements that promised equality or the end of mass poverty and elitist privilege, wealth, and power—favored these movements over those that stressed the importance of a liberal state. In the course of the twentieth century, the Americans became aware of the limited applicability of their own revolutionary tradition.

9

The Constitution

The confederacy that the Americans created at the start of their rebellion finally received its constitutional frame when the "Articles of Confederation" were approved—with the settlement of western land claims—by all of the new states, in 1781, the year the fighting stopped. During the 1780s, Congress, consisting of delegations chosen by each of the states' legislatures and each with one vote, provided a mixture of effective and ineffective governance.

Some states were lax in selecting and sending their quotient of delegates. Some delegates were themselves lax in attendance and being present for voting. Congress could exercise only that authority given to it by the Articles; the states retained all other powers. Even so, Congress in the 1780s did what it had been doing during the revolution and what the old imperial government had done before that: It was responsible for relations with other nations and with the native population, for postal communications, for weights and measures, for coinage.

In order that Congress avoid exercising those powers that had created the imperial crisis of the 1760s and 1770s, the unicameral government was given no authority to tax (it had to requisition the states for revenues) and no authority to raise and maintain an army and a navy (it had to rely on the states to fill national quotas from their own armies and navies). Congress did not enact laws, but passed ordinances for which it had no national force to compel compliance. And, because an amendment to the Articles required the unanimous consent of the states, efforts to find a reliable source of revenue failed when an amendment granting Congress the right to levy import duties did not gain the necessary unanimous consent of the states.

Ironically, the two great achievements of government under the Articles involved actions for which Congress had no express authority to act. In both cases, the politicians who sat as delegates acted pragmatically and effectively to deal with two major problems: the need for a national banking and credit system and the need for a national policy respecting the public lands.

Superintendent of Finances Robert Morris devised a scheme for a national bank that was quasi-public and quasi-private, even though performing public functions. The new bank provided loans for those in commercial life at the same time that it served as a deposit for government funds. Morris' model was Britain's national bank, the British having been the first Europeans to develop an institution of this kind. (This was the first of several national banking systems that shared this private/public character.)

Congress, after much debate, decided that the new territory granted by Britain at the peace treaty of 1783 would not remain in a subservient "colonial" status, as the erstwhile colonists themselves had been within Britain's European-style overseas empire. As Russia had been doing in its expansionist overland empire, America too would expand through the *addition* of territories, which, at a requisite level of population, would be admitted to the union as states with equal standing. The novelty in the American scheme was that the new territories, as states, would be indistinguishable from the original union of states, whereas in the expanding Russian empire, additional territories typically contained new ethnic and racial groupings, though over time, ethnic Russian migrants mixed with these other groups. Without a monarch or an aristocracy, Americans never thought of their expanding nation as an empire. Furthermore, the public lands in the new territories were to be sold to settlers at auction in an orderly fashion, with the proceeds to provide revenue for Congress. (Although there would be debate at the time of subsequent territorial accessions, later U.S. Congresses reconfirmed this basic policy.)

So, acting beyond its stated powers, Congress nonetheless forged two very basic policies that would remain central to all subsequent governmental activity: (1) that the national government would continue to be active in regulating the economy in a mercantilist manner, that is, it would favor a mixed economy marked by the interaction of both private and public sectors (the national bank being the classic illustration of this position) and (2) the American union would be expansionist, but in a way that veered away from the European norm, as a growing nation of equal states.

But, in the sphere of international relations, Congress was almost wholly ineffectual. It was unable to agree on any response or to provide direction for its Secretary of Foreign Relations with respect to British and Spanish incursions on American territory. The Spaniards closed the mouth of the Mississippi River, claimed much of the southwestern part of the British-ceded lands as their own, and tried to aid secessionist movements in the old southwest. The British maintained troops in forts that were clearly within American territory under the terms of the peace settlement and did so with the explanation that their action was the means by which to pressure the American government to force individuals to repay their prewar debts to the British and the state governments to compensate the loyalists for having confiscated their property.

During the 1780s, debate grew concerning the overall performance of Congress. The "Continentalists" were those who argued that the new national government was too limited in power to govern a large nation effectively. The "Localists" were those who insisted that Congress had sufficient power; that it was unable to become tyrannical, as the old imperial government in London had; and that in any case the national and state governments together had sufficient power to govern appropriately. When a proposed constitutional amendment failed to be enacted, some continentalist-oriented politicians called for the states to send delegates to a special, constitutional convention to review the Articles.

The convention of delegates—55 in number—met in the summer of 1787 in Philadelphia. These men were among the ablest of the politicians of their time. Most were of the elite—the planter-merchant group who had dominated colonial life. They were experienced in political life, but were also aware of European philosophy and history. And though much of what they did reveals their awareness of political activity in the colonies and during the revolution as well as their constant reference to the recent state constitutions and the Articles themselves, it is also clear these men were aware they were creating a new nation-state and tried to base it on the best philosophical ideals of Europe. It is this fusion of the practical with the ideal that makes the U.S. Constitution what it has been as a durable frame of government.

The delegates were agreed that there should be a new constitution and a new government and not just a revision of the old (even though they had not been chosen with this as the stated objective). They agreed that the new government should consist of the classic three organs responsible for the three main functions of government: the administration, enactment, and adjudication of the laws by an executive, legislative, and judiciary, respectively (whereas the old government was a unicameral, or legislative, one). And they agreed that the new government should be elected (in various ways) and thus directly responsible to the people (rather than merely delegates chosen by state legislatures as in the past), and that it should also have substantial powers (that the old Congress had lacked): the power to tax, to raise and maintain armies and navies, to regulate commerce.

The work of the convention was done in committees that examined state constitutions and the Articles as guides, but drew on their members' own abundant political experience and familiarity with European political philosophy to produce segments of a wholly new frame of government. The committees' presentations were further debated and voted on by the whole convention. The resulting document has the appearance of a hacked-up lawyer's brief—long, detailed passages appear next to abbreviated statements; some sections appear in a superabundance of detail, others are tantalizingly terse or vague. Everywhere the new constitution betrays its origins in a forum of debate and compromise.

On two issues, the convention was so divided that it could have ended before agreement on a final draft was achieved. The first was the question of slavery: What political expression should its existence merit? The compromise between hostile Northern spokesmen and favorable Southern delegates was that the slave trade would end by 1808 (20 years after the new government began), but that three slaves would count as one voter for purposes of establishing electoral districts for representatives, so that there would be more representatives in areas in which there were slaves than there would be elsewhere. The second issue for which compromise was found was another question involving representation: How would the small states of the new union keep from being overwhelmed by the representatives of the larger states if representation were based on numbers? The solution was to limit representation in the Senate or "upper" chamber of the new Congress to two per state, to be chosen by the state legislatures.

The final document established a new national government whose structure was based in many ways on what the drafters derived from their colonial experience in government. The executive, or President—like the Royal Governors before him—was to be independent of the legislature, or Congress, which was—as before—to have two chambers, and the judiciary was to be independent of both the executive and legislature in turn. Each organ of government was to be chosen in a distinctive way: the House of Representatives, in electoral districts, by all those who could vote; the Senate, by state legislatures; the President, by an electoral college, whose members were elected by the voters of each state; and the Justices of the Supreme Court and the Federal Courts, nominated by the President, with the required approval of the Senate. Thus, though there were to be no hereditary offices, something that characterized European governments, with their monarchs and aristocracies, officials of the new American government were to be chosen by different groups of people—some by the whole electorate, others by special groups who, it was felt by the drafters, would have a greater capacity to select those who would serve in the higher offices.

So, the new government was to be, in the manner of its composition, neither simply "popular" nor in any way hereditary. What was distinctive about the newly planned government was not only its nonhereditary and thus republican character, but—even more so—the separation of power and the checks and balances that were to exist among the three organs of the government. It is in this aspect of their constitution making that the drafters drew most heavily on their knowledge of the history and philosophy of Europe. As a group, they were extremely concerned that the new central government not be able to become tyrannical, as the old imperial government had been. In order that this not happen, the powers of government must be checked, balanced, separated. The new government must be strong enough to govern effectively for the nation's welfare, but must never be so strong that it could jeopardize by means of tyrannical actions the liberties of its citizens.

There were several ways the drafters chose to prevent this from happening. Not only was each organ chosen differently, but each was chosen for terms of differing lengths—Representatives for two years; Senators for six years; Presidents for four years; Justices for life. Proposed legislation had to receive the approval of both houses of Congress and the President. If the President vetoed a bill passed by Congress, Congress could override his veto with a two-thirds vote. The President could make treaties with other nations, but those agreements had to receive the Senate's approval. Only Congress could initiate the appropriation of funds for foreign relations. The President could be removed from office for "high crimes and misdemeanors"; Justices of the Supreme Court could also be removed if convicted of a major crime; and Congress itself had the right to deny a seat to any of its elected members.

The powers that each organ of the new government was to exercise were unquestionably drawn with colonial and revolutionary wartime experiences in mind. The President, though not hereditary, was meant to serve as titular or ceremonial head of state; he was to administer the national laws and could veto bills sent by Congress for his approval; he was to present an annual message to Congress on the "State of the Union" (with suggestions for legislative action); he was to be chief diplomat and Commander-in-Chief of the armed forces; and he was to appoint (with the Senate's consent) the officials of the executive branch.

The Congress was given specific powers—to tax, to regulate commerce, to oversee postal communications, to coin money, to keep weights and measures, to raise and maintain armed forces, to declare war and peace—but it was also commanded to do everything "necessary and proper" to carry out its powers. This combination of specific powers and vague implementary authority has created flexibility in the decades since 1787, but also debate and confusion over the appropriate extent of the national government's constitutionally sanctioned authority and jurisdiction.

The Supreme Court's Justices were given authority to adjudicate cases arising under the Constitution and the nation's laws. The drafter's made national laws and treaties the "supreme law of the land," state laws notwithstanding. State governments were left to function as they had, unobstructed in their operations and exercise of power, except where they directly conflicted with national activities.

The framers—or Founding Fathers—thus created the blueprint for republican government in which *political* power was checked and balanced, in order to prevent tyranny and maintain liberty. But the framers did not similarly treat *private* power, economic power. Because wealth and its acquisition and accumulation was itself perceived to be a liberty, and because the drafters were themselves from the elite that dominated all aspects of life in the new nation, they exhibited no concern about the concentration of private power in an elite. Their constitution contained statements concerning the protection of property, and Congress was given the authority to "regulate interstate and foreign commerce." The framers did not perceive that those who possessed concentrated economic power should be checked and balanced in ways similar to those who were given public office, or political power. The liberal state whose outline the Founding Fathers presented for ratification thus made important and lasting distinctions between public and private power, between the political and economic spheres of life. Political power must always be contained and limited; economic power would not be.

The procedure for ratification that the drafters devised was shrewd. Mindful that Congress under the Articles had great difficulty in gaining the required unanimous acceptance of the states for its constitution and had been unable to find the necessary unanimity for any constitutional amendments, the convention of 1787 decided to declare the document operative when two-thirds of the states ratified it. In order to gain popular acceptance, the convention asked each state legislature to call a special ratifying convention whose elected delegates would decide the fate of the proffered new frame of government. The delegates so chosen did not debate and vote along occupational lines: farmers, lawyers, doctors, craftsmen, merchants, planters, landowners—all groups voted both for and against ratification. The factors that determined an individual delegate's vote were as varied as those that went into the earlier decision of whether to proclaim one's loyalty to or independence from Britain.

In the conventions called by states that had been weak or exposed under the decentralized confederation of the 1770s and 1780s, delegates *tended* to favor ratification. Delegates in the conventions from states that had felt strong under the confederacy *tended* to oppose ratification. But, these were tendencies only. Rhode Island and North Carolina were the last two states to ratify, and neither had been a notably strong or independent state. Many delegates determined their positions after the conventions began, in response to the debates that occurred both at the conventions and in the press of the larger population centers. The ratification process prompted Americans to engage in a full-blown discussion of the nature of politics, a discussion that was fuller and deeper than any since that time—appropriately so, since the voting population was being asked to determine what kind of government would be best for it.

The "Anti-Federalists" (the localists of the 1780s) were those in the conventions as well as political and editorial spokesmen in the wider community who were opposed to ratification. Their first argument was that what the drafters had done was illegal because the convention had been called to examine the Articles in order to find ways to improve them, not to institute an entirely new frame of government. In any case, the Anti-Federalists opposed a national government of such power as the Federalist had drawn in their constitution. The proposed government could become tyrannical, just as the old British imperial government had, mainly because the Federalists had not bothered to add a Bill of Rights (as the new states had in their constitutions of the 1780s), which enumerated the civil liberties that the proposed government could not infringe.

Furthermore, the proposed government would be so strong and its powers were so vaguely defined that it would soon dominate state and local government and overpower a federal system that would, before long, disintegrate. The Anti-

Federalists were convinced that only the rich and powerful would be chosen as members of the new government and would at least be beholden to special interests that could influence the nation's politicians in the capital, far removed from where most voters actually lived. Certainly they believed that the Electoral College would choose only influential and famous persons as President, that the state legislatures would elect the same kind as U.S. Senators, and that the President would act in the same manner when appointing Supreme Court and Federal judges.

The Anti-Federalists did not believe that the republican form of government that the Federalists were offering would be a durable enterprise. Historically, republics had flourished within small territories where representative government was based on small, largely homogeneous populations. A republic of the scale the Federalists envisioned would either break up into anarchistic pieces or be held together by a centralized, autocratic authority.

The Federalists, the drafters whose constitution was being discussed and their allies, countered each of the Anti-Federalist arguments. As for the assertion that the convention's work was illegal, the Federalists argued that the state legislatures had all agreed to issue the call for a ratifying convention. If the political community had been decisively against what the convention was offering, surely the call for delegates would never have been made. As for the argument that the national government would overwhelm the federalist system, the Federalists insisted that the new government was encased in specified powers, strictly limiting its authority so far as the internal governance of Americans was concerned, that state and local governments would continue to exercise primary authority over such matters, that that national government's main focus would continue to be on international relations, and that the only time its power would be extended would be in response to national crises of whatever kind.

As for the fear that only the rich and powerful would emerge from the proposed electoral system, the Federalists preferred to think that only the wisest and ablest of men would emerge from such a winnowing process, that national office would cap careers grounded in local and state service.

As for the insistence that republican government wouldn't last when established for a large and possibly growing nation-state, the Federalists argued that republican government would work best over a large territory containing a population of varied interests. This plurality of interests would ensure that power would not become monopolized and then abused by a majority that would not protect the rights of minorities (something that had occurred in small republics). These varied economic and social interests ensured that society in a large republic would be "checked" and "balanced" and "separated," just as the republican government that would serve as its protector and regulator would be. Great, divergent interest groups—whether rich, middling, or poor; agricultural or commercial; ethnic or religious—would find political spokesmen who themselves would be divided and balanced within the new government.

All of this worked mightily against tyranny—of the majority or of any particular interest. Such a government—so filled with checks and balances and separations—would be unable to become tyrannical. Therefore, there was no need for an explicit Bill of Rights, in contradistinction to what the Anti-Federalists were arguing. However, Federalists in certain states let it be known that they would favor such a bill, as amendments to the new constitution as soon as it became operative.

Indeed, the Federalists were fiercely determined that the document be ratified, and, as politicians and delegates, they indulged in any means at their disposal to ensure a favorable outcome. Delegates voted for or against ratification on the basis of a range of influences—what they took to be in the best interest of their state; the force and appeal of either the Federalist or Anti-Federalist case during the debates held inside or outside of the conventions; a sense of how the new constitution would likely affect their own interests as individual delegates. The outcome was highly favorable in some state ratifying conventions, close in others, and protracted in still others.

* * *

Once ratified, the Constitution quickly became accepted as the foundation for American government. "Constitutionalism" became the most powerful sentiment in American politics: whether something was "constitutional" or acceptable within the American political system was the most basic test anything political could be put to. Like the Declaration of Independence, the Constitution has become secular scripture, the final source of authority for any of the operational aspects of American political life. Like the Declaration, it has, since the 1940s, occupied an honored place, under glass, in a secular chapel at the National Archives.

All of this is in striking contrast to the republics of Middle and South America, where constitutions were promulgated and abandoned with astonishing regularity. Spain's erstwhile colonists, once they had gained political independence, from 1810 to 1826, allowed various governmental bodies to devise constitutions that were filled with imported ideas. Eschewing local experience, these state makers drafted frames of governments filled with borrowings from the already-existing constitutions of the United States, France, and Spain. The Spanish had filled their colonial administrations with "peninsular" colonists (migrants from the homeland), which meant that the colonial native-born white population emerged from their successful rebellions with very little direct political experience of their own. The *caudillos* who typically established autocratic rule after independence did not feel bound by the formalities of written frames of government.

Politicians in the United States, united in their loyalty to the Constitution, have divided from the inception of the national government in 1789 over how to *interpret* the document. "Nationalists" believe the national government's powers must be interpreted broadly, so that national problems and interests can be dealt with in a uniform and positive way. "State rightists" have been concerned that there not be a concentration of power at the national level of government that would lead to tyranny, that state and local government maintain primary authority in the internal governance of Americans, and that the "federal" system be fully sustained.

But all who have been involved in the American political system since the 1780s have shared a belief in the fundamental and sacred character of the Constitution as the foundation for the entire political system. This shared belief has given durability and legitimacy to a federalized governmental system that has become, during the twentieth century, the oldest in the world to have been continuously operating under its original constitution. In a global context, the American Constitution became a model for other new nations that began as empires disintegrated during the nineteenth and twentieth centuries and has been referred to on those occasions when even established nations have reconfigured their governmental systems in response to some crisis. The combination of a written frame of government that has also received popular approval, that is, the conjunction of a constitutional order with popular sovereignty, has become one of the most influential features of the American political system.

* * *

As the system has evolved, neither the Anti-Federalists nor the Federalists have been accurate forecasters. The national government did not overwhelm the federal system and became dominant in domestic governance only in the economic crisis of the 1930s. National legislators, judges, and Presidents have been rich and powerful and have favored the interests of the rich and powerful, but they have also worked to extend legal protection to minorities of a racial and gender and ethnic kind, to regulate economic activity in a fair manner, and to provide for the welfare and security of all citizens. Republican government has endured in a large, continentwide republic, but though power has been divided among varied interests represented politically in a multitiered and thus divided system, there are some matters on which the American population as a whole has reached a consensus and, in these cases, minority rights often have not been protected. The Federalists and Anti-Federalists were thus flawed futurists, both underestimating the actual complexities of life under a constitutional system whose most basic source of stability has been the reverence with which Americans have held their Constitution itself.

10

Republicanism

Americans for many decades stressed above all else the republican character of their political system. Not until after World War I, when Europe's imperial powers started to unravel and when monarchs and aristocracies were no longer at the center of political power, did this emphasis begin to wane. The United States was unique in the world: a new republic in a political world still dominated by dynastic kingdoms. Neither older (the Swiss and the Dutch) nor newer (South and Middle American) republics were founded with a proclamation that the nation was special, was the embodiment of the highest of Europe's political ideals: the first state dedicated to liberty and its defense. The American government was without an aristocracy or a monarchy; was wholly elective, not partially hereditary; was limited in power through checks and balances, the separation of power, and a federal system.

When Americans compared their system of government to those of the Europeans, they continued to stress what the rebels during the war for independence had emphasized: American purity versus European corruption, American liberty versus European tyranny, and now American republicanism versus European dynastic kingdoms. Republicanism was the politics of the future, and America was in the vanguard. Its republican citizens were hard-working, virtuous, independent, resourceful, prosperous, property-accumulating individuals who were to be sharply distinguished from the downtrodden, burdened "subjects" of Europe's kingdoms. For the propertied, adult, white male, republican citizen, the American republic promised equal participation in the world's largest and most open political community, the only one based entirely upon elected representatives.

Throughout the nineteenth and into the twentieth centuries, America's politicians continued to perceive the United States' republican form of government as distinctive in the Europeanized world and, indeed, until World War I much of Europe was still divided politically into dynastic states, with monarchs and hereditary aristocracies still wielding important political power. France's alternating monarchical and republican government since 1789 was symptomatic of the durability of a political system whose polities only gradually shifted their locus of power from hereditary elements to elected ones. Dutch and Swiss republicanism remained anomalous in a continent filled with empires and kingdoms. New Zealand and Australia and Canada and South Africa were seen as dominions within the British Empire. World War I and the peace settlement that followed resulted in the collapse of the European system in the central and eastern parts of the continent. But, government by directly elected, popularly chosen officials was still fragile in Europe and the political culture of much of the continent was still receptive to varied forms of authoritarian government. By the 1920s, only the north and west of Europe seemed to have generated a securely "democratic" polity.

So, even though—after World War I—Americans could no longer perceive their republicanism as an unusually distinctive entity, throughout the decades between the Civil War and the Depression, national politicians could proclaim the virtues of a republican, federal system of government that had become democratized—through universal white-manhood suffrage and mass political parties—significantly in advance of all of Europe, and in particular, Britain (the source of America's political culture), the Netherlands, or France. However, in the late nineteenth century, those influenced by a social Darwinist view argued that the Anglo-Saxon "race" had—in both Britain and America—exhibited a distinctive tendency to develop political systems in which human liberty could flourish, something only heightened by the United States' involvement in World War I as Britain's ally.

American republicanism was strongly linked to capitalism during these decades, more so than in the more complex political culture of Europe, where a wide spectrum of both representative and authoritarian governments existed. And, within the representative governments, there were multiparty systems representing a wide array of political positions. European politicians represented a large spectrum of opinions on capitalism, everything from the highly favorable conservative view to the equally hostile socialist and communist view. Politically, the European heartland was more complicated than the white settler societies on its frontiers.

In the more liberally oriented states of western Europe, universal manhood suffrage and then women suffrage were granted by the time of the depression of the 1930s. But, by World War I, there was a resurgence of authoritarian governments, with the coming to power of communists in Russia and of fascists in Italy and Germany and the profusion of radical, reactionary, leftist authoritarian, rightist militarist, monarchist, and antimonarchist movements elsewhere. Europe contained complex political impulses, everything from the extreme democracy of the socialists to the autocracy of the communists, fascists, and monarchists. Political systems in the crowded polities of Europe gyrated in varied directions over time. The political cultures of the white settler societies were much simpler by comparison.

Between World War II and 1989, the American government was the political leader of the democratic governments of western and central Europe. During these years the European heartland was divided into democratic and communist states, with the Soviet government exercising the same sort of domination over the communist states as the Americans did over the democratic ones. Never before had the political culture of Europe been so reduced and simplified. European polities bifurcated and, in the weakness produced by the devastation of World War II, became allied with either the democratic or the totalitarian states that had emerged from World War II with the greatest political and military power. Those with the strongest tradition of constitutionalism and democracy were nearer to the United States, those with the weakest traditions of this kind were in the borderlands of the Soviet Union. The Cold War divided western civilization down the middle, creating within it a fundamental division between polar opposite political systems.

The defeat of Nazi Germany and Imperial Japan in 1945, the collapse of the Communist governments of Eastern Europe in 1989–1991, the unraveling of the European empires in Africa and Asia from the 1940s to the 1970s and the creation of a republican type of government in such former colonies as India and its later subdivisions, the movement in the South and Middle American republics away from government by military coup—all of these developments have had the effect of spreading functioning republican forms of government into several parts of the world since World War II. Americans were long able to portray themselves as the fortunate inhabitants of the world's only large-scale, significant, "working" republic in a world awash with various kinds of authoritarian governments, whether ruled by hereditary elites or by self-appointed autocrats. But, first in Europe and then elsewhere, durable representative government has emerged midst much complexity in the political arrangements by which people in other national and imperial polities have organized themselves since the American nation began in the late eighteenth century.

11

Federalism

The creation in the 1770s and 1780s of a republican form of government for a large and growing nation was an innovation of importance, but in another sense the political system that has existed under two constitutions since 1781 has been thoroughly traditional, and that is, in its federalism. Human polities of substantial size have always been so organized. In the colonial period, England's mainland North American colonists existed politically in a federal system that extended from municipal to county to provincial to imperial levels of government. The burst of constitution making that occurred during the late eighteenth century did nothing to alter this common political setup. The only change was that new "state" governments proclaimed themselves within the borders of the old provinces or colonies.

What was distinctive about American federalism with respect to the federal systems of the larger and more powerful European states was its bottom-heavy character. With the notable exception of the tiny (and republican) Swiss federation, the national authority in such well-developed states as Britain, France, Spain, Holland, and Russia had already created a degree of centralization that the Americans were to approximate only during the twentieth century. But the Americans shared this decentralized federalism with other white settler societies on the frontiers of Europe—with Canada, Australia, New Zealand, even with such racially mixed nations that emerged in South America as Argentina. Decentralization on Europe's frontiers related to size and scale, even though in Europe each polity developed according to an internal dynamic, where spacious and autocratic Russia was more centralized than confined and politically mixed Britain, for example.

The new American national governments, created first under the Articles of Confederation and then under the Constitution itself, were governments of limited and defined power, reflecting a deep suspicion of strong central authority born of the Revolution as well as a practical recognition that a large republic whose national government was set up not to be autocratic had to have a vibrant and many-layered political system. And so, state and local governments exercised primary authority in most areas of governance until such crises of the twentieth century as world wars and great depressions provoked the national government to greatly extend its ambit of constitutional power.

Nothing that the new national government did in any sphere of domestic governance equaled in importance these activities of the state governments, except for its fostering and protection of foreign commerce, which was a significant part of its authority over *foreign* relations. Even the civil (as opposed to the nationally administered criminal) justice system was under the jurisdiction of state courts. Local governments—a mixture of governmental bodies (derived from English practices) at the town, city, and county levels—also exercised an array of powers, varying from region to region, state to state.

Nothing more dramatically indicates the bottom-heavy character of the American federated union than the smallness of the governmental community in Washington, D.C. Physically designed to mirror the constitutional separation of powers, Washington quickly became two separate social communities hovering around the executive mansion on one hill and the legislative capitol building on another, separated by a swamp that later became a "mall." Washington throughout these decades remained a scattered village, and both the legislators who stayed in boardinghouses around the capitol and the executive department officials and foreign diplomats who resided in homes around the executive mansion typically had short office-holding careers, often expressing their dismay at having to live in such a small, provincial, ill-appearing place.

The public buildings in the nation's capital were only slowly built, and government personnel remained few in number. Washington as a capital was an accurate mirror of a constitutional system that retained most power (in all but international relations) for state and local governments and of a nation that was notably decentralized, conspicuously lacking the national institutions, activities, and groups of Europe's dynastic kingdoms. For the American people, Washington was insignificant, far away, and generally unknown as a physical or social reality—no more a dominating presence than the national government itself was. And within Washington itself, the geographically and constitutionally and socially separated Presidential and Congressional communities functioned effectively only with the strenuous efforts of concerned Presidents and Congressional leaders. Both within and without, Washington existed as the symbol of a decentralized nation-state.

Washington as a community grew steadily between the 1860s and the 1920s, reflecting the augmented size of the national government itself, which in turn mirrored the enlargement of governmental activity. Congress itself grew in size with the population and with the admission of new states (until 1912), but so did the bureaucracy of the executive part of the government, as regulatory agencies and new "cabinet" departments were added. And so too did national lobby and "pressure" groups, which began to open headquarters in the capital city. Improved communication and transportation systems—trains, telegraphs, and, increasingly, after the turn of the century, telephones—linked Washington to citizens in all parts of the nation, either through direct travel or communication and through the reports of news agencies that appeared in various newspapers and through national magazine articles.

During recent decades, Washington as a physical and social community has grown with the ever-greater role that the national government has played in the nation's life. As a capital city, Washington has become one of America's metropolitan centers, the focal point of a national governmental bureaucracy, of countless lobbying groups, of a huge press corps. The federal political system since the 1930s has "flipped": instead of being "bottom-heavy," it has become "top-heavy," with the national government the *locus* of political power.

12

Constitutional Interpretation

Americans have regarded their Constitution as a sacred document, as the source of all legitimate political authority, as the basis for all government policy and for all the rights and obligations of the citizenry. It is revered as the earliest and most durable of all the written documents or constitutions that others have since created as the foundation for their governments. As pioneers in the making of constitutional frameworks for the modern nation-state, Americans have been proud of their accomplishment. Because they based the Constitution's legitimacy on popularly elected ratifying conventions, Americans have also been the champions of "popular sovereignty," of the notion that frames of government, foundations of polities as they are, must also have the approval of the people to whom they apply to gain needed legitimacy.

American citizens were united on the efficacy of the Constitution, but their reverence for the document was tempered by the realization that, like religious scripture, the Constitution has to be interpreted. They believed it should remain as the legitimating source for the political system as a whole. But, how would a document, produced in a particular time in a particular set of circumstances, retain their allegiance into an indefinite future. The amendment process was rather cumbersome and has been activated relatively rarely. Amendments have usually resulted from Congressional proposals approved by three-quarters of the state legislatures. Beyond this kind of formal change that has been undertaken within prescribed procedures has been the vexing question of interpretation. The words of the Constitution have always had to be interpreted by public officials and ordinary citizens alike. How would the document's meanings evolve in an ongoing way?

From the beginning, politicians with a philosophical cast of mind have divided into two positions on how to interpret the Constitution. The nationalist position, best articulated by the first Secretary of the Treasury, Alexander Hamilton, the second Chief Justice of the Supreme Court, John Marshall, and long-term Speaker of the House and later Senator Henry Clay, was that the document should be interpreted loosely. If it were to last for the ages, then politicians and citizens alike should interpret its language broadly, allowing the new national government to exercise its authority to the fullest possible extent. Nationalists believed that the framers intended the new political system to embrace a vibrant central government that would be responsive to the shifting needs of a large, varied population. The state rightist position, best explained by Presidents Thomas Jefferson and James Madison, was that the Constitution should be construed strictly. The federal system that the Constitution retained will be healthy only as long as centralized power doesn't become abusive. The great danger is an overactive, distant, central authority: the Revolution itself provided lasting evidence for that. The Constitution created specific powers for the new national government, enumerated grants of authority that must be strictly adhered to if the American system of government is to be sustained as the framers intended. In a loose, sprawling, variegated republic, local and state governments, close to the people, must exercise the most authority in the internal governance of Americans.

President Washington came to perceive the union from the vantage point of the Presidency as a "nationalist"; that is, he came to believe that the new national government should *use* its powers to create a strong union out of a loose, decentralized republic. He therefore believed the Constitution ought to be construed broadly. This perception was shared by all of his successors, at least while in office, through to John Quincy Adams in the late 1820s. Jackson was the first to bring to the Presidency a definite "states' rightist" or strict constructionist view of the Constitution and of the national government's role in the American political system. Jackson was convinced that the broad exercise of national power had led to the government's favoring powerful special interests. He believed that the aim of the national government should be to refrain from so acting, so that state and local government would remain the focus of power within the American political system. Since Jackson's successors remained, as Jacksonian Democrats, committed to this perception as well, and since they dominated the Presidency, except for two terms, until the Civil War, the Presidency did not regain the nationalist orientation it had had from the 1790s to the 1820s until after the War.

Chief Justice John Marshall, like the contemporaneous Presidents with whom he served, was a nationalist, and, in a series of cases, he and his court indicated that the Constitution must be construed loosely, that the national government must be allowed to interpret its powers broadly. Coincidentally, Marshall's long-time successor as Chief Justice, Roger Taney (1834–1862), exhibited a states'-rightist orientation, once again contemporaneously with Presidents who (with few exceptions) shared his outlook, that is, Jacksonian Democrats, who adhered to their mentor's precepts. Marshall was appointed by the nationalistically oriented President John Adams and served until his death in 1834. Taney was appointed by the states'-rightist-oriented President Andrew Jackson and served until his death in 1862. The result was that the Presidency and the Supreme Court passed through similar phases: in both organs of government, nationalism predominated from the 1790s to the 1830s and states' rightism predominated from the 1830s to the 1860s. By contrast, many Congressmen did not act on the basis of such overall positions. To the extent the major parties articulated a basic philosophy, the Federalists, and later the Whigs, and still later the Republicans subscribed to a nationalist view, whereas the Jeffersonian Republicans and the Jacksonian Democrats favored a state-rightist view.

With the crisis of the Civil War from 1861 to 1865, the nationalist position was triumphant within the Union government, as Lincoln believed his administration had to assume wide authority to deal with widespread civil rebellion. But, in the decades after the Civil War, the states'-rightist position gained ascendancy in both major parties and among Presidents and Supreme Court Justices as well. Not until the progressive reform movement infected the Presidencies of Theodore Roosevelt, William Howard Taft, and Woodrow Wilson in the years after 1900 did the nationalist view influence the Presidency again, as these Presidents began to perceive national problems that needed in their view to be dealt with by an active federal government, fully and imaginatively using its authority. But the states'-rightist position was very resilient, and there were many politicians from 1900 to 1930 who continued to argue against significant enlargements of federal authority legitimized through the loose construction of the Constitution.

Only in the crisis of the Great Depression did President Roosevelt and the Democratic Party subscribe fully to the nationalist position, as have Democratic Presidents and philosophically oriented Democratic Congressmen since that time. By construing the Constitution broadly, Roosevelt and his Democratic successors have presided over an activist national government and have greatly enlarged the authority of that government by enacting legislation that involves many dimensions of the lives of Americans. By contrast, Republican Presidents and reflective Republican Congressmen have at least superficially and formally adhered to a states'-rightist view in their opposition to a loosely construed constitutional underwriting of significant enlargements of federal authority, conjuring up benign images of an older republic with a bottom-heavy federalism.

The nationalist and states'-rights positions have been the filtering mechanisms through which thoughtful American political figures have interpreted the Constitution for other politicians and for the voting public. In this way, particular policies have been dressed up with a Constitutional justification. This prism, this filtering process has provided a needed sanction for policy initiatives that have created political division or controversy. Because politicians could take widely varying positions on policy proposals and still all argue that their views were "constitutional," the nationalist and state-rights positions constituted an ideal pressure valve, allowing for varied interpretations of the Constitution in the ongoing process of lawmaking and judicial adjudication.

Nationalist and states'-rightist interpretations of constitutions were not a distinctively American phenomenon. Such debates have taken place in all the markedly federalist nations of Europe and its offshoots, especially in Canada and Australia, two other sprawling, continentwide confederations on Europe's frontier. All three of these new nations represented a coming together of preexisting states, which bonded politically within a constitutional framework. One significant distinction is that the United States was formed after a revolutionary separation from Britain, whereas Canada and Australia were formed under the auspices of imperial Britain, by means of Parliamentary legislation.

13

Philosophical Positions

In the United States, at least, the nationalist and states'-rights positions became entangled with the two most influential philosophies of government that had developed in Europe by the late eighteenth century: liberalism and conservatism. Shifting away from defenses of absolutism and the divine right of kings, various observers, commentators, writers, philosophers, and critics put together two contrasting views of what government's place in society should properly be. Reflective Americans were aware of these views and advocated policies or defined government's role with reference to them. Though most American politicians have been pragmatic in their cast of mind, a minority have been principled liberals or conservatives.

For liberals, the power and authority of government must always be limited, must never impinge on the liberty of citizens, must in fact always protect that liberty. Liberals believed that the state should protect property and leave economic enterprise to flourish in a setting of free trade. As a political standpoint, liberalism was extremely congenial to the development of capitalism and was quite antagonistic toward the kinds of economic regulation that had marked mercantilistic governmental activity in Europe during the seventeenth and eighteenth centuries. Liberals were very concerned to limit public power, governmental authority, in order to protect the liberty of the individual citizen. But liberalism had little to say about private power, about economic elites of any kind, whether landed, mercantile, or industrial. Liberalism didn't have much concern for those who were propertyless or who, under industrialization, became wage earners without owning what they produced and who were without economic security. Liberalism didn't confront its own contradictory advocacy of equal legal and political rights for all citizens in a society with huge social and economic inequities.

Conservatism—beginning with Edmund Burke's late-eighteenth-century formulation—stressed the organic nature of society, the way its parts interact and evolve over time. To conservatives the state must never be used to support sudden, violent, wrenching change. Society by nature consists of a hierarchy of institutions, groups, and activities, some of which are more important and have more authority than others. The rights and responsibilities of various groups differ, are not the same, and have evolved slowly over long periods of time. Society changes, truly changes, slowly, not as the result of the efforts of revolutionists who seek to redraw its boundaries all at once in a violent spasm of change. Such efforts are doomed to failure and only succeed in rupturing the orderly working of society for a brief time.

In this context, America appears as a liberal state, one dedicated to limited government, checked and balanced, with power separated among various organs, a state whose primary purpose was to further the liberty of its citizens. Without either a feudalistic or a communistic past, America burst forth into the world of modern nation-states as the first liberal state from its very inception. By contrast, other areas along Europe's frontier—Spanish and Portuguese America, French Canada, and Dutch South Africa—all remained conservative, traditional, hierarchical societies, even when conquered by the British, as the French and Dutch settlers were. During the course of the nineteenth century, Britain became an increasingly liberal nation, and as the British shed their white colonies in North America and Australasia, New Zealand (1852), Canada (1867), and Australia (1901) became liberal states as well. Even though the conservative-minded Loyalists migrated to British North America after the Revolution, their presence did not produce a durably conservative society or even a continued commitment to a definitely conservative creed. The prevailing liberalism of both the United States and Britain was a potent outside influence in the shaping of attitudes toward government in the new Canadian nation. In all of the former British dominions, there has been continued support for both liberalism and conservatism throughout the nineteenth and twentieth centuries, even though liberalism has been the dominant philosophy.

In the United States, the states' rightists espoused the liberal cause throughout the nineteenth century. Jefferson and the Republicans, as they emerged in the 1790s, staked out a perfectly liberal position: As states' rightists, they supported the defense of liberty by opposing the broad exercise of power by the new national government, whose authority should be strictly interpreted and limited to what the Constitution unambiguously confined it to. The internal governance of Americans should be carried on by state and local governments, those nearest to the people. Government should favor open commerce among nations and refrain from regulating and protecting economic development. Nothing could have been more liberal than these positions. Throughout the nineteenth century, these liberal prescriptions were, in fact, descriptions of how the American governmental system operated. As espoused by reflective Jeffersonian Republicans and Jacksonian Democrats, liberalism and states' rightism remained conjoined until the twentieth century.

But, conservatism also had advocates in the United States during the same period. The nationalists—such as Alexander Hamilton, John Marshall, and Henry Clay—were thoroughgoing conservatives. Nationalists argued that the strong central authority that marked Europe's imperial powers during the seventeenth and eighteenth centuries should be continued in the form of a new national government in the United States that would use its power to create a vibrant, modern republic. Just as the imperial authorities of yore, through mercantilistic policies, created through legislation a "common market" within their empires, so too should the American government use its authority to create a protected economy within the new nation. Just as imperial authorities, as imperialists, had tried to create an imperial economy, so too should national authorities, as nationalists, try to create a national economy. This conservative tradition of favoring the exercise of power by an activist, strong government did not mean that advocates of conservatism thought such political activity in any way altered the hierarchical character of society. Conservatives hoped that the exercise of such power would protect and encourage the development of a strong, nationally oriented business community that would be close to a strong, nationalistically oriented government. A great government-business alliance would lead America into becoming a modern state and a modern, industrialized economy. A naturally hierarchical social and economic system should above all else be harmonious, and government should do nothing that would create disharmony among the various elements and interests within American society.

This neat fit, this symbiotic relationship between the states' rightist/liberal and nationalist/conservative positions that became a deeply grooved coupling during the course of the nineteenth century, ruptured in the twentieth century. The associations "flipped," as liberalism came to be associated with the exercise of strong, activist, central governmental authority and as conservatism became linked to either an antigovernment or a states'-rightist posture. The attitudes toward government have become completely reversed. Liberals have had a positive view of government, whose power should be used to provide for the security and welfare of all citizens, whereas conservatives have had a negative view of government, which, at all levels, should avoid excessive regulation of or interference in the lives of free citizens.

Such liberal and nationalist Presidential spokesmen as Republican Theodore Roosevelt (in the 1900s) and Democratic Franklin Roosevelt (in the 1930s) argued that a liberal state must not only protect its citizens' liberty, but, through governmental action, maintain their social and economic security and welfare as well. This position involved a seismic change in the nature of liberalism, both in the United States and in Europe and other white settler societies as well. But so too has the shift in conservatism to an antigovernment posture. Throughout the twentieth century, as the liberal state in the Europeanized portions of the globe became the welfare capitalist state as well, conservative spokesmen have continued to argue for smaller, more limited government, government that regulates less, government whose ambit of authority shrinks. The liberal outlook is progovernment: government is benign and beneficial and is the repository for public responsibilities, the custodian of those values—humaneness, fairness, justice—that are basic to community life. The conservative outlook is antigovernment: government is inefficient, bureaucratic, impersonal, tends to do too much too badly, and has a propensity for becoming too powerful and for curbing individual freedoms and liberties.

Unlike the long states'-rightist/liberal ascendancy of the nineteenth century, in the twentieth century, conservatism and liberalism have struggled for dominance as philosophical positions that explain and guide the forging of public policy and the position of government in American life. From 1900 to 1930, a liberalism with a progovernment stance either accepted bigness in the economy and in the society (in Theodore Roosevelt's formulation) or contested that bigness (in Woodrow Wilson's definition), and both were strongly contested by a conservatism of an increasingly antigovernment posture. It was the Great Depression that completed the transformation of liberalism and conservatism in America. Under Franklin Roosevelt and Harry Truman and, later, under John F. Kennedy and Lyndon Johnson, the liberal/nationalist connection was firmly established, as was the linkage between conservatism and states' rights among the political opposition. Conservatism and states' rights were influential to some extent under Dwight D. Eisenhower and Richard Nixon, but especially under Ronald Reagan and George Bush, when the whole concept of the nationalist/liberal state in its modern welfare capitalist form was questioned.

Liberalism and conservatism have not by themselves ever *determined* governmental policy, but they have created philosophical justifications for particular lines of public policy, have provided overall explanations for the appropriateness of certain kinds of lawmaking. Whether legislators favored or opposed legislative proposals could be justified, made to seem consistent, be given wider coherence, with reference to a particular philosophy of government. But such considerations have always coexisted with legislators' practical concerns and constituency pressures.

* * *

Other philosophical positions developed in Europe during the eighteenth, nineteenth, and twentieth centuries have had far less impact on the American political system. Both liberalism and conservatism were centrist positions, quite congenial to a population that never experienced feudalism at one extreme or communism at the other. The spectrum of political philosophy was much wider in the European heartland than in the frontier white settler societies. In Europe, a monarchical/aristocratic political and social order continued to be defended right into the twentieth century, especially where it continued to flourish in eastern Europe, though in western Europe such defenses veered toward a justification of constitutional monarchism as the nineteenth century evolved and liberalism strengthened. As capitalism spread, socialism and then communism emerged as critiques of a new economic order. Socialists argued that political democracy should be conjoined with the public ownership of basic economic activity, whereas communists argued that a necessary dictatorship of the Communist Party should accompany the violent overthrow of any capitalist-dominated political system and the resulting public ownership of the means of production. In the early twentieth century, a resurgence of authoritarian government—fascism—arose in the wake of the collapse of central and eastern European empires after World War I. Fascism was above all a defense of dictatorial, one-party, centrist states, closely allied with large combinations of industry.

Neither communism nor fascism had much impact in America, or in any of the white settler societies. Both positions were too extreme, too distant from the workable arrangements of liberal states that contained ongoing debates between liberalism and conservatism. Even the socialist alternative was confined, as in Europe itself, to the conjunction of labor union movements and laborite political parties that were able in many western and central European nations as well as in Canada and Australia and New Zealand to legislate in piecemeal fashion either the nationalization of certain kinds of economic activity or the institution of social welfare and security mechanisms. Only in the United States did socialism fail to underlie a major political party, as a conservative labor union movement supported political candidates in the major parties who would, in turn, support, the legitimization of labor unions and social welfare legislation, without in any sense creating public ownership of the economy. In its lack of reception for socialism, the United States was quite distinctive.

The result has been the continued absence of a democratic "left" in the European manner. Such proposals as a wealth tax to diminish the concentration of wealth, a national corporations incorporation law that would bring large corporations more directly under national governmental supervision, the stimulation (through tax policies) of the founding of firms owned and managed on a "co-operative" basis, and the creation of an enlarged "public" sphere to operate "essential" services of all kinds—none of these proposals has even become a regular part of the public discourse or the basis of serious legislative bill making. America, seen by many Americans as the Europeanized world's greatest "liberal experiment," has, in the course of the twentieth century in fact become the most conservative of all the European-derived nations. The development of American political, diplomatic, economic, and military power—at its peak, from the 1940s to the 1970s—occurred at the same time that America lost its position as the vanguard, as the utopia, as the experimental edge of the world's dominant civilization to the much older center of that civilization—Europe.

14

Governmental Structures

For all the novelty of having created a large republican state and an elected, not hereditary, national executive, the political system that the Founding Fathers instituted was in many important ways a reflection of the European political world of its time. Representative government elected by propertied, white, adult men existed within many mixed political systems in states all over Europe. Within that wider context, what linked Americans to their specifically British colonial past was also significant. The framers of the Constitution thought they were drawing on the best in European political thought in their state-making activity, but many of them were also seasoned politicians who had participated in the political life of the English colonies and drew heavily upon that experience in crafting their new state. Not only did the new American political system everywhere bear the marks of its colonial origins, certain aspects of it were directly patterned after British models. This was especially true of the judiciary. The legal precedents that formed the basis of judicial decisions in particular cases were wholly British in origin, so the nonlegislative law interpreted by judges was a British importation. Later efforts to "codify" these legal precedents by various state-level judges—and thus make them more "American"—were only partially successful. The new state governments, in terms of their structures, were direct copies of the provincial governments they replaced, with directly elected Governors replacing the appointed royal ones.

Since the new national government created by the Founding Fathers was deliberately meant to be a government limited and defined in its powers, it is not surprising that in fact it was rather fragile throughout the decades from 1789 to 1861. Nothing about it became a well-settled tradition before it unraveled with Southern secession in 1860–1861. At the outset, nobody knew whether the new government would work, how well it would work, or whether it would endure. And, even as it successfully operated during these decades, political party systems were created, collapsed, and were created again; Supreme Court decisions were ignored by Presidents and party leaders; opposition parties sought amendments that would substantially alter the structure and functioning of a still recently created government; each major party thought of itself as being a party of the people and accused its opponents—in the manner of the rebels of 1776—of favoring measures that were autocratic, even tyrannical. This was a young political culture, and it had not grown to maturity by the time it came apart.

And yet, when the rebellion against federal authority was suppressed and the Confederate government was defeated, the reunited political system that resumed operation in 1865 was exactly like the one that had operated before. Though immature, the American polity had developed by the 1860s enough resiliency to survive political insurrection. It is important to note that the political system as a structure of government has never been seriously criticized by its citizens, not even during the time of the Civil War, when the Constitution of the new Confederate government was patterned after the already existing Union one. Critics of the American political system have sought to extend citizenship to others or to make the existing Constitution a better basis for protecting the rights of aggrieved groups. But, there has never been a serious or significant movement to scrap the Constitution and to start over.

The initial task of the new government was to fulfill the promise the Federalists had made to the anti-Federalists that the Constitution would explicitly, through amendment, provide protection for enumerated civil liberties. As formulated in the first Congress (which referred to the Bills of Rights in the various state constitutions) the list consisted of the freedom *of* expression, belief, assembly, and bearing arms and of the freedom *from* arbitrary search and arrest and unfair punishment. By its first major act, the national government proclaimed the new republic to be libertarian in nature.

But, the Constitution not only designed a government whose aim was to "secure the blessings of liberty"; it also gave that government specific powers to provide for the defense and general welfare of its citizens. Furthermore, each organ of government was defined and given certain kinds of authority. But, these constitutional provisions were cryptically or vaguely stated, and even such simple terminology was naturally *interpreted* by those chosen to fill the offices of the national government.

The office of President—as the executive—was the newest organ of government in the sense that of all the parts of the national government it exhibited the fewest antecedents under the Articles of Confederation or during the colonial era. The Presidency was like the royal governors and the British monarch in its executive or administrative function, and, like them, the President could veto legislation enacted by the legislature, though his veto could be overridden. Unlike the monarch, the President was not hereditary, although he could be reelected without limit. Though elected, he was chosen by an "electoral college," consisting of presumably experienced political figures, who would choose experienced, able men. But, the development of political parties soon resulted in the replacement of a deliberative electoral college with slates of electors pledged to vote for the candidates put forth by the parties. The President was to give an annual state-of-the-union message to Congress, administer the laws, appoint and receive ambassadors, appoint officials to the executive department (with the concurrence of the Senate), and serve as Commander-in-Chief of the armed services. Though there is not an explicit constitutional provision, all occupants of the office have also served as titular head of state at official ceremonies.

George Washington, Commander-in Chief of the Continental Army, hero of the revolution, President of the Constitutional Convention, was the unanimous choice of the first and second electoral colleges, and it was widely felt that the credibility of the new government depended upon his willingness to serve. As for the more ceremonial aspects of the new office, Washington created a greater formality than any of his predecessors cared to follow. During his years in office, he held formal levees, not unlike those of European royalty, and sought acceptance for a monarchical-sounding title in his communications with Congress that the legislative body refused to provide. Washington's successors sustained the Presidency's ceremonial role, but in a less formal manner. Inaugurations became the chief celebratory linkage between the national executive and ordinary citizens, and the inaugural address gradually took on the character of an address to the people containing the new President's general observations on the political life of the nation.

Washington quickly turned the Annual Message to Congress into a policy-making instrument, outlining both foreign and domestic problems and sometimes suggesting legislative solutions, something all of his successors have done as well. Washington—with his abundant military experience—was the first, and the last, President actually to command the armed forces when they were in a combat-ready position (to suppress the tax revolt of 1795). Not even his successors who were former Generals in the decades through the Civil War—Jackson, Harrison, Taylor—chose to perform this function. Washington established the executive departments of the government (with Congressional approval). Though the number of such departments was added to from time to time, as a result of what his successors understood to be the growth of governmental responsibilities, the administrative procedures Washington developed—that the "Secretaries" would meet with the President to inform him on the administrative activities of their departments and to advise him on matters they felt needed executive action—remained basic to each succeeding Presidency.

Congress created committees to receive appropriate portions of the President's Annual Message and to indicate to the House and Senate whether legislation was desirable. These committees drafted bills and, after 1816 (under Henry Clay's Speakership), they assumed the power to initiate legislative proposals without reference to Presidential recommendations. So, after a brief period of passivity, Congress, after 1816, shared with the President the power to plan and recommend particular laws.

Senators and Representatives voted on legislative proposals the way they did in response to varied influences: their party's position on a given issue and how high a priority the issue had on the party's agenda; the President's views, usually expressed in his Annual Message; the persuasiveness of those who took positions on particular issues during Congressional debates; the pressure of constituents made by means of petitions, conversations, and letters; a Congressman's commitment to a certain set of principles. When the parties nominated Congressmen and supervised their campaigns and succeeded in getting them elected (either by voters or by state legislatures), the parties did not thereafter automatically command or demand loyalty from the sitting Congressmen affiliated with them. Party leaders did not usually insist that Congressmen exhibit the same identity during their Congressional session that they had during the electoral campaign. The reason for this was that everyone recognized that the political system was organized in such a way that individual Representatives and Senators were automatically open to influences beyond party affiliation. Presidents and party leaders sometimes attempted to make particular issues matters of party identity. The more an issue seemed distant or abstract or philosophical, the less an issue provoked constituency pressure because of its palpable local effects, the easier it was for leaders to succeed in this kind of endeavor.

This meant that Congressional actions lacked the predictability and regularity of the Parliamentary system emerging across Europe, where party loyalty became a defining feature of the political parties that emerged during the nineteenth century. In the United States, by contrast, the views of an individual legislator mattered; debate could be crucial; constituency pressure could be intense. Most Congressmen were characterized by their pragmatism, arriving at positions as a result of a shifting mixture of influences. But, there were also rare Senators and Representatives whose commitment to nationalism or states' rights was so firm that their voting records were consistent and steady. In short, most Congressmen were pragmatists; only a few were ideologues. In either case, the way Congress reached a decision on a piece of legislation was the most distinctive aspect of the structure and functioning of the American government if viewed in the context of European civilization as a whole.

The Supreme Court lacked a well-defined identity during the early decades of the republic. It did not have its own physical location, operating out of the basement of the capitol building, and there was no "judicial community" to match the Congressional and Presidential ones. As was the case with the President and Congress, the Court's duties were not clearly defined by the Constitution and were naturally a subject of interpretation. The provision that the Court must "adjudicate cases arising under the Constitution and its laws" was interpreted by Chief Justice John Marshall (1800–1834) to mean that the Court could declare "unconstitutional" and thus nullify any laws enacted by national, state, and local governments whose terms conflicted with the Constitution itself.

Throughout the nineteenth and twentieth centuries, the Court has retained its independence as the final arbiter of constitutionality. When Franklin Roosevelt tried to "pack" the court in 1934 by introducing a bill that would have suddenly expanded its membership and allowed him to nominate justices with a philosophy congenial to the New Deal, Congress and the public rebelled and the bill was withdrawn. At the same time, the Court moved into its own building and took on its own physical identity. The prevailing views of the justices have gyrated between an activist view, that the court should, through its adjudication of cases, interpret the laws in such a way that social, economic, and political problems are confronted, and a passive view, that the court should strictly interpret the cases before them as points in law and should avoid decisions that pertain to matters that the legislative and executive branches should address.

As for law enforcement agencies, the continued existence of vigilante movements during the seventeenth, eighteenth, and nineteenth centuries attests to the vitality of a popular attitude toward authority that found its fullest expression in the rebellion of 1775–1781. That popular attitude was that when government was not operating properly (as it often did not in frontier areas), the populace itself should create their own. The prevailing attitude toward law enforcement was revealed in the continued existence during these centuries of the rudimentary mechanisms by which laws were upheld by governments at all levels. The national government had no police force, except for small numbers of federal marshals, unless the government decided to "call up" the militia to suppress domestic rebellions. The state governments had no police force either and were similarly reliant on the militia. Counties and municipalities had sheriffs and constables, but, until the ethnic and racial riots of the 1830s, not even the largest urban centers had a trained police force. Certain states and cities built prisons, beginning in the 1830s, responding to a new perception that criminals should be incarcerated and then rehabilitated, and during the remainder of the nineteenth century, both professional police forces and jails spread throughout the union at the local and state levels. The states retained their earlier control over the adjudication of the civil law, whereas the new national government was given under the Constitution the authority to deal with the criminal law. A federal prison system was built during the nineteenth and twentieth centuries to overlay a state one. But, the federal government has never created a general national police force, as most other Europeanized nations have, relying instead on its federal marshals and on agencies created for special purposes, most notably the Federal Bureau of Investigation, created in 1922. That law enforcement agencies were of a rudimentary character until the 1830s suggests that Americans long continued to be anxious about the use of professional armed forces in domestic situations.

15

The Party System

One of the most important elements of the American political system was not favored by the Founding Fathers and received no sanction in their Constitution: political parties. During the eighteenth century, there were political factions in England and in other developed states of Europe, as indeed there had been in colonial assemblies. But these were parliamentary groupings, not ongoing organizations seeking the election of like-minded legislators. What was distinctively American was the creation by 1800 of full-fledged political parties, that is, permanent organizations whose task was to nominate and elect to office their own political candidates and who did so in the context of a mass electorate. It was these political parties that in turn created, by the 1830s, the first political democracy in the Europeanized world, the counterpart to the communal democracies of tribal societies. In this way, the political life of white Americans connected in a fundamental way with the past of their subjugated colored castes: the black African slaves and the native American tribes.

But, though the new American political parties originated as ideological in their orientation, that is, out of antagonisms based upon sharply contrasting positions on the new national government and its proper role in American life, the parties rather quickly changed into pragmatic, centrist, vote-seeking machines whose fiercely competitive nature brought political democracy into being. As nonideological entities, the American parties veered sharply away from European and even other white settler society parties, which, as electorates expanded in the American manner, became steadfastly ideological within the context of a multiparty parliamentary system. In the distinctively American system, the parties nominated and elected politicians, but weren't able to command their unity and allegiance thereafter, whereas in the European parliamentary system, wherever it has taken root, parties and their elected members have remained loyal to their stated positions. European parties have insisted on party loyalty and have usually been successful in this endeavor. American parties have only rarely sought to attain such a goal.

The American system, from the beginning, has been a two-party system. Other parties have never challenged the supremacy of the major parties, both because "third" parties have lacked organizational resiliency and because, as they emerged, the major parties prevailed upon the states (who have primary constitutional authority on the manner and timing of elections) to adopt an electoral system that declares as victors Congressional candidates with a plurality, and not a majority, making it impossible for new parties to challenge the old parties in runoffs or to elect members on the basis of proportional representation.

By the 1830s, American republicanism became transmogrified into American democracy. The republican ideal of the late eighteenth and early nineteenth centuries was the existence of virtuous, property-holding citizens electing disinterested, virtuous, prominent leaders imbued with civic duty, governing in the public interest on behalf of all. By the 1830s, the political parties created a white man's democracy in which adult white men were equal in their right to vote and chose others who, like them, were ordinary citizens, holding office and performing tasks that all could perform, representing different interests in a population that no longer revealed an overall public interest, that no longer was managed from above by a natural aristocracy of talented individuals, that no longer divided into property holders with a place in the political community and those other white men without one.

The American political community expanded in piecemeal fashion when state constitutional conventions held in the decades after 1789 gradually altered the suffrage requirements by including all adult white men (who were not mentally incompetent or criminals) without reference to property-holding qualifications. The arguments proponents made were of both an idealistic and practical character. Some asserted that the revolution's ideology involved the equality of men and that the great new republic, as the world's first liberal state, ought to have a political system that involved all white adult men equally, without distinction. Others were responsive to the competitive two-party system that emerged during the 1790s and again during the 1830s. To the extent that either of the major national parties sought votes among a propertyless urban and immigrant population, it seemed desirable, for practical political purposes, to enlarge the electorate. In any case, an electorate composed of all white men was a significant change from the colonial experience and differed notably from contemporaneous European practice.

But, there was no consensus beyond this enlargement. When the woman's-rights movement appealed to the Declaration of Independence as implying male and female equality and thus as sanctioning suffrage for white women, few responded positively, so deeply ingrained was the reality of social hierarchy based on gender. When the Northern states ended slavery, whether in constitutional conventions or by legislation or by judicial interpretation, so powerful was racism and so durable was the existence of a racial caste, that suffrage for blacks was granted only in New England, where there were the fewest African Americans.

Those with the suffrage were most apt to vote when there were two national parties, almost even in strength, and actively competing all over the Union. The adult white men who could vote did not support legislation that was different in kind—more popular or more radical—from that enacted by more avowedly elitist European governments. America's federal system of republican governments was confined by a constitutional order that sanctioned lawmaking quite similar in kind to that practiced by European governments.

The American electorate did not vote along occupational lines: planters, merchants, doctors, lawyers, landowners, farmers, craftsmen, industrialists—none voted as a group for a given party. The only groups who tended to voted together were small immigrant-ethnic-religious ones who had a high degree of self-awareness and shared anxiety in a somewhat alien setting: e.g., the Irish and German and French immigrants or the pietistic sects. Also, there was significant family continuity in voting. Most individuals weighed the personality of the candidate, the political allegiance—if any—of their own father and grandfather, the positive or negative connotations of the overall images of the parties candidates were affiliated with, the likelihood that a candidate or his party would either aid or harm the voter's basic interests.

Indeed, American politics played a varied role in the lives of those who could vote. In the absence of other national institutions and groups and activities, the national government was the only vehicle through which Americans could express their identity and loyalty. The government was the forum for the articulation of nationalist sentiment by that portion of the population that belonged to the political community. The most significant expression of that national affiliation were campaigns and elections, during which American voters experienced their membership in the national community. Campaigns and elections also dramatized life, gave participants the feeling that they were part of a great national event, and provided a social and cultural setting that linked individuals to groups with a national concern. Participation in campaign clubs, parades, and political gatherings of all kinds provided voters with the secular equivalent of religious processions, camp revival meetings, and church services.

The politicians elected to the various levels of government continued to be out of the planter-merchant elite until the 1820s. Voters deferentially elected such persons because they continued to feel that the "best sort" should occupy office as a community service. This meant that political-economic-social-cultural-religious power was *combined* in a single leadership group. In the new republic a national political career capped an earlier involvement in local and state politics. Jefferson was a prime example, but there were many others. The elite ran the early national parties through the caucus system, were chosen Presidents and Senators, were elected Representatives, were selected as vestrymen and deacons in churches, were at the apex of commercial and agricultural enterprises of great complexity, and presided over social and cultural activities that were the American counterpart of the court societies of Europe.

Gradually, but noticeably by the 1820s, the type of person elected to political office changed. Politicians became careerists: those trained in law who sought a career in making, administering, or adjudicating law. This was a long-term shift: Jackson, President on the 1830s, was still like Jefferson; Lincoln, President in the 1860s, definitely was not. Politics as a career underwent the narrowing and specialization that began to permeate all occupations after the early nineteenth century. The lawyer-politicians who increasingly came to characterize those who served in government during the 1830s, 1840s, and 1850s, by their very presence, broke the link between political and economic, public and private power that had characterized the elitist-oriented politics until the 1820s.

It became less and less typical for the most powerful merchants, planters, and the new industrialists to pursue a political career. They did not need to in order to protect or further their interests, for the careerist politicians basically shared the economic elite's social and economic outlook and certainly had no desire to alter in any important way the fundamental arrangements of life in America. The careerists were basically pragmatic opportunists who sought wealth, status, and power through the holding of political office. The successful merchant, planter, or industrialist was as much a model for such politicians as for other segments of the population.

It was in this context that American political and economic, public and private life shredded apart. The careerist politicians, thus, did not pursue policies that were more popular or radical than the elitists had before them. Both were constrained by a constitution that confined legislation to particular areas.

Moreover, the typical careerist created political parties that were publicly displayed through their convention systems as democratic, but that, in reality, were managed from the top as fully as the caucus system had been under elitist domination. The careerists curried popular support through mass party organizations, whereas the elitists had expected voters to elect them deferentially. But, both groups wanted to exercise the power that came with the occupancy of political office. Careerists declared that not just a trained elite, but any ordinary, virtuous citizens should be able to perform the duties of political office, but nevertheless were as interested in sustaining or attaining wealth, power, and status as the earlier elitists. In short, the sort of person who was elected to office changed between the 1790s and the 1860s, but the way the political system was operated did not.

Political parties were not envisioned by the Founding Fathers, even though they were aware of the existence of parties and factions in the British House of Commons and in their own erstwhile colonial assemblies. But, "party" had a negative connotation for these state makers. Party connoted factiousness, divisiveness, lack of independence. They hoped the new government would consist of wise individuals whose decisions would be guided by reason and a dispassionate assessment of the best interests of everyone concerned.

Certainly President Washington, who had been President of the Constitutional Convention, was notably hostile toward the notion of party. Ironically, it was the domestic and foreign policy formulated within his own administration (policies often propounded by Secretary of the Treasury Hamilton and approved by Washington) that so deeply divided his "cabinet" and Congress that the opposition formed the first mass political party in the history of Western civilization. These Republican opponents and Federalist adherents (under the overall leadership of Washington's successor, President John Adams) developed in the late 1790s from the top down, from the cabinet to the Congress to the nation-at-large. They were ideologically oriented, with the Federalists nationalists and the Republicans states' rightists.

However, from a wider, European perspective, these parties shared a basic allegiance, in spite of Republican fears, to the new, liberally oriented republic: their major distinction was that the Federalists had a positive perception of the national government and emphasized its authority under the Constitution, whereas the Republicans looked with suspicion on that government, and relied on state and local governments as the appropriate instrumentalities for the furtherance of the common weal. Just as was the case with resisters and rebels during the 1760s and 1770s, so too during the 1790s, the Republicans became increasingly convinced that the Federalist administration and its Congressional affiliates were abusing power, were becoming arbitrary, even tyrannical, and would, if unopposed, destroy the new republic (just as the imperial British government's policies after 1763 came to be perceived as a grand design in tyranny).

Galvanized by this conviction, the Republicans organized the first mass political party in the Western world, appealing to a distinctively large American electorate, and succeeded in 1800 in electing their leader, Thomas Jefferson, as President, as well as a majority of Senators and Representatives to Congress. But, neither Jefferson nor his Republican successors Madison and Monroe nor the Republicans in Congress remained ideologically pure. The Federalists also organized a mass party and tried to win subsequent elections by showing that the Republicans were themselves becoming too dictatorial and powerful. When, after 1800, both major parties became popularly oriented and competitively sought to gain electoral victory, they undermined both their adherents' ideological commitments and the elitist nature of politics. Henceforth, parties competed for votes, denounced elites elected through deference, and were pragmatic rather than ideological in character.

The first major parties, managed by Congressional caucuses, were fragile institutions, not generally regarded as having true legitimacy, and were usually unable to command the loyalty of their elected members in Congress. When the Federalists opposed the War of 1812, their disloyalty to a victoriously concluded conflict undermined their credibility, and they simply shredded apart as a national institution. Politics after the war became partyless and faction-ridden, first in Congress and then in the Presidency, whose occupant by 1824 was elected from a field of five candidates. By 1828, however, state factions coalesced around the candidacy of Andrew Jackson and the incumbent, John Quincy Adams.

And though, by the 1830s, in what would later be called "platforms," the Jacksonian Democrats propounded and revived state rights principles and their opponents, the Whigs, articulated a rejuvenated nationalism, the second major parties were basically pragmatic in their orientation, focused on winning elections through popular appeal. The convention system gave them a democratic look, even though in reality they were managed from the top, and (as was the case in the first system) they continued to present themselves as parties of the people and to brand their opponents as aristocratic enemies of the populace.

Even considering the extent to which adherents of the two parties could be associated with contrasting nationalistic and states'-rightist principles, what they shared was of more importance than what divided them (as in the first party system). Both Democrats and Whigs supported the republic and its political system and the overall role of government in it; both were liberal in orientation. But the Whigs revived the nationalism first propounded by the Federalists and the Democrats restored the states' rightism earlier developed by the Jeffersonian Republicans.

What sharply divided the second from the first party system was its "legitimacy": people active in the political community came to accept parties as a legitimate, ongoing, institutionalized part of the system, even though they were wholly without Constitutional sanction. Parties, like the politicians themselves, were a pragmatic means of making the system work; the experience of the partyless 1820s demonstrated what chaotic situations could arise without the presence of these vitally important organizations.

The slavery issue divided the major parties along sectional lines, with the Whigs splitting apart in 1854 and the Democrats in 1860. Civil War occurred as soon as there were no remaining national parties. The Republicans were a northern sectional party from their inception in the mid-1850s, and Lincoln's election to the Presidency as a sectional President in 1860 hastened secession. In general, the national parties united a federated, decentralized political system and provided the mechanisms whereby candidates to national office were nominated and elected. Because they sought to win office and to govern, the parties were, perforce, centrist, moderate, heterogeneous in character, with a mixed appeal to a varied electorate (though an electorate confined to white, adult, male voters).

Minor parties arose to represent the interests of special groups (outside of the electorate) whose objectives or interests could not be dealt with by the major parties in a constitutional system that limited, circumscribed, and defined the power of the national government in any case. In this way, groups such as anti-Masons, abolitionists, nativists, women, and free soilers all found political means to make their appeal in a public manner, even though the major parties found what these groups advocated to be too contentious to act on. The common weakness of all "third party" movements—as parties—was a failure to develop and maintain a strong and durable organization. By nature more crusades and causes than electoral devices, they consisted of people more interested in furthering reformist ideals than in developing lasting political organizations.

* * *

After the Civil War, national political parties continued to bind the system together, operating as before, on local, state, and national levels. Unchanged too was the chief *function* of the parties: to nominate and elect candidates, but not to command their loyalty to clearly defined "party" positions on particular issues after they became elected members of the national government. As was the case before the Civil War, efforts on the part of Presidents and party leaders to maintain party loyalty in voting was only one factor influencing the way Congressmen actually voted. Other factors continued to be constituency pressure—now much more directly exerted by the newer means of communication and transportation—and the attraction of positions enunciated by party leaders and in Congressional debates prior to voting.

The only issue in which the major parties maintained consistently opposite views in "platforms" and policy statements was the tariff: the Republicans favored protection, the Democrats espoused free trade. But, even in this case not all Democratic Congressmen voted one way and all Republican Congressmen another. No party leader or President could ever command total loyalty to a particular position among his party's adherents in Congress, and yet no President in this period tried to gain the loyalty of cross-party coalitions of either conservative or liberal members of Congress either. This was because most Congressmen and Presidents were too pragmatic to be neatly labeled as either conservative or liberal.

Issues rarely attracted or repelled national politicians on a clearly liberal or conservative basis in any case. The party system brought out a politician's flexibility, not ideological fixations. Even those who favored or opposed one issue largely on the basis of ideological considerations would not necessarily be the same ones who divided on the same basis on another issue. There weren't many consistent and clear liberal or conservative Congressmen at any time during these decades, and even Presidents who can be regarded as taking such stances were at times accommodating and moderate. The chief result of political debate and action—however initiated—was legislation that gained the approval of the President and a majority of the Congress—a pattern that emphasized the balancing of many factors and pressures and influences.

Whether conservative or progressive, most of the Washington political community believed that government ought to be managed by the rich or the talented. In sharp contrast to what the Jacksonian Democrats had argued during the 1820s and 1830s, national politicians in the late nineteenth and early twentieth centuries argued that ordinary citizens lacked the capacity to deal with the complexities of making, administering, and adjudicating the law. This perception united "bosses," genteel reformers, progressives, and conservatives and brought American politicians in harmony with those who governed in Europe. On both sides of the Atlantic, politicians agreed that political change should be managed from above, whether government's power was wielded by hereditary or elected officials.

The parties were managed at every level—national, state, and local—by "bosses" who were, though they always exercised power in a personalized manner, sometimes corrupt and descended directly from the highly oligarchical organization of the first popular party of the antebellum era—the Jacksonian Democrats. It was partly in response to the irregular and corrupt activities of these bosses that reform-minded "progressive" politicians, after 1900, successfully persuaded the voting public, through changes made to state constitutions, to institute the referendum and recall and thus to further democratize a party system whose democratic structure (the convention system) had been a facade for internal control by small, autocratic groups.

However managed, the two major parties continued to survive challenges from such minor parties as the Populists (in the 1890s) and the Progressives (in 1912 and 1924), parties that would have pushed reform far beyond anything Democratic or Republican politicians supported. These minor parties continued to fail for the same reasons earlier movements had failed: through either absorption or disintegration because of organizational ineptitude and reformist brittleness, purity, and—hence—divisiveness. The major parties survived and flourished because they continued to reflect the varied composition of the electorate as conglomerates that performed the post electoral coalition building that the more ideologically oriented and more numerous parties in the European-derived Parliamentary systems elsewhere were forced to perform in order to govern.

The appeal of the two major parties—just as before the Civil War—to the electorate was varied, inconsistent, muted, tailored to popular concerns on a regional, state, and local basis. Those who voted divided almost equally between the Republicans and the Democrats in both Presidential elections in the years between the Civil War and 1896, when the merging of a reformist third party (the Populists) and a major party (the Democrats) united more moderate voters than was usual in support of the other major party. Voting patterns between 1866 and 1896 were remarkably consistent, with much evidence of voting habits extending from one generation to the next. Supporters of the main parties divided about evenly in Northern and Western regions of the nation. Only in the South was there a heavy preponderance of voter preference for a single party—the Democrats—and there only after reconstruction had ended in the late 1870s. White Southerners united in both national and state elections in opposition to the party that had enforced a harsh peace settlement.

Except for this one important instance of regional identification dictating party allegiance, the white Americans who, as voters, supported the two major parties did not divide into occupational or class groupings (which was another continuation of a pre–Civil War phenomenon), though self-conscious ethnic, racial, and religious minorities continued to exhibit a tendency to support either the Republicans or the Democrats. For example, those Americans from Ireland maintained their long-standing loyalty to the Democratic Party in these years. Other recently arrived immigrants and the ethnic communities they and their progeny created were less united in their political affiliations, perhaps because they lacked the forced cohesiveness of the Irish, whose long-standing visibility was based upon a common poverty and Catholicism and antagonism toward the British, the root group of native-born Americans.

The reasons for an individual voter's party preference were varied and complex, and the major parties' pragmatic, largely nonideological appeal for popular support assumed that the voters' allegiances would be on other than occupational or class bases. Because each of the two parties appealed to virtually half of the electorate, party competition—outside of the South—was especially keen between 1866 and 1896, and voter turnout during these decades was higher than it ever was before or has been since. Popular campaign activity, first developed by the Jacksonian Democrats and their Whig opponents before the Civil War, was greatly augmented as party "clubs" were organized and sponsored parades, social gatherings, rallies, and speeches, and, as a still-partisan press articulated the party's objectives and instilled both loyalty and a will to participate in the party faithful.

This peak period of party competition and voter turnout coincided with the presentation of typically bland, durable, innocuous candidates selected by "boss"-managed party organizations, all of which indicates that these "bosses" understood how to involve large numbers of ordinary citizens in the outwardly democratic forms of party activity (where elected delegates had the ultimate responsibility for electing party officials and nominating candidates for elective office) as well as in the campaigns and elections themselves. By contrast, voter participation steadily declined after 1900, during the very years that "progressive"-minded politicians argued for government by the well-trained and virtuous and succeeded in introducing the referendum, recall, woman suffrage, and the popular election of Senators. Nor did voter participation notably rebound with the decline of "progressivism" during the 1920s. As the progressive notion that government should be managed by those with the training and talent for it gained acceptance, popular participation in campaigns and elections declined.

The American political system has placed a high priority on a pragmatic approach to governing. The entrenched two-party system works against the development of ideologically pure political movements; those who seek to govern naturally develop a pragmatic outlook and avoid ideological rigidities. The parties, as the mechanisms by which people became elected to public office, have continued to be varied, coalitional, heterogeneous entities. A socialist movement has not been able to operate effectively within such a system. By contrast, in democratic Europe's multiparty Parliamentary system, socialists not only have gained a prominent place, but have augmented their power through coalitions with other ideologically oriented parties. In Europe, the compromises needed for ideologically driven Parliamentary government to function were made after elections, during legislative sessions, as majority coalitions forged policies that had been created by no one party. In the United States, the parties themselves were vehicles of compromise during campaigns and elections, and, once elected, Congressmen were subjected to a variety of influences before arriving at positions on issues.

European polities became democratized in the sense of having mass electorates either during or after industrialization, with the result that political movements sought to mobilize newly enfranchised industrial workers. By contrast, the American party system interacted with a large electorate long before significant industrialization had occurred in the United States, so that the major parties had been significantly involved with the very voters whose occupations became defined by industrialization. American laborers have lacked the cohesion of European groups, a cohesion that helped make possible the linkage between workers and specifically labor parties. In America, the working class has exhibited an ethnic, racial, and religious variety and diversity that worked mightily against the kind of unity for political purposes that marked the relationship of that class to politics in parts of the European heartland.

Earlier socialist formulations involved the communalist socialist groups, such as the North American followers of Owen and Fourier, who built utopian local communities, just as the Puritans had in seventeenth century New England. After the Civil War, Marxist-inspired Communist and Socialist movements were founded by immigrants who had experience in craft unions, usually in Germany and were well versed in a Marxist view of life (Marx himself having been a German). These political movements, in contrast to their locally oriented precursors before the Civil War, were national in scope, reflecting the overall enlargement in the scale of every dimension of life in the United States. The Communist or Socialist Labor Party, founded in 1877, came under the leadership of Daniel De Leon and favored nonviolent, electoral change with Marxist objectives, however. In 1897, Eugene Debs founded what by 1901 was named the Socialist Party of America with more flexible, moderate objectives.

As the progressive impulse grew stronger, the Socialist Party became more popular in elections—at all levels—and, just before World War I, reached its peak of electoral significance. A significant number of Socialists were elected to office in all levels of government during these years, and voters in many municipalities agreed to the establishment of publicly owned utilities: Socialism at the local level. But, both the Communist and Socialist parties were tremendously adversely affected by World War I. Socialist leader Debs was charged, sentenced, and jailed under the Espionage and Sedition Acts, and the Socialist Party itself was effectively outlawed by the Wilson administration and its war policies. Many active Socialists opposed the war, and, after it, some of the more radical joined the new Communist Party, which was formed out of allegiance to the Bolsheviks in the "Soviet Union."

The only parties dedicated to the transformation, rather than the maintenance or reform, of the basic economic-social-political system, the Socialist and Communist Parties—between the 1870s and the 1930s—had little impact on American political life. Only with the rise of the progressive impulse or spirit did significant numbers of Americans provide electoral support for candidates who sought to fundamentally alter their pattern of life. With the amazingly rapid growth of a chauvinistic, intolerant nationalism, such political dissent was made to appear dangerous and "un-American." Nothing illustrates the rapid decline of political radicalism better than the fact that in 1912 Eugene Debs was a serious candidate for President, whereas during America's brief period of involvement in World War I, he was jailed for presumed opposition to that involvement.

* * *

What Europe has had since 1930, but what America has lacked, is a strong Communist and Socialist movement (on the "left") and a strong monarchical or Fascist movement (on the "right")—in short, Europe has had in recent decades a much *wider* political spectrum than Americans have had. Monarchical and particularly Fascist movements have been minor, but persistent, since the defeat of the Fascist-led governments in World War II. But, the Communist parties in such leading non-Communist European states as France and Italy were major political presences throughout the Cold War era (1945–1990), both as parts of the Third International and as part of the political cultures of their own nations.

Even more significant have been the Socialist Parties of many non-Communist European states, leftist parties that have often been a major component of governing coalitions. And though in much of non-Communist Europe there was in the 1980s a conservative reaction to the long development of the welfare capitalist state, just as there was in the United States (Reagan) and Canada (Mulroney) in North America, the fact remains that Europeans have gone further in developing welfare states than Americans have, and this has been so because of the existence of a much stronger Socialist movement.

Nor has the American labor movement provided a basis for an indigenous socialist movement, as has typically been the case in Europe. American labor unions have also been pragmatic in character, and their leaders have usually sought to operate safely within the capitalist system, seeking to enhance their members' economic benefits (such as wages and hours of labor and working conditions) and supporting labor-friendly politicians within the ensconced two-party system.

That system after 1930 has remained institutionally stable in the sense that both major political parties have retained their organizational resiliency. Because of their capacity to lure volunteers and financial contributions, the Democrats and the Republicans have continued almost to monopolize the process whereby candidates are chosen and campaigns are managed. This near-monopoly has continued to serve as a barrier to the multiparty system, which predominates in Europe. Third parties (Henry Wallace's Progressives, Strom Thurmond's State Rightists, the candidacies of George Wallace, Eugene McCarthy, John Anderson, and Ross Perot) have focused on particular causes and have been ideologically clear and organizationally poor, just the opposite of the major parties, which have remained pragmatic, centrist, vote-gathering apparatuses.

Since the Depression of the 1930s, the Democrats have been the more liberal and the Republicans the more conservative party with respect to "platforms" and legislative initiatives. During these years, the parties can be said to have "appealed" to a certain type of voter. The Democrats evoke a response from "outsiders," those seeking a better position or opportunity or more security or assistance from a government that is looked upon as a good and beneficial institution, the repository of the best dreams and hopes for all Americans. By contrast, the Republicans elicit favorable reactions from those who have already considered themselves "mainstream" Americans, who aspire to higher status with less governmental regulation of their private lives, and who perceive government as a "necessary evil," as an institution that, since 1930, has tried to do too much and has done what it has done badly, with excessive bureaucracy and waste and inefficiency.

Until the 1950s, there was a rather large, regional exception to even these generalizations, however: the South. Still responsive to the heritage of Confederate defeat by a Republican-led Union, generally conservative or moderate white Southerners continued to support the reformist-dominated Democratic Party in national elections until Dwight Eisenhower's Presidential campaigns demonstrated that a moderate, "above-party" popular leader was worthy of Southern allegiance, even if he wasn't a Democrat. Thereafter, the Republicans' more conservative Presidential candidates gained substantial support from white Southerners, though popular Democratic Presidential candidates from the South—Lyndon Johnson in the 1960s, Jimmy Carter in the 1970s, and Bill Clinton in the 1990s—have still been able to garner majority support from the region.

Since the 1960s, there has been an operational two-party system in all parts of the nation. Through all these changes, however, the two major parties have remained organizations consisting of regional, state, and local units, with differing personalities, interests, and preoccupations. The polyglot, heterogeneous, coalitional nature of the parties has meant that—as before—they have attracted a variety of candidates and, if successful, officeholders and a variety of voters for a variety of reasons. (Only the blacks have tended to vote as a block, and they have usually supported the more liberal Democratic candidates.) The result, as before, has been that the legislative record of elected Republican and Democratic Congressmen (and women) has typically been erratic by any strict standard of ideological correctness.

The nature of campaigning has significantly changed since the 1930s. During the Depression and World War II and its aftermath, the party organizations were dominated by officials who used the Post Office as a major source of patronage and communication (a practice originated by the Jacksonian Democrats in the 1830s) and who appointed most delegates to the national conventions. The parties' conventions and campaigns were reported over radio and through newspapers and magazines. Campaigns were conducted by means of train travel to many particular locations. Since the 1950s, however, increasing numbers of primaries have extended the campaign season and ever fewer delegates are chosen by party committees, thus steadily reducing the importance of the national conventions; campaigns have involved airplane travel, often confined to major population centers; and television reporting has extended the print and aural coverage of party activities to a visual one.

More importantly, candidates have increasingly relied on advertising and less on formal speeches and statements to convey their positions, which has meant that the cost of campaigning has increased dramatically. The result has been that, although candidates have been chosen by a more popular and democratic system (that is, increasingly on the basis of primaries), the sheer cost of being elected to office has prohibited those who are not personally wealthy or who do not have the influence or popularity to attract significant financial support from being candidates for office—in all levels of the federal system. Those who have been financial contributors to candidates since 1930 were not strictly limited in the amount of their aid until the 1970s, and with the proliferation of pressure groups and lobbyists in Washington and the state capitals, individuals and groups with money available were in a position to influence candidates and officeholders far more than those without such resources.

In the 1970s, in the aftermath of the "Watergate" scandals (in which the Nixon administration indulged in illegal spying activity on the opposition Democratic Party offices), the Election Expenses Act was passed, limiting the amount each individual and group can legally contribute to a national campaign (Presidential or Congressional), granting individuals tax credits for voluntary contributions, and making candidates eligible for matching contributions from the national government itself. But these reforms have in no way reduced the high cost of becoming a candidate for national office.

In a global context, America's Democratic and Republican parties remain distinctive in their lack of party discipline, which in turn reflects other peculiarities of the American political system. But the Democrats and the Republicans have been joined since the late nineteenth and throughout the twentieth centuries by many other mass parties in other democratized parts of the world.

16

Governmental Functions

It is important to recognize that power exercised at *all* levels of government (and not just the national)—what government within the American system actually did—was quite traditional, quite like what was done in European governmental systems. The range of governmental activity evolved out of a common European political culture that the Americans' forbears experienced as colonists during the seventeenth and eighteenth centuries. Just as the colonists lived in a political world in which governments performed various functions at the municipal, county, provincial, and imperial levels, so too did politically independent Americans occupy a polity with governments operating at the local, county, state, and national levels. At no time during the nineteenth and twentieth centuries have the functions of government in America *at all levels* differed from those exercised by the various levels of government within European polities, or from those in other white settler societies. What differed from nation to nation was the *level* at which particular functions were performed. Government activity that in America and other loosely federated European frontier nations was performed by state (or provincial) and local government, in the more centralized polities of Europe was within the purview of national governments.

In no part of the Europeanized world during the past two centuries has there been a desire on the part of those who actually governed to change in any significant way the capitalist, increasingly industrialized or mechanized economic system and the form of wealth and power it generated. Whether politicians wanted the economy to grow and develop without significant regulation or wanted government to guide that growth and development and provide for the security and welfare of those harmed by such activity was as much a European as a white frontier phenomenon during these centuries, though the mixtures and cycles varied from one national political system to another.

The most striking and fundamental political development since the late eighteenth century has been something that all Europeanized governments, all federal systems have shared: the pronounced enlargement in the overall role of government and the concomitant ascendancy of the national government within these federal systems. In this, government in the United States has reflected a much larger trend, as governments everywhere Europeans have been dominant have augmented their scope in many ways since the time of the French Revolution, extending public responsibilities into areas that had been privately managed.

Americans have tried to adhere to a strong, deep antigovernment tradition, demarcating their governments and the legitimate exercise of public power within constitutional boundaries. The national government in particular was a government of defined power, and many dimensions of American life were presumably beyond the purview of governmental action at the national level. State governments have become experimental on particular occasions, but they too were confined by Constitutions that defined and limited their powers as well. But, during the 1930s and early 1940s, Americans created a "welfare-capitalist" state that much of Europe was already in the process of instituting. And, since World War II, Americans have involved their national government, with its newly augmented central authority, in matters hitherto beyond its purview, in activities that had been locally or privately managed—education, health, the arts, and recreation—or in new areas of public concern that were clearly national (or international) in scope—most notably, the environment.

All such governmental activity has involved an augmentation of the scope of government and a corresponding growth in the authority of the central government. Each change has been a matter of controversy, debate, and political division, but the overall trend has been in favor of the enlargement of the role of government in American life. In the process, the line between what is "public" and what is "private" has revealed a diminishing private sphere, to the point that, since the 1970s, it has been routine to refer to the "public" and "private" sectors with respect to almost any human activity, and, indeed government has a role to play in almost everything Americans do.

From the perspective of national government only, the American government—as well as the Canadian and Australian—has been much slower to develop the functions and authority of European national governments in Europe's more centralized polities. But this kind of distinction has become far less significant during the twentieth century, when two world wars and the Great Depression brought notable enlargements of federal authority in many parts of the Europeanized world.

The dynastic, despotic states of early modern Europe gained power and authority in the way they functioned chiefly by developing their war-making apparatus in a highly competitive state system. The creation of professional armies in turn led to the development of various forms of revenue-collection services. During the nineteenth century, as capitalism moved from commerce to industry and agriculture and as the electorate expanded in response to popular pressures, national governments in Europe worked to develop through a combination of private and public means the "infrastructure"—that is, the founding of public school systems, the legalization of national languages, the institution of modes of transportation, the protection of contracts, the provision of military security, and the administration of justice—and in so doing created modern nation-states while fostering the growth of industrializing economies. Capitalist enterprise of all kinds—commercial, industrial, and agriculture—was nurtured through a moderate intrusion of public authority, which cleared away internal impediments to such activity while avoiding excessive control of the kind that would have stifled capitalistic growth. In the process such governments subverted the authority that had been exercised by various subnational groups: the churches, the landed aristocracy, municipal councils, urban guilds. National governments established professional bureaucracies to administer a growing array of governmental agencies. These governments also standardized customs services, installed border guards, issued passports, and regulated the movements of citizens and foreigners and goods of all kinds in and out of their borders. During the late nineteenth and first half of the twentieth centuries these same governments went on to regulate industrial activity, protected labor union movements, and provided for the security and welfare of their mass electorates.

During the course of the nineteenth century, European national governments enlarged their power and functioning in ways that seemed far beyond the Constitutional authority of the new national government in America. In America, the nation expanded without creating a large, permanent military establishment. In America, the nation industrialized without a significant enlargement of the federal government's regulatory or protective authority. America seemed to become a modern nation without the augmentation of national power that marked the transformation of European dynastic states into modern nations. But this was true only if the process is viewed from a national perspective. The American federalist system, at its state and local levels, was as active in this process as national governments in Europe were. When the Great Depression of the 1930s brought a significant enlargement in national power in the United States, the role of government in the development of a modern nation didn't change. What changed was the *level* at which power was exercised. The American federal system of government, operating at all levels, dealt with the onset of industrialization, the regulation of industry, the protection of labor unions, and the institution of welfare and social security schemes—and even the creation of a huge military, all as European governments had.

But the timetables for this enlargement of political authority varied from polity to polity, revealing distinctive political cultures and traditions among the nations of Europe and the white settler societies along Europe's frontiers. For example, in France and Germany, activist governments were used to exercise authority through well-developed bureaucracies. By contrast, in Britain, governmental authority was more diffused and decentralized, less authoritarian. Even though the British national government had long exercised its power in significant ways, government in Britain continued to function within the context of a fully operating federal system. Across the Atlantic, in the United States, one of the features of the American governmental system that stood out most clearly among Western nations was an extremely decentralized federalism.

The degree of industrialization, the extent of the political activism of the business community or of the labor movement, the size of the socialist or labor party, the role of the citizenry (that is, whether pressure for change came from "above" or "below," from government officials or from popular pressure)—in all of these aspects, the timing for the enlargement of political authority varied considerably from polity to polity. For example, a new German national government preemptively acted to mollify a politically active, cohesive labor movement and to undercut the popularity of a socialist opposition. In contrast, the British government, acting sporadically over a period of more than a century, sometimes instituted such changes, but also tried to be responsive to popular pressures, while maintaining continuity and consensus for a population that was commonly perceived as having varied classes with varied interests. In the United States, the enlargement of power came later in the process of industrialization, mainly during the economic crisis created by the Depression of the 1930s. Such change was initiated by government officials who investigated problems, but who didn't usually have to respond to popular pressures from a divided, ill-defined "business" or "labor."

The chief distinction between Europe and America was the relative lateness of American governmental action: not significantly different in the matter of industrial regulation, more so in the matter of union protection and social security and welfare, hugely so in the matter of a large professional army. The national government lacked the capacity—lacked its own "infrastructure"—to move quickly into these areas during the nineteenth century. Industrialization matured only during the very late decades of the century, and when the scale and scope and concentration of industrial enterprise seemed to threaten the existence or operation of a free and open capitalist system, the American federal system of government started to bestir itself, though it wasn't until the Great Depression that it was goaded into the kinds of actions that European governments, responsive to a somewhat earlier industrialization, had already begun to take. Similarly, the United States was the Western Hemisphere's preeminent power for a century, from 1815 to 1914, before it seemed necessary to create a significantly large military and intervene in Europe during World War I in order to sustain the overall balance of power there that had guaranteed the United States's preeminence in its hemisphere for the previous century. And, it wasn't until World War II that America's geographical isolation from European powers seemed vulnerable and that a huge military force was needed to defeat aggressors who, if they controlled the Eurasian land mass, could pose a threat to America's security in an age of long-distance air and sea power.

As the American national government enlarged its authority in the manner just described, it increased its capacity to deal with the concerns of the electorate.

Through this entire trajectory of growing governmental activism, a sequence of different political agencies dominated the process by which power at the federal level was enlarged. During the nineteenth century, the major political parties, even with their looseness and lack of discipline, and the federal court system, through judicial interpretation, were the key institutions in the forging of government policy as America turned from being a predominantly agricultural and commercial society to an increasingly industrialized one. The federal administration itself lacked the scope and scale to exercise national power of the kind that state and local governments were already exercising. After the turn of the century, however, growing numbers of reform-minded observers, intellectuals, and critics argued that the federal government should increase its capacity to deal with what had become problems with national dimensions by legislating into existence administrative agencies whose trained personnel would regulate and protect various social interests and groups.

These reformers allied with progressive politicians who, from time to time during the course of the twentieth century, have dominated the Presidency, the Congress, and the Supreme Court, and who, at various points, have enlarged the authority of the federal government. Not until the crisis generated by the Great Depression of the 1930s was there the administrative capacity in Washington to sustain a national government with predominant authority in a hitherto bottom-heavy federal system. The federal bureaucracy has continued to perform this function since the 1930s, though they have never supplanted their predecessors: the federal courts and the major parties still play a role in the expansion of federal power.

17

Domestic Policy

Under the decentralized American federal system, state governments—from the 1790s to the 1860s—took the lead in regulating and fostering economic and social development. These governments incorporated or issued charters for banks and transportation and industrial corporations, private schools, orphanages, insane asylums, hospitals, charitable units, and private institutions of all kinds. Incorporation or charter issuance involved a commitment by these private groups to abide by certain public standards. The state governments themselves founded jails, poorhouses, insane asylums, orphanages, old people's homes, public schools—an array of public institutions for the deviant and dependent groups in the population, groups that in the colonial period had typically been dealt with in the context of the better-off families. This enlargement of government in the social dimension of life was almost entirely the work of the states.

So too was theirs the *primary* responsibility for the regulation and fostering of economic activity. State governments issued charters or incorporated (at first by special acts, but, by the 1830s, by "general incorporation" laws) banks, road or canal or railroad companies, and industrial firms. These same governments issued licenses for those trained in specific ways for particular trades and professions. This regulatory function was supplemented by aid in the form of the subscription of public tax revenues to private banking and transportation corporations. State politicians believed that banking and transportation were of vital and basic importance to economic development and, though private groups should create and sustain banking and transportation facilities for the profit to be garnered, the public's interest in the success of this costly and rather risky enterprise was of such magnitude that public funds ought to be invested alongside private funds.

It is important to note that both the Civil War and the "Reconstruction" of the Union during the 1860s and 1870s constituted a crisis for a *federal* political system. The secession of the Southern states disrupted the functioning of the American political system for the four years of civil war. Parts had seceded from the whole, states from the nation. The problem after the war was a political one: how to reconstruct the Union. Lincoln's plan was pragmatic, simple, forgiving in tone. Whenever 10 percent of the voters (excluding Confederate office holders) in a former Confederate state took an oath of allegiance to the Constitution (including the laws, proclamations, and subsequent amendment ending slavery) and the Union and received a Presidential pardon, that state could be readmitted to the Union. The plan of Andrew Johnson, Lincoln's successor, was only slightly less so. Presidential reconstruction would have been speedily accomplished.

By contrast, Congressional reconstruction was punitive in tone. Under the leadership of the "Radicals," the sizable Republican majority in Congress united in response to evidence of continued Southern opposition to the ending of slavery and to a new President who seemed implacably hostile to Congress. By 1867, Congress enacted its own reconstruction program over Presidential vetoes. The motives and goals of the Radical Republicans who designed the program were mixed: a hatred of slavery and Southerners, a love of power, an idealistic view that saw victors and virtue punishing the vanquished and wickedness. Various Reconstruction acts set up a militarily occupied region (something like what happened in Germany after World War II). Reconstruction was sustained by a combination of effective Congressional leadership, ineffective Presidential leadership on the part of Andrew Johnson, and popular hatred of Southerners and of slavery.

Congressional Reconstruction produced biracial political equality in the South, but this significant change did not outlast the military occupation of the South because popular support was not deep or sustained enough for national political power to be used to bring about genuine, lasting racial equality.

Reconstruction governments in the South were based upon black suffrage and Southern white voters who favored "positive" state government of the kind that voters elsewhere supported, as state governments around the Union significantly extended their role in the development of transportation and educational systems and in the provision of "social services." Black participation as voters and officeholders was not basically different in character from white voting and officeholding. But, Southern whites were also responsive to racism and to the terrorist groups (like the Ku Klux Klan) who intimidated blacks. As in the North and West, so in the South, after military occupation ended, there wasn't the will or interest or support among Southern whites to sustain a political, economic, and social life that embraced racial equality.

And yet, government and politics retained its profoundly *federal* character throughout the decades following the Civil War, for state and local government continued to exercise paramount authority in the internal governance of the American people. The national government continued to operate under a constitution that specified and delineated (even if sometimes in confusing ways) its proper powers, and there were no sustained crises—except for the one and a half year involvement in World War I—that prompted national politicians to interpret the national government's constitutional edict in the manner that Lincoln had during the Civil War: as being flexibly defined in order to justify significant enlargements of authority for the duration of a crisis. The "war boards" of World War I and the immense augmentation of power they were granted over the economy reveal the basically pragmatic character of American politicians, but also the temporary nature of important increases in national authority. A distrust of centralized political power was deeply embedded in the consciousness of politically active citizens, was indeed as old as the republic itself, and remained a defining feature of the American political system.

Reformers after 1890 sought to increase the authority of the national government to take into account the enlargement of scale that increasingly marked the economic and social aspects of American life, and Progressives were the most influential advocates of this course of action, especially during America's brief encounter with World War I. But, it was the Depression of the 1930s and World War II that produced crises of such a magnitude that Americans were galvanized into sanctioning—in dramatic and abrupt ways—both the enlargement of governmental authority and the emergence of the national government as the preeminent level of government, developments already clearly visible in Europe.

These crises provoked *national* responses, and from 1930 to 1945, American politicians and voters acted accordingly. Once enlarged and centralized, governmental authority has continued, since World War II, to expand in response to other problems that have arisen in an increasingly "nationalized" populace. What in Europe occurred sporadically and gradually over a long period of time, from the late eighteenth century onward, in America occurred more abruptly, under the spur of particular crises, in spite of a durable antipower, anticentrist tradition.

Beginning in the 1930s, the national taxing power has been so extensive that many state-level governmentally financed "programs" and activities are partially funded by grants from the national government. State and local governments have shared in the overall augmentation of governmental functions, but have largely ceased to act independently of similar national regulations and expenditures. This fundamental shift in the nature of the federal system has mirrored, though belatedly and under the initial spur of crisis, the "nationalizing" tendencies evident in all dimensions of American life.

As the reach of national governmental authority has grown, the federal system has, since the 1930s and 1940s, assumed a top-heavy aspect, with national funds generated from a far-ranging national revenue system assigned to state, county, and local governments that maintain programs defined by certain national standards. So, the federal system, though altered, still functions, and indeed, the more conservative Presidents since World War II (especially Eisenhower, Nixon, and Reagan) have indicated—though in word more than in deed—their loyalty to that system. State and local governments have also grown both administratively and in the range of their activities, but rarely do they act without the benefit and support of national grants-in-aid. American federalism has come to be a system in which, typically, all three levels of government use their taxing power and Constitutional authority to participate in particular programs or activities.

By the 1960s, the "liberal"-dominated Supreme Court, with Earl Warren as Chief Justice, decided that the rural elements in the population of the American states had devised a variety of means to retain voting districts (such as by county) that favored the shrinking rural population over the growing urban population and that such devices were unconstitutional, as each vote should be equal in value to every other. The effect of this decision has been to foster the growth of legislatures and legislation more favorable to the large urban majorities in many states.

* * *

The Constitution provided the new national government with certain powers that were "enumerated" in the document, powers that European central governments routinely exercised in the late eighteenth century. But, though the American government was to be a government of limited, defined powers, the drafters of the Constitution wavered between being explicit and allowing the new government needed flexibility to deal with future crises and complications. The two most important and ambiguous "couplings"—of specific powers with vague means of exercising them—were that Congress could collect taxes "for the common defense and general welfare" and could do anything "necessary and proper" in the execution of its particular spheres of authority.

The most contentious issues of national politics did not necessarily relate to the controversial exercise of Congress' enumerated powers. (The Founding Fathers linked the power to legislate to Congress alone, not to the President.) As was the case with the confederate Congress of the 1780s, the most important issue from the 1790s to the 1860s involved a matter not listed among the Constitutionally sanctioned powers. Slavery was referred to here and there in the Constitution, but nowhere in provisions defining Presidential or Congressional authority in relation to it. And yet slavery was the issue that undermined the whole political system. Even the banking issue—which, after slavery, perhaps most deeply affected the political life of the nation—was not derived from any Constitutionally defined power. Issues arose because Presidents (in Annual Messages), Congressional leaders (in committee reports), and party leaders (during campaigns and elections) felt strongly that a matter of public concern could be dealt with in some way by the national government. Among the mix of factors that determined the course of political action taken on particular major issues were the impact of particular personalities (Presidents and Congressional, judicial, and party leaders); the imperatives of party politics; constituency pressures;

the lure of ideological commitments; and the effectiveness with which particular positions were made in the political and public debates.

There were shifting political contexts during the decades from the 1790s to the 1860s from which contentious issues arose. In the 1790s, Alexander Hamilton and Thomas Jefferson personified contrasting visions of what the new republic should be. It was their efforts to foster and protect those contrasting visions that created the nation's earliest political divisions.

Hamilton had the perspective of someone born outside the nation (in the British West Indies) and exhibited an older imperial bias. He was the (illegitimate) son of a Scottish merchant. Washington's aide-de-camp during the Revolution and appointed by the first President as his first Secretary of the Treasury, Hamilton came to the most important position (in domestic affairs) in the new national government with an already-formed political nationalism. Hamilton was disappointed that the Constitutional Convention had not created a stronger national government. His model in all things political and economic and social was Britain, the very imperial power that the Americans had revolted from in order to create "a more perfect union."

From the beginning of his years in office (1789–1795), Hamilton believed that the new national government must exercise its powers to the fullest Constitutionally sanctioned extent. He envisioned a strong, not a weak, decentralized, and fragmented, political union whose government assisted in the creation of an integrated modern economy, one that quickly industrialized as Britain itself was doing. A powerful and modern national union and economy could be created out of loosely connected, undeveloped ones if the new government forged an alliance with those who had the capacity and talent to invest in and manage large-scale enterprise. Politicians and businessmen of talent formed, Hamilton believed, a natural or symbiotic relationship. Each group benefited from a close alliance with the other (so unlike Washington's abhorrence of entangling alliances in foreign affairs). But, Hamilton was convinced that the "business community" of the late eighteenth century in the former colonies was a fledgling one—hesitant, uncertain, unimaginative, reluctant to take risks.

To create the union and the economy he envisioned, he proposed in reports submitted to Congress that the national government redeem the revolutionary war certificates, at face value, to their current holders (and not to those to whom they had been originally issued for services rendered during the war); that the old states' war debts be assumed by the new national government (no matter how little or how much they had already paid off); that there be a new national bank, quasi-private and quasi-public in character, that would hold the government's funds and issue sound loans to a hopefully expanding business community; and that Congress enact "protective" tariff duties, allowing American firms to develop, thus ending American dependence upon Britain's more advanced, industrializing economy.

As these reports flowed into Congress, Jefferson (in the cabinet) and Madison (in the House) became increasingly alarmed. Thomas Jefferson—who emerged as the chief "opposition" spokesman—was the most intellectually oriented of all the Virginia planters who dominated Southern political life until the 1820s. As coauthor of the Declaration of Independence, he was extremely sensitive about any policies that could be construed as arbitrary or tyrannical in nature. Jefferson believed Hamilton's proposals—in their cumulative effect—were like those of the British imperial governments in the 1760s and 1770s. Hamilton's interpretation of the Constitution and his requests for legislation threatened the delicate balance of a decentralized federal political system and unfairly favored and promoted the interests of a commercial elite.

In reaction, Jefferson became a fierce defender of the status quo. He envisioned a perpetual, decentralized union without industry, without urbanization, a republic of farmers (and planter elites) whose national government's powers were strictly limited and balanced and whose hallmark was liberty for white men. Any political development that jeopardized the continuation of this kind of republic was to be determinedly combatted. Jefferson's and Hamilton's visions were widely assimilated by segments of the small national political community in Philadelphia during the 1790s. These visions provided a basis for the political debates that produced Cabinet, then Congressional, and then party divisions, ending the political unity of 1789 and bringing a deeply ideological hue to the issues of the first decade of national political life.

The election of Jefferson to the Presidency in 1800 created a major political question about the future of the young American political system: What would happen when power shifted peacefully and legitimately from one party to another when those parties were deeply antithetical ideologically? Would Jefferson try to undo all the legislative accomplishments that the rival Federalists had achieved during the 1790s? The answer was that Jefferson and the Republicans in Congress and the Cabinet became pragmatic in office. The ideological fervor of the late 1790s was not sustained thereafter. Many Republicans believed, with the passing of the Federalist threat, that "party" was not a necessary feature of republican government. And when the Federalists—after 1800—curried popular support as the Republicans had earlier, thus setting up a competitive two-party electoral system, elected Presidents and Congressmen did not generally give top priority to adherence to principles during campaigns or in office.

No major domestic issues emerged from 1800 to the War of 1812 because there were no impassioned and committed Presidents or Congressional leaders devoted to the enactment of legislative programs (as Hamilton had been in the 1790s). Only the War of 1812 and the painful reality of a woefully unprepared nation galvanized the pragmatic President Madison into a postwar plea (suffused with nationalistic sentiment) that the union become self-sufficient and strong in order to ward off future enemies and intruders. Madison's solution was to revive Hamilton's program (a strong defense establishment, a national bank, and a protective tariff) and add to it the financing of a national transportation system. This display of Presidential nationalism was presented in the midst of the disintegration of the first party system, however, as the "disloyal" Federalist opponents of the war disbanded in bits and pieces during the immediate postwar years.

Congress became factionalized around would-be Presidential candidates in the 1820s. The issues that were dealt with emerged as a result of Presidential encouragement (such as internal improvement bills) or constituency pressure (such as tariff bills). When "party" revived around the candidacies of Andrew Jackson and John Quincy Adams in the late twenties, party leaders again took a deep personal interest in some issues (for example: Jackson on the bank and Clay on public lands), and even tried to commit their party colleagues to a particular position on them. The interest of the parties became a factor in the emergence and intensity and duration of particular issues in the thirties and forties, and, indeed, parties themselves became acceptable features of the political system.

But, party loyalty was never fully achieved, and the second major parties continued to seek popularity, which blunted efforts to sustain ideological purity and adherence to principles. Constituency pressure, the personalities of political leaders, and the emergence of unforeseen problems also were features in the development of controversy and debate. By the 1850s, the slavery issue divided the major parties along sectional lines (the Whigs in 1854 and the Democrats in 1860), thus destroying the only national institution that had provided the means for a functioning political system. Slavery came to dominate public debate to the near exclusion of other issues, a domination that led to the destruction of the system itself.

So, there were shifting contexts within which particular major domestic issues ebbed and flowed as matters of public concern from the 1790s to the 1860s.

All of the major issues that the new American government dealt with between 1789 and 1861 were the concern of national governments all over the westernized world during these decades. As European and white settler society governments consolidated their authority and tried to deal with increasingly complex capitalist economic systems, all of them grappled with such questions as: How public or how private should the banking system be? Should tariffs protect the domestic economy from foreign imports or should they generate revenue? To what extent should public funds be invested in various modes of transportation? However distinctive the new American government might have been in its republican and then democratic nature, in its decentralized federalist makeup, the issues it grappled with were standard ones for national governments in Europe. Other issues were those that Western frontier governments shared, issues involving the public lands and the native populations and the black African slaves. The American government was distinctive in certain respects, but its domestic policies, though the product of a particular constellation of circumstances that existed only in the United States, were nonetheless focused on issues that resonated over large parts of the westernized world.

The banking issue was without a Constitutional foundation in the sense that the national government (like the Congress under the Articles of Confederation) was given no authority to create a banking system. Hamilton's proposal in 1791 was that Congress create a national bank and branches that would be both private and public, though performing public functions—a perfect example of his overall plan to forge a government-business alliance. Officers were to be both government and stockholder appointees; stock had to be in the form of government bonds. The bank was to serve as a deposit for government funds and was to loan the government money. But it was also to act as a creditor for men of commerce who needed loans and who would—because of their faith in the soundness of the bank—hand on the bank's loan notes as a kind of currency, failing to redeem them in gold and silver coin, and thus increasing the money supply as the economy expanded.

Jefferson and Madison thought the bank proposal was unconstitutional and that such an institution would favor the interest of commerce over agriculture. Hamilton's proposal was approved by Congress, but of all the domestic issues of the 1790s, banking was the greatest factor in the creation of a political opposition. And yet, when Jefferson became President, he did not attempt to dismantle the national banking system. The Bank of the United States' (BUS) charter was of 20 years' duration and wasn't to be renewed until 1811 in any case. Jefferson's attitude toward the bank was a good example of his pragmatic position with regard to the Federalist legislative attainments of the 1790s. When the bank's charter was presented for renewal in 1811, Jefferson's successor, Madison, took no discernible position on the matter. The bank recharter bill was defeated because those Congressmen responsive to the interests of state banks outnumbered those whose allegiance was to the continuation of the national banking system.

During the War of 1812, the absence of a national bank created difficulties for a government waging war, there not being any dependable deposit for government funds, source for loans, or regulator of credit and currency for commerce as a whole. Madison presented a proposal to Congress in 1816 for the recreation of a BUS, quite similar in nature to the old, and a largely partyless Congress agreed. When Nicholas Biddle became President of the BUS, the bank gained an articulate spokesman and defender of its interests, as well as a friend of those who became leaders of the Whig opposition during the 1830s. Andrew Jackson, elected President in 1828, hated the national banking system and its President. Jackson believed that the bank represented foreign interests (in the form of its investors), was a largely private body performing public functions, and was the prime example of the pernicious effects of political nationalism, of an unconstitutional institution that favored the rich and powerful. Government, Jackson believed, should return to old republican principles, stay out of the affairs of private citizens, and refrain from acting in unconstitutional ways by creating institutions that favored the rich. Moreover, state banks were unduly restricted by the operations of the national bank. Some of the most powerful and vocal state banking interests were strong Jackson advocates.

So, Jackson vetoed the Whig-sponsored charter-renewal bill in 1832, and

Congress failed to override his veto. He then made the bank issue *the* party issue, insisting that all Democrats nominated for Congress agree with his position. In so acting, he chose an issue on which it was relatively easy to gain party loyalty because the question of whether or not there should be a national banking system could be argued in terms of the national interest by those representing or hoping to represent many areas of the country where banking was not an important local issue. When reelected in 1832, Jackson then placed the government's deposits in specially designated banks (tested for political loyalty of their officers) and, in a Specie Circular, forbade payment in anything but gold and silver coin for public lands. Jackson's successor, Van Buren, was finally able to persuade a majority of Congress to pass a bill setting up an Independent Treasury system, special deposit facilities for government deposits only. And though the Whigs repealed this legislation in 1841 under Whig President Tyler, Democratic majorities reenacted the proposal under Democratic President Polk in 1846. No Whig effort to revive a national banking system succeeded before the party itself disintegrated in the mid-1850s.

It is clear that Jackson, Van Buren, and Polk were genuine states rightists who had a deeply engrained bias against a national bank and the expanding paper currency it spawned. Jackson's position on banking hardened into party dogma, and none of his successors wavered in their commitment to opposing a national system. How much effect did government policy have on the economy? Certainly there was not any clear relationship between economic growth and the existence or nonexistence of a national banking system. There were no economic contractions from 1811 to 1816 or from 1832 to 1862 (the periods during which there was no BUS), except for the depression of the late 1830s and early 1840s and the brief downturn of 1857–1859. Moreover, the depression of 1819–1822 occurred while there was a BUS. It was widely felt that the existence of the BUS created a sounder credit and currency system, that state banks would not be as apt to make excessive loans if the BUS and its branches regularly presented state bank notes for redemption. But, the economy expanded from the early 1840s to the late 1850s with only state banks in operation. So, in this most contentious economic issue, the sporadic actions of the national government, inconsistent as they were, had no obvious and continuing impact on the growth of the economy.

The debt issue was related to the bank issue insofar as both involved credit and the currency, but the government's debt was not entirely dependent on the state of the banking system. Debt became a matter of contention, debate, and action at different times from those that the national bank emerged as a major political issue. When Hamilton proposed to pay off the Continental Congress' bonds at face value, he argued that those investors who gambled on the future of government in the new nation should be rewarded and thus made reliable creditors of the government in the future, when other bond sales would be needed. Indeed, Hamilton envisioned a regular issuance of bonds, something that would link investors to the government and its financial needs indefinitely.

But, the opposition argued that this proposal ignored the soldiers who originally held these debt certificates, which had been issued in lieu of pay. The soldiers were great patriots who deserved—at last—the monetary reward the debt certificates promised, even if the soldiers had sold the bonds to speculators at a fraction of their face value. Hamilton's proposal passed Congress, as did his proposition that the new national government "assume" the war debts of the state governments. The opposition argued—in vain—that the various states had already paid off their debts in varying degrees and that therefore it was unfair for the national government to assume debt burdens of widely differing magnitudes.

When Jefferson became President, he and his successors—Madison and Monroe—all reduced the national debt to the point that after Jackson became President, instead of a debt, there was a surplus. All these Presidents acted out of obeisance to the Republican doctrine that the national government be frugal and minimal in its needs and revenues. Ironically, it was not Jackson, but Henry Clay, the leader of the Jacksonian opposition in the early 1830s, who proposed that the national government distribute this surplus among the states based upon the size of their Congressional representation and made this proposal the first test of party loyalty for the emergent Congressional opposition. With Washington under an almost-continuous Democratic domination until 1861, the tradition of frugality worked against a resurgence of governmental expenditures, and the debt issue never became important again—until the Civil War.

The tariff issue was based upon the Constitution itself in the sense that Congress had been granted the power to levy tariff duties. What made the exercise of that power a matter of contention was Hamilton's argument for protection: that Congress ought to fix high duties on imported products that were essential to domestic production if the United States was to become an industrializing nation, as Britain was, and if the new republic was to maintain its independence in times of crisis because of economic self-sufficiency. Hamilton was confident that the domestic industries so protected would develop products of the quality the British had already attained. He was prescient in believing that the earliest labor force for machine production would be women and children, as native farmers and craftsmen were sufficiently economically well-off to avoid such alternate labor opportunities.

The opposition to Hamilton's tariff proposal argued that the Founding Fathers intended tariff duties to be a leading source of revenue, not a means of protecting fledgling domestic industries. Republicans denounced protection as another indication of Hamilton's favoring a special interest group (early industrialists) at the expense of the larger population, who would be forced to pay high prices for shoddy domestic products so that in some distant time the United States would achieve economic self-sufficiency. Hamilton's tariff proposal did not receive Congressional approval, but, by 1816, when large-scale group investment began to turn from long-blocked commerce and shipping to the factory production of textiles, the kind of domestic industry Hamilton envisioned was starting to appear.

There were ever-higher levels of protection in the tariff bills of 1816, 1820, 1824, 1828, and 1832—all the product of constituency and interest group pressures on particular Congressmen, as well as the continued advocacy of Presidents Madison (after the War of 1812, when he argued for the necessity of economic self-sufficiency in essential products in case of future crises), Monroe, and Adams—all of whom adopted a nationalist posture on this issue. Jackson, by contrast, sought to avoid openly advocating protection. He was a states rightist by inclination, though his own military experience in the War of 1812 made him sensitive to the need for economic self-sufficiency in times of national crisis. The Constitution clearly gave Congress the authority to levy tariffs. The question remained: Was that authority to be exercised for revenue raising purposes only, or could it be broadened to embrace protectionist levels as well?

Jackson's Annual Messages, as they referred to the tariff, were ambiguous. He was acutely sensitive—as a political matter—to the indubitable fact that Jacksonian Democrats were deeply divided into protariff and antitariff factions. And yet, he did not veto the 1832 tariff bill, which brought protectionist levels to a new high, perhaps because he was aware that the tariff—of all the great domestic issues—was most susceptible to local and constituency pressure (product by product), and thus least amenable to the force of party principle or Presidential leadership. It was not until South Carolina (under the extreme states' rightist Vice President John C. Calhoun's political leadership) "nullified" the Tariff Act of 1832 that Jackson responded to the issue, and even then, he deferred to Henry Clay's efforts at compromise. Clay's solution, which became the Tariff Act of 1833, progressively lowered the tariff duties for the ensuing 10 years.

When the Whigs dominated Congress in the early 1840s, they raised duties once again (with their President, John Tyler's, concurrence), but when Democrats became the majority party once again (under President Polk), they lowered duties significantly in 1846. The tariff duty level remained low until the Civil War, as the Whigs lacked a majority under Taylor and Fillmore from 1849 to 1852 and the Democrats dominated the Presidency and Congress from 1853 to the outbreak of war. By the 1840s, even the tariff issue became susceptible to party discipline and loyalty, though many Congressmen continued to vote on the basis of local interests.

What was the effect of these sporadic, shifting—first toward protectionism and then toward revenue-only—legislative acts on the development of the economy? Once again, there was no clear connection. The protectionism of 1816 to 1832 does not appear to have significantly aided the development of domestic industry any more than the revenue tariffs of 1833 to 1861 appear to have deterred the growth of that industry. It is clear that the tariff issue was not a sectional one (except in the crisis of 1832–1833). The preponderance of protectionist pressure did come from Northern districts, but, when Northern and Southern politicians divided over the slavery issue in the 1850s, they did not also debate the question of protection as a sectional matter.

The internal improvements issue was only indirectly related to one of Congress' explicit powers. President Washington hoped Congress would develop the postal road system, which it clearly had the authority to do. Hamilton himself never reported on the matter, perhaps because he believed it was within the purview of the Postmaster General's department. But, transportation could not long be subsumed under communications, as an aspect of the postal system.

Another Secretary of the Treasury, Jefferson's Albert Gallatin, issued a Hamilton-like Report on Roads and Canals in 1808, urging Congress—with appropriately added constitutional authority—to finance a national transportation system. Gallatin's constitutional scruples guided Presidents Madison and Monroe as both adopted a nationalistic outlook at the same time they wanted to adhere to old republican principles. The resolution of this particular dilemma was for Congress to propose a Constitutional amendment explicitly granting itself the authority to finance such a program. When Madison proposed—after the War of 1812—that there be a nationally financed "internal improvements" program, he also requested an appropriate Constitutional amendment. When Congressional leaders drew up an internal improvements bill and gained Congressional approval, but without reference to an amendment, Madison successfully vetoed it, as did his successor, Monroe, when a similar bill was presented to him in 1822. However, in 1824, Monroe did approve of a "general survey" bill as a preliminary step toward a national system of roads and canals. John Quincy Adams, the most nationalistic of all the Presidents before the Civil War, did not insist on such an amendment, and he approved of several bills dealing with particular projects: a piecemeal approach.

Internal improvements was not an issue that could inspire party loyalty to a high degree, so great were local pressures. Jackson, a states' rightist by inclination, did not try to commit his party to a particular position on the matter. But, he himself forged one in his annual messages, in which he declared that harbor and river projects, because they partook of foreign commerce, were eligible for national funds, whereas road and canal projects within particular localities were not. Another factor in the making of Jackson's position was that strong Jacksonian supporters were from states that had already built a road or canal system or that didn't need them. In a partisan political move, Jackson vetoed a road bill that involved his opponent Henry Clay's home state and announced his views on the internal improvements issue.

Thereafter, Jackson and his Democratic successors opposed national funding for roads and canals. Van Buren, Polk, Pierce, and Buchanan all adhered to Jackson's states'-rightist position on this as on other issues. The Whig Presidents—Harrison, Tyler, Taylor, and Fillmore—were more favorable toward such bills, but, since the internal improvements issue was not one in which

Congressmen easily allowed party loyalty to override local interests, none of the Presidents was able to make the issue one strictly identified with party.

Sporadic appropriations for a "National Road" from Washington westward were the only evidence of federal funding for internal (as opposed to external) improvements before the 1850s, when Democrats led by Senator Stephen Douglas favored a nationally funded transcontinental railroad through the western territories of what was by-then a continental republic. It was Douglas—in his position as Chairman of the Senate's committee on territories—who linked the internal improvements issue with the fateful slavery issue when, in 1854, he drafted the Kansas-Nebraska Act, which organized the old Louisiana Purchase into territories (on the basis of popular sovereignty) so that planning a transcontinental railroad could proceed. But the fact remains that it was the state governments that provided most of the public funding for transportation systems of all kinds before the Civil War.

The public lands issue emerged directly from the exercise of a Constitutionally sanctioned power of the national government. But the various public lands acts passed during the decades following 1789, extensions as they were of the land ordinance of the 1780s, created little controversy in Congress and among the parties before the 1830s. Each successive act reduced both the acreage required for each purchase and the minimum price per acre, and the auction system, established in the earliest act, was abandoned by 1820, having become a basis for speculative ventures more than a means for actual settlement by serious settlers. All these changes were evidence of a sporadic but sincere effort on the part of most Congressmen to match government policy with the real needs of those who wanted to settle on the public lands.

But, lurking behind the surface of this instance of Congressional harmony was the vexing question of whether the government's land policy should have as its aim the garnering of a major source of revenue or the facilitation of settlement over these vast tracts of resourceful land. Henry Clay—leader of the emergent opposition to Jackson and his Democrats in the early 1830s—tried to make public lands policy a test of party identity and loyalty (linking this issue with that of distribution of the surplus as party issues). Clay wanted the minimum price high enough so that the sale of public lands would be a major source of the government's revenues. Public land policy was a relatively easy matter to define as a basis of party loyalty because local or constituency interests were not likely to be very evident on something so distant from the immediate concerns of most of the electorate. Congressmen were able to take a larger view and could be responsive to other pressures, such as the demand for party loyalty.

But, Jackson failed to perceive the issue as Clay did and did not even have a well-defined position on the matter. Jacksonian Democrats in Congress were thus not united in opposition to Clay's party. But, some western Democrats—such as Senator Thomas Benton—favored both "graduation" and "preemption"—that is, (1) a gradual lowering of the price of the public land, until it would be given away to serious settlers, and (2) the granting of legal titles to squatters, those thousands who had gone ahead and settled on desirable plots of land without bothering to adhere to the rules established by the various land acts. And though Congress did not pass a new land act during Clay's and Jackson's years of rivalry, by the 1840s it did enact temporary preemption acts, until, under a like-minded President, Polk, it passed a permanent Preemption Act, in 1848.

By the mid-1850s, the desire for legislation granting free land to actual settlers passed from the western Democrats to the newly formed Northern sectional party, the Republicans, who favored what they called a "Homestead Act" (which was enacted during the Civil War). So, public land policy only became contentious in the 1830s, during the time of the emergence of the second party system, when the until-then-latent question of whether the government's policy should be to facilitate settlement or to generate revenue was made into a partisan political issue. Indirectly, the public land issue was linked to the slavery issue in the sense that the most contentious question in American political life from the 1820s to the 1860s was: What should the status of slavery be in the territories, where the public lands were sold, squatted on, and settled?

The "Indians" issue was located uneasily between the foreign and domestic affairs of the national government. Presidents in their Annual Messages treated Indian affairs alongside foreign relations. There were regular references to Indian "nations," and the political instrumentality for dealing legally and formally with the Indian tribes was the same as that for dealing with foreign relations: the treaty. And yet, there were basic differences in the position occupied by the native American population from that of, say, the British, the French, or the Spanish. The Indians were located *within* American territory, and, though displaced and removed and kept apart from the European migrants and their descendants, they are most sensibly perceived as a geographically segregated, but *domestic* minority, and thus part of the caste system, just as the black slaves were.

Congress had clear, Constitutionally sanctioned authority over Indian relations, and, in a series of acts, beginning in the 1790s, it determined the nature of trade with the tribes (establishing registered traders and even, for a while, national trading posts). Various Presidents and their territorial governors went on making treaties for the lands of particular tribes and sometimes the presence of settlers or troops along frontier areas led to war with apprehensive tribes. Congress also passed a Civilization Act in 1819, setting up a fund to pay missionaries who tried to Christianize certain tribes and to finance efforts by the government's Indian agents to teach tribes European-derived methods of agriculture and the private ownership of property. The Presidents, Secretaries of War, and Superintendents of Indian Affairs who initiated and gained Congressional approval of these policies were motivated by a desire to be philanthropic, to aid the native population, to civilize it, and to remove it from what was perceived as its savage state through a beneficial educative process, after which the Indians might be able to gain full admission to white society.

But, government policy changed in the 1830s and, in the process, Indian relations became a contentious issue in the partisan politics that so marked that decade. Andrew Jackson regarded the Indians as childlike primitives whose ignoble savage nature he had experienced in military conflicts earlier in his life. Jackson sought to remove the "civilized" tribes that the state of Georgia had attempted to control through legislation that contravened earlier treaties. President Jackson ignored the earlier treaties, which were protective in character, sided with Georgia's government, and introduced a removal bill (with the tribes to be taken to a reservation carved out of public lands in present-day Oklahoma). He made the bill a test of party loyalty, a seemingly good choice because it was relatively easy for Congressmen to respond to larger considerations than constituency pressures on a matter that little affected most of the electorate. But Jackson's proposal itself generated a lot of controversy, and a significant number of Democrats were unable to support a bill that appeared so unjust to the Indian tribes (as the emergent Jacksonian opposition also argued). Opponents insisted that the removal bill ignored the national treaties and sanctioned a takeover of Indian land, a move favored by a state government that had clearly overstepped its Constitutional bounds. Jackson's bill passed Congress, and the removal that followed was a kind of forced march involving the spread of disease and major accidents involving faulty equipment.

During the 1830s, 1840s, and 1850s, the national government continued to make treaties with particular tribes as a result of which most of the land east of the Mississippi River was ceded to the national government so that white settlers could move progressively westward. This process continued without significant political controversy. Only Jackson's forced removal policy generated political division of any consequence. Otherwise, the American government acted on the basis of a broad consensus: that the Indian lands should be ceded; that Indians should be traded with (in a regulated manner); that the frontiers should be defended; and that the Indians should be civilized, but apart from white society, as the tribes were moved steadily westward.

By contrast, the slavery issue deeply divided national politicians every time it assumed a political form. White Americans were racists in the sense that all agreed that blacks were inferior; most also believed that this was likely to be a long-term, persistent state of affairs. Certainly there was no government-sanctioned "civilization" program for blacks, as there was for natives. Natives and blacks were both elements in the caste system, but whereas the native population was a geographically displaced caste, blacks—as slaves—were a physically, economically, even politically *integrated* one. What divided Americans was not racism (which, in various forms, was universal), but the desirability of the continuation and augmentation of the system of slavery. The political system was enormously sensitive to this division of opinion.

Only a comparatively few Americans ever became abolitionists, but this reform group became, during the 1830s and 1840s, effective propagandists and agitators, ceaselessly arguing that slavery was wrong, directly conflicted with the highest religious and secular ideals of the republic, and must be abolished immediately. The abolitionists prodded many Northerners, in whose region slavery (never very entrenched) was abolished in various ways by the 1820s, to adopt an antislavery attitude, which was based on partly humanitarian (slavery was too cruel and inhumane), partly moral (it was bad to enslave another human being), and partly materialistic (slavery was, as a labor system, the very antithesis of free labor) considerations. The abolitionists also prodded Southerners into a defensive proslavery position, for which spokesmen garnered scientific (phrenology), historical (all civilizations contained the institution), economic (slaves were better treated than the new wage laborers in the early factories), and philosophical (liberty must be earned; whites were serving as tutors for a primitive, childlike race) evidence.

The abolitionists challenged, but never obliterated, an earlier position on slavery, that of the colonizationists, Northerners and Southerners, who claimed that the final solution to the intractable slavery *and race* problem was to send blacks back to Africa, just as the Indians were being moved ever westward.

All of these positions on slavery found political expression, but the problem for national politicians was to recognize ways in which the U.S. government could act, because the Constitution, other than recognizing the existence of slavery and proscribing the end of the slave trade, did not grant Congress any explicit authority over the institution. Most white Americans—even those with an antislavery or colonizationist (if not abolitionist) position—agreed that the American government had no authority to abolish slavery where it already existed. But, some Northern politicians believed that Congress had the power to *contain* slavery, to keep it from spreading as the Union expanded. That power, so it was argued, derived from Congress' undoubted authority over the territories.

In 1819, Missouri sought entrance into the Union, and antislavery Northerners in a largely partyless Congress introduced a bill barring slavery from the new state. Proslavery Southerners argued that Congress had no authority to interfere with the movement of property—in this case "chattels"—from one location to another. Speaker Henry Clay led those moderates who sought a compromise solution, which was that Missouri be allowed to enter the Union as a slave state, "Maine" (whose politicians sought separation from Massachusetts) as a free state, and that the rest of the Union be divided along the 36–30 latitude to the westernmost territory, with free (above the line) and slave (below the line) areas.

The new parties of the 1830s—the Democrats and the Whigs—tried to manage this potentially explosive and sectionally divisive issue in somewhat different ways. The Jacksonian Democrats agreed to remain silent on the issue and even successfully imposed a "gag" rule on antislavery petitions sent to the House of Representatives. Jackson's Postmaster General Amos Kendall blocked antislavery writings from reaching Southern post offices. The Whigs, less centralized than the Democrats, were less able to remain united on the issue, and, from an early time of their existence, there was a tendency for Whigs in Congress and in the Presidency to assume openly pro-or antislavery positions.

When the territories added as a result of the Mexican War were organized, some Northern antislavery politicians again introduced a bill that would have made slavery illegal. Once again, proslavery Southerners argued that Congress had no such authority. Once again, a dying Henry Clay, along with Stephen Douglas, led the moderates who successfully sought compromise, the heart of which was that California territory would be a free state and the inhabitants of New Mexico and Utah territories would be allowed to practice popular sovereignty (that is, the people there would decide the question of what slavery's status would be). When, in 1854, Douglas, as Chairman of the Senate's committee on territories, introduced the Kansas-Nebraska bill and gained Congressional approval for it, he reopened the slavery question by allowing the procedure called popular sovereignty to apply to those territories as well.

Douglas led the Northern Democrats, who were not morally sensitive to the issue, believing that slavery would exist where it was economically feasible and would fail to develop where it was not economically feasible. The Whigs—never strong at the top or center—split apart on this resuscitation of the slavery issue. The Republicans swiftly emerged as a Northern, sectional, antislavery party whose chief objective was for Congress to use its legitimate authority over the territories to bar slavery from those areas in order to contain it within the states where it already enjoyed Constitutional protection. (On economic issues, the Republicans tended to support a nationalist position, which they inherited from the Whigs and the Federalists.) The Northern Democrats (under Douglas) and Southern Democrats (under Presidents Pierce and Buchanan) became estranged as Kansas Territory divided into pro- and antislavery factions, each with its own constitution and territorial legislature. The administrations of the Democratic Presidents in the 1850s, Pierce and Buchanan, became pro-Southern in outlook and favored the Southern position, that Congress had no authority to forbid slavery from entering the territories, a position given judicial sanction in the Dred Scott case, decided in 1857. Douglas felt betrayed, arguing that the Democratic administrations had not given popular sovereignty a fair chance to succeed. Douglas's Northern Democrats became a much reduced portion of Congress in the elections following the Kansas-Nebraska Act, suggesting that popular sovereignty was not a position with large support in the electorate.

But, Douglas insisted on being the Democratic candidate in 1860 and, in so doing, he forced the Democrats to split into two factions, with a Southern candidate (Breckenridge) as well as a Northern one. With Bell as the Union Party (consisting of the old Whig remnants) candidate, and Abraham Lincoln the Northern Republican Party candidate, there was a four-way electoral contest. Lincoln won, outpolling Douglas and Bell in the more populous Northern part of the Union. For the first time in the history of the republic, a President was elected who was widely perceived as being dangerously hostile toward Southern interests.

Lincoln, as President-elect, advised party leaders in Congress not to compromise on the party's basic principle: the containment of slavery. The Republicans had a distorted view of political reality in the South. Having mistakenly believed in the mid-and late 1850s that pro-Southern Democrats constituted a "slavocracy," or slave power that was conspiring to subvert freedom everywhere in the Union, the Republicans went on to just as mistakenly assume that Southern politicians were united in their desire to secede from the Union in 1860–1861. As a result, Lincoln did nothing to reassure Southerners that he would not, as President, interfere with slavery where it legally existed. But, the Southern secessionists' view of Lincoln's Republicans involved distortion as well. Those Southerners who favored immediate secession pointed to Lincoln's election as the proximate cause. They mistakenly believed that Lincoln and his party were basically abolitionists and that a Republican administration would tyrannically threaten the entire Southern way of life. The secessionists created widespread anxiety in the South and succeeded in undermining Southern political support in Congress for compromise.

Thus, the secessionist Southern Democrats and the Northern Republicans both subscribed to a conspiratorial view of their political opponents, thereby helping to assure the failure of those moderates who made compromise proposals. In this, the extremists in both sections shared with the rebels and the British ministers during the 1760s and 1770s the distorted conspiratorial view of the opposition and, in the process, eradicated the understanding needed for serious attempts to resolve complex differences short of violence and war. When Senator Crittenden (Clay's successor from Kentucky) made a series of compromise proposals, the moderates were outvoted by the extremists of both sections.

All Southern politicians agreed with John C. Calhoun, who provided the theoretical and constitutional justification, that the states had the authority to secede from the Union, just as they had formed the Union by calling for ratifying conventions. But, Southerners were divided into secessionists and conditional unionists by 1860–1861. The conditional unionists wanted Southern leaders to avoid secession and to make continued efforts to keep the Union whole for as long as possible. The delegates of the secession conventions formed by the seceding states were divided and, though the division varied from state to state, generally the secessionist delegates represented the areas of heaviest concentrations of slaves and the antisecessionists represented those parts of the South that were predominantly white. The lower Southern states—where slavery was most fully developed—seceded first and with the most lopsided voting in the conventions. Lincoln, as President, succeeded in retaining for the Union those borders states—Maryland, Delaware, (West) Virginia, Kentucky, and Missouri—with significant secessionist movements, by moving in the Union armies and summarily imprisoning secessionist leaders.

A comparison of the causes of the American Revolution and the American Civil War illuminates the nature of both conflicts. In the case of both events, a part sought to secede from the whole. In both instances the "rebels" fought for their political independence in order to escape from a tyrannical central government. The earlier rebels perceived tyranny in the actual policies of the imperial British government; the later rebels tried to avoid the tyranny they felt sure would follow if they remained in a Union governed by a party that was fundamentally hostile toward Southerners. In both conflicts, the government of the whole refused to accept secession by the government of the parts that favored rebellion, refused to allow such secession to be peaceful, and fought to end what the central authorities regarded as an illegal rebellion.

In both instances, both the central authorities and the rebels believed they were fighting for a cause. In the case of the earlier rebels, the cause was for greater liberty; in the case of the later rebels, the cause was the freedom to have slavery. In both cases, the central governments believed they were fighting to preserve an entity that was the best of its kind, whether an empire or a nation. But, in at least one sense, the way the conflicts came about differed. A moderate political leadership emerged among the leaders of the resistance movement before the Revolution and retained its leadership throughout the conflict that followed, whereas the moderates from both the North and the South, who found common ground in the form of compromises on the slavery issue during the 1820s, 1830s, 1840s, and 1850s, lost control of the situation by 1860 and were outflanked by radical secessionists in the South and Republicans in the North.

* * *

In the Civil War that followed, the Union (or North) brought far greater resources than the Confederacy (or the South): in population, there were 22 million living in the states loyal to the Union and 9 million in the seceded states, 3½ million of whom were slaves. Most of the manufactured products (nine-tenths) were of Northern origin. But, the resources of both sides were decentralized and fragmented: manufactured products were still mostly produced in widely scattered shops, not mills and factories; railroads and canals and roads were still confined to particular areas. For both sides, the production and transportation of wartime commodities and the deployment of troops were hampered by localized facilities. Unequal resources did not dictate the outcome of the war, though the longer the war lasted, the more likely the Union's superior resources would accrue to its favor.

Other factors determining the outcome were the will of the populace and its leaders to wage war, the talent of field commanders, the capacity of the Presidents, the workability of the whole governmental systems, and the situation with respect to foreign (European) powers. For the Confederacy to establish with credibility its independence, it needed early, decisive military victories and equally swift recognition from and support of the European powers. But, the Confederacy failed to achieve either objective. The reason for its failure had as much to do with the overall political situation as with the existence of resources heavily lopsided in favor of the Union side. Basic to the outcome of the war was the fact that the Union government performed more effectively than did the Confederate.

Lincoln's Presidency was fundamental to this distinction. Lincoln focused on his authority as Commander-in-Chief: he believed he had to act in decisive ways in a national crisis. Other aspects of his office did not greatly interest him, and he allowed Congress to initiate domestic legislation not directly related to the war effort. Lincoln's concentration on his duties as Commander-in-Chief brought to the Union cause unity of authority and clarity of direction. Lincoln, from the outset, defined one war aim: the preservation of the Union. From this he never deviated. To him, the Union was indissoluble. The rebellion, like that of 1775–1781 (from the perspective of the central authority of that time), was illegal, and, as the duly constituted authority, it was his constitutional duty to end it—though he never adequately explained why the rebellion of 1775 was justified and that of 1861 was not.

Lincoln was a political nationalist, with a nationalist's definition of the Union as a perpetual, popular political instrument (a view given earlier substance in the utterances of Hamilton, Marshall, Clay, and Webster). Republican government—especially at the national level—was government "of the people, by the people, and for the people." Republican government had allowed self-made men, like Lincoln himself, the opportunity to rise politically, economically, and socially, and it must not be allowed to "perish from the earth" in a world still filled (outside of the Western Hemisphere) with nonrepublican, monarchical, dynastic states. Nationalism was thus combined in Lincoln's utterances with democracy—for white men.

Nothing, not even the vexing slavery issue, must be allowed to interfere with the Union's war aim. Lincoln admitted that slavery was the cause of the war (and it remains the only issue that has ever led to breakup of the American polity). But, his actions with respect to this institution were confined to what he perceived to be appropriate wartime measures, as further means to bring about Union victory. Emancipation came in early 1863, only after the practical question of how to define the status of the slaves within the Union lines arose, and only after Lincoln was convinced that emancipation would boost troop morale and be received favorably by the Northern civilian population and by the English, the nature of whose relationship to the Union was crucial throughout the war.

As President, Lincoln had the capacity to articulate the Union's war aims in messages to Congress, statements to editors, and speeches at gatherings in a clear, memorable way—Presidential pronouncements that filtered down and out to the populace. Lincoln was also an enormously effective pragmatic politician who, in his rise to the Presidency, mastered the intricacies of an especially complicated political system and quickly learned how to operate it while President in an emergency situation. His greatness lay in his ability to be the practical manager of a many-layered government as much as in his gift for defining an uncomplicated war aim to which he was able to commit a majority of both the populace and the politicians within the shrunken Union. Lincoln chose the leaders of all the Republican factions to his cabinet and most became effective wartime Secretaries of their respective departments. The President allowed them to be their own managers, seeking their advice on matters of general policy in cabinet meetings, but always making up his own mind on the crucial issues.

Similarly, Lincoln allowed Congress to initiate legislation that his party favored. When the Southern Democrats exited from Congress at the time of secession, the Republicans were left with a sizable majority in both houses of Congress. There was a strong sentiment in the party for the kind of nationalistic legislation that the Whigs (under Clay) and the Federalists (under Hamilton) had favored. During the war, a diminished Congress enacted, with Lincoln's approval, legislation creating a new national bank, a protective tariff, and free public land for genuine settlers. What Lincoln did not allow Congress to direct, however, was the war effort, even though the radical Republicans set up a joint Committee on the Conduct of the War and investigated the Administration's wartime management.

In the case of both the Cabinet and Congress, Lincoln succeeded in his effort to retain overall leadership, and never allowed any faction of his party to dictate policy. The President also worked effectively with state Governors, maintaining their loyalty and commanding their obedience to governmental regulations for the raising of troops. As Commander-in-Chief, Lincoln had to deal with politically appointed Generals, but he kept badgering the early field commanders to fight and quickly promoted a General—Grant—to the top position when he fought effectively. By renaming the Republicans as the Union Party, Lincoln successfully linked the administration with patriotism, while the Democratic opposition was exposed as favoring a negotiated peace. The President was easily renominated and reelected, and his party retained its commanding majority throughout the war.

By contrast, the Confederacy was hampered by its dedication to states rights at the same time it had to have a central government with sufficient authority to wage war. Its Constitution was patterned after the older "Union" one, stripped of ambiguous phrases that in any way allowed the "national" government to jeopardize the legitimate power of the states. Moreover, the man elected President—Jefferson Davis—lacked Lincoln's capacity to articulate the Confederacy's war aims and to inspire confidence in the government's capacity to achieve that aim. Davis was a meddler in the management of his own administration's departments, thus reducing his effectiveness as an overall director. He bunched his ablest Generals in the eastern theater of the war, thus hastening the fragmentation of the Confederacy's territory. And, he sparred with several state Governors who objected to troop requests containing occupational exemptions for groups judged to be too vital for armed service. And, Davis lacked Lincoln's ability to find politicians who could perform effectively as cabinet Secretaries. However, Davis generally gained the approval of the Confederate Congress for his proposals and there was never—during the life of the Confederacy—a major organized opposition to his administration in that Congress. But, the larger point remains: the Confederate Government did not—as a whole—operate as effectively as the Union's.

This discrepancy can be seen in every major aspect of the war. In the financial dimension, the Union's Secretary of the Treasury, Chase, successfully garnered the needed resources through a combination of means—higher tariff duties, the first tax on incomes, the issuance of widely dispersed government bonds, and the introduction of greenbacks (notes with no promised redemption). There was inflation because of the relative scarcity of civilian goods, but it never became severe chiefly because those in the Union territory could at least attempt to produce goods civilians wanted. By contrast, the Secretaries of the Treasury in the Confederacy presided over a steadily deteriorating financial situation. The Confederacy lost valuable currency because the Union blockade kept the South's valuable staple crops (mainly cotton) from being exported. With a slim basis for a currency, Confederate officials tried everything they could think of as a means to gain financial resources for the government. They taxed property and occupations (accepting payment in commodities) as well as incomes; they presented vast issuances of government bonds, which, when sold, quickly dropped in value, as confidence in the government's ability to repay was undermined. Tax collectors became very unpopular federal officials and evidence of tax avoidance was substantial.

So too, in the matter of supplying the armies and navies: the Union's effort was far more successful than the Confederacy's. Secretary of War Stanton succeeded in establishing procedures for the making of war contracts, and, though the Committee to Investigate the Conduct of the War found evidence of graft and corruption and the presentation of shoddily made goods, the army and the navy were adequately supplied, both by a still notably decentralized economy and by the importation of munitions from Britain. By contrast, the Confederates were largely cut off from such foreign imports and had to rely heavily and dangerously on a single iron works for armaments. The Confederacy was effective in developing war-related production as far as it did, given the almost total absence of manufacturing of any scale before the war. But hasty conversions did not result in sound and durable munitions and supplies, and as the war became a protracted conflict, adequately supplying the army and navy became increasingly difficult.

In the matter of the recruitment of soldiers and sailors, both sides acted similarly and achieved similar results. Any discrepancies involved size: the Union had far more manpower to draw on. Both sides began with regular armies augmented by volunteers, and when that system did not generate sufficient troops, both sides turned to the draft and bounties for enlistees. Men were given the choice, that is, of either being paid to give up some of their freedom (by enlisting) or losing some of their property (by hiring a substitute, if drafted.) This meant that draftees tended to be the poor, those who either could not, or would not, hire substitutes. Poor immigrants (mainly Irish) in New York City rioted against the draft in 1863. The Confederate government exempted those in certain, "crucial" occupations from the draft, something that caused a lot of resentment. But, as skewed in favor of those with means as the draft was, its main purpose was to induce voluntary enlistments. A further inducement was the bounty, a sum of money paid to each enlistee. The enticement was abused, however, and there is evidence for a substantial amount of "bounty jumping," as soldiers deserted their units and signed up for others.

Considerations of class and money were thus basic to the recruitment process, but the question of why men enlisted, fought, and died for political abstractions—the Union and the Confederacy—is more complicated than pecuniary considerations. There is no doubt that men enlisted on both sides in the early phases of the war because they thought the conflict could lead to a quick, glorious victory for their side. Loyalty to the Union and to the Confederacy and their constituent parts (states and localities) was strong, certainly strong enough to be evoked in a crisis. But, as the war became protracted, Lincoln concluded that the abolition of slavery would add appeal to the Union's cause, whereas the Confederate government continued to rely on the loyalty of those who became enlistees and draftees to their beloved "homeland." It seems clear that soldiers reenlisted out of loyalty to their units, their fighting "buddies" and that the continued association with this group was the paramount consideration in the making of a veteran.

In the course of the war, two great citizen armies (quite unequal in size by the war's later phases) engaged in much combat. But, the outcome of battles and campaigns and the war overall had more to do with the quality of the commanders and the soundness of the strategies they developed. On the Union side, Lincoln became impatient with rule-bound commanders (especially McClellan) who were slow to engage the enemy, slow to pursue him after the battle. Lincoln wanted a commander who would use the Union's superior manpower and unrelentingly fight until the enemy no longer had the capacity to wage war. The early Union commanders were, in his view, excessively bound by the carefully laid-down rules of professional warfare learned from Europe at the Military Academy at West Point.

Grant was different. As a commander in the Western theater, he fought continuously and used manpower relentlessly. Lincoln appointed Grant as his chief General and gave him the command of the Army of the Potomac, which had fought Lee's Army of Virginia in the eastern theater of the war. Grant continued to attack frontally and massively and gradually ground down Lee's ability to fight back.

Lincoln had an overall sense of strategy to which he adhered throughout the war (a strategy not very dissimilar to the one the British attempted to pursue during the Revolution). He believed that the Confederacy should be blockaded and then fragmented through well-focused incursions. The first of these was directed down the Mississippi River and was successful in the sense that the

Confederacy west of the Mississippi was cut off from the remainder. The second such incursion involved Tennessee toward Georgia. The third was from Virginia toward Georgia. A fragmented Confederacy would lack the capacity to wage war and would surrender; the "rebellion" (in Lincoln's terms) would be over. This is exactly what happened, but the plan took far longer than Lincoln at first imagined.

On the Confederate side, Lee and his principal lieutenants were effective commanders in the sense of becoming masters of maneuverability (like Washington during the Revolution), making the most of their increasingly inferior numbers. But, Davis bunched his ablest field Generals in the eastern theater of the war, thus weakening the defense of the West, where the Union's first incursions were. Davis' strategy was to defeat the Union's armies whenever they tried to penetrate Confederate territory, until such time as the Union relinquished its attempt to defeat the new nation-state by means of military conquest or until European powers—such as Britain and France—recognized and aided the Confederacy, making Union efforts at conquest futile. In short, militarily the war for the Confederacy was a defensive one. But, Davis and his commanders failed to achieve even their limited military objectives.

As for the navies, Secretary of the Navy Gideon Wells on the Union side built up a naval fleet out of old merchant ships and successfully blockaded the Confederate coast, whereas the Confederacy converted its merchant shipping into coastal raiders, which prayed on the Union blockade, but not with great effectiveness. (This was a reversal of the kind of naval forces the rebels and the British had had during the Revolution.)

In the diplomatic sphere, once again there was a marked discrepancy between Union success and Confederate frustration and failure. The European powers had a unique opportunity to break up American hegemony in the Western Hemisphere. A Union reduced to two parts would not have continued to be the colossus of the Americas that it had swiftly come to be. But, Britain—with the world's largest navy—would have had to do all that the Confederate government had hoped it would before the American power center could have been regarded as permanently sundered. Instead, the British—as they had since 1815—gave priority to considerations of trade over geopolitical concerns and simply recognized that a state of belligerency existed and went no further. The Union government, ably represented by Charles Francis Adams, had as its major diplomatic objective the maintenance of British neutrality. Trade flourished between the British and the Union, with the importation of British-made munitions a crucial factor in the Union's victory. Only twice was this arrangement endangered. When the Union navy captured Confederate agents on their way to seek British recognition and aid, the Union government released them when the British protested. And when Lincoln's administration learned that the British were building ships to be used as Confederate raiders and protested, the British agreed to sell the ships privately in Britain.

The Confederacy's diplomacy was a desperate attempt to gain both recognition and aid from the European powers. The British remained unconvinced of the need for such assistance, even having found additional supplies elsewhere for the staples of which the Confederacy hoped to remain the indispensable supplier. The French, under Louis Napoleon, did hope to become active once again in New World affairs, but without the concurrence of the British, their efforts were limited to the sending of a puppet Emperor to the debt-ridden Mexicans. Without aid from the British of the kind envisioned by Davis, the Confederacy was doomed, especially with a crumbling will to fight a Union army under the command of a General who knew how to use its superior resources and a Union government steadily directed by a determined President.

The Civil War was the costliest of America's wars in terms of the loss of life relative to the whole population. As many died during the Civil War as in World War II, when the population was much greater. As a result of the Civil War, the South was devastated physically, economically, socially, and politically. The institution that had given the region its identity was ended, along with all the property slavery represented. Seldom in human history has an elite group of consequence to a whole population lost its property (or at least its chattel property) all at once and without any compensation. The Civil War represents the last time Americans living in different regions destroyed the national political system rather than confront a vexing public issue that divided them along sectional lines. The American political system was too disjointed, too fragmented and decentralized to withstand such divisiveness. Most power had remained at the local and state levels.

But the war did not have major political, economic, and social consequences for the nation's future. The political system endured, with wartime Presidential preeminence giving way afterward to Congressional hegemony. There were no major economic changes as a consequence of the war: the economy continued to evolve in its capitalistic way toward industrialization and corporate concentration, processes little affected by the war itself. Neither was American society greatly changed by the war: Americans were still a people of classes and castes, based upon wealth and race. Growing urbanization and increasingly sophisticated technology were symbiotically related to the changing nature of industrialization, and not to a cataclysmic civil war. Even within the defeated Confederacy, once the military occupation was ended (by the mid-1870s), Southerners reestablished a political system whose practitioners were assiduous in restoring and maintaining a region based upon white supremacy, as had their antebellum predecessors. Former slaveowners became large landowners; former slaves became sharecroppers. By the 1890s, those who had been black slaves and their progeny became a segregated caste, far more separated from Southern whites than the slaves had ever been.

In sum, the Civil War did not produce major change, except as a precedent for the perpetuation of national authority in response to rebellion or secession. Unlike the Revolution, when a part (rebelling colonies) successfully seceded from the whole (the British Empire), in the Civil War, the whole (the Union) sustained itself, crushing efforts to dismember or fragment it. But, the Civil War has perpetuated itself in popular culture as a folk memory of a time when the inhabitants of two regions within the nation were so agitated over a question that divided them that they attempted to create two nations and fought a bloody civil war, which the North won and the South lost. Memory of the Civil War keeps alive regional identities long after the circumstances that produced the conflict have ceased to exist—the memory of two peoples in one nation: one victorious, progressive, successful; the other different, apart, lost.

* * *

Between the Civil War and the Great Depression, there were several shifts of mood among national and state politicians. The preponderant "spirit" of political life changed from conservative (1865–1890) to a mix of conservative and radical (1890–1900) to progressive (1900–1918) to conservative (1918–1930) again.

Those who articulated a conservative position, as the Jeffersonian Republicans and the Jacksonian Democrats had earlier, emphasized minimal government. Such spokesmen favored a laissez-faire approach to the way that government should relate to the economy and the society. This outlook or perception was buttressed by a popular and broadly social philosophy—Social Darwinism—which stressed that human societies develop best naturally, without government interference, and that the strongest individuals emerged as preeminent in the human world, just as was the case in the animal world. Proponents agreed that the United States was destined to become the most advanced nation in the world.

What had been liberal became conservative: what Jeffersonians and Jacksonians offered as means of protecting the interests of those who had not yet become successful, post–Civil War conservatives offered as an appropriate role for government in a social and economic setting dominated increasingly by big corporations. The old states'-rightist position became a justification for minimalist government at a time of rapid concentration of private or nonpublic wealth and power, something that conservative spokesmen said was a natural part of the evolution of modern society. True liberty, they argued (as had Jefferson and Jackson in a time of much smaller enterprise), can flourish best when those engaged in economic and social activity have the widest possible freedom.

The radical position (adopted by the Populists and the farmers who supported them in the 1890s) was that the social/economic system was so off-course, so dominated by corporate power, that a significant enlargement of governmental authority was needed if America was ever to create a just society. If certain sectors of the economy were persistently unresponsive to the public will and the commonweal, then the national government should assume direct control of those sectors.

The more moderate "progressive" outlook avoided the matter of direct governmental control (except during America's brief involvement in World War I, when politicians influenced by such views favored the establishment of governmental boards with significant authority over the actual functioning of the economy, going far beyond what those of Populist views ever imagined in the 1890s). Progressivism, which appealed to urban middle-class citizens, was an impulse to reform American life, but not to alter its basic structure, something that would occur in the case of government ownership. This progressive outlook was strengthened by an increasingly popular, nondeterministic social philosophy that countered "Darwinism" with a contrasting perception of the world as one open to human intervention, experimentation, and improvement.

Progressive-minded politicians sought to make the political system itself less corrupt, more efficient, more the work of virtuous and trained personnel, but also more democratic, more responsive to what they hoped would be civic-minded voters through the adoption of such devices as popular primaries for political parties, the referendum, the recall, woman suffrage, and the direct election of U.S. Senators. Progressives also favored government regulation of the economy, though they divided over whether simply to regulate firms of a greatly enlarged scale or to become more activist and break up monopolistic enterprise and thus restore a more openly competitive economy. Progressives also believed that American society should be characterized by its sense of social justice, that those who were harmed by the capitalist system should receive protection by government (such as the prohibition of child labor).

Politicians influenced by this impulse also believed that government should be able to extend its activity through the addition of public services as there seemed to be need for them (such as the building of "public ways" or highways, the regulation of food and drugs, the conservation of natural resources, and the creation of recreation and wilderness areas), all of which meant that Progressivism, like political nationalism between the 1789 and 1861, emphasized a broad, open view of the Constitutional mandate for a federal political system. Once again, there was a fundamental reversal: political nationalism had been opposed as elitist and conservative and authoritarian and dangerous to liberty; progressivism as a nationalistic force defined activist government as liberal: strong government was democratic and popular, defending and furthering the public interest against the amassing of power by special interests (which was exactly the same argument that Jackson had used in the 1830s *against* the development of big government).

The conservative impulse was the strongest between 1865 and 1900. Most national politicians in diverse ways shared a largely conservatively oriented belief that the government in Washington was one of limited, defined powers; that the economy should be allowed to grow and change without significant government regulation, interference, protection, or ownership; and that the state and local governments should provide whatever social welfare agencies were clearly needed. However, it was in the context of this political consensus that certain state governments challenged the status quo by enacting laws regulating corporations. An even greater challenge, though an unsuccessful one, was mounted during the 1890s, when the populist reform movement criticized the national government for not acting on behalf of a citizenry increasingly under the control of large transportation, industrial, and financial corporations.

The progressive impulse that gained strength after 1900 also involved the development of an activist government, one that would be rationally managed, yet fully responsive to the popular will, an honest, efficient, administratively sound public mediator-regulator-umpire that would exercise sufficient authority to prevent monopoly, sustain competition, and provide the citizenry with the services it wanted and needed. Progressivism affected politicians at the municipal, state, and national levels, with the direction and timing of its influence from the local through the state and finally to the national levels of government. By the time of its waning, it had influenced politicians at all levels to act in accordance with its prescriptions.

The resurgence of the conservative impulse during the 1920s followed the massive disillusionment with progressivism that came as a result of the impact of World War I on American life: namely, the emergence of a narrow, exclusionist nationalism and the failure of Wilson to effect an internationalist, idealist peace settlement. But, even in the twenties, there continued to be evidence of various municipal and state governments that bore the impress of a reformist or progressive outlook.

These varied political impulses thus affected politicians at various times during these decades at every level of a highly *federal* political system. The relative strength of each of these impulses shifted over uneven periods of time, creating "cycles" or "seasons" of innovation and conservatism. As each impulse in its turn gained the ascendancy and influenced politicians in varying degrees to behave and act in certain ways, this process seemed to set up a reaction, a counterpressure, so that the opposite impulse gained strength. The impulse to reform the system and the impulse to conserve the status quo thus *coexisted* in unequal strength. Their dialectical impact kept the overall course of domestic policymaking within a moderate, centrist compass.

However, it is important to note that American politicians continued throughout these years to be pragmatic and opportunistic in character, so it is not possible to refer to specific Presidents, Governors, jurists, and legislators simply as "reformers" or as "conservatives," as if by labeling them, their behavior and careers suddenly become consistent and explainable. There were too many conflicting pressures and influences for any politician to act entirely within the molds created by these labels. It is far more accurate to focus on political "impulses" that *in varying degrees* governed political behavior.

But, whether the dominant political spirit or impulse was liberal or conservative, the role or function of government (at all levels) steadily grew during these decades: what governments *did* was incremental and irreversible. Once the political system assumed a particular task, it maintained that function, whether the prevailing political temper was reformist or in favor of the status quo. The national government remained a government of defined, limited powers situated at the apex of a federal state whose constitutional arrangements divided power among four levels: national, state, county, and municipality. This meant that the major political issues of these decades (as was the case before the Civil War) always related in some way to Constitutionally derived structures and powers.

As before, federal policies mirrored European developments in many ways. European and white settler society governments continued to grapple with ongoing economic issues involving currency, banking, tariffs, and transportation: Should the currency be hard or soft, of gold and silver coin or of paper money—or a mix of both? How public or how private, how national or state or local should banking and transportation systems be? How protectionist or revenue-generating should tariffs be? In polities around the westernized world, various mixtures of currency and of banking and transportation systems developed in these decades, but a definite pattern emerged on the question of tariff policy. All of the nations with significant industrialization, including the United States, went through a period of high duties, of protection for youthful domestic industries. This was a widely shared form of economic nationalism. The only nation to escape it was Britain, with its peculiar conjunction of industrialization linked to worldwide trade.

With respect to a newer issue, a more recent policymaking area: the regulation of industry, there were significant differences of emphasis that mirrored differing national political cultures, though all governments again had to deal with the question of how public and how private the system should be. Because Americans have divided power among the elements of a decentralized federal system, their industrial policy naturally involved local communities and the states and the courts—all before the federal government began to act, and when it did, it focused on the desirability of maintaining the free market and open competition and thus acted to prevent monopoly or unified control, which restrained both the market and competition. By contrast, the British have emphasized the importance of the free individual, so that their industrial policy has focused on the entrepreneur more than on the market, and so the government has acted to create conditions that allow particular firms to survive through periods of economic growth and contraction. In still another contrast, the French have emphasized the supremacy of the nation, and so France's more centralized political system has led the government to favor giving national technocrats a much greater role in the forging of industrial policies that have involved significant public regulation, if not outright ownership.

But, with the improvements in communication and transportation that speeded up the transcontinental and transoceanic movement of ideas, activities, people, and goods, there was extensive international borrowing of policy innovations during these decades. There came to be a rather common phenomenon of legislation enacted by one national government being passed on from one nation to another, sometimes in spite of traditions of rivalry and distrust. For example, Britain's early factory legislation turned up in France, Germany, and elsewhere by the 1870s. Germany's pioneering compulsory state social insurance was later borrowed by both France and Britain. Denmark's novel old-age pensions were adopted by New Zealand and then Britain. France's "subsidarism" (that is, state revenue being put into ongoing private social insurance schemes) was taken up by Denmark, the Netherlands, and some of the Scandanavian nations.

In matters directly involving the United States, labor legislation united the Wilson administration and the Campbell/Bannerman and Lloyd George governments in Britain and the rapidly rising labor-socialist parties elsewhere in Europe. In the most radicalized polities in the westernized world—Australia and New Zealand—came early recognition of the legitimacy of labor unions and, at the turn of the century, the institution of compulsory arbitration mechanisms for the settlement of labor disputes. Civil service reform was a transatlantic (North America) and transpacific (Australasia) movement. Among political reforms, the secret ballot was borrowed from Australia, the initiative/referendum/recall from the Swiss provinces. Local socialism in America, that is, publicly owned utilities and transportation systems, drew on the experiences of municipalities in Britain and Germany (in the Rhine Basin).

In short, the policymaking of the American government, the matters that became political issues, were common to governments in much of the Western world, although the Americans, because of their particular circumstances, forged their own mix of policies within these wider commonalities. There was a transatlantic and transpacific legislative interconnectedness, transoceanic Western political "membrane," selective in nature: sometimes permeable, sometimes impenetrable; sometimes precedents were exchanged, sometimes they were extracted from their context; sometimes such models were blocked or transformed or exaggerated. Sometimes, circumstances converged in such a way that there were orgies of significant legislation, as in Germany in the mid-1880s, in Britain from 1908 to 1911, and in the United States from 1914 to 1916, but far more typical was the slow evolution of government policy by means of legislation enacted sporadically over long periods of time.

The Wilson administration was well aware of the Lloyd George government's legislative accomplishments, which were themselves an amalgam of reform initiated elsewhere: old-age pensions (borrowed from New Zealand), compulsory wage earners' health insurance (borrowed from Germany), wage boards empowered to establish legal minimum wages (borrowed from Australia), state-run employment offices (borrowed from Germany), a state-administered unemployment scheme for high-risk trades (new!), school meals and school medical facilities (new!), progressive land and income taxes (new!)—quite an astonishing list.

The movement for the reform of the structure and functioning of government developed in the 1870s and 1880s as an elitist response to the corruption of a popular and effective "boss"-dominated party system whose hallmark was patronage. The elitist reformers (or "mugwumps") succeeded in persuading Congress and President Grover Cleveland to enact the Civil Service Reform Act of 1885, which introduced classifications for national government positions that henceforth would be occupied only on the basis of merit, not party service. Later, elitist progressive reformers—still responding to the "bossism" that remained in the political system—persuaded the major parties in some states to introduce popular primaries and certain state governments to enact initiative, referendum, and recall measures and were successful in gaining necessary Congressional and then state approval of constitutional amendments that mandated the popular election of Senators and extended the suffrage to women.

Both groups of reformers—mugwumps and progressives—believed that government ought to be administered by honest, efficient, well-trained individuals who governed effectively for virtuous citizens (including women) and to "initiate" legislation when their elected politicians ignored public need, to "recall" corrupt or incompetent officials by removing them from office, and to institute "referenda" whenever there was an important matter that a certain number of citizens thought the citizenry itself ought to vote on itself in an election. Mirroring the racism of white Americans generally, these reformers limited their reforms to native-born, white citizens; blacks and natives were regarded as inferior groups incapable of participating in republican government.

Ironically, the entire movement to effect more honest, efficient, and responsive government was led by "gentleman reformers," just as the "boss-" dominated political system the reformers sought to alter was directed by an elite as well. There was further irony in the fact that popular participation in elections was notably higher in the pre-1900 era when bossism most fully characterized the system than in the reformist era of 1900–1918. But, whether the dominant spirit since 1918 has been liberal or conservative (or even moderate), these reforms of the systems have remained—or been extended.

Similarly, the movement to regulate the economy and society has been of an incremental, irreversible character. In this particular issue, form has generally preceded effective functioning as the national government was initially concerned to give the appearance of providing regulation long before creating the actual means of doing so. Nothing more clearly reveals both the power of corporations and the essentially pragmatic character of business-minded national politicians in these decades than the tentative, halting, uncertain manner by which Congress and the Presidency and the Supreme Court extended national regulative authority, all of which was based on the Constitutional provision that "the Congress shall have the power . . . [to] regulate commerce with foreign nations, and among the several states."

The bipartisan Anti-Trust Act of 1890 was a response to the emergence of monopolistic industrial corporations. The act forbade monopolies that "restrained" interstate or foreign trade. But, not until the progressively oriented Presidencies of Roosevelt and Taft did the national government make the act operative by bringing suits involving trusts to the Supreme Court. In 1903, a Bureau of Corporations was founded to study and report on the activities of interstate corporations. In 1914, under Wilson's Presidency, a Federal Trade Commission replaced the Bureau and was given the power to define unfair trade practices. In the same year, an Anti-Trust Act outlawed price discrimination, "tying" agreements, interlocking directorates, and the acquisition of stock in competing corporations whenever any of these practices lessened competition. By contrast, in the conservative 1920s, Secretary of Commerce Herbert Hoover promoted the "trade association" movement in which corporations in a given field gathered and shared information in sales, purchases, shipments, production, and prices in an effort to stabilize costs, prices, employment, wages, and markets.

Essential to the development of national corporations was the national transportation system provided by the railroad corporations that themselves began to display monopolistic tendencies in the late nineteenth century. The national government responded both to the unique place that the railroads occupied in the emergent industrial system and to criticism from farmers and small industrial firms that the railroads favored other large corporations by enacting the bipartisan Interstate Commerce Act of 1887, which established an independent regulatory commission—the Interstate Commerce Commission—to investigate the "freight" traffic of railroads and prosecute violators of the law, which henceforth required rates to be "reasonable" and "just" and forbade rebates or discrimination or agreements to fix rates.

In 1906, under Theodore Roosevelt's Presidency, the ICC was given direct authority to set minimum rates. In 1910, under Taft's Presidency, the Commission was empowered to initiate rate changes, its regulatory authority was extended to communications (the telephone and telegraph companies), and a Commerce Court was established to deal with appeals to commission rulings. During World War I, under the Railroad Administrator, the national government operated the railroads as a single system, giving priority to military traffic. And, after the war, in an act of 1920, the ICC was given authority to eliminate wasteful competition and to fix minimum and maximum rates as well as dividends for stockholders. Thus, in periods of either liberal or conservative dominance, the governmental regulation of railroad transportation sporadically increased.

In response to growing concern about public health, in 1906, Theodore Roosevelt extended government regulation to food and drugs. The Meat Inspection Act required meats in interstate commerce to be nationally inspected, and the Pure Food and Drug Act forbade the production and sale of "adulterated, misbranded, or harmful foods, drugs, or liquors."

But, all these regulatory efforts were usually ineffective because all the Presidents in these decades appointed men to these commissions who were sympathetic to corporations, who were eager to find ways for corporate managers to live within the governmental restrictions placed upon them, and who had a strong propensity to avoid using the authority granted to them by the national government. This was the case even during the height of progressivism. None of the Presidents insisted that their commissioners be men who regarded their position as adversarial. On this matter, national politicians and corporate owners and managers shared the same perspective and values from the 1860s through the 1920s.

Progressive-minded Presidents—Roosevelt, Taft, Wilson—argued that, with the emergence of large corporations, the national government should itself expand its role and size and assume the authority to regulate corporate America, and like-minded Congressmen agreed. But, politicians and businessmen were too alike for there to be effective regulation of the latter by the former. However, even when in the 1920s Secretary of Commerce Hoover focused on the development of voluntary trade associations, "liberal" politicians remembered the *principle* of government regulation. For them, the experience of World War I was a compelling precedent for the dramatic exercise of national political regulatory power.

Other major national political issues were more cyclical than incremental in character. Both the monetary and tariff issues involved Congressional and Presidential responses to varied pressures and interests and resulted in legislation that ebbed and flowed between protectionism and free trade or between gold and silver coinage and the issuance of paper money, depending upon the relative strength of those who supported the contrasting positions. Such legislation did not require new governmental bureaucracies and functions, both of which tended to remain, even with a shift of political sentiment.

Congressional authority over the currency was Constitutionally unambiguous. ("The Congress shall have power . . . [to] coin money, and regulate the value thereof.") From 1865 to 1900, Congress was responsive to the public controversy aroused over the merits and demerits of "hard" and "soft" currency, gold or silver coin and paper money. Money became, for some Americans, the cause of all economic advancement or deprivation. The public controversy over the nature of money and the monetary responsibilities of the national government reduced the complexities of economic life to distorting simplicities, but made the money issue one of dramatic political significance, so politicized, in fact, that it absorbed and rendered impotent the most important reform movement of the late nineteenth century: Populism.

The "greenbacks" issued by the Union government to pay some of its bills during the Civil War were not redeemable in specie (coin) and thus circulated (at a value less than gold) as money, making it relatively easier for debtors to repay loans to creditors. But, President Grant was responsive to conservative "hard money" advocates who argued that only gold provided a sound currency, and Congress in turn responded to his request for redemption of "greenbacks" in specie by passing the Redemption Act of 1875. A minor party—the Greenback Party—kept the monetary issue alive by advocating the continued issuance of an unredeemable paper currency that would result—in their view—in a desirable expansion of the money supply.

At the same time silverites argued that the issuance of silver coin would also help to expand the currency commensurate with economic need and growth. Congress responded again (over President Hayes' veto) with the Silver Purchase

Act of 1878. By the 1890s, distressed, debt-ridden farmers (along with silver-mining interests) agitated for an inflation of the currency through the coinage of silver. A currency expanding beyond economic growth would raise prices and make it easier for farmers to gain the profits needed to pay their debts. Congress enacted another, strengthened Silver Purchase Act in 1890, with the silver to be paid for by the issuance of Treasury notes redeemable in gold and silver.

But, these measures did not resolve the basic problem with the currency in the late nineteenth century: its chronic, deflationary inflexibility; its tendency to grow in volume more slowly than economic activity. This lack of a political resolution was yet another indication of the national government's inability (given the nature of the political system) to move beyond tinkering with issues that provoked serious public controversy. Between 1865 and 1890, the amount of currency in circulation (greenbacks, national bank notes, gold and silver coins or certificates) per capita actually decreased. Greenbacks were fixed at a certain level by 1878; national bank notes, based on government bonds, contracted in volume as the government paid off its bonds; and silver purchase acts provided too little coinage to offset the overall contraction of the currency.

In the economic depression of the mid-1890s, a monetarily conservative-minded President Cleveland was able to convince Congress to repeal the Silver Purchase Act so that the government wouldn't have to continue to pay out gold for the treasury notes issued in payment for silver. When, in 1896, the Populists joined the Democrats in support of the silverites' position and the Republicans, by contrast, favored the gold standard, a Presidential election became a rare forum on a major political issue, and the public voted decisively against the silverite position. By the late 1890s, currency inflation came from a rapidly growing supply of minted gold from the discoveries of the 1880s and 1890s in Alaska, the Yukon, and South Africa. In 1900, Congress passed the Gold Standard Act. The currency issue then vanished along with the popular controversy over the urgency of currency expansion or currency stability.

An issue related to currency had a much briefer life in the decades between the Civil War and the Great Depression: banking. The bank issue, which had been so closely linked to party loyalty before the Civil War, did not remain a touchstone of party loyalty after the war. The national banking system of 1862 gained the support of both major parties. Before 1900, only the Populists questioned its soundness, supporting in its place a variant of the prewar Jacksonian Democrats Independent Treasury System.

As a result of a sharp, brief economic downturn in 1907, which threatened the banking system, a National Monetary Commission was created. The Commission recommended in 1912 that a National Reserve Association with 15 branches be created and that there be changes to the national banking system that would require the pooling of bank reserves as well as the maintenance of a flexible currency. This report brought varied reaction from several groups. Radical agrarian spokesmen—heirs of the Populists—thought that the entire banking system should be placed under direct government control. But, Democratic progressives in Congress joined the Wilson Administration in favoring a mixed system, in the sense of its being both public and private, as well as mirroring the federal system itself.

Legislative action took the form of the Federal Reserve Act of 1913, which established 12 Federal Reserve Banks owned by the member banks of their district and capped by a central Federal Reserve Board. Each member bank had to subscribe a portion of its capital to its reserve bank and keep on deposit a portion of its reserves. The Federal Reserve Banks issued notes whenever they made a loan to member banks. These notes were based on government gold and on promissory notes signed by borrowers from the member banks and had the effect of expanding both the money supply and bank credit as the economy expanded.

In response to pressure from farm interests, which had been ignored in the earlier legislation, the Wilson administration supported a Federal Farm Loan Act in 1916, setting up a Federal Farm Loan Board and 12 Federal Land Banks, offering farmers loans of 5 to 40 years' duration at low interest rates. The Warehouse Act of 1916 authorized national licensing of private warehouses (for the storage of farm produce), with national support of their receipts as collateral for short-term bank loans.

Overall, the banking legislation of 1913 and 1916 was a progressive, reformist resolution of problems facing the banking system: Government regulation over banking was extended, but banking remained basically a federal and a private system. But, as in the case of the antitrust and interstate commerce issues, the banking issue led to the creation of new government agencies and functions, which, once established, remained through the ebb and flow of reform and conservatism.

Another issue of these decades involved—like the monetary issue—a clear-cut grant of authority to Congress: to impose import duties on foreign-made commodities entering the United States. The tariff issue had a longer, more continuous "lifeline" than any other major issue during this period. Unlike the antebellum period, when tariff legislation was too localistic in its effects to become a matter of ongoing national party policy, the major parties came out of the Civil War with contrasting positions on the tariff. During the Civil War, in the Union, the Republicans had favored mildly protectionist duties and had enacted legislation that made the tariff a source of wartime revenue as well as a basis for protection of domestic industry from foreign competition. After the war, the Republicans tried to sustain their linkage to rapidly developing industrial producers who would benefit from such protection. By contrast, the Democrats' most solid support came from the South, whose economy remained dominated by staple-crop producers who continued to advocate that there be open access to international markets for commodities in great demand elsewhere, a demand that could be adversely affected by protectionist policies, which could provoke retaliation and protectionism in other nations.

Throughout these decades, all of the Republican Presidents (except for Taft, who was influenced by the progressives' free-trade outlook) favored protection; the two Democratic Presidents—Cleveland and Wilson—favored free trade. But, the tariff legislation that was fairly regularly enacted by Congress was still the product of constituency pressure as much as it was a matter of party policy. Congressional voting on this issue was never solely a matter of party affiliation, though pressure from Presidents and party leaders was also a factor.

By 1890, tariff legislation raised duties on manufactured goods to nearly 50 percent. The act of that year added agricultural products and empowered the President to raise duties on basic imported commodities as a counterpressure to those national governments that raised import duties on American products to high levels. Taft failed to persuade Congress to significantly lower the tariff duties in 1909, but Wilson succeeded in 1913 in wresting from Congress duties that were on the average under 30 percent, with a free list that included important consumer products and raw materials. But, after World War I, a protectionist policy again prevailed. Secretary of the Treasury Mellon favored high duties for the infant and innovative chemical and metal industries, and the legislation of 1922 restored to industry its pre-1913 levels of protection. By the early 1930s, even in the face of depression, national legislation brought average industrial and agricultural duties to the all-time high of over 50 percent.

So, with the exception of 1913 to 1921, when a progressive-minded Democratic President and strong party leader was able to deflect the protectionist tendency of Congress toward his goal of free trade, the overall direction of the tariff was upward, toward high duties, which protected domestic industries and even agricultural products, well beyond the "infant" stage of development. Protection became a panacea—like monetary policy—for economic well-being, a simplistic safeguard against complicated problems. Groups pressured Congress for protection more out of anxiety and uncertainty than economic understanding. Republican protectionist tariff policy was nationalistic in its impact: the national government must provide the security needed for the development of American industrial and agricultural corporations, free from the complexities of the world's economy.

Just as one of the chief goals of foreign policy was to protect the expansion of the economy abroad, so one of the chief features of domestic policy was to protect industry from foreign competition. But, prevailing attitudes on monopoly meant that national politicians also believed that American corporations had to compete with one another. Ironically, protectionists strove to free American enterprise from the need to compete with the products of similar enterprises elsewhere in the world, at the same time that there was a consensus that monopolistic corporations—free of competition—shouldn't be allowed to exist *within* the United States.

Direct national aid for (in addition to regulation of) transportation was not a continuous matter during the decades after the Civil War, as it was before, when "internal improvements" divided constitutionally strict constructionist Democratic Presidents from Congressmen eager to extend national funds as needed capital for risk-filled road and canal corporations. Constitutional sanction for such legislation was equivocal in the sense that Congress was only given the power to establish post offices and post roads. No overall national program of aid was ever enacted. Proponents of national and successfully initiated state-level programs argued that transportation was too basic to economic and social development to be left entirely to private initiative. Their solution characterized all proposals made during the nineteenth century that involved government aid: a mixture of public and private funds invested in (or gifts of public land appropriated to) various kinds of transportation corporations—roads, canals, and railroads.

During and after the Civil War, the national government copied this kind of state aid and donated public lands along predetermined transportation routes carved out of remaining national territories and made public loans, both as financial inducements for private corporations to link the Pacific Coast to the eastern railroad system. State and local governments continued to provide various forms of aid to railroad companies.

When motor vehicles developed after 1900 as a major alternative to rail transportation, state governments created departments of highways to construct public ways for the new vehicles. This was an innovation in the way governments involved themselves in transportation. Before the Civil War, state governments had appropriated funds, but roads had been built and maintained by various mixtures of private corporations and local governments. But, automobile, truck, and bus travel had a much wider ambit than had movement by horse and wagon, and so state governments decided to construct their own systems of public ways.

During the nineteenth century, the national government never appropriated funds for a national postal roads network. By contrast, President Wilson and Congress enacted the Federal Highway Act of 1916, which contained the first significant national-state "matching grant" program. States whose highway departments met certain national standards were given matching national contributions for expenditures on road construction and maintenance, though such funding was restricted to "post roads." As motor vehicle traffic continued to grow, additional Highway Acts in the 1920s extended national aid through the establishment of a national system of highways, funded and built directly by the national government.

Thus, governmental aid to transportation in these decades, though its source mirrored the "bottom-heavy" character of the federal political system (outside of foreign relations), was continuous. And, as the forms of transportation became wider in scope and scale, aid became progressively more national in its origins. This happened without a major political controversy and developed without reference to the ascendance among national politicians of conservative, moderate, or progressive moods.

National political policymaking during the decades after the Civil War affected in various ways the owners and managers of economic units of various types and sizes—whether handcrafted or mechanically made products and services; whether single ownership, partnership, or corporate firms. The major political issues of these years involved the question of how much government should regulate or aid such entities. But, national governmental action also affected two groups beyond owners and managers: wage laborers, who worked for corporations, partners, or individuals, and farmers who, while owners, believed that agriculture remained a fundamentally distinctive occupation, deserving of special treatment and protection by government.

Even when farming became increasingly mechanized and when large-scale specialized farms attained a notable economic complexity, farmers of all kinds continued to believe that the production of food and cloth should be recognized by all as America's basic way of life, which could nevertheless be easily threatened by economic developments of an industrial and financial nature. When farmers organized into organizations—"granges"—of a broadly social character, they nonetheless pressured state governments—sometimes successfully—to enact legislation regulating the railroads, which, they argued, were unfairly favoring big industrial corporations in the rates they charged. These concerns brought national action in 1887, with the passage of the Interstate Commerce Act and the establishment of the Interstate Commerce Commission.

Farmers continued to be concerned about the effects of currency, banking, and transportation on their livelihood. Farm prices remained chronically low through these decades of increasing agricultural mechanization and specialization, as supply often outran demand and as the currency (before 1900) didn't expand with economic growth. During the 1890s, farmers, especially those from specialized crop areas of the Midwest and South, organized the populist reform movement, which favored a strengthened national government that would have the authority to deal with the adverse consequences of rapid industrialization. Populists advocated government ownership of the transportation and communication systems, the coinage of silver to expand the currency, and an eight-hour workday.

The absorption of the Populists by the Democrats in the 1896 election and the rise of a "progressive" reform spirit among urban middle-class politicians in both major parties after 1900 meant that politically induced reform of American life became the focus of groups other than farmers, at the start of the twentieth century. But, it was farmers who formed the first significant reform party whose aim was to increase the power of the national government to deal with the rapidly shifting scale and scope of economic activity. However, a significant part of these developments was the dramatic diminution, by the late nineteenth and throughout the twentieth century, in the number of farmers relative to the total population. What had been a broad reform movement when farmers still thought they were typical, average Americans, turned into an interest group ever more conscious of its disadvantageous position in an increasingly nonagrarian population.

By the 1920s, a "farm bloc" formed in Congress. The Cooperative Marketing

Act (1922) exempted farm cooperatives from the antitrust law. Cooperatives were organized from the late nineteenth century onward by farmers who believed that cooperatives were the most effective means of dealing with purchasing and marketing operations. Pressure for "parity"—to raise farm prices to the point that they had the same purchasing power as other prices—led to Congressional efforts to enact legislation allowing farmers to sell surpluses on world markets in order to raise domestic prices. After President Coolidge vetoed such bills, arguing that they involved too much government interference, President Hoover agreed in 1929, and the Agricultural Marketing Act set up a Federal Farm Board, both with a revolving loan fund to help cooperatives market major commodities and with the authority to set up "stabilization" corporations that could buy surpluses and keep them off the market. In these ways, farmers became another special-interest group pressuring the national government to act for its benefit, just as other "owners" did.

In these decades, wage earners operated as craftsmen in merchant- or master-owned shops, as machine operators in factories and foundries, as laborers on construction sites of many kinds, and as farm laborers. Wage labor spread wherever owners had the entrepreneurial skills to organize and sustain large-scale operations. But, the "laborers" who acted in a political context could be individual craftsmen (and thus "owners"), groups of craftsmen in a shop, or wage earners. There was an ongoing confusion over who was a "laborer," something that worked against group unity of the kind that allowed farmers and "businessmen" to perceive themselves as groups. The craftsmen who formed the loose National Labor Union in 1866 provided support for the short-lived National Labor Reform Party in 1872 and persuaded Congress to enact an eight-hour day for national employees and to repeal the Contract Labor Law, passed during the Civil War to facilitate the importation of labor.

But, neither the broadly social Knights of Labor nor the more narrowly economically oriented, craft-based American Federation of Labor took on a political orientation—at least on the national level. Under Terence Powderly's Presidency, the Knights of Labor welcomed all wage earners and supported the eight-hour day and mechanics lien laws (to ensure payment of wages), but were handicapped by poor leadership and organization. Under Gompers' long-term Presidency, the American Federation of Labor sought to negotiate contracts with owners over wages and hours and working conditions, rather than support a special, labor-oriented political party, and, in any case, was largely restricted in membership to the transportation and building trades.

Though Gompers and the American Federation of Labor favored strikes or work stoppages as a last resort, there was wide consensus among national politicians and jurists that strikes were illegal. The Supreme Court sometimes found striking labor unions—like monopolistic corporations—"in restraint of trade" under the terms of the Anti-Trust Act of 1887. Governors and Presidents sent in troops to keep order during the more contentious work stoppages. At the optimal moment of "progressive" political influence, President Wilson and Congress enacted the Child Labor Act, prohibiting from interstate commerce products manufactured by children under the age of 14. During World War I, when the national government assumed a great deal of authority over the operation of the economy, the National War Labor Board encouraged conciliation of wartime labor disputes and mediated those that could not be privately settled. The War Labor Policies Board standardized wages, hours, and working conditions in "war" industries, while the U.S. Employment Service found workers war-related employment.

But, with the exception of the brief World War I period, national governmental policy did not usually focus on wage earners. From the perspective of Washington, those aspects of American economic life that could be affected by governmental activity were largely confined to owners, not those who were paid wages, as if the political system as established was incapable of dealing with an economy that was not comprised of proprietors.

Other groups that induced governmental activity during these decades were defined by caste: a gender caste and a racial caste. Various woman's-rights movements influenced courts and state governments to gradually change the legal status of women from that of a nonentity (apart from her husband) to a person with standing in law. The most dramatic advance for women came with the passage of a Constitutional amendment in 1920 granting them the right to vote. Progressive-minded politicians favored this action and supported the inclusion of (white) women in an enlarged political community.

Significant elements of the national (Northern) political community supported equal rights for blacks after the Civil War. In the late 1860s, Republican-dominated Congresses passed civil rights legislation and Constitutional amendments: ending slavery, forbidding segregation in public places, and guaranteeing equality under the law, voting, and officeholding. But neither the courts nor state or national governments had the political will to sustain this "first reconstruction" beyond the time of the military occupation of the South, because of the endemic racism of the population. So, when white Southerners introduced segregation toward the end of the nineteenth century, neither the courts nor the national government tried to stop the practice. Indeed, the Supreme Court in 1896 gave its judicial approval. Though the Populists showed some interest in uniting blacks and whites in a biracial political reform movement, the Progressive-minded politicians were racist, and nothing in their prescriptions for a reformed and improved America indicates that they in any way wanted to change the racial caste that encased American blacks (even though they favored improvements in the position of women).

* * *

When either a crisis (1930–1945) or an uncharacteristically lopsided division between the parties (Democrats over Republicans: 1964–1968; Republicans over Democrats: 1981–1986) or between liberal- and conservative-oriented politicians (liberals over conservatives: 1964–1968; conservatives over liberals: 1981–1986) has occurred, *both* the Presidents (Roosevelt, Johnson, and Reagan) and the Congress were active in either extending (1930–1945, 1964–1968) or diminishing (1981–1986) the authority of the national government within American society. The Supreme Court, with its own rhythm and timing and depending on its composition, has gyrated in its major decisions on the constitutionality of particular matters brought before it between liberal and conservative interpretations, and on some particularly deep and complicated political controversies, the Court has itself been the chief national instrumentality for the forging of a national "position" on issues that the President and Congress have either avoided or have believed were proper subjects for judicial and not legislative action.

In the decades since 1930, there have been gyrations between periods when the liberal or conservative impulses dominated national politics, as was the case between the Civil War and the Depression. However, such gyrations were complicated by the continued strength of a moderate, pragmatic political outlook, whose adherents did not feel obliged to be consistent and loyal to either liberalism or conservatism.

Reformers were clearly in command of the national government during the Depression of the 1930s, but by 1938 a reaction to important and continuous political change set in and the reformers lost their lead to a conservative coalition of Republicans and Democrats, which remained in evidence through World War II and its aftermath. From the late 1940s to the early 1960s, a more moderate Congress predominated, as neither reform nor conservatism evoked broad popular appeal. Reform was again prominent under Lyndon Johnson, in the mid-1960s, when the Republicans became associated with an extreme form of conservatism under Barry Goldwater's leadership, and Democrats were able to win lopsided "liberal" majorities. When the Republicans became more moderate, so did Congress, which remained so until the 1980s, by which time conservatism again dominated the Republican Party. But this time, under Ronald Reagan's leadership, conservatism was a public reaction to "big" government and became an asset to the Republicans, not a liability, and Congress became notably conservative.

The domestic legislation of the national government after 1930 has had the effect of making that level of government preeminent within the American federal system, something that did not happen for a century and a half after the founding of the new nation. The crisis that was produced by a deep and lasting depression followed by the greatest of all America's and the world's wars overrode the deep allegiance Americans had given to a decentralized federal state, and a newly empowered national government aided, preserved, and stabilized a capitalistic economy at the worst time in its history by legislating into existence a "welfare capitalistic" state.

Both the Presidency and the Congress were dominated by pragmatic reformers who, by experimenting with the relationship of the government to the economy, hoped to rejuvenate and improve a system that had seriously malfunctioned in the United States, as well as around the globe. During the 1930s, new legislation greatly extended the ways the national government aided and regulated the economy and society at the same time that the economic and social welfare and security of Americans became subjects of national programs. The result was that a capitalistic economy was preserved and rejuvenated (by World War II's mammoth productivity), while Americans who failed to function within the system were provided with a minimum of state-sponsored benefits to keep them from becoming abjectly poverty-stricken. Officials in Roosevelt's administrations drew openly on the progressivism of both the Theodore Roosevelt and the Woodrow Wilson varieties as well as on the experiences of the war boards in World War I as guides for action.

But, once again, policymaking in the 1930s needs to be seen in a wider context, because there continued to be many crosscurrents and much borrowing from others. Roosevelt drew liberally on European experiences for a wide variety of his proposals for reform, and officials of his administrations were aware of earlier legislative breakthroughs that European governments had experienced, especially the gush of social welfare legislation that the Lloyd George government had managed to crowd together from 1908 to 1911, and saw their own Depression-generated rush of major reform legislation from 1933 to 1938 as an even greater achievement in that the American government was trying to create the kind of welfare capitalist state that European and Australasian governments had come to over a longer period of time, in sporadic bursts of legislative activity.

Much of what the American government did during the Depression of the 1930s governments elsewhere in the westernized world also did in an effort to end the Depression and to sustain the industrial capitalist system. There were parallel legislative programs dealing with the monetary and financial systems, welfare and unemployment, public works, national industrial recovery, agriculture, labor, and housing in Germany, Italy, France, Britain, Australia, New Zealand, and Canada—enacted by governments that were widely varied in their makeup: all the way from fascist to various kinds of united fronts to reformist. All governments in the industrialized world tried to end the greatest crisis ever faced by the economic system that all shared, whatever their political complexion, and in that effort sought to sustain their popularity during a time of social upheaval as well as sharp economic decline. In the process, there was much awareness of what other governments were doing and much evidence of the cross-fertilization of legislative proposals.

The abandonment of the gold standard; the securities, agricultural, and public housing legislation; regional planning (the Tennessee Valley Authority)—in all these areas of policymaking what the American government did reflected prior experiences among Europeans. But influence flowed both ways, and the United States itself became admired and imitated for its Depression Era innovations, its social experimentation exported to some extent. There were other "New Deals," and visitors flocked to witness what was going on. British and Canadian and other social democrats looked to Washington for usable blueprints. The United States became a haven for the politically oppressed at this time. So, reform occurred under the spur of a deep depression, but it occurred in an international context. What one government did was noticed by others. The Americans may have "caught up" with Europeans and Australasians, but they did so without being isolated and unaware of global developments.

The "New Dealers" acted to reform the financial aspects of the system. In 1933, the government abandoned the gold standard by canceling the gold clause in public and private monetary obligations, impounding all gold in the Federal Reserve System (in Fort Knox), and setting a high price for an ounce of gold ($35 per ounce). Such measures, it was hoped, would make the money supply more flexible. In the same year, the government also established the Federal Deposit Insurance Corporation to guarantee bank deposits (up to $5,000) to help restore the public's badly shaken faith in banks and passed a Federal Securities Act requiring "full disclosure" of information about new stock and bond issues sold in stock and bond exchanges. In 1934, a Securities and Exchange Commission was created to regulate those institutions. The Banking Act of 1935 strengthened the Federal Reserve Board's control over the monetary system (and in particular over reserve requirements and rediscount rates).

The Revenue Act of 1935 raised surtax rates on very high incomes and steeply graduated taxes on higher incomes to a maximum of 75 percent; raised estate and gift taxes; and increased corporate taxes for the larger corporations, with an "excess profits" tax on corporate earnings above 10 percent. This act served to work against, as Roosevelt put it, "an unjust concentration of wealth and economic power."

The national government also enacted legislation to protect and aid home ownership, which had become the chief form of property for middle-class Americans, since most had—by the 1930s—ceased to be farmers with the aim of owning their own farms. The New Deal could draw on several generations of European housing policies: Austria's socialist-inspired, tax-subsidized working-class housing rented at levels so low that even unskilled laborers could afford it; Britain's mixture of philanthropic housing companies that cleared slums and rebuilt low-cost tenements and of local councils who built and rented working-class houses; France's policy of providing cheap public loans to noncommercial builders of workers' houses; Germany's public investment in nonprofit or limited-profit working-class building associations and private efforts of co-op building societies, which pooled weekly dues of working-class members and invested funds in the building of co-op tenements.

In the United States, a strong real estate lobby and building and loan associations lobbied hard against the kind of working-class housing that had become fairly common in Europe, and the New Deal's housing bills were whittled down to cheap public housing for the poor. The Home Owner's Loan Act of 1933 allowed persons whose capacity to pay off their house mortgages was in jeopardy to refinance their homes with mortgages at lower interest rates guaranteed by the U.S. government. The Housing Act of 1938 established a U.S. Housing Authority in the Department of the Interior, which subsidized low rents for low-income persons and granted long-term loans to local agencies that assumed part of the cost for slum clearance and public housing.

As for industry and business, the government during Hoover's Presidency, in 1932, set up a Reconstruction Finance Corporation to make emergency loans for banks, life insurance companies, mortgage institutions, and railroads. In 1933, under Roosevelt's Presidency, the government passed the National Industrial Recovery Act, which established a National Recovery Administration. The 'NRA'—an offspring of the War Industries Board of World War I and Hoover's voluntary trade associations of the 1920s—set up committees representing management, labor, and government for each major industry. These committees drew up binding "codes of fair practice." Early codes fixed prices, limited production, allocated resources, endorsed collective bargaining, and included labor standards of maximum weekly hours (40), minimum weekly wages ($12, in the South, or $13 elsewhere), and provisos against child labor (under age 16).

But, the codes provoked opposition from small firms whose spokesmen argued that large corporations dominated the code authorities, that allocations froze the existing industrial structure in place and limited production, that price fixing made it impossible for smaller companies to compete, and that further investment in industry would be discouraged. When the Supreme Court declared the act unconstitutional in 1935 on the grounds that Congress had exceeded its power under the "commerce clause," the 'NRA' was already unpopular. Though the National Industrial Recover Act was the only important piece of government legislation specifically aimed at regulating and aiding business and industry, the government continued to act on behalf of laborers and farmers, in order to more equally balance the power of the three great economic interest groups within the national economy.

The New Deal's agricultural policies reflected policymaking efforts across the face of the westernized world. European governments protected farmers during the 1920s, blocking off European markets to staple crop producers elsewhere, burdened as these producers were with high fixed costs and an inability to buy industrial goods. After the onset of the Depression, various governments passed high tariff duties to protect farmers, as well as granting subsidies to farmers when tariff protection was too risky. Farmers in Asia, Africa, and the Americas, who were exporters of raw materials and agricultural products, tried to limit production in order to stabilize prices, but they did not succeed. Europeans, who were importers of such products, sought to protect their own farmers, who were relatively inefficient, by means of tariffs, quotas, and subsidies, which were narrowly nationalistic policies, but which worked to a degree. All such efforts crippled international trade and hampered a recovery.

Western governments also attempted to put into place the same sort of proposals that they had considered in the previous decade. There were various commodities (such as tea, wheat, and rubber) agreements whose aim was to adjust production to demand. Producers of staple crops for export attempted to raise prices by reducing supplies, but to the extent that higher prices were achieved, demand was reduced further. Protectionist European agricultural policies injured the food exporting areas and added to the costs of their own consumers.

The Agricultural Marketing Act of 1929 in the United States was based upon the Canadian Wheat Pact. In 1933, Roosevelt's agricultural policy centered on the Agricultural Adjustment Act, which compensated farmers for voluntarily reducing production. Seven basic commodities were initially included, with the money for benefit payments coming from a processing tax levied on each commodity. The act allowed the national government to "dump" surpluses abroad at below-market prices—all with the objective of achieving parity. Producers in commodities in excess supply were polled, and if they agreed, acreage was reduced by a specified percentage. This was a scheme for paying farmers not to grow crops and was part of a worldwide response to the Depression. The AAA was a plan for subsidizing agriculture through the reduction of production to bring down supplies to the level of current demand. Many other nations organized and controlled their domestic markets as well. The Farm Credit Administration was also created in 1933 to supervise the refinancing of endangered farm mortgages with government-sponsored loans at lower interest rates, in order to preserve farm property in the same way that house property was being preserved during the same years. A Commodity Credit Corporation extended loans on crops kept in storage and thus off the market. The Rural Electrification Administration provided funds for rural cooperatives to establish electrical systems in rural areas.

When the Supreme Court declared the Agricultural Adjustment Act unconstitutional because farm production was intrastate (and not interstate), the Soil Conservation and Domestic Allotment Act in 1936 omitted processing taxes and acreage quotas, providing benefits for soil conservation practices. The second Agricultural Adjustment Act, in 1938, reestablished the earlier programs, but left out a processing tax, deriving payments from general revenues. The government had to hold a plebiscite among particular groups of growers and win a two-thirds majority before applying marketing quotas to a given crop. As for poorer farmers and farm laborers, the Resettlement Administration, established in 1935, offered loans and grants to keep such persons off relief and, in 1937, the Farm Security Administration (set up under the Farm Tenant Act) made available rehabilitation loans to preserve marginal farmers and to allow tenants to purchase their own farms, but the Farm Security Administration turned into little more than a relief agency, and farms continued to become fewer in number and larger in size.

As for labor, the New Deal, once again, had varying European and Australasian precedents to draw on, particularly in the area of labor-capital mediation, everything from New Zealand–style compulsory arbitration to the personal intervention of government leaders (as in the case of Britain) to networks of industrial courts, conciliation bureaus, or legally mandated workers' committees. Long after governments elsewhere in the Western world had legitimized labor unions, the federal government in the United States remained inactive, in the face of fierce corporate hostility. The American resolution came in 1935, with the National Labor Relations Act, which gave workers the right to bargain collectively through their own unions and prohibited employees from interfering with unions' activities. The National Labor Relations Board was established to supervise plant elections and certify unions as bargaining agents (when a majority of workers approved). The Board could investigate actions of employees and issue "cease and desist" orders against specified unfair practices. The act also salvaged the labor guarantees of the National Industrial Recovery Act, whereas the Public Contracts Act applied 'NRA' wage and hour standards for work under government contract. In 1938, the Fair Labor Standards Act, applying to firms operating in or affecting interstate commerce and phased in over several years, set a minimum wage (40 cents) an hour and maximum work week (40 hours), and prohibited child labor (under age 16).

As for relief for the unemployed and poor, under President Hoover, in 1932, the Emergency Relief and Construction Act provided Reconstruction Finance Corporation money to states for relief loans, authorized loans for state and local public works, and provided funds for federal public works. Under the Roosevelt Presidency, the Civilian Conservation Corps gave work relief under a quasi-military direction to young men (aged 18–25) with a variety of jobs in forests, parks, and recreation areas. The Federal Emergency Relief Administration granted (rather than loaned) states relief money for various work programs (education, student aid, rural rehabilitation, and transient relief). The first direct, national relief agency was the Civil Works Administration (1933–1934), which provided temporary jobs for those able to work.

The National Industrial Recovery Act created the Public Works Administration, in 1933, with funds for public buildings, highway programs, and flood control. Harold Ickes, Secretary of the Interior, used the Public Works Administration indirectly for work relief, though funds were directed toward well-planned, permanent "improvements." In 1935, the Works Progress Administration was created (to replace the Federal Emergency Relief Administration) and was headed by Harry Hopkins, who favored temporary public works, but the Works Progress Administration also built public buildings, bridges, roads, airports, and schools. It also, under the National Youth Administration, gave part-time employment to students, set up technical training programs, and provided aid to jobless youth. Finally, it extended the range of government by providing funds for artists through its Federal Theatre Project, Federal Arts Project, and Federal Writers Project. The government in the 1930s Depression became an employer of last resort, providing jobs and in some cases training to many of those who could not otherwise find either. Though the "relief" programs were meant to be temporary, they established a precedent for national governmental action with respect to poverty and unemployment.

The government's long-term solution to the heightened sense of economic insecurity that took hold during the deep and prolonged Depression was the Social Security Act of 1935. Once again, the New Deal could draw on several strands of social insurance policymaking that had evolved in European and Australasian capitals since the late nineteenth century. The United States was the last of the Western industrialized nations to embark on a legislative program in this area, and did so only under the spur of the Depression, so powerful was the tradition of opposition to government assistance.

Government in the westernized world didn't invent social insurance; the laborers themselves created the earliest forms of insurance against the risks of labor. The earliest European government-mandated social insurance programs involved the public subsidization of already existing insurance schemes that had been developed by mutual assistance associations for various groups, whether occupational, ethnic, or religious. There were, at the most primitive level, "slate" clubs (named after the slates that hung on the pub wall), whose workmates contributed to a common fund at a year's start from which death or sick payments could be drawn, with the surplus, if any, divided at year's end (all of which made the clubs a cross between a gambling club and a mutual assistance fraternity). In Germany, there were *Hilfskassen*; in France, there were *sociétés de secours mutuel*; in Britain, there were "friendly" societies; and in the United States, there was a great variety of such organizations, lacking an overall name—but, whatever they were called, all were mutual assistance associations, a banding together to mutualize the risks endemic to wage labor—sickness, accident, joblessness, the enfeeblement of old age, or the death of a wage earner.

But, European governments also set up state-run insurance schemes, either legislating compulsory employee and employer contributions, or (more rarely) even financing the schemes directly out of general revenues without any contributions at all. Sometimes programs were locally or provincially run, but sometimes they were national operations. In a given polity—in Britain, in France, in Germany, say—old age, sickness, accident, and unemployment schemes varied in how they were financed, and were introduced and later changed at different times.

The Americans were the slowest of all the westernized nations to deal with social insurance and drew on an array of models that Europeans and Australasians had already created. The American version of social insurance was instituted all at once in the Social Security Act of 1935. The act's provisions reveal how sensitive national authorities still were to the divisions of power within a vast federal system, something that didn't similarly confine most westernized national governments. Under the terms of the act employees and employers contributed payroll taxes to fund the annuities paid to retirees (after the age of 65). The act also established a shared national-state plan of unemployment insurance for those who had worked but who had lost their jobs. Finally, the act committed the national government to contribute to welfare programs. Those unable to work would remain a state responsibility, while the national government would provide work relief for those able to work. The law inaugurated national grants-in-aid for public assistance programs involving the aged, dependent children, and the handicapped. By the terms of this act, the national government became directly involved in the provision of social and economic security and welfare of the population.

Finally, the New Deal reformers, in 1933, instituted regional planning through the creation of a multipurpose public corporation (the Tennessee Valley Authority) that developed the entire watershed of a major river by building dams; fostering navigation, soil conservation, and forestry; and providing cheap electrical power in a meshing of public planning and private industrialization. The TVA was a notable precedent for regional planning of a mixed public-private character, but national politicians in the 1930s did not copy this showcase by making additional proposals that would have involved other parts of the nation.

Since the late nineteenth century, polities all over the westernized world have created welfare capitalist states with similar arrays of social security and welfare legislation. What has differed has been the timing of these political activities. Those European states with the strongest central governments, with the capacity to institute such programs, tended to act earliest: Germany, France, Britain—all had the central administrative apparatus that enable those governments to embark on significant enlargements of their authority. Among the white settler societies on Europe's frontier, New Zealand alone had an early capacity to act, as in 1876 its central government took over the functions of the provincial governments, which were abolished.

With a strong anticentrist tradition to contend with, not until the Great Depression did the American government, in peacetime, dare to significantly augment its authority over the internal governance of the American people, which meant that the significant moves in America toward the creation of a welfare capitalist state came in a concentrated form in the 1930s, much more concentrated than was the case in other westernized polities.

This great outpouring of reformist legislation was generated by a President and a Congress willing to act boldly and experimentally to aid, preserve, and improve the basic economic and social system that they were all beneficiaries of. Roosevelt was perhaps the greatest master of the American political system who ever occupied the White House, though Lincoln was probably his equal under very different, but similarly trying circumstances. Roosevelt attracted capable people, many from academic life, to serve as advisers, and he welcomed varied opinions and fresh ideas. Out of such turmoil came much experimentation, which is what Roosevelt wanted. His was a pragmatic temperament; he did not have a theoretical cast of mind; and his philosophy was simply to help the American population to survive their worst economic crisis and to make the American system work better.

Roosevelt worked effectively with Congressional leaders, and his frequent news conferences and "fireside chats" on network radio were enormously successful means of communicating more directly with the population. He inspired hope in a frightened and fearful public, and his great popularity was a reflection of his actions and legislative accomplishments, but also of the optimism he inspired that economic calamity could be overcome. He was also a generally strong party leader, sustaining the loyalty of party chieftains throughout the nation, whether they were conservative, moderate, or liberal in outlook, or Southern, Western, or Northern in location. The only important occasion on which his command of the political system faltered was when he tried to "pack" the Supreme Court (that is, to add seats, and presumably sympathetic appointees, to the Court's quotient of nine seats) after the Court's conservative majority had declared two major pieces of New Deal legislation unconstitutional. Even though he had been reelected with a "landslide" majority and was still enormously popular, the public outcry in reaction to his court-packing plan was so pervasive that he abandoned the proposal.

Roosevelt's New Deal liberalism was located at the center of the political spectrum during the 1930s and was a considerably greater political force than the conservatism espoused by members of both major parties. The Communist and Socialist movements—on the "left"—and Huey Long's Share Our Wealth program and Father Coughlin's National Union for Social Justice and Francis Townsend's Townsend Plan—on the "right"—all gained popular support at a time of grave economic crisis.

By 1938, the public reaction to a half-decade of major reform was strong enough for a conservative coalition of Southern Democrats and Northern Republicans to assume effective control of Congress. This coalition did not seek to "undo" New Deal reforms, but rather to turn back any further reform proposals. During World War II, this coalition supported the war effort and favored the kind of government control of the civilian economy that would have horrified them during the Depression itself, as the economy was directly operated by public authorities with respect to the allocation, production, and rationing of goods as well as price/wage controls. For conservative Congressmen, the war-making power of the national government and the great objective of defeating clearly aggressive enemy nations overrode their natural propensity to oppose an enlargement of governmental power.

After the war, the Truman administration presided over an orderly though not full demobilization, with combatants receiving a "GI Bill of Rights" under the Serviceman's Readjustment Act (1944), with funds for education, vocational training, medical treatment, unemployment insurance, and loans for building homes or starting businesses. In the decades since World War II, if domestic policy is viewed from a Presidential perspective, governmental activity until the mid-1970s was cumulative, expansionary, though the rate of change waxed and waned. Reform-minded American policymakers were influenced during the 1940s by the Beveridge Report, issued in Britain in 1942 as a blueprint for the enlargement of the welfare capitalist state as it had evolved in Britain, at least. Beveridge argued in favor of a universal, state-financed children's allowance; a system of free, public medical insurance; and the systematic governmental responsibility of full employment. While the Labour Government of Clement Atlee enacted many of these recommendations into law, the Truman administration was aware of these proposals and wanted to extend the New Deal in similar ways. Truman, at various points, sought to add government-guaranteed employment for the unemployed, a national health insurance plan, a plan to provide subsidies for farm incomes, and various civil rights proposals. But, Congress was too conservative to do more than extend or enlarge already existing New Deal programs.

Eisenhower's moderate views favored neither drastic extensions of already existing activities, nor the wholesale dismantling of previously enacted legislation, and Congress shared his outlook. Kennedy was liberal enough to favor new proposals, but it wasn't until his assassination and the unpopularity of a seemingly extremely conservative Republicanism under Goldwater's leadership—that is, until the mid-1960s—that national politics were sufficiently imbued with a reformist outlook for an extremely able director of the political system, a former New Dealer, President Lyndon Johnson, to lead an unusually liberal Congress into significant extensions of the New Deal. These extensions involved aid to education, the establishment of a health care system for the aged and the poor, antipoverty programs involving local community agencies, civil rights for blacks, and ongoing aid to the arts. Even Johnson's successor, Richard Nixon, though generally more conservative in outlook, was pragmatic enough to respond to pressure for further reform or at least innovative governmental regulation, in particular in the area of environmental degradation caused by pollutants, from a gradually more moderate Congress.

The Presidency suffered from Nixon's resignation (to avoid a likely indictment and removal from office) in 1974, and Nixon's successor, Gerald Ford, was—temperamentally, philosophically, and out of prudence as well—the most passive (and, as it turned out, interim) President since the 1920s. And his successor, Jimmy Carter, was so pragmatic and without settled views on anything involving the government that the remainder of the 1970s, following Nixon's resignation, was a period of drift with respect to domestic policy.

By 1980, both a vocal and popular conservative President, Ronald Reagan, and a much more conservative Congress were elected. For the first time since 1930, there was a consensus in the national government in favor of the disbanding of liberal programs, of the deregulation of what had come under government regulation, and of reductions in the size and function of the national government itself. Reagan's conservatism—that big government was part of America's problem, and not its solution to problems—for at least six years (1980–1986) seemed to be the dominant perception of national politicians. The conservative ascendancy of the 1980s had a fairly limited impact, though from a longer perspective, the conservatism of President Reagan and Prime Minister

Margaret Thatcher, in Britain, spawned a much deeper and longer effort to reduce the size and scale of national governments, to impose limits on the public authorities of the welfare capitalist states, and even to diminish the public sector in the developing nations of the world.

Throughout these decades, Congress evolved at various times from having a conservative to a liberal to a moderate character, but though ideological outlook was an important element in the legislative behavior of significant numbers of Congressmen in these years, so too were other factors, such as constituency pressure, party loyalty, or Presidential exhortation. The legislative proposals that have come out of Congress and the Presidency in the decades since World War II have been the product of various influences, some harmonious, others conflicting. But, the legislative or lawmaking, administering, and adjudicating mechanisms of the national government were shaped by more than the pressures exerted upon Congressmen, Presidents, and Supreme Court Justices.

"Government" became far more than elected and appointed officials during the decades following World War II. It became a huge, growing bureaucracy, with thousands of ongoing "civil servants" who advised Presidents, legislators, and jurists and performed the ongoing governmental functions. Some of these governmental employees were academically trained, but whether out of universities or of some other institution, those who worked "for" the government increasingly became "experts," trained specialists. Government policy, in brief, was greatly influenced by people who were not elected to office and did not have to respond directly to popular pressures.

Another group who shaped in significant ways what government did were lobbyists of an increasingly numerous and varied kind. Washington has come to abound in "associations" and "institutions" of many identifiable groups in American society. All have to register and subscribe to certain standards. But, as they propagandize for their group's interests, lobbyists inject yet another element into what "government" is. Congressmen and Presidents, in addition to being influenced by their constituents, whether on a national, state, or local basis, and by other pressures, have responded to the efforts of lobbyists.

All of these "elements" of government have been in evidence throughout the twentieth century and, in embryonic forms, during the latter stages of the nineteenth century, but not until the post–World War II era did they became major, obvious components of the national political institutions of Washington.

In financial matters, government policy—much influenced by the academically trained economists on many staffs around Washington and especially on the Council of Economic Advisers, founded in 1947 as part of a much emasculated Employment Act—has involved both fiscal (taxation and spending) and monetary aspects. *All* Presidents and Congressional leaders after World War II have been aware of the great economic effects of the size of the money supply and of the scale of the government's spending policies. In terms of a theory developed by John Maynard Keynes during the 1930s that increasingly influenced the government's economic advisers after World War II, in periods of economic decline, it was beneficial for government to deliberately increase spending or to cut taxes in order to stimulate the overall demand for goods and services, but when the economy was becoming overstimulated, taxes should be raised in an effort to curb demand and stave off inflation.

Truman used Presidential pressure to keep down wages and prices during the demobilization process after World War II. A financially conservative Eisenhower administration manipulated fiscal and monetary policy to keep inflation very low, but tolerated an unemployment level of 7 percent during the 1958–1959 recession. Kennedy cut taxes to successfully stimulate demand during the 1960s, but Johnson's policy of increasing expenditures for the war in Asia while not increasing taxes led to inflation and then, throughout the 1970s, to "stagflation," a combination of relatively high inflation and unemployment. A pragmatic, erratic Nixon tried but failed to reduce the federal deficit by raising taxes and lowering expenditures; encouraged the Federal Reserve Board to reduce the money supply by raising interest rates, after which the economy quickly went into recession; and froze wages and prices for 90 days, thereafter establishing a mandatory guideline for wage and price increases under the direction of a special agency.

Ford tried the passive policy of "voluntary" wage and price restraint, which failed abysmally. Carter attempted to deal with increasing unemployment by cutting taxes and increasing government spending, but then reversed himself as inflation soared, delaying tax reductions and increasing government spending. A conservative Reagan looked with favor on the Federal Reserve Board's tight monetary policy after 1980 and, as interest rates soared, inflation rapidly declined, but bankruptcies and unemployment rose and another recession resulted (1981–1982). As a low-inflation economy revived, Reagan cut taxes, especially for the top income bracket Americans in a revival of 1920s-style conservative fiscal policy, and successfully stimulated demand.

As for foreign trade, the General Agreement on Trade and Tariffs of 1947 established periodic "rounds" of tariff agreements among as many of the nations of the world that wished to participate. American negotiators favored low duties and worked steadily against protectionist proposals from either domestic or foreign sources. The prevailing belief, leading to historic major-party bipartisanship in Congress and in the Presidency, was that—overall—the American economy, the largest in the world, would benefit most from an open, not a protectionist, position in these international trade negotiations.

America's post–World War II hegemony was confirmed in 1944 when the Roosevelt administration at a conference at Bretton Woods, New Hampshire, pledged the convertibility of dollars into gold at $35 per ounce, thus making the U.S. dollar the standard by which other currencies were valued in international currency exchanges. But, by the 1970s, foreign competition from a rejuvenated Japan (and other nations along the Asian perimeter) and from a physically rebuilt and increasingly economically integrated Europe had much reduced that hegemony.

In 1971, in recognition of this shift in economic power, Nixon took the United States completely off the gold standard; that is, the U.S. government refused thereafter to convert dollars held by foreigners into gold, thereby ending the linkage between the U.S. dollar and the global currency exchanges. Under the new arrangement—more appropriate to a world no longer with a single economic giant—all currencies "float" (relative in value to one another), and all nations deposit international monetary exchange funds in case governments want to buy or sell their own currency in an effort to stabilize or increase its value.

The New Deal legislation provided guarantees and protection for the nonbusiness elements of the economy and society, and no important legislation since World War II has *basically* altered the government's relationship to business and industry, labor, and agriculture. In the case of labor, there have been two major acts, both passed at times of unpopular union unrest or racketeering or corruption or monopolistic practices and both amount to a counterweight to the obviously prolabor legislation of the 1930s.

The Act of 1947 banned closed shops (in which nonunion workers could not be hired), but allowed a "union" shop (in which newly hired workers were required to join a union) unless banned by state law, and defined unfair labor practices (just as the Act of 1935 had defined unfair business practices)—secondary boycotts, pay for work not done ("featherbedding"), and contributing to political campaigns (except for voluntary union "political action" committees). Union leaders were required to take an oath that they had not been members of the Communist Party. Employers were permitted to sue unions for breaking contracts, to petition the National Labor Relations Board for votes on specific unions as collective-bargaining agents, and to speak during union campaigns. The Act forbade strikes by national employees and imposed a "cooling off" period of 80 days on any strike that the President deemed dangerous to national health and safety. The Labor-Management Act of 1959 safeguarded democratic procedures in unions, penalized the misuse of union funds and the coercion of union members, and excluded from office persons convicted of certain crimes.

As for the poor, Lyndon Johnson's "War on Poverty" extended aid to those in poverty in a variety of ways that went well beyond the relief legislation of the 1930s by involving local community groups in the administration of national funds. Under the terms of the Economic Opportunity Act a corps for youth was instituted, as were job-training programs, work-study projects for students, loans to those willing to hire the hard-core unemployed, a domestic peace corps ("Vista"), and a variety of community action programs.

The other "traditional" area of major legislation since World War II has been the government's transportation and communication policies. It was the moderate to conservative Eisenhower administration that proposed and got Congressional approval for the Federal Highway Act of 1956, which authorized the national government to pay for 90 percent of the cost (and the state the other 10 percent) of a limited-access interstate highway system to serve commerce and defense as well as privately owned automobiles. The St. Lawrence Seaway was built as a joint Canadian-U.S. effort during Eisenhower's Presidency and opened oceangoing commerce into the heart of the continent. And, since the 1930s, the national government has steadily provided funds for the construction and maintenance of airports. The only form of transportation to be generally neglected have been the ailing railroads, and even rail transport was aided when remaining passenger lines were amalgamated into the publicly owned Amtrak system.

The government's communication policy has been to regulate broadcasting—both radio and television—through the Federal Communications Commission and telephones, but the U.S. Post Office was changed into the U.S. Mail Service, a private corporation placed under government regulation. In all areas of transportation and communication (except for newspapers, magazines, and books, which continue to remain outside of government supervision because of the earlier-established Constitutional guarantee of freedom of the press), the national government since 1945 has assumed some regulatory authority and assistance, but shuns outright control or ownership.

Other areas of major legislation since World War II all involved significant extensions of national authority and have come as a result of pressure from reform groups or from reformist-minded Congressmen and Presidents. Civil rights were advanced, first by a liberally oriented Supreme Court in its decision that separate educational facilities were unequal and unconstitutional (1954) and in later decisions involving the busing of students to achieve racial equality in the schools of a particular area. But, the Civil Rights Acts of 1964 and 1968 were a response from an unusually liberally oriented Congress and a liberal President to growing pressure exerted by a large reform movement. Discrimination in all public accommodations was outlawed, nationally assisted programs and private employers were required to eliminate discrimination, the Equal Employment Opportunity Commission became the agency to administer the new ban on job discrimination, and certain devices used to keep citizens from voting were eliminated.

The National Defense Education Act of 1958 provided national funds for scientific and technical education needed for national security (the Soviets having become pioneers in space travel, beginning in 1957). The Elementary and Secondary Education Act of 1965 provided aid to education for the first time, extending that aid to "poverty impacted" school districts regardless of their public or parochial character. A Medicare Program for the Aged (1965) and Medicaid (a nationally funded medical program for low-income persons) (1965) initiated the use of national funds for the first time directly in health programs. The National Endowment for the Arts and Humanities was the first ongoing commitment of national funding for the arts. And, under Nixon's Presidency, the Anti-Pollution Acts of 1970 and 1972 extended national authority to the regulation of the ways Americans used the environment itself. And all the while, these new areas of legislation led to a new form of government bureaucracy, to new agencies, such as the Environmental Protection Agency, or to new "cabinet" departments.

The policies of the federal government since World War II have reflected the enlargement of the reach of government that has marked the policymaking of national governments all over the world in recent decades, including the large, nonwesternized parts of the globe. Whether communist, socialist, or capitalist in orientation, governments everywhere have legislated in some manner on most aspects of human life. This enlargement of the scope and scale of government was so extensive that it ran beyond the revenue that was supposed to pay for it. The welfare capitalist state was predicated on the presumption that there would be steady economic growth and, thus, the basis for increasing wealth that could be taxed to pay for a steady enlargement of governmental services. But, by the 1970s and 1980s, governments in both the developed and undeveloped parts of the world had become large in both size and indebtedness, as revenues chronically ran behind expenditures.

The sheer size and complexity and taxation rates and indebtedness of government led to a reaction in the Western world during the 1980s, led by British Prime Minister Margaret Thatcher and U.S. President Ronald Reagan (though Reagan greatly increased the national debt to pay for an enlarged military establishment in the years before the collapse of the Soviet Union). With the collapse of most Communist governments in 1989–1991, many governments in various parts of the world have since moved to reduce their cost and size, even devolving control over certain programs to state or provincial governments. National governments all over the westernized world have failed to further increase taxes, as resistance from wealthy and middle-class taxpayers has increased, and have moved to balance their budgets and close out state-run programs and agencies. Their example has influenced many governments in the developing parts of the world to move in the same direction.

All of this is a vivid indication that domestic policy in the United States has become an exercise that is carried on with an increasing awareness of how American policies fit or don't fit into larger, global trends and developments. Such policies are still made in the United States, as is the case in other nations, but they are made in a world whose economy and society in all their bewildering varieties are nonetheless exhibiting patterns that are beyond the control of individual national governments, even the government of the strongest—economically and militarily—nation on earth.

18

Foreign Policy

Under the Constitution, the national government's primary authority was in the sphere of foreign relations. Everyone in the political community agreed that this was so, and the government's primacy was never questioned or debated. Not even committed nationalists argued that this primacy extended to domestic affairs, where everyone agreed that power was shared with state and local governments. Therefore, it was generally assumed that the most decisive and important actions taken by the national government would involve the new republic's relations with foreign political entities of many sizes and shapes. Those who developed foreign policy after 1788—the Presidents as well as Congressional leaders with a special interest or an appropriate committee assignment—took account of at least four factors when assessing what to do in any situation involving foreigners. Evolving circumstances between 1789 and the 1860s, when the nation was embroiled in a great civil war, compelled American policymakers to ask certain questions that related to each of these factors.

One was security: Was the nation's security being threatened? Was it likely that it would become threatened without some retaliatory American response? Another was economic expansion: What position would best protect and further American commerce abroad? How could the United States remain neutral and act as traders to all belligerents when European powers were at war with one another? A third was territorial expansion: Could additional territory that American citizens were finding attractive be secured peacefully, through negotiation? Under what circumstances was such additional territory worth negotiating for, or even going to war for? A final factor was ideological: Since the American republic was in the vanguard of liberty and had a special mission in the world, when was it a part of America's destiny to extend the republic to others who would benefit? When was that destiny "manifest"?

None of these factors—security, commerce, territory, or ideology—was peculiarly American. Governments all over Europe, and, as the nation-state system spread abroad, elsewhere as well, acted out of consideration for similar kinds of national interests. However, the American government joined a much smaller number of national governments in its sporadic, though persistent expansionist policies. Such governments responded to popular pressure for additional territory and commercial supremacy. The British, the Dutch, the French, the Spaniards, the Portuguese, the Russians, the Germans, the Japanese, the Chinese—all have expanded territorially and commercially since the founding of the English North American colonies. All believed they were a special people, superior to whatever "natives" stood in their way, and were destined to spread out beyond their existing territories and to become economically and militarily dominant in expanding spheres of influence. What is peculiar about the Americans is that they were the only white settler society to imbibe this thoroughly European (and to some extent Asian) trait. Canada, Australia, New Zealand, South Africa, Brazil, Argentina—none of the other polities that grew out of European migrations has shared the American propensity to grow and to dominate.

All Presidents and Congressional spokesmen acted out of consideration for security, territory, commerce, and ideology, though the mixture and relative importance was always changing. It is too simplistic to find a basic theme in American foreign policy during these years. That policy was determined by ever-shifting circumstances with varying influences involving security, trade, territory, and ideology. If there is one recurrent theme—one characteristic that marked the government's achievement of its goals, it is not economic or territorial expansion or warmongering, but rather opportunism. The most notable achievements in American foreign policy came when American Presidents and diplomats noticed and took advantage of situations in which foreign governments were too preoccupied with their own problems to deal effectively with the Americans. This opportunism was the counterpart of the same trait that characterized the careerist politicians who became numerous beginning in the 1830s and was linked to the pragmatism that defined the American political system as a whole.

In one sense American foreign policy mirrored British imperial policy of the seventeenth and eighteenth centuries: The American government, like the British before it, was the only expansionist state in the Western Hemisphere to conquer or negotiate for territory originally held by the colonists of other European powers. In gaining Florida, Louisiana, and northern Mexico, the Americans annexed land originally settled by transplanted Spaniards and Frenchmen.

Europe was engulfed in wars from 1789 to 1815, and that fact provided the context in which American foreign relationships initially developed. The new republic was the first independent colonial offshoot of imperial Europe, whose powers were, from the 1790s to the 1810s, almost continuously engaged in the fullest and deepest warfare of their two-and-a-half century era of dynastic struggles for predominance in Europe. What should the American response to this situation be?—that was the basic question facing the American Presidency until the general settlement of 1815. Washington's responses were so effective that they became the basis for everything his successors tried to accomplish until 1917, when the American government intervened in World War I.

The most immediate problem was to deal with the incursions made in the 1780s on American territory by the two European powers who retained colonies in the Western Hemisphere—Britain and Spain. To Washington this was a matter of security: Would the United States have sovereignty over its own territory or would it not? The British continued to occupy frontier forts in the old northwest in order to force compensation for departed Loyalists and British creditors. Washington's envoy, John Jay, successfully negotiated a treaty in 1795 at which time the British, involved in a war with France, decided to withdraw from U.S. territory without any agreement that the debts and compensation would in fact be made. Opposition to the agreement erupted in both the Cabinet and Congress over Jay's failure to negotiate a trade treaty with the British that would have opened up the British Empire to American commerce.

In the meantime, the Spaniards continued to block the mouth of the Mississippi River to American commerce, the Spanish authorities still claiming portions of the Southwest as Spanish territory. Washington's envoy, Charles Pinckney, like Jay, successfully negotiated a treaty with the Spaniards in 1796. Spain was distracted by a war with France and agreed to open the Mississippi River to trade and to end its claims over the disputed territory. Washington—in a two-year period—thus established full sovereignty over American territory, an action all of his successors would uphold as a minimum definition for national sovereignty in international relations.

But, the situation Washington had to confront in the 1790s involved more than the presence of European powers in the Western Hemisphere. In Europe, the leading powers were at war with revolutionary France, with whom the United States had a treaty that obliged the American government to become France's ally in time of war. The question of what course of action the United States should pursue divided Washington's cabinet. Secretary of State Jefferson argued that the treaty was a solemn international obligation, the first great act with a foreign state made by the newly independent American government, back in 1777. The French Alliance had been an indisputably crucial factor in the victory gained by the rebels. How could the American government ignore France, now that *its* revolutionary movement was at war, likewise struggling for survival? But, Alexander Hamilton, Secretary of the Treasury, argued that the French government that Congress had negotiated with in 1777 was no longer in existence, that the United States was thus freed from its treaty obligations, and that if the United States were to become allies with anyone in Europe, it should be the British, whose colonists the Americans had recently been (with all that implied with respect to bonds and ties).

Washington reached his own decision. His Neutrality Proclamation of 1793 declared that the new American republic must be independent of all "entangling alliances" with European powers and must therefore remain neutral during the power struggles of the European heartland, until the time the republic had matured and had sufficient strength to avoid being a junior partner of any of the great powers abroad. Washington's largeness of view, his capacity to place the fledgling republic within the context of European civilization as a whole, and his insight into what was required as a diplomatic posture to best secure the future of the American nation in the wider world—all made his proclamation a starting point for any of his successors who had to deal with crises involving Europe.

Washington's immediate successor, John Adams, was wholly focused on transatlantic problems. The French seized American shipping on the basis of newer (and, to the French) necessarily looser rules of war for neutrals trading with the enemy in the midst of what was now all-out, unrelenting, limitless warfare. After the French government unsuccessfully tried to bribe the American negotiators Adams had sent to France in an effort to end what from the American perspective were offending practices, the U.S. government retaliated by creating a naval department and attacking French warships in the Atlantic. The Adams administration was confronted with the first "wartime" crisis of the new American government and was quite uncertain how much freedom the political opposition should be allowed in such a situation. The administration was able to pass into law the Alien and Sedition Acts of 1798, which substantially restricted opposition to government policy during the undeclared war.

The opposition Republicans were highly agitated by the restrictions placed upon their activities as legitimately elected political opponents. The political crisis created by the enactment of the sedition legislation galvanized—more than any single political act of the 1790s—the Republicans into action and led directly to the creation of the first mass political party in the history of modern European civilization. The Republicans were convinced that these acts were tyrannical in nature and that to save or secure the republic, the Republicans had to organize and to defeat the Federalists at the next elections. Indeed, Republicans in two state legislatures—Kentucky and Virginia—succeeded in passing resolutions indicating that the states were the final arbiters of the constitutionality of any legislation, just as they had had to ratify the document in the first place. The Sedition Acts, in this view, were unconstitutional.

The crisis abated when Napoleon became First Consul in 1799. In the Convention of 1800, the United States and France agreed to abrogate their treaty of alliance (continuing their trade treaty, however) and to stop attacking each other's shipping. When the Republicans elected their leader Jefferson as President in 1800 the basic situation in Europe did not change, as France (under Napoleon) conquered much of Europe, with Britain as its implacable and unconquerable enemy. In this situation, *both* Britain and France adopted looser laws of war for neutrals trading in war zones. To both governments, older, tighter definitions had to give way to newer ones because the character of war itself had changed into protracted, all-out conflict with conquest as the objective.

Contraband had to include any items that might help the enemy wage war. Blockades must include whole coastal areas, not just harbors. And, (for the British) impressment of seamen must be pursued in the most expeditious manner, because the navy was losing seamen to English-speaking America at an alarming rate.

To Jefferson and his Republican successor Madison, these changes in the rules worked significantly against the enlargement of American commerce in war-torn Europe. America remained neutral, and the American government's diplomacy was directed toward the protection of American commerce as it grew in response to the needs of a disrupted Europe. Both Jefferson and Madison—and their emissaries—believed that the most effective way to protect and aid American commerce was to insist that the European belligerents honor the old (1756) rules of war, which placed fewer restrictions on neutrals trading to belligerents in wartime. Mindful of the telling effect of the economic boycotts organized by the colonial resistance movement of the 1760s, the Republican administrations employed a seasoned pro-French, anti-British, and thus increasingly skewed response to what were *both* British (Orders-in-Council) and French (Berlin and Milan Decrees) restrictions.

Napoleon decided to sell to the U.S. government all of the Louisiana Territory in 1803, when Jefferson sent an emissary to negotiate a removal of French trade restrictions at the mouth of the Mississippi River. The negotiator took advantage of Napoleon's preoccupation with European conquest, and Jefferson, though he doubted that, as President, he had authority to make such an agreement, decided to send the proposal to an approving Senate on the pragmatic grounds that this great inland valley was too valuable to ignore. On the matter of policy differences over trade, Jefferson convinced the Congressional Republicans to support an all-out embargo against both belligerents in 1806, but, by the end of his terms in office, he was convinced the embargo was a failure and had it repealed. Madison applied a more selective embargo in 1810, as a result of legislation committing the American government to an embargo on the other belligerent if either one decided to end its trade restrictions.

By 1812, Madison was convinced that the British—who continued to impress what the U.S. government regarded as American citizens and whose navy was stronger and, thus, whose trade restrictions were more effective—would not change their policies. Since the diplomatic situation was intolerable, he asked Congress to declare war because of these irreconcilable grievances—much as Polk would later determine to ask Congress for war because the Mexicans would not cede one-third of their territory as a result of diplomatic efforts.

Many Republicans in Congress supported Madison because they believed the British had not treated the United States as a fully sovereign nation and, therefore, the nation's honor had to be upheld. But "peace Republicans" joined the Federalist opposition as a negative response to Madison's request for a declaration of war. Both groups served as spokesmen for the coastal commercial interests for whom war, even with its likely blockade, was perceived to be even less desirable than British and French trade restrictions had been. Ironically, the British had revoked their Orders-in-Council before Madison issued his war message, but because transatlantic communications were of six weeks' duration, Congress declared war before news of the British action arrived in the United States.

During the war that ensued, Madison was not a very effective Commander-in-Chief (the first time that that particular duty of the Presidency was performed). The Republicans had reduced the navy (created during the undeclared war with France from 1797 to 1799) to a fleet of coastal gunboats, had maintained only a skeleton army, and had kept defense expenditures to a minimum. The nation was not prepared to wage war. Its commanders were aging veterans from the late eighteenth century. Congress was divided among "war hawks," who wanted to provide the means for a successful fighting effort, peace Republicans, and Federalists, who argued and voted against such measures, and others who were successfully wooed by both of these groups.

Some Federalist state governors in the Northeast, where opposition to the war was greatest, delayed acting on the requests of the Madison administration for troops to augment the initial federal force. Certain militia groups refused to fight beyond their state's boundaries. Some merchants traded with the enemy through remote border areas adjacent to British North America. Troops were not able to move expeditiously from one area to another because there was no network of roads and canals linking the nation. Since the national banking system had ended in 1811, there was no dependable basis for the government to borrow or even store its funds. In sum, the United States was greatly fragmented, and its government lacked the capacity to wage war effectively.

And yet, Madison persevered. He appointed many "Secretaries" to his "cabinet" offices of War and the Treasury and had to deal with old, ineffectual generals. But, he did have a strategic sense: he believed Britain could be defeated if its supply lines were severed along the St. Lawrence River, preferably at Montreal. However, his generals lacked the capacity and the means to coordinate such an attack. Still, whenever Madison spotted an able young general or admiral, he gave such talented commanders combat responsibility. Perry and MacDonough won naval engagements in the Great Lakes and Lake Champlain. Scott was victorious on the Niagara frontier. Jackson repulsed the British at New Orleans. The Federalists, who met at Hartford, Connecticut, and proposed amendments to the Constitution that would have limited the powers of the Presidency and thus hopefully check what they believed had become a too powerful Republican Party, were discredited as a disloyal opposition when the war ended.

The British were involved with Napoleon and were never able to focus their full attention on the North American sideshow war (as wars in the Americas had been before the fateful Seven Years' War). Nevertheless, the British tried to blockade the American coast, hoped to strike inland from their colonies along the St. Lawrence River and the Great Lakes, and, when that failed, by 1814, had designed a grand strategy of attacking the United States along its border, both coastal and inland. When the able young American commanders repulsed these military efforts, a war-weary Britain negotiated for peace. After protracted negotiations, the two sides settled for the "status quo antebellum," leaving unsettled all the major issues of the war. The real peace treaty was a series of separate agreements reached by accommodationist-minded diplomats over a period of years, beginning with the convention to disarm in the Great Lakes (1814), and continuing with a trade convention (which excluded Britain's empire) (1815), and concluding with a boundary agreement along the 49th parallel and the joint occupation of Oregon territory (1818).

During the post-Napoleonic era in Europe, there was a basic shift in the context within which American diplomacy operated. The powers of Europe created alliances whose objective was to keep any single power from dominating the continent, as France in its revolutionary and Napoleonic era had. When Spain's Middle and South American colonies rebelled and established republics superficially akin to the American republic, the question was whether Spain would launch an invasion to reclaim its colonies. The Americans were sympathetic to the Spanish rebels, and Speaker of the House Henry Clay led those in Congress who urged that there be a speedy recognition of the newly independent republics, even though the Monroe administration advocated delay. In the meantime, Secretary of State Adams was able, in 1819, to negotiate the acquisition of Florida from a distracted Spain. Florida was at the entrance of the Caribbean and was thus of strategic importance to the United States' security.

The lesson of the War of 1812 for Madison was that the nation must in the future be prepared for war and should, therefore, have adequate armed services, a national bank, and a national transportation system. Madison prevailed upon Congress to pass appropriate legislation (except for an impasse over the constitutionality of a nationally funded transportation system). But, what about the long-term position of the United States vis-à-vis the European powers (especially Britain, France, and Spain)?

Secretary of State Adams envisioned a continental republic, and he believed that, in order to secure it, the U.S. government had to negotiate boundary treaties with Spain and Britain (which he did in 1818 and 1819). But, Adams also believed that in order for the United States to become the dominant power in the Western Hemisphere, it was unnecessary to have a large defense establishment or to be powerless in the event of further colonization efforts on the part of the receding European powers. Adams believed that Britain would not support such recolonization schemes, that it was more interested in trade than in colonization, and that without the support of Britain's navy—the world's largest—any such colonization efforts by Spain and France would not succeed. So, he wrote as a part of Monroe's Annual Message of 1823 that Europe would not be allowed to recolonize the Americas and that the United States would remain uninvolved with European alliances.

Adams was right. As a result of the loss of most of Britain's mainland North American colonies in 1783 and the subsequent loss of most of Spain's Middle and South American colonies between 1810 and 1826, the character of European expansion altered its form. It was in the Western Hemisphere that European domination of others had evolved into its most mature political shape: colonies whose territories completely replaced the polities of the native population. Nowhere else in the world had the Europeans more completely assumed direct authority over the indigenous peoples of other continents. The successful rebellion of their colonists during the half century between 1776 and 1826 meant that Europeans experienced a major setback in their durable quest to dominate the populations of the rest of the globe. At that point, a much reduced European imperial presence consisted of British North America, various Caribbean island possessions, and Russian settlements that had spread along the Pacific Coast virtually overland from Siberia. What would the European powers do to recoup their losses, to regain the momentum they had long enjoyed in their penetration and subsequent domination of other people and other lands and waters?

As Adams understood, the British were in the pivotal position. With the world's largest navy, the British could decisively support or oppose schemes to regain lost colonial worlds in the Americas. In the decades after 1815 and the defeat of Napoleon, British policy with respect to the Americas fundamentally shifted, as successive British ministries markedly emphasized an important aspect of European expansion other than the maintenance of colonies, and that was the economic penetration of the erstwhile colonial sphere of the Western Hemisphere. Rather than support schemes by which the European powers might regain their former colonial empires, the British wanted to augment their economic power by expanding trade with all parts of the world.

And so, when there were short-lived and quickly put-down rebellions in parts of British North America in 1837, led by those who felt unfairly constricted by a system of colonial government that vested ultimate authority in unelected councils and appointed Governors, the British government, fearing another American-style rebellion, appointed Lord Durham to report on the situation. Lord Durham recommended that "responsible" government be instituted in the British colonies (at least in North America), that is, that local ministries be responsible to an elected lower house of Parliament and truly govern within the colonies themselves. The British established such a political system, and when similar white-dominated British colonies were established in the temperate zones of Australia and New Zealand, the British created responsible government there as well.

All of this was in sharp contrast to areas of the world where tiny elites of Europeans continued, even after the setbacks in the Americas, to dominate large native populations: the Dutch in the East Indies, the English in India. During these decades the English moved through every form of European domination in their dealings with the Indians within the subcontinent of Asia: from trading depots and military fortifications, to trading companies (the East India Company), to alliances with and conquests of particular Indian states, to full-scale British colonial rule, replete with Governor-Generals and other resident officials.

So, the movement toward evolutionary colonial self-rule was restricted to those areas—like the United States—with large, transplanted white populations.

In harmony with other still-colonized areas of the world featuring tiny white elites and masses of impoverished native populations, the former Spanish colonists who established the other republics of the Western Hemisphere during these years produced a political system within which *caudillos*, or strong leaders, emerged. The *caudillos* continued the patriarchal pattern of the past and retained rule by an elite, allying themselves with the rural aristocracy, the Catholic church, and the army. The army was the only truly national institution, and its strength only revealed the weakness of other political elements. Elections were not regular or honest, and revolutions or palace coups became the customary means of bringing about political shifts. The military had the dual role of guaranteeing order and changing governments. *Caudillos* worked with the military, which was well provided for.

Monroe's "doctrine" (as it later came to be known) did not mean that the U.S. government favored the immediate territorial expansion of the republic, whether westward, southward, or northward. Jackson was more interested in the removal of trade restrictions within the British Empire, which he successfully negotiated in 1830, by which time British shipping interests gave way to open free-trade advocates. Jackson refused to recognize rebellion to the South when Texan rebels gained their independence from Mexico in 1836, as did his successor Van Buren. Similarly, when there were rebellions to the North, in British North America, Van Buren remained strictly neutral and quickly settled a boundary dispute with the British in Maine.

It was only when, during the 1840s, American settlers in Texas, Oregon, and California led movements in favor of annexation to the United States of British (the jointly occupied Oregon territory) and Mexican territory and when Presidents Tyler and Polk favored territorial expansion for agricultural (the Texan plains) and commercial (the Pacific Coast harbors) purposes that American diplomacy became expansionist in character. Whig President Tyler persuaded Congress to annex Texas on the basis of a simple agreement and not on the basis of a more-difficult-to-obtain treaty. By the 1844 election, the Democratic Party became committed to expansionism and nominated Polk, while the Whigs chose an antiexpansionist position and nominated Clay. Each party appealed to the public for support on the basis of party positions on the territorial issue.

When Polk was elected, he drew back from extremist demands for all of Oregon and all of Mexico; his objective was to obtain through diplomacy the portion of Oregon that Americans settlers already inhabited and the northern part of Mexico that contained the harbors and fertile valleys of the Pacific Coast. He negotiated with a willing Britain a division of Oregon territory along the line of American and British settlements. But, when the oft-changing Mexican government refused to sell its northern tier of states to the United States, Polk decided to ask Congress for war. When the Mexican army moved onto territory claimed by the Texans, Polk was able to present to a nearly unanimously favorable Congress a request for war in response to an attack by Mexico.

In the war that followed, a politically unstable Mexico fought with an old-fashioned, European-styled army, comprised of an aristocratic officer corps and soldiers from the poorer segments of the population. The United States presented, for the third time in its history, a militia-augmented army, whose soldiers believed that they were fighting racially inferior Mexicans in order to enlarge the blessings of American republicanism. Polk was, unlike Madison, a quite effective Commander-in-Chief. He chose able commanding generals in Scott and Taylor, led determinedly a largely united Democratic Party in Congress that successfully supported war measures over the steadfast opposition of the Whigs, and persistently pursued a strategy of attacking and invading Mexican territory until, with the capture of the capital, the Mexicans negotiated for peace. An impatient Polk repudiated and then agreed to the settlement reached by this negotiator (Trist): Mexico ceded the territory Polk had wanted for a sum of money.

In the years after the war with Mexico, the Democrats continued to adhere to an expansionist posture, with both security and territorial objectives. For example, Pierce's administration favored the purchase of Cuba and Buchanan's administration planned to turn the northern tier of Mexican states into a protectorate. The Whigs, by contrast, adhered to their antiexpansionist position. For instance, Taylor's administration negotiated a treaty with the British in 1850 to share the responsibility of building and protecting a canal through the Central American isthmus.

Britain, with its powerful navy, had played the role Adams had envisioned in 1823: it had favored trade over further colonization. When the United States expanded across the continent, it became the only great power in the Western Hemisphere and, unlike Europe's powers, was unchecked and unbalanced (as it own government was supposed to be). The United States had achieved this unique position in the political world with the smallest armed services in modern history—in sharp contrast to both the European powers and the other American republics.

* * *

After the Civil War, the one area of uncontested authority that the national government continued to exercise within the American federal political system was the conduct of foreign relations. And within the government, the Presidency continued to initiate policy and remained responsive to the earlier mix of influences—security, economic expansion, territorial expansion, and ideology. The development of steamships as the basis of oceanic travel brought the Eurasian geopolitical world closer to American concerns. Though Europe remained the center of political-economic-military power, in Asia, two additional centers of power—a declining China and an ascendant Japan—were of concern to a government whose territory—after 1848—faced both the Pacific and the Atlantic Oceans. The Caribbean remained at the center of the government's concern over security. Political, economic, or social instability in that area of independent hemispheric nations could create the possibility of foreign intervention.

The United States, as it gained economic eminence during the late nineteenth and early twentieth centuries, remained the only political power in the world's geopolitical areas without the countervailing presence of other powers. This distinctive situation made it possible for the U.S. government to exert political influence vastly greater than the armed services the government ever felt it necessary to train and equip. As long as Britain—who continued to have the world's most powerful navy until World War II—opposed direct European intervention in the Western Hemisphere, the United States went on having a minuscule armed service to serve as the coercive base of American diplomacy.

Indeed, the fundamental element of American foreign policy from the 1870s to the 1940s (and World War II) was borrowed from the British. Just as the British government worked after 1815 to expand trade on the basis of commercial agreements with the preindustrialized world and opposed further territorial annexations in a world kept free of war between competing industrializing powers, so too did the American government favor such a world order. The government wanted equal access to the preindustrial world for the purpose of expanding American commerce, but it was unwilling to build up its military strength to ensure that such a world existed, preferring to rely (as it had since the 1820s) on Britain's preeminent military position. When a prolonged price depression gripped the industrialized world from the 1870s to the late 1890s and investment in the preindustrial world seemed attractive and competition between the European powers intensified, Britain's policy failed, and imperialistic expansion involving much of Africa and Asia ensued.

American relations with Canada (as British North America became known at the confederation of the British provinces in 1867) remained largely stable and peaceful. Among the European powers, only Spain maintained possessions in the hemisphere—most importantly Cuba and Puerto Rico, at the gateway to the Caribbean, the very area in which the American government felt most strategically vulnerable. When the Cubans revolted and sustained an insurrectionary force over many years, there was widespread American sympathy for the rebels, who, when captured, were cruelly treated in concentration camps. But, even though Spain, by 1898, decided to concede defeat, President McKinley asked a willing Congress for war.

Various factors united most national politicians behind war. Spain was perceived by many Americans as being obstreperous and inhumane. The prevailing ideology sanctioned a bellicose response. A "social Darwinian" geopolitical philosophy defined the United States as being in the vanguard of white civilization, with a duty to civilize, Christianize, and stabilize the world, to act as its moral and political policeman. Though anti-imperialist spokesmen denied that the

United States had such a duty and asserted the superiority of an isolationist position, theirs was a minority voice in the clamor over what to do about Spain's rebelling empire.

In the brief, decisive war that followed, the easily victorious American forces were still based upon voluntary units quickly filled by young men convinced that this particular war was just and glorious. In the peace settlement, the U.S. government made Puerto Rico and the Philippines colonies and Cuba a protectorate, and in this way dealt with imperialist ideology, security concerns, and territorial expansion all at once. Though the United States became an imperialist power without a design or plan for doing so, it did its "duty" by governing more primitive populations, improving government services and standards of health and education. It also better protected the Caribbean strategic gateway by gaining total or partial control over the key islands and expanded territorially in both the Western Hemisphere and the Pacific, thus acting in the manner of empire builders elsewhere in the world.

But, the United States never became an imperialist power in the classic European sense. The American government never created a permanent imperial bureaucracy and, until the conquests of 1898, American expansion involved a contiguous continental empire wrested from Britain, Spain, Russia, and Mexico, an empire consisting of lands that were turned into territories soon admitted into the Union as equal states. The Americans never annexed or conquered whole polities, but incorporated peripheral or exposed parts of empires. Its only significant overseas possession, the Philippines, was administered as a colony in the time-honored European (particularly British) manner, with sustained efforts to improve the health and education of the population, even though American authorities were plagued by a protracted Filipino insurrection. But, the islands were given their independence in 1946, as the European imperial powers themselves moved toward the devolution of their empires.

By 1904, President Theodore Roosevelt declared, in a "Roosevelt corollary" to the Monroe Doctrine, that the U.S. government might intervene in a situation in which European involvement in hemispheric affairs became overt. American trade with South and Middle America grew throughout the late nineteenth and early twentieth centuries, the South and Middle Americans trading basic commodities for American industrial products—thus placing themselves in a position similar to the ones that the colonists had with respect to Britain during the seventeenth and eighteenth centuries. The political expression of that relationship was the formation of the Pan-American Union.

But, when certain central American nations—Haiti, Santo Domingo, Nicaragua—became deeply indebted to Europeans and Americans, Presidents Taft and Wilson sent in marines as a military occupying force and installed American customs officials to oversee debt payments from revenues generated from trade. This was the kind of intervention envisioned by Theodore Roosevelt, who himself wrested from a politically chaotic Colombia a Canal Zone, where he had the long-envisioned canal link between the Pacific and Atlantic Oceans built, thus greatly facilitating trade, particularly American foreign commerce. When Mexico entered a prolonged period of instability, President Wilson tried to support the faction that passed his test for morally acceptable government, but disentangled himself when the situation in Mexico became more stable. Throughout these decades, the United states involvement in South and Middle America reflected the varied concerns of American Presidents and Congresses: security, ideology, and territorial or economic expansionism.

In Asia, the same mix of influences was in evidence, except for security. The absence of any nearby islands along the Pacific Coast meant that American foreign policy with respect to Asia lacked the strategic considerations that were frequently present in dealings with South and Middle America. When Hawaii was annexed, after American immigrants pressured for such an action (in the same way that pioneers in Texas, Oregon, and California petitioned for annexation in the 1830s and 1840s), and when the Philippines was made a colony after the brief war with Spain in 1898, the United States had expanded territorially in the manner of—but far from the same scale as—the powers of Europe. Americans could civilize and Christianize the primitive Filipinos and Hawaiians and used their territory as naval bases.

But, the overriding interest of the U.S. government in Asia during these decades was the expansion of trade, an emphasis clearly seen in the long-term adherence to an "open door" policy respecting China. As the European powers and the United States established militarily protected spheres of influence for trade purposes in a weakening China, the U.S. government, through its Secretary of State, John Hay, announced its support of a policy of equal and fair treatment for all who wanted to trade in these zones, a policy the government did nothing to enforce, but proceeded at frequent intervals to proclaim. In the Pacific and with Asia, the United States's lack of any substantial military force worked against the enforcement of policies in any way antithetical to the European powers, who did station armed forces in Asia.

The time-honored American propensity to proclaim a policy that was beyond its military means to enforce worked in the Western Hemisphere largely because of British concurrence. In Asia, such posturing was a sham and could be exposed at any time there was a large military force trained and equipped by a government antithetical to American interests (as defined by the U.S. government). Such was the case with Japan by the 1930s.

With respect to Europe, American policymakers adhered to another time-honored position, that of noninvolvement in European alliances, tensions, crises, and wars—at least until 1917, when the United States entered World War I on the side of the Allies. The basic situation had not changed since 1815, as the European nations continued to be "balanced" in power through alliances that evolved and shifted from time to time, but, by their very existence, provided a basic geopolitical stability. All American policymakers after 1865, as had been the case before the Civil War, were agreed that the U.S. government's best position was to remain neutral and to do everything in its power to foster trade, to protect American economic expansion. In a basic sense, U.S. foreign policy with respect to both Asia and Europe, that is the entire Eurasian landmass, was the same: stay uninvolved diplomatically, while furthering American commercial interests.

Not even the outbreak of World War I changed this. Wilson was as committed as his predecessors had been to a policy of neutrality. What worked against the continuation of that policy was the widespread popular sense that Britain and France were *preferable* to Germany, were historically closer to America and its development. American trade and loans gravitated toward the Allies, creating a heavy imbalance. The Central Powers *seemed* more belligerent when Germany developed a policy of unrestricted submarine warfare. Though Germany was using a new weapon of warfare in the most effective way (if warnings were issued, submarines would lose their effectiveness) and was retaliating against what it had already declared to be illegal American trade with the enemy, the American public was repulsed by the prospect of civilians suddenly being lost at sea by weapons of war. When Wilson asked for a declaration of war, a newly united Congress quickly obliged.

Twice in American history—in 1812 and in 1917—the national government's effort to remain neutral and increase trade with the European belligerents in the midst of a major war failed. In both cases, the European nations at war enlarged their definition of blockades and contraband in order that they be appropriate for what to them was a *major* conflict. In both cases, the American government treated the two sides unequally. British policy was perceived to be the major irritant in 1810–1812; German policy was seen as far more hostile than the British in 1914–1917. But, the United States in 1917–1918 was notably more effective in waging war than the Madison administration had been. Though the United States became involved with European hostilities in 1812–1814 and in 1917–1918, American combat moved from the United States itself to Europe, where the Expeditionary Force under General Pershing, retaining a distinctive identity, played a crucial role in the final assault on the German forces in 1918.

The Wilson administration was forced to provide centralized planning for a still largely decentralized nation and was quite sensitive to deep traditions of local and regional autonomy. But, developments in communication and transportation and the attendant enlargement of scale in economic, social, and cultural life meant that Wilson could focus all of American life on war in a way that was unimaginable during the War of 1812, a century earlier. The Wilson administration drew on the earlier World War I experiences of the European belligerents as the basis for America's war mobilization. The first massive extension of federal authority in the United States was very much an extension of European wartime innovations.

Recruitment of a voluntary army buttressed by the draft was left to local boards under overall national supervision. The administration's war boards utilized the existing telegraph and mail service as well as the developing telephone to dictate wartime production needs. Under the War Industries Board's supervision, the purchasing bureaus of the United States and of allied governments submitted their requirements to the board, which in turn set priorities and planned production. The board had authority to allocate raw materials, instruct manufacturers what to produce, and, with the approval of the President, fix prices. Corporations—both owners and wage earners—came under the regulation of distant government regulatory agencies. A newly created U.S. Employment Service supervised the creation of an enlarged wartime labor force, which included women and, through recruitment drives in the South instituted by various Northern firms with war-related contracts, blacks and Mexicans as well, though the hostility of white laborers occasionally led to race riots in new black urban neighborhoods. War bond drives brought widespread popular financial (and patriotic) support for the war effort, beyond ordinary taxation. A Committee on Public Information used every means of communication at its disposal to instill in citizens the "American" version of the war, enlarging patriotic sentiment and feeding a growing intolerance of dissent.

Wartime Washington became a "progressive" utopia: a government that instituted national planning and defined the national identity and goals. But, the reform spirit got increasingly mixed up with patriotism, with "Americanism," and became increasingly hostile toward those who opposed the war or challenged prevailing definitions. World War I led, thus, to the apotheosis of "progressivism" in the United States at the same time that it led to a resurgence of intolerance, a growing insistence on an orthodoxy, an "American" truth. Americans in World War I and its aftermath tried to create a unified, harmonious, closed orthodox *national* community in the same spirit of reform, with the same kind of utopian impulse as the Puritans in seventeenth-century New England had in their local communities.

Anything Germanic was popularly equated with disloyalty. Under the Espionage and Sedition Acts, criticism of government leaders and war policies was greatly limited. These acts were similar in intent and in effect to the Alien and Sedition Acts of 1798, during the first war (undeclared) with a European power, with France. The impulse of both the Adams and the Wilson administrations when the United States got directly involved in a European war was to sharply limit dissent. The Sedition Act of 1918 prohibited the advocacy of cutbacks in production or anything that would obstruct the sale of government bonds and prohibited saying, writing, or printing anything "disloyal, profane, scurrilous, or abusive" about the U.S. government, the Constitution, or the U.S. Army or Navy. More than 1,500 prosecutions led to more than 1,000 convictions. Leaders of the Industrial Workers of the World went on trial and were convicted. The Socialist leader, Eugene Debs, was convicted for encouraging draft resistance. The Supreme Court upheld the constitutionality of these acts. When the Communist Party attained power in Russia during the war and started an international communist movement, Communists in the United States became a new target as the war ended. Attorney General Palmer summarily deported radical aliens, and local police forces in many cities raided presumed radical headquarters, sweeping up 5,000 suspects, often without arrest warrants.

Wilson's rigidity in pursuing a peace settlement without the presence of the Republican opposition leaders resulted in the Senate's refusal to accept the treaty. Public opinion was too divided for there to be a consensus for a treaty that set up an ongoing international organization that would monitor international relations and try, through what Wilson called "collective security," to avoid national wars thereafter. Wilson was the first significant internationalist in the American Presidency and tried to create a peace settlement that would sustain the United States' involvement in world affairs through his proposed "League of Nations" as well as through an international commitment to free trade, or the removal of trade barriers. Nationalists, such as Theodore Roosevelt and Senator Henry Cabot Lodge, were concerned about the loss of national sovereignty that would result from the adoption of such a scheme. Lodge and his supporters focused on aspects of the treaty that in any way seemed to limit the application of national sovereignty in future U.S. policymaking, and their position reflected the deep division in the American public.

But, American opinion was not notably divided over the territorial settlements that Wilson and the other peacemakers made out of the former empires of central Europe. Indeed, Americans generally supported the "war guilt" clause Wilson's fellow peacemakers insisted upon, and American diplomats in the 1920s worked out various plans ensuring that Germany continue to repay the victorious Allies what the victors had determined was the cost of the war. But, American insistence on German reparations only increased German resentment toward the Allies. Having rejected the treaty and its league and free trade, American policymakers during the 1920s went on to extend to the world its Asian-made peace-by-proclamation policy.

The Peace Pact of 1928 was the widest application of a policymaking impulse designed to maintain peace through pious declaration, without any of the enforcement machinery envisioned by Wilson, but now developed by a largely powerless (and American-less) League during the 1920s and 1930s. Similarly, the Naval Disarmament Treaties of 1922 not only led to minimal naval cutbacks, but committed certain powers to aid others in the event of aggression without any mechanism for the maintenance of collective security in a crisis.

In sum, with the large and traumatic exception of World War I, between 1865 and 1930, U.S. foreign policy exhibited certain basic ingredients, at least outside of the American sphere of influence. Within that sphere, in South and Middle America, there was active and continuous American intervention. But, beyond the Western Hemisphere, American policy reflected a desire to protect the expansion of the American economy abroad. Policymakers proclaimed the need for peace among the nations of the Eurasian landmass at the same time that they neglected to develop armed services or forge international alliances or arrange for American membership in international organizations. The basic current in

United States foreign policy *remained* isolationist, neutralist, noninvolved in the wider world. The United States thus developed economic power far out ahead of its diplomatic and military power, thus becoming the first major nation in the modern world to disassociate one from the other.

* * *

Only in the area of foreign affairs has Presidential dominance usually been conceded by the judicial and legislative branches. Since the 1920s, the *typical* posture of Congress on significant matters involving foreign relations has been bipartisan, though there have been a number of specific occasions when the tradition of bipartisanship has broken down, as politicians espoused sharply differing views on the proper course of action for the administration of the time to take. Still, through all of the decades since 1930, American foreign policy has been deeply marked by Congressional consensus and Presidential continuity. "Liberal" and "Conservative" positions there have sometimes been; Republican and Democratic party differences have sometimes existed. But, such divisions have meant far less in foreign relations than in domestic policy. Presidential preeminence has been seriously challenged only once, as a result of the "loose" Congressional resolution that led to what became in its final stages a very unpopular war in the Asian perimeter of the Communist power centers. But, in general, in foreign relations, national politicians have usually followed Presidential initiatives, and those Presidents have been remarkably consistent in adhering to a given, overall policy during a period in which the United States has been a "superpower" (militarily and economically).

Since 1930, the preeminent position of the President in the conduct of foreign relations has rarely been questioned by Congress, which has usually accepted a Constitutionally sanctioned division of power. And, in most basic positions forged by the Presidency in the American government's dealings with other national (and, after 1945 and the creation of the United Nations, international) governments, the posture of Congress has been to be bipartisan, though there have been disagreements over emphasis and the means to achieve various foreign commitments.

America's position as the leading power (economically, if not militarily) of the Europeanized world was evident from the time of World War I, but in the 1930s, isolationism was pervasive and popular. The American government at times worked informally with the League of Nations, but the nation's basic policy with respect to foreign alliances and involvements in foreign wars was "neutrality" encased in two laws enacted in 1935 and 1939. Franklin Roosevelt even refused, in 1933, to participate in an international economic conference intended to deal with the deepening worldwide depression of the 1930s. It was widely believed that America's participation in World War I had been a mistake, a fateful aberration from the nation's sound and fundamental posture—noninvolvement in European alliances and disputes.

Just as Americans continued to support an anticentrist, antipower, antistate tradition long after their lives were in fact "nationalized" or organized on a continental scale, so too did they retain their allegiance to an isolationist tradition long after their economic power made them deeply involved in Europe and other parts of the world. Even in America's "sphere of interest," in South and Middle America, the "Good Neighbor" policy was established, which was a pledge from Roosevelt's administration that the United States would no longer interfere in the internal affairs of the nations of the Western Hemisphere. This constituted a considerable veering away from the Roosevelt Corollary to the Monroe Doctrine. The only instance of an "internationalist" orientation during the 1930s was Roosevelt's agreement—on Secretary of State Cordell Hull's insistence—to trade reciprocity, that is to a mutual lowering of trade barriers with individual nations. In adhering to a time-honored principle of the Democratic Party, Roosevelt concluded that freer trade would benefit Americans and help to revive the world's economy.

But, when Germany and Japan displayed expansionist tendencies during the mid-and late 1930s, Roosevelt tried to find ways of aiding those who opposed these aggressive nations. He eroded the Congressional consensus in favor of a neutralist posture by arguing that America's security could be in jeopardy in an age of airplanes and submarines if the Eurasian landmass were controlled by hostile states, a position that triggered a major Congressional debate. He persuaded Congress to establish a lend-lease program with Britain (under which British naval bases were leased to the United States in exchange for the lending of warships) and a conscription system.

Japan and Germany continued to conquer adjoining nations in Europe and Asia, and, when Japan attacked the American Pacific Naval Base at Pearl Harbor in Hawaii, Roosevelt was able to argue that America itself had been a victim of such aggression, thus uniting Congress and the American public behind a declaration of war against both Japan and Germany, in the same sort of way that Polk had been able to gain wide support for a war declaration when the Mexican army crossed the United States' new border in Texas in 1846.

During World War II, the Roosevelt administration drew upon the experience of the Wilson Administration in World War I, as well as on its own experience with new agencies established in response to the Depression of the 1930s, and set up an array of government boards. These organizations were headed by the War Production Board, which directed the conversion of industry to war production, and by special administrators who instituted rationing for civilians and promoted the wartime production of such scarce and important commodities as oil. The Office of Price Administration (and, later, the Office of Economic Stabilization) set price ceilings and further developed a civilian rationing system. The War Labor Board tried to keep wages in line with price levels, and, at times, the government, under the War Labor Disputes Act, seized key industries (such as coal mining and the railroads) threatened by strikes.

The conservative-dominated Congress dismantled what it felt were "nonessential" New Deal agencies. Senator Harry Truman led a Senate War Investigating Committee that had the task of reporting on waste and inefficiency in the war effort. Roosevelt and Congress divided over how best to finance the war. The President preferred taxes, which would also retard inflation; Congress feared taxes more than deficits. The result was a series of compromises in the form of revenue acts that greatly broadened the tax structure, lowered exemptions, instituted payroll deductions, and increased surtaxes to over 90 percent in the highest bracket. About half the government's wartime costs were covered by taxes, the other half by borrowing, with much raised (as in World War I) by war bond drives that involved thousands of ordinary citizens and by government notes that were bought by financial institutions.

The wartime economy brought millions of people fully into the economic system who had been on its margins before the war. The government's tax policy actually reduced the share of the income received by the wealthiest 5 percent, from 24 percent to 17 percent of the total, and thus to some extent "democratized" economic life. The Roosevelt administration emphasized that the war was a "crusade" against totalitarian aggressor nations, and the civilian population responded with enthusiastic support in senses that were both civilian (rationing, war bond drives, defense work) and military (enlistments were high, as young men and women eagerly joined in a campaign to defeat clear aggression.). Women and blacks entered the wartime labor force in large numbers, and blacks became more vocal in their opposition to discrimination, to the point that Roosevelt issued an executive order forbidding discrimination in defense work and training programs and established a Committee on Fair Employment Practices. The government did not attempt to suppress wartime dissent as had occurred in World War I. The war was widely supported throughout the civilian population, as German and Japanese aggression seemed real, even threatening. Japanese-Americans, for whom there was much fear and racial prejudice, were forcibly moved from the Pacific Coast to "war relocation camps" in the interior, for security reasons, with no effort on the part of the government to uphold their civil liberties.

President Roosevelt and Prime Minister Churchill combined the command structures of the British and American armed forces, but their ally, Soviet leader Stalin, remained aloof, even refusing American aid. The American, British, and Soviets were the major opponents of the German and Japanese aggressors, but Stalin's totalitarian government felt alien to the British and American governments, whose ancient bonds reasserted themselves in this time of crisis. For the Soviets and the British and the Americans, the alliance (of the "Allies") was one of convenience and, during the course of the war, the three leaders, in "summit" conferences, determined that their goal was the "unconditional surrender" of the "Axis" nations' armed forces. Churchill and Roosevelt designed, and persuaded other nations who opposed Germany and Japan to subscribe to, an "Atlantic Charter" (the self-determination of all "people," equal access to raw materials, economic cooperation, freedom of the seas, and a new system of general security), based upon Wilson's 14 points as well as New Deal goals.

The question of what constituted the most effective strategy was a contentious one throughout the war. From the American and German perspectives, it was a two-front war. American leaders came to feel that in Europe, with the Soviets on one side and the British on the other and with American aid, the Germans could and should be defeated first. In the Pacific (America's other front), the Americans were the primary opponents of the Japanese because the Soviets and the British lacked the resources for a two-front war—in Europe and in Asia. The American command concluded that the Pacific war should be given a lower priority than the European conflict. The British agreed, but disagreed with the Americans over what constituted the best strategy in Europe.

The Americans and Soviets (who had been directly attacked and supported any strategy that would hasten the end of the war) favored a direct attack on the European mainland, agreeing that two giant "pincer" movements, one from the Soviet east and another from the French west, would be the most expeditious way to crush Germany's military power. The British didn't believe that the Allies were ready for such a move. The Americans relented and agreed to attack Axis forces in northern Africa and in Italy, thereby delaying their direct assault until the third year of American involvement in the war. The "pincer" strategy was finally successful, however. After a year of combat in both the western and eastern theaters of the war in Europe, Germany surrendered.

In the Pacific, the American air and naval forces pushed back Japanese forces by successfully employing a policy of "leapfrogging" around various Japanese island conquests without bothering to conquer the islands themselves. With the aid of two atomic bombs, the Americans launched a direct attack on the main Japanese islands and induced the Japanese to surrender before the Soviets were able to enter the Pacific war.

After Germany's and Japan's unconditional surrender, the allied victors divided Germany (and Austria) into occupied zones, and General Douglas MacArthur was appointed Supreme Commander in Japan. The political leaders of Germany and Japan were tried and convicted of crimes against peace, humanity, and the established rules of war. After the war, the victors ended their occupations of Germany (as well as Austria) and Japan by 1955, except that the Soviet government, in the midst of a "cold" war with the American government, maintained the independence of their zone, the eastern zone of Germany.

History's greatest war involved 70 million combatants, 17 million military dead, 18 million civilian dead, one trillion dollars in military expenditures, and two trillion dollars in property losses. The United States' costliest war produced nearly 300,000 combat deaths and over 100,000 other fatalities, but the Americans suffered far smaller loses than any of its major allies or enemies, and American territory escaped entirely the destruction incurred on the other nations on whose territory the war was fought.

The war left the United States the strongest nation on earth militarily and economically, and the Soviet Union, despite the fact that its people suffered the heaviest losses of the war, became the greatest power on the entire Eurasian landmass. The "cold war" that followed shortly after World War II was the consequence of basically different perceptions of geopolitical reality between the governments of the United States and the Soviet Union. American policy-makers favored democracy and capitalism and the self-determination of "peoples" and believed that any words or actions that would enhance these phenomena were desirable. Accepting the reality of American power, they became committed to a policy of the "containment" of Communist-dominated states in the Soviet Union and, by the 1950s, in eastern Europe and China as well. The American government hoped that such confinement would eventually lead to the internal disintegration of the Communist "faith," with its goal of world domination. This was the globalization of Lincoln's policy of the containment of slavery within the American nation. Lincoln had also believed that, if contained, slavery would progressively alter its nature in an ongoing process of redefinition.

To "contain" the nations with Communist governments, Presidents Truman and Eisenhower and their Secretaries of State, most notably Dean Acheson and John Foster Dulles, and other policy advisers broke decisively with deeply held traditions and made the United States, commensurate with its military and economic power, the leader of the non-Communist world. The "idealistic" international impulse (which had guided Wilson during and after World War I, as well as Roosevelt in the 1930s and 1940s) found expression in the American commitment to the United Nations, founded in 1945 and housed in New York City.

The United Nations is a form of international government, with a legislature (the General Assembly), a judiciary (the affiliated, but separate International Court), and an executive (the Secretary General and the Security Council), with administrative agencies (such as the Food and Agriculture Agency, International Labor Office, World Health Organization, Education, Science, and Culture Organization). And, as a result of war-end conferences, the United States agreed with many other nations to subscribe to an International Monetary Fund and a "World Bank."

But, the "realistic" geopolitical impulse (which had influenced Theodore Roosevelt and, later, Franklin Roosevelt, in the 1930s) was also expressed, in a series of regional treaties binding the United States to the security of other groups of nations: the Organization of American States, in 1947; the North Atlantic Treaty Organization, in 1949; the South East Asian Treaty Organization, in 1954; and the Middle East Treaty Organization, in 1955. From time to time various Presidents—Truman, Eisenhower, Nixon—have issued statements, later called "Doctrines" (like Monroe's), proclaiming that it was America's intent to prevent the conquest or subversion of independent states by aggressive, usually Communist groups.

The Soviet government, by contrast, came out of World War II reaffirming its faith in a universally applicable communism as a political ideology and its commitment to its own "sphere of influence," that is, to the establishment and maintenance of a tier of friendly, subservient, Communist-led states around its periphery in order to avoid further catastrophes of the kind that had occurred when an aggressive Germany had twice invaded its territory in the first half of the twentieth century. In other terms, the government that Joseph Stalin, Nikita Khrushchev, and Leonid Brezhnev dominated as General Secretaries was responsive to the same mixture of idealistic and realistic impulses as the American government was in these same decades. The Soviet government set up the Third Comintern (or international body of Communist parties) at the same time that it formed the Warsaw Treaty Organization in 1955, consisting of the Eastern European nations with Communist governments, as a regional pact to serve as a counterpoise to the North Atlantic Treaty Organization.

The United States and the Soviet Union became known as "superpowers" and attempted in the late 1940s and the 1950s to woo the entire world into supporting their ideology and their military and diplomatic and economic leadership. The domestic effect of the "cold war" within the United States was pronounced. In ways reminiscent of what happened in the aftermath of World War I, an anti-Communist crusade gained momentum in the decade after World War II. A House Un-American Activities Committee constantly investigated alleged subversive activities within the national government, especially while Senator Joseph McCarthy was its chairman, but the committee failed to find Communist agents in the government. In 1947, President Truman issued an executive order establishing procedures for an employee loyalty oath program, and all government employees were investigated by 1955, but no spy ring was uncovered. In 1949, the leaders of the American Communist Party were convicted under an act of 1940, which outlawed conspiracies to overthrow the American government.

The Internal Security Act of 1950 (passed over President Truman's veto) made it unlawful for a group to try to establish a totalitarian dictatorship in the United States. Communist and Communist-front organizations had to register with the Attorney-General, and aliens who had belonged to totalitarian parties were barred from entering the United States. In 1953, President Eisenhower, in another executive order, broadened Truman's criteria of "disloyalty" with a new term: "security risk." Employees of the national government were dismissed because of dubious associations or personal habits that might make them careless or vulnerable to blackmail. When Senator McCarthy was censured by the Senate in 1954 for his conduct, the anti-Communist crusade lost its momentum.

By the 1950s, it also became clear that the "underdeveloped" parts of the world contained nations whose political leaders sought to retain their independence from both Soviet and American influence. This "third" or "nonaligned" or neutral world was treated by the American government, in competition with the Soviet government, to a succession of military and economic assistance programs—foreign aid—whose objectives were to relieve poverty and gain the support of the governments involved in matters of diplomacy and trade.

After World War II, the American government decisively broke with tradition by not demobilizing, recognizing its new, global diplomatic and military responsibilities. The Department of Defense and the Central Intelligence Organization were created shortly after the war to reflect and make more efficient the large armed forces and intelligence-gathering services created during World War II. The Americans actively developed atomic weaponry, but the Soviets soon revealed that they too had the capability of producing the same weapons. An arms race continued apace, especially after the failure in 1946 of a fearful and suspicious Soviet government to agree to the plan introduced by the United States, then with monopolistic control, to internationalize the control of atomic energy through the United Nations Atomic Energy Commission.

But, only once did nuclear weaponry itself become the basis of a diplomatic crisis between the American and Soviet governments. In 1962, the Kennedy administration insisted that Soviet leader Khrushchev remove Soviet missiles from Cuba, and Khrushchev did so, rather than risk a nuclear confrontation.

The combination of mounting public pressure exerted by various peace and disarmament groups with a growing awareness that both superpowers had nuclear arsenals of globe-threatening dimensions created an atmosphere conducive to arms reduction negotiations. In 1963, President Kennedy and Soviet leader Khrushchev agreed upon a Test Ban Treaty, barring atmospheric testing of nuclear weapons. In 1972, President Nixon negotiated a Strategic Arms Limitation Treaty with the Soviet government, an agreement that began to limit the arms buildup by setting limits on the number of various kinds of nuclear weapons that the two governments would maintain.

After 1985, the Soviet political and economic system rather suddenly unraveled under General Secretary Mikhail Gorbachev's leadership. Domestically, the political structures developed by Lenin and Stalin disintegrated. By 1991, the monopolistic power of the Communist Party was shattered and the party temporarily outlawed. The central government was soon thereafter eliminated as the Commonwealth of Independent States became an umbrella organization among sovereign republics, whose political leaders, in varying degrees, are committed to the creation of democratic political states and capitalistic, "market" economies.

Internationally, the Soviet government ended its hegemonic control over Eastern European Communist-led states, and, in 1989 and 1990, the Communist governments of the area quickly collapsed, replaced by governments that, in varying degrees, are similarly committed to democracy and capitalistic, market economies. The Soviet government, under Gorbachev's leadership, also entered into several nuclear and conventional arms reduction agreement with the Reagan and Bush administrations, in an effort to reduce the cost of defense and, as the republics assumed authority, also reduce the risk of nuclear war as a result of political chaos.

From the American perspective, these developments—the effort to democratize and privatize the Soviet Union and to disband Soviet control over an international Communist movement—constitute an admission by both the Soviet leadership and people that communism, in the deepest sense, had failed to provide them with the kind of life they wanted. By contrast, the American policy of containment was a resounding success (in sharp distinction to Lincoln's earlier effort to contain slavery within the United States).

During these decades, American policy developed in more specific ways in response to more specific circumstances in the various geopolitical regions of the world. In Europe, the United States, British, and French governments allowed the occupation zones of Germany to be amalgamated into a Federal Republic of Germany modeled after the American political system, whereas the Soviet zone was turned into the German Democratic Republic with a Communist government. The Americans decided to aid the economic recovery of a war-ravaged Europe through an assistance program—the European Recovery Program—in which grants were offered to all European governments (the Soviets and the Communist-led states of Eastern Europe refused to participate). In 1949, the North Atlantic Treaty Organization bound the leading non-Communist states into a military alliance with the United States. By the 1950s, the economic infrastructure of western and central Europe had largely been rebuilt. Economic assistance and a military alliance brought to these parts of Europe the kind of prosperity and stability that American policymakers sought.

The European Common Market was created and has progressively integrated the economies of member states in the years since. A European Parliament was also formed, but political integration has thus far lagged behind economic. Since World War II, the U.S. government has had to deal with an increasingly unified western and central Europe.

As for Eastern Europe, the United States government did nothing to stop the Communist parties that emerged under Soviet military protection from assuming control of the national governments of that area after World War II. Though President Eisenhower's Secretary of State Dulles issued statements supporting "liberation movements" in the Communist part of Europe, American policy remained basically unaltered until the end of Soviet Communist military and diplomatic control of the area in 1989. Since then, the United States has provided economic aid as the newly democratized governments in the region try to supervise a shift to a capitalistic, market economy.

In Asia, the Americans replaced the British, the French, and the Dutch as the leading non-Communist power, but refused until 1979 to recognize the Communist government of China, after the Communists had defeated the American-backed Nationalists in 1949. The United States tried to contain Communist influence by participating in two Asian wars on the continent's periphery, in Korea and in Vietnam. When Communist movements in those two nations threatened to dominate by military conquest, the Americans intervened to assist those who opposed the Communists. But, American intervention was limited in nature. American policymakers were determined that such Communist movements had to be defeated without risking a major war with the Communist superpowers, the Soviet Union and China.

In Korea, this policy led to a military stalemate and a divided nation. In Vietnam, it resulted in a Communist takeover and an American defeat. The great popular revulsion toward the second Asian war in Vietnam meant that no American administration after 1975 acted to contain Communist movements elsewhere in the world through the use of American combat troops. Recent Chinese Communist efforts to include private economic activity in a carefully controlled setting, while steadfastly opposing any political democratization, have brought American East Asian policy into a period of flux.

In southwestern Asia, where the Americans also assumed the position of being the leading Western power, a position inherited from the British, the U.S. policy has been to maintain regional peace and stability, to serve as a moderating influence midst ongoing Jewish-Arab enmity, and to protect the leading outside source of energy and power for American industrial uses (oil).

In South and Middle America, the United States, while supporting the Organization of American States, has on several occasions violated the spirit of the treaty of 1947 by unilaterally intervening in the internal affairs of island nations or by covertly aiding anti-Communist or anti-Socialist elements who have fought against their governments. American Presidents have—throughout these decades—continued to perceive South and Middle America as lying within the American sphere of influence, even though the United States is officially committed to noninterference. When the Soviet government introduced missiles into Cuba (the only nation in the Western Hemisphere at that time with a Communist government), President Kennedy reacted on the assumption that this was an unacceptable incursion into the American "sphere" and forced General Secretary Khrushchev to retreat. Kennedy's Alliance for Progress was a later-day European Recovery Program for the Western Hemisphere, but the poverty and overall lack of economic development in Latin America doomed this effort.

In Africa, the collapse of European colonialism and the emergence of the Organization of African Unity during the 1960s and 1970s led the United States to recognize a newly politically independent continent. Its policy during the Cold War years was to counter Soviet foreign aid with American foreign aid and to oppose Communist insurgency movements wherever they developed.

* * *

Around the globe, the Cold War, an age of two superpowers, has given way since 1991 to an ill-formed new age of regional political organizations (such as the European Political Union, the Organization of American States, and the Organization of African Unity), regional military or economic alliances (such as NATO), and international organizations (such as the United Nations, the International Monetary Fund, the World Bank, and the World Trade Organization). From an American perspective, the Soviet-led Communist enemy is gone and has not been replaced by any other political antagonist with a global reach. Political crises in the 1990s have been local, and the United States' role uncertain. Elsewhere, national governments have been contested from within when politically vulnerable by resurgent provincial (or state) governments wanting more authority or by ethnic separation movements or by terrorist activities, and impinged on from without when in economic crisis by austerity programs dictated by the International Monetary Fund or the World Bank.

There is a reservoir of hostility toward Westerners among those who live in all the other great civilizations of the world, all of which came to be dominated either politically or economically by the West. This hostility has assumed its most pronounced form in the Islamic world, long the major antagonist of Western supremacy. Such enmity could lead to conflict along the "fault lines" between the other civilizations and the West. But, since the whole globe has become so subjected to such varied influences, so interpenetrated with ways of living whose origins lie in many parts of the globe, what works against major intercivilizational conflict is the patch-quilt pattern of life now exhibited all over the world.

It is not clear whether the nation-state system itself is in danger of being undermined, on one side, by organizations of a international scope that exercise significant power and thus diminish the sovereignty and authority of national governments, and, on another side, by a process of the devolution of power to smaller political units—states or provinces—or to national polities shrunken by ethnic or racial territorial divisions, and, on yet another side, by the growth of regional polities that emerge from continental associations of an economic or military kind. If any one of these developments becomes significant, the United States, as the world's last superpower, could become a bastion of national sovereignty in a world increasingly marked by the undermining of such authority.

PART II

AN AMERICAN GEOGRAPHY AND ECONOMY

Political entities have never fitted geographical areas very well. It is very rare for well-demarcated political borders to neatly encompass a particular geographical formation, be it river watersheds, mountain ranges, plateaus, coastal areas, lake districts, deserts, forests, or grasslands. Certainly this has been true of those white Europeans who have settled on the territory of what became the United States, where Americans have shared the Great Lakes, Plains, and Rockies with Canadians and various deserts and mountain ranges with the Mexicans. Only to the east and to the west have Americans been able to claim the natural oceanic borders of the Atlantic and Pacific.

The Americans established a nation that spanned a continent in an astonishingly short period of time. An eastern seaboard colonial empire, from Maine to Georgia, all east of the Appalachian Mountains, suddenly became a continental nation, assuming its current continental borders in the 50-year period between 1803 and 1853. Within these boundaries are contained all of the major kinds of land formations of the earth, except for the arctic and the tropical. Vast midlatitude forest lands cover the entire eastern half of the continent and much of the Pacific Coast. The western half of North America is much more varied. It includes deserts, grasslands, and huge mountain ranges.

The native North America tribes had lived for many centuries on all of North America's topographical areas. It is revealing that much of Northern Europe—the area that includes Britain, the Netherlands, most of France and Germany, and some of Scandinavia—is also midlatitude forest lands. All of the white settler societies founded by mass infusions of white European immigrants were located in this particular kind of geographical area: South Africa, British North America, Australia, and New Zealand—all contained such forest lands. Only the Portuguese and Spaniards, whose homelands had a special Mediterranean landscape, ventured into areas quite unlike what they left behind, and it was they who failed to generate the kind of mass migrations that the English, French, and Dutch succeeded in varying degrees to produce.

All of the white settler societies that became continental in scope—Russia, the United States, Canada, Australia, and South Africa—also shared continental settings that included grasslands, deserts, and mountain ranges, as well as midlatitude forest lands. The settlers in each of these societies also had to deal with the geographical consequences of these varied settings. All had "wests" or "easts," that is, frontier areas whose settlement involved coping with topographies significantly different from the European heartland's.

The black African slaves came as forced migrants from tropical and grassland settings to forested lands. Later Oriental immigrants from China came from the only other area of the earth covered so extensively with midlatitude forested land, though they tended to settle from the western to the eastern parts of North America and thus, at least initially, came to a quite different geographical setting. Later white European immigrants from southern, though not eastern, Europe came from a Mediterranean area and thus, except for those who went to the West Coast, also settled in a substantially new topography. Thus, among the various groups of migrants who have come together in the United States, the dominant northern Europeans flocked to a geographical zone much like the one they left behind, whereas other migrants typically confronted quite different settings.

From the perspective of climatic zones a somewhat different picture emerges. The eastern half of the United States is humid, that is, has precipitation year-round, but divides between continental (with either warm or cool summers) and subtropical (with hot summers) areas, roughly along the lines created by the Potomac, Ohio, and Missouri River systems. Northern Europeans came from a marine west zone (with balmy summers and mild winters) and could easily adjust to the northern continental zone, though winters were colder and summers were hotter than in Europe. But, settlement in the subtropical zone was more difficult because of the very hot summers. The black African slaves, from a tropical climate, could more easily adjust to semitropical weather. The southern English colonists and, later, southern Americans have had the kind of climate that prevailed in northern Argentina and southern Brazil and southern and central China and southern Japan. But, whereas the Spanish and Portuguese settlers moved to a semitropical climate that wasn't a lot different from the Mediterranean climate of southern Europe, the southerner English colonists and, later, Americans represent the largest group of European migrants who have settled in a climatic zone significantly different from the one they left behind in Europe.

The climatic area of the United States most like northern Europe was the marine West Coast climate of the Pacific Northwest, and most like southern Europe was the Mediterranean climate of parts of California. But white European settlement started to the east and (in the case of the Spanish and Portuguese settlers, to the south) of these areas. Most Europeans did not settle in the climactic zone they left behind: relatively few southern Europeans—the Italians and the Greeks—settled in the Mediterranean areas of the Pacific Coast; similarly, there weren't many northern Europeans who headed for the Pacific Northwest, even when it became known to white migrants.

Neither geography nor climate determined what the various groups who have identified themselves as Americans did with the land they settled on. The polities, societies, economies, and cultures that various human groups have developed in the various geographical and climatic zones of the earth have been bewilderingly varied; there have certainly not been particular types of societies to match particular kinds of geographical and climatic settings. This can be seen with special clarity in the contrasting attitudes that the native North American tribes and the European migrants had toward nature and the use of the land they occupied.

The prevailing attitude among the English colonists and their white American successors was to be dominant over nature, to use and improve the land, to amass wealth from it. In this, Americans have been energetic Europeans, applying with particular force a work ethic with a religious sanction behind it. In their effort to gain wealth from the land, Americans have gouged, scarred, and polluted their landscape, but they have also been in awe of whatever wilderness has remained, have seen it as sublime, as evidence of God's presence, and have created nature parks in order to preserve it. In their schizophrenic attitude toward nature, white Americans have gone from one extreme to another. As preservers of nature, they have been more radical than the native tribes, who tried to exist in nature, leaving traces of their living on it, but never drastically altering it, always respectful of it.

Though Americans have thought that there is an "American geography," there are no geographical land formations or climatic zones that have been encased within U.S. borders. Americans have shared their geography with other politically defined groups to the north and to the south, and, in this, they are like most politically defined groups in the world.

* * *

Since ancient times, economic life has consisted of an overlay of barter and market economies, at least in mature traditional societies. By contrast, the original tribal societies of African slaves and North American natives contained simple barter arrangements. Europeans after 1500 were traditional in the sense that they shared with various Asian and North African societies a vigorous market economy that coexisted with barter activity. What was new in Europe, and to a much lesser extent in parts of Asia as well, was capitalism.

Capitalism involved the accumulation of wealth to the extent that its possessors could make choices as to which large-scale enterprises, if invested in, could produce large-scale profit. Europe became the center of capitalism after 1500 because it contained a society whose political and economic elites encouraged capitalistic activity. In mature Asian societies, there were traces of capitalistic endeavors, but, by contrast, states there usually discouraged such enterprise. From its inception, capitalism has exhibited contradictory manifestations: it has been both national and worldwide, both private and state-based, both competitive and monopolistic. Governments have from the beginning played a role in the development of the capitalist economy, aiding and protecting it, regulating it, both enhancing and limiting its effects on society.

Unlike feudalistic and communistic arrangements, capitalism has typically separated the private management and ownership of the economy from its public regulation. The capitalists and the politicians have usually been distinct groups; private and public power has been separate. However, there have been overlappings in the membership of the two groups, who have usually shared a common perception of what a well-functioning capitalist-dominated economy consists of.

European capitalism has constituted a world system, that is, a complete, self-contained unit of economic activity. Europe's capitalistic world system has been mightily expansionist, with a European center and a growing periphery, first in the Americas and then in Asia and Africa, wherever Europeans sought to dominate others. Capitalism developed slowly until the nineteenth century, and it flourished only where a certain combination of factors existed: access to materials that could be produced and traded on a large scale, good transportation and communications networks, the presence of governments that protected private property and could offer tariffs and military security in the face of both political and economic competition from others, and the existence of individuals or groups who were willing to risk capital on new kinds of investment. Capitalism has had several, overlapping phases of development, and it has relatively slowly, but steadily evolved since the sixteenth century.

The first area of economic activity suffused with capitalistic endeavor was long-distance trade, which met the criteria for something that was of a large-scale both in its volume and in the margin of profit that could accrue to the merchants involved. Merchants found materials for both elite and ordinary customers in a Europe whose population overall was becoming increasingly involved in a market economy. The commercialization of agriculture and trade produced workers with the capacity to buy and sell goods and services with money.

The English colonists replicated Europe's economy by becoming engaged in both barter and market activity—and capitalism. Coastal merchants in the colonies copied mercantile endeavors in Europe, shipping raw materials to European markets. Colonial merchants had a place on the periphery of a larger European-centered mercantile capitalist world. The European merchants, with their colonial counterparts, established corridors of trade involving coastal cities and huge hinterlands in their colonies in the Americas during the seventeenth and eighteenth centuries.

When England and then other parts of Europe became industrialized, when goods were produced on machines by wage labor, capitalism added an industrial orientation, with mass-produced products sold to customers in the very areas that had become industrialized. There was a long prelude to industrialization in the areas where it first appeared. "Protoindustrialization" involved several kinds of activity: significant concentrations of craft laborers who together manufactured large and complicated products for one owner in one building; merchants capitalists who developed a "putting out" system, making use of the home labor of many craftsmen and farmers, selling what they produced in much wider markets; milling activity with water-power-driven mechanisms that mass-produced certain goods. What was fundamentally different about industrialization itself was that, wherever it flourished, it undermined earlier, feudalistic forms of economic and social life, creating in its place a new kind of "modern" economy and society. By contrast, merchant capitalism and protoindustrialization existed within what continued to be a basically feudal society.

Wherever industrialization developed, it produced an explosion of occupations and workers with money to buy and sell goods and services. This new occupational structure and the accompanying preoccupation with commodities, consumption, and money became the bases for modern societies. Similarly, machine production, wage labor, and a vast growth in productivity and economic specialization characterized a new economy. Industrialization was a fairly easy process to copy by those in areas where circumstances were favorable to its growth, areas where capitalism had already developed. Britain's early primacy could not last, but was sustained for a considerable time by that kingdom's preeminence in trade and empire. Wherever it flourished, industrialization initially favored the owners and managers of industrial firms who could hire laborers from a large pool and who benefited from a legal system that was hostile toward combinations of workers. Industrial workers in turn benefited from a notable regularity of income, but were dependent upon owners for work. Everyone benefited from the huge expansion of products at affordable prices.

From the outset, though, industrial capitalism was contested by those threatened by the changes it produced: agrarian interests, artisans and craftsmen, the Catholic Church, traditionalists, utopian socialists, populists. Over time, labor union movements have developed and governments everywhere have consciously intervened in the workings of the industrial capitalist system, to control and limit the operation of the market in order to establish tolerable working conditions for the mass of the population. Governments have tried to deal with some of the problems that industrialization has created: its threat to the environment, its reckless consumption of nonrenewable resources, its pollution. Other problems have been beyond the reach of governments: the system's overwhelming focus on material values and its placement of the majority of people in uninteresting work.

Americans copied the Europeans, developing industrial capitalism as well, extending the European capitalistic center to the American frontier periphery, the first such extension. As European expansion continued in Asia and Africa during the nineteenth century, capitalists developed further corridors of trade for materials wanted in the industrialized world through the creation of a succession of port cities with linked hinterlands. As had been the case in North and South and Middle America, so later in Asia, and in Africa—everywhere the pattern was the same. Similarly, the American South and West provided materials needed in the urban and industrialized portions of the Northeast and Midwest and Pacific Coast. As industrialized America spread southward and westward through the twentieth century, the heartland of European- and now North American–centered capitalism was thereby enlarged.

The United States thus moved from the periphery to the center of the European capitalist world system. From its inception, this system plunged beyond political boundaries. It has never been contained within them, has never found political expression in an empire. Its expansion is partially attributable to its capacity to vault outside of any given political jurisdiction, to deal with various governments for various advantages. As a system, it has coexisted with European-style governments, societies, and cultures, in a symbiotic relationship at once congenial to and competitive with these other elements of European civilization.

It is important to emphasize that capitalistic endeavors continued to coexist with barter and market activities throughout the seventeenth, eighteenth, and nineteenth centuries. Until the twentieth century, the more localized forms of the barter and market economies were more widespread and certainly involved far more people than capitalistic enterprise, especially in the tribal and traditional areas of the globe where nomads and peasants continued to engage in pastoral and agricultural activity. And, even where capitalism got established and created large-scale mercantile, industrial, and financial enterprises, it must be remembered that such activities coexisted with multitudes of small-scale local and regional firms still operating within the context of a small-scale market economy.

Americans have always been part of both smaller and larger economic worlds, and American economic activities are most meaningfully observed from those smaller and larger perspectives. There has never been an American national economy as such. There has been economic activity that has been intensely local or at most regional in scope—or international in scale. The national corporations that emerged in the late nineteenth century developed continental markets, but were rarely confined for very long solely to the United States in the sale of their products.

As the federal and state governments extended their regulation of economic activity—through tariff duties, incorporation laws, the monetary system, fiscal policy, subsidies, regulations of many kinds—a governmentally regulated economy emerged in America during the course of the late nineteenth and the twentieth centuries. But that did not mean that the economic activity that occurred within American national borders was different in kind from what occurred in other jurisdictions in the Europeanized world.

Even among the white settler societies, American economic life was not unique. The Americans, as the most populous of those societies, were the first to move toward modern, capitalistic, industrialized economic activity, but British North America was not far behind. Australia, New Zealand, and South Africa moved out of a phase of being corridors of raw material supplies for capitalistic, industrialized zones elsewhere to one of a self-sustaining industrialization of their own by the late nineteenth century.

Finally, northern Argentina and southern Brazil led the way for South America by the early twentieth century.

So, though Americans have identified with an "American" economy that has been coexistent with the territory of the United States, in fact economic activity within the United States has been basically the same as activity within the European economic world system. The "American economy" is a fiction—a powerful one, created by Americans to match their nation and thereby to extend American-ness beyond its natural political dimension. That this creation didn't match reality attests to the power of a politically based sense of national identity.

19

The Environment

The native population of Eastern North America that the Dutch, French, and English dealt with tried to live in harmony with nature, which was filled with spirits that had to be honored and appeased.

Native Americans as agriculturists slashed and burned trees, thus reducing the nutrients in the soil and hastening the need to move on to fresh land. In this way they cleared fields for farming, which featured light plowing and the hilling and mixing of various kinds of crops whose nutritional value was thereby enhanced. The land was little altered by these practices. Animals fed on the shrubbery that grew around the cleared fields. The natives moved away when a field started to diminish in fertility. Over time, the forest was allowed to grow back.

Similarly, native crafts did not involve metal, as the native population had not developed the capacity to mine and purify ores, and thus did not alter the earth's surface in areas where there were minerals. Even their houses and transport—bark tepees or communal longhouses and canoes—did not affect the natural setting beyond the stripping of certain kinds of trees.

By contrast, the predominant attitude of the English colonist and their white American successors toward the natural world was a religiously sanctioned view that human beings should dominate the earth and the plants and the animals on it, by working hard, soberly, industriously, dependably, reliably, and continuously. From the beginning of white settlement, land was not only a necessary source for sustenance and the basis for the primary occupation of most of the population, but it was also a commodity that was bought and sold for its speculative value.

The English colonist deep-ploughed permanent cleared fields, fenced in other fields as permanent pasture for livestock, failed to rotate either crops or grazing fields in any systematic way, and consumed vast quantities of timber for their houses and as fuel—all of which led to soil erosion and depletion and the steady abandonment of agricultural land along the Atlantic coast and the movement of settlers westward. Colonial mining operations, iron foundries, and limestone kilns all further scarred the landscape. In their haste to gain dominion over nature and to accumulate wealth and status, the English colonist altered the environment in a way that stood in sharp contrast to the relationship of the native American population to the natural setting of the North American continent.

Soil erosion and depletion continued during the nineteenth century as settlement moved westward across the continent. But, by the 1860s, agricultural experimental stations (sponsored by the national government) advised farmers on crop rotation, which had already received scientific study—especially in England—and was thereafter practiced by increasing numbers of farmers who became informed on ways to avoid the wearing out of their soil. By the late nineteenth century, there was no longer any need for farmers to abandon their acreage for this reason, at least. However, mining and forestry operations still involved considerable scarring of the landscape, and pollution of the atmosphere occurred as steel foundries burned off impurities. When coal became a fuel for steam and electrical production, it too polluted the atmosphere as it provided the heat to generate the compression to turn the wheels of trains or activated the turbines that produced electric power.

Americans have also developed systems of water control that have altered their environment. Applying increasingly sophisticated dam technology to their waterways, the English colonist and the Americans, from the seventeenth century onward, have dammed rivers and lakes to produce waterpower for milling operations and early factories, to provide energy for the creation of hydroelectric power, and, in the semiarid areas of the western half of the continent, in the dry plains, and in the Pacific coastal valleys—to create a source for irrigating croplands and for augmenting municipal water systems. The consequence of all these efforts has been to alter the landscape and, in the case of the semiarid western half of the continent, to lower the water table significantly.

Since the late nineteenth century, a fast-growing chemical industry has produced synthetic materials of many kinds, some of which (such as plastics) are not biodegradable, others of which (such as fertilizers) have added pollutants to the soil and water. More sophisticated industrial processes (such as the refinement of materials through intense heat) have produced pollutants that have befouled the air and water and plants of many kinds. The gas-fueled internal combustion engine in motor vehicles, as well as coal-fueled hydroelectric plants, have polluted the air.

By the 1970s, the full impact of modern industrial processes on the environment was beginning to be perceived by both the scientific community and the general public. The entire industrialization of the economy, the mechanization of production, the generation of power based upon oil and coal and nuclear energy, the creation of certain manmade chemical products—all together had by then the cumulative effect of distorting the ecobalance; that is, the relationship of human activity with its natural setting had been upset. The cyclical nature of natural processes within the earth's ecosystem has been threatened by the very human activity that Americans had long valued as among life's highest aims: collectively to develop the earth's resources for human use and, individually, to accumulate wealth (and therefore status) and comfort.

Pollution has been a long-term, deep-rooted problem that Americans share with others in the advanced industrial areas of the world. It has become abundantly clear that one of the greatest consequences of industrialization has been the pollution of the environment as a result of a number of industrial processes and synthetically made products and chemicals. The pollution of the air, soil, and water and their illness-causing effects on the humans and animals and plants that live around them can now be seen as a major result of the industrialization of the globe, especially the industrialization since the 1920s and 1930s, when synthetic materials and chemicals were created and when the large scale use of fuel-burning vehicles and hydroelectric and mining and metal plants was initiated. Those who live in industrialized economies have disrupted the ecosystems of the earth and caused illness among themselves.

The U.S. government's Environmental Protection Agency (created by executive order in the early 1970s) and its antipollution legislation have caused industrial operations to be somewhat less harmful to the environment. Crop rotation, reforestation, and mine-site redevelopment have become standard practices, and pollution emissions have been legislatively restricted, but the pollution of the environment has continued at a rapid rate, and many of its effects are still unknown. The American and Soviet governments—and, to a much lesser extent, other governments as well—produced nuclear weaponry that, if used, would threaten the continued existence of the ecosystem of the planet. The Americans and others throughout the industrialized parts of the world have also created peaceful economic processes and products that pollute and thus threaten that same ecosystem. In these ways, the political and economic activities of the Americans have become meshed—perhaps fatefully—with those of others around the globe.

* * *

These ways of utilizing the natural resources for the enhancement of wealth, the movement of people and products, and the mechanical production of commodities—all without regard for the ecological consequences—triggered a "conservation" movement whose advocates began to argue by the late nineteenth century that the natural resources of the continent (and the animals that exist within them) must be preserved and protected as well as used for the economic betterment of the human beings who call themselves Americans. Originating with naturalists and scientists and trained government officials, the conservation movement was concerned about the inefficiency and waste of America's natural resources.

Conservationist focused on the need to protect wilderness areas, parts of the American landscape unaltered by human development. The favorable attitude toward the wilderness that conservationists exhibited involved a major shift in human perception. Since the dawn of civilization humans everywhere had been fearful of the wilderness, a fear rooted in human psychology and in a deeply felt need to control the environment. The wilderness was equated with the unknown, the disordered, the uncontrolled and was filled with negative connotations. In prehistoric times, humans tried to move onto open environments. Thereafter, the dark, forested wilderness evoked for them a fear of wild animals and unknown sources of fright.

An appreciation of the wilderness is, therefore, a quite recent phenomenon. Small groups of late-eighteenth-century deists and nineteenth-century romantics and nationalists extolled the wilderness in America as the unsurpassed example of God's creation of a natural world unaltered by human life. By the late nineteenth century, naturalists such as John Muir established a cult of the wilderness, the popularity of which was made manifest in the founding of associations such as the Sierra Club and the Wilderness Society. Beginning in the 1880s, the first national parks system in the world developed with the setting aside as wilderness areas of designated parts of the public lands. The conservation movement created, in effect, an "American Commons," a patch quilt of public land parcels and other governmental properties that by the late twentieth century included 40 percent of all U.S. land!

Gifford Pinchot, appointed by President Theodore Roosevelt as Chief Forester of the Forestry Service, became the early champion of restricting public lands from commercial use, though the conservation movement split between those who wanted to preserve public land for continuous, though noncommercial, public use (like Pinchot) and those who wanted public land permanently set aside as wilderness areas. By the 1950s and 1960s, preservationists pressured the national government to enact the Wilderness Act (1964), which established a wilderness system. The conservation movement took on a popular dimension by the 1960s and 1970s, when those in what became known as the "counterculture" turned away from many aspects of their society and showed an appreciation of wilderness settings.

During the 1910s and 1920s, the science of ecology emerged with Alex Leopold as its most effective spokesman. As a U.S. forester and wildlife scientist, Leopold developed the single most important idea about land since the creation of private property, much more important than the creation of an "American Commons" had been. Leopold proposed that there be a "land ethic," that is, the conviction that we belong to the land as much as it belongs to us. The land is part of "our" community. The prosperity and health of the land is as important as the prosperity and health of the human community. Land is more than a storehouse of economic resources. It is an interconnected, interdependent community of living organisms on which human survival depends. The great danger to the relationship between humans and their environment is that human activity might lead to ecological degradation.

During the 1970s, the "environment" replaced the "wilderness" as the prime concern of those who sought to preserve nature. David Brower became the best-known figure of the environmentalist movement, but, unlike the earlier conservationists, environmentalists became a mass crusade during the 1970s. This second movement was concerned, not with inefficiency and waste, but with the quality of natural resources, with the ecological effects of pollutants. The focus of the environmentalists was on the ecology and the need for balance between human activity and the natural world that surrounds it. In this context, wilderness protected the diversity of ecosystems by existing outside the conformities of human civilizations. Wilderness and civilization benefited from each other.

Ironically, wilderness has become so popular with civilized people that they threaten to overrun it. Both uncontrolled recreational activities and economic development threaten the existence of wilderness areas. Recently, a debate has flourished between those who argue that wilderness is for people (the anthropocentric view) and those who argue that wilderness is for the good of nature (the biocentric view). From an international perspective, nations that have wilderness do not want it, while nations that want wilderness do not have it. Wilderness enthusiasts in developed parts of the world subsidize actual wilderness areas in undeveloped parts of the world. Well-off wilderness enthusiasts travel to see wilderness elsewhere, away from urban centers.

* * *

One view of nature that has prevailed among white Americans since the eighteenth century is that the natural world has an order and a structure that encompass the earth's human population. The universe is governed by natural laws, and humanity's earthly environment reflects that fact, with its seasonal cycles and its climatic and topographical continuities. During the eighteenth and nineteenth centuries, naturalists—amateur scientists—tried to describe and, by describing, to understand the natural world. But, they were also struck by its boundless mystery and its infinite grandeur, an entity vastly greater than anything human, evoking wonder, but also demanding respect and care. Professionalized scientific inquiry was also based upon a presumption that there were natural laws that governed all aspects of the natural world. Physics and chemistry and biology and geology—all of the sciences that took on a separate existence during the eighteenth and nineteenth centuries—probed a deterministic, rule-bound natural world. Reflective American nationalists thought that even nature was distinctive in America. Just as nature was complete, eternal, and perfectly ordered, so too could human nature perfect itself in America's "Garden of Eden." America would provide the world with a model society.

This view of nature has been progressively undermined by three developments that have had an increasingly telling impact on the way humans behave toward the natural world: the belief that humanity should dominate the natural world, the rapid growth of specialization in the ways humans interact with their natural environment, and the emergence of scientific indeterminancy, that is, the growing belief among scientists—physicists, chemists, biologists alike—that reality is chaotic, not determined.

The benign view of nature referred to above coexisted with another view, expressed in both religious and secular language, that humans are the lords of existence and should dominate their settings—all the plants and animals, all the land and water and air. Ordinary Americans usually believed that God's laws gave order and structure to their natural environment, but they also believed that the earth and its ingredients existed for their comfort and their wealth-garnering enterprises. In their agricultural, extractive, and industrial activities, Americans, like other westerners, altered, gouged, and polluted the earth.

In the process they became increasingly specialized. Even general-purpose "agrosystems" are ecosystems reorganized for agricultural purposes and are thus truncated versions of original natural systems, rearrangements of natural processes. And when agriculturists specialize and produce particular crops for commercial purposes, still further are they removed from a holistic connection to nature. The land becomes a commodity, a basis for creating wealth for producers who no longer have a vital concern about the place of their specialized activity in the context of a vastly larger and infinitely more complex world. Extractive and industrial activity has only heightened this process of specialization, with human artifices greatly enhancing our power over the natural world. Technology has made specialization immeasurably more sophisticated. In short, industrial capitalism has on the practical economic level reinforced the idea that humans must dominate nature, that natural resources exist for human consumption.

Industrialized society, of which America has become a leading part, seeks a disequilibrium between human economic enterprise and the natural world. In those areas of the world dominated by industrial capitalism, innovation, change, and adjustment have become the norm. Through the eighteenth and nineteenth centuries, these effects of industrialization were contrary to prevailing scientific views of nature, which stressed order and stability. But, in the twentieth century, this lack of synchronization has become increasingly less pronounced as first one and then another of the sciences has become less deterministic and more open to a chaotic natural universe revealed by increasingly sophisticated instruments that take human observation far beyond what human senses can reveal. Whether in physics, chemistry, or biology, a chaotic reality lurks beneath a seemingly ordered universe. An "undetermined" nature is far more congenial to human economic domination of the natural world than the older, deterministic view of nature had allowed for.

As late as the 1960s and the 1970s, practitioners of the new science of ecology still perceived equilibrium and balance in ecosystems, but since the 1980s, this view has been challenged by those ecologists who have embraced chaos theory. If the universe itself is undetermined, is in flux and constantly changing, then what humans do to nature can also be creative and probing and altering. The future is open, for both nature and humanity. There is also evidence of a harmonious relationship between industry and the ecology in the growing corporate and political support for the notion of "sustainable development," that is, the assertion that industrial capitalism can flourish in an environmentally friendly way. But, the rhetoric of sustainable development has run ahead of the reality of continued industrial and agricultural and extractive pollution. The test of corporate friendliness toward the maintenance of environmental quality comes whenever profitability is adversely affected by particular industrial practices.

20

Territory

There are no records of the exact boundaries of the hunting and fishing territories of the native North American tribes, but tribal peace depended on their having a common understanding of the shape of such territories. The English, from the their discovery of lands in the Americas to the royal sponsorship of colonization, made large, continentwide land claims in North America, claims that individual colonial governments were quick to assume. It was these overlapping land claims that led certain states to withhold their approval of the first "American" constitution, drafted during the Revolutionary War.

Even with surveying, disputed land claims besmirched the record of the young American government after political independence had been gained. The Spaniards claimed land in the southwest after the revolution; the state of Maine's border was in dispute between British North America and the United States in the early 1840s; the newly admitted state of Texas' disputed border with Mexico was the immediate cause for the war declaration with Mexico in 1846. As has been typical of all but island polities, America's national boundaries were drawn without geographical coherence: to the North, from the Atlantic Coast, dividing the Saint John River watershed, across the top of Lake Champlain, across the middle of the Great Lakes, across both the Plains and the Rockies at the 49th parallel, to the Pacific Coast; to the South, across mountains and deserts as the continent narrowed into Mexico, and across the middle of the Rio Grande River.

Similarly, subnational political territories—those of the states, the counties, and the municipalities—were defined without reference to the contours of geographical areas. The boundaries of towns and cities and counties have changed over time, either through annexation (in the case of municipalities) or through division (in the case of counties). By contrast, the original states as well as all of those added to the union through the admission process have all steadfastly maintained their geographically idiosyncratic boundaries, with the lone exception of Virginia, which divided during the Civil War.

As the English Atlantic seaboard colonies became the continental United States in the seven decades following political independence, Americans lived among all the major types of geographical areas on the earth, except for tropical and arctic settings. With the admission of Alaska and Hawaii in 1958, it added those two kinds of topography as well.

But, most of the land in the Americas originally claimed by the Portuguese, Spaniards, Dutch, French, and English was not situated in moderate, European-like climatic zones. Most of the land lay in semitropical and tropical climates, areas not naturally appealing to transplanted Europeans. In these areas, the white Europeans who settled developed a society that differed sharply from the one that emerged in the temperate zone of what became British North America and then the United States.

This semitropical/tropical colonial society included the Spanish and Portuguese colonies, but also the southernmost English ones. This geographical division ran along a line that divided the English colonies into two different zones, making basic features of life in the southern English colonies the same as in the Spanish and Portuguese colonies. Geography and politics were out of synchronization in ways that profoundly affected the future of what became the United States.

21

Occupation

Many of the early English colonies gave away land as an inducement to settlement. The headright system, developed by Virginia, and copied by many of the other colonies, gave 50 acres to any man who would emigrate or arrange to have someone else emigrate under his auspices. The Puritan-dominated colonial governments of New England gave land to those who founded towns. Elsewhere in the colonies, those who founded towns often paid preexisting owners for the land platted (or surveyed) for sale to others.

After the revolution, the Land Ordinances of 1784 and 1785 prescribed the manner of surveying and selling the public land in the territory west of the Appalachians ceded by the British in the peace treaty of 1783. All land was to be surveyed in a great rectangular grid pattern throughout the Northwest Territory and sold at public auction to genuine settlers. Under the national government after 1789, a series of Public Land Acts progressively lowered the price per acre and the minimum acreage per purchase in an effort to induce settlement.

Many settlers "squatted," that is, moved onto the land ahead of surveying and sale, occupying parcels whose shape reflected the contours of the land, rather than a relentless, irrelevant grid, and established farms whose acreage reflected economic need. Congress responded with Preemption Acts during the 1840s, acts that gave squatters legal entitlement on improved lands. By 1862, the Union government responded to pressure for free public land and enacted the Homestead Act, which gave 160 acres of the remaining public domain to genuine settlers. After the Civil War, such laws as the Timber Culture Act of 1873 and the Desert Land Act of 1877 extended the provision of free land to areas where the government required settlers to grow trees or to irrigate, in the prairies and deserts.

Land policy came full circle from the time of initial white coastal settlement to the time that the nation embraced a continent: from free land to free land. National policy after the revolution tried to balance the need for a national revenue with the objective of inducing genuine settlers to inhabit and improve the land. Public land legislation failed consistently to keep up with the optimum conditions that would have produced the highest volume of settlers with the highest amount of public revenue. Congress as a legislative body was somewhat out of touch with shifting conditions on the lands it tried to sell; most of its members were from districts and states that were considerable distances from the actual land being sold. It seemed easier to package and sell land on the basis of a simple formula.

Placed in a global context, the American government's land policy was meant to favor the family farmer, the homesteader, the independent agrarian. Such a policy, if successful, would have sustained the kind of agriculture that prevailed in northern and western Europe.

Small farms were in fact typical to the north and to the east of America, where rich, arable land was spotty, and even in the forested Ohio River valley. But, policymakers could not control speculation and the desire for large landholdings that animated those who became the owners of plantations with slave labor in the broad valleys of the South or of large mechanized farms with wage laborers in the huge plains of the Midwest. In America and elsewhere on the frontiers of Europe, wherever an elite could exploit a rich resource and could best do so by establishing large estates—farms, ranches, plantations—with either slave labor or wage laborers operating either manually or with machinery, they moved swiftly to gain control of as much land as they could. Instead of a land of small farms, America became the setting for a mixture of large and small agricultural operators, of plantations amidst ordinary farmsteads, of homesteaders located near ranchers and large, commercial farmers, all of whom usually peacefully coexisted in a common effort to gain wealth, unless they were in direct conflict for the same land, as was the case with the homesteaders and ranchers on the plains. The family farm, predominant in northwestern Europe, was mixed in with large-scale enterprises in North America, where plantations and mechanized grain farms and ranches were modifications of the large landholdings of eastern, north-central, and southern Europe.

Under the influence of a generation of imperial reformers who believed that British-sponsored settlement abroad should reflect the increasingly middle-class orientation of the motherland's society, British authorities in the early and middle nineteenth century sought, like the American government, to produce in their empire the kind of farming population that American policy favored. But, in New Zealand agricultural settlers were a mix of relatively small-scale operators and large-scale sheep ranchers on "stations." In Australia, once white settlers occupied the agricultural land of the coastal areas for mixed farming, "squatters" headed for the outback, inland from the southeastern coastal area, and became, not American-style homesteaders, but "pastoralists," large-scale sheep farmers, counterparts on their "stations" of American planters on their plantations. Australian state governments (each of whom legislated land policy on its own), enacted American-style preemption acts and set up a licensing system. In South Africa, British authorities allowed the Dutch settlers who moved inland (the Trekboers) to maintain large farms with black African laborers.

In the late nineteenth century, the new Canadian government enacted homesteader legislation to attract settlers to the plains from the farmlands of central Canada or from migrants of a "preferred" or British source. But, unlike the United States with its continuous agriculturally suitable land, Canada consisted of scattered arable areas: Atlantic coastal and river valley strips, the St. Lawrence waterway, the enclosed Great Lakes peninsula (southern Ontario). The movement of agriculture westward was interrupted by the huge, infertile shield around the lakehead. As in the United States plains, so in the Canadian: government homesteader policy did not lead to an influx of small, independent family farmers, but rather to the establishment of large, mechanized farms whose owners used wage labor.

In the former Spanish empire, in South America, independent national governments drew on a different model in forging land policies. A tiny, powerful, usually white, landed elite sustained its great power in every sphere of life in the decades after independence. In monarchical Brazil, the authorities allowed a "squatter" elite (as in Australia) to gain legal title to vast tracts of land in the southern plateau inland from the coastal mountains, which became sugar and coffee plantations and cattle ranches. In decentralized Argentina, provincial governments allowed a well-established landowning elite to gain title to huge areas of the pampas, the most agriculturally fertile land on the continent. Both the Brazilian and the Argentinian governments welcomed white immigrants from southern Europe (mainly Italians), who came during the decades after 1880: in Argentina, as temporary tenant farmers who grew wheat or became laborers on the great cattle ranches that this elite developed on the pampas; or, in Brazil, as wage laborers on coffee plantations and cattle ranches.

Throughout the vast lands of the white settler societies, those of British origin in particular, government policy was to favor the continuation of small-scale agriculture, but everywhere on that frontier governments acquiesced in the desire of some to own and manage large enterprises. Governments were caught in the cross-currents of two contradictory and very basic impulses: to keep alive the tradition of the independent family farmer and to allow all to speculate on or to develop and improve land—to enhance its value, to make it productive, and to get rich and powerful in the process.

22

Settlement

At the time of contact with migrant Europeans, the native populations of North America were either nomadic hunting and fishing tribes, who did not produce settlements of any durability, or seminomadic agricultural tribes, who created seasonal villages, one for the growing season, another for cold weather, a pattern repeated until the soil became depleted and the tribe moved on to another area. Only in what became the American southwest did tribes, whose lives were marked with some of the complexity that tribal life had exhibited before the arrival of the Spanish and Portuguese in parts of Middle and South America, establish permanent settlements. This overall situation contrasted to that of the black African slaves who came from western Africa, from tribal societies where permanent villages were the norm.

Similarly, European settlers all over the Americas wanted to build permanent settlements, but many who settled in the English colonies went directly out to rich agricultural land and lived in scattered farmsteads. As long as agriculture remained the prime occupation, there was a large rural population in the colonies and, later, in the United States, a population that didn't inhabit clustered settlements of any kind. During the colonial years, settlements of all kinds provided services for the rural, farming population. Especially notable in the mid-Atlantic colonies, but present everywhere, water-powered mill sites became the heart of small mill villages where craftsmen and others served the economic, social, and cultural interests of those who lived out in the countryside. These settlements were everything from service centers at crossroads (a church, a school, a tavern, a courthouse, a store), to mill villages, to rather substantial market towns and county seats or state capitals or forts, to urban centers with large concentrations of public buildings and residential structures, providing an array of economic, social, and cultural services. In the Southern colonies, where staple crop agriculture prevailed, settlements beyond the size of crossroad hamlets were quite widely spaced.

At first, when settlement was confined during the colonial period to the Atlantic coastal area, such urban settlements were port cities, but as settlement moved inland, cities grew up where there were breaks in transportation, at lakeheads or at river mouths or bends or at the meeting point of railroad lines. As the great inland valleys became settled, Americans went on an orgy of town founding, especially in the areas to the north of where slavery and staple crop agriculture prevailed, making settlements every so many miles apart (serving a manageable "catchment" area of farmers) across a huge swath of valley and plain, establishing a large number of market towns and county seats across northern Missouri, Iowa, western Illinois, southern Wisconsin and Minnesota, and the eastern parts of Kansas, Nebraska, and the Dakotas. In the semiarid plains and in the Rocky Mountains, settlement took a very scattered form, sometimes the result of the efforts of railroad companies looking for agricultural development along their lines across the plains, sometimes the result of mineral companies seeking workers in remote mountainous mining areas. Settlements in the Pacific Coast valleys were, once again, service centers for farmers.

With the exception of (1) religious or ethnic groups who settled on their own and of (2) various levels of government who designated certain settlements to be capitals on the county, state, and national levels and who created forts and, later, military bases—with these exceptions, most settlements in America performed an economic or, more rarely, a social function: as centers for production and marketing, for professional services, for cultural or educational activity, for retirement, or as locations for various kinds of social institutions and for vacation or resort facilities.

There was nothing particularly or distinctively American about this array of settlements. Even the existence of a large rural population was something shared with others along Europe's frontiers and, indeed, within Europe itself as the peasant village gave way to rural dispersion. Nor is the herding of the population into a very limited number of urban areas unique in any sense to North America. A quickly accelerating migratory flow into urban areas as agricultural activity in rural areas sustained fewer and fewer farmers is a global phenomenon, affecting industrialized areas all over the globe. Even urban areas in the undeveloped world, wherever agriculture has ceased to absorb most of the population, have been flooded with rural migrants who have moved toward cities that don't yet have much industrial capacity.

* * *

As for the layouts of their settlements, Americans have drawn heavily upon European models. Many settlements were not planned and have involved the building of structures in a linear fashion along a roadway or around a crossroads or irregularly around a mill or, later, an industrial facility. There have been many hamlets in agricultural and mining or forestry or fishing areas that also exhibit this lack of overall design. Even settlements that grew into cities sometimes had a helter-skelter layout (for example, Boston), reminiscent of the market-or bazaar-centered medieval cities of Europe and of the Islamic and southern Asian worlds.

But, many American settlements have been planned, designed from their origins, and in this endeavor Americans have drawn heavily on European models. The most basic plan has always been the grid, the rectangle, usually with some sort of central square: settlements from the Atlantic Coast to the Pacific Coast have featured this simple design (Philadelphia was a notable early model). The Spaniards decreed that all of their colonists' town foundings should proceed according to a carefully prescribed plan—featuring the grid and a square—and most of the settlements annexed to American territory were quite faithful copies of the original sixteenth-century prescription. By contrast, the French, some of whose settlements were also later incorporated into American territory, favored a linear pattern of one main street with structures situated along it, a planned version of what could be simple happenstance in a unplanned settlement. But, Americans have also imported more sophisticated ideas in the planning and design of settlements, particularly from England and France. The radial pattern, with circles instead of squares and streets in angles toward those circles, was a variation sometimes followed. This more grandiose scheme was sometimes favored by governments that planned capital cities (such as the nation's capital in Washington, D.C., and such early colonial capitals as Annapolis, Maryland).

The most significant modern variation on these kinds of designs has been the curvilinear street layout, a largely post–World War II invention. Many settlements across the North American continent now feature a schizophrenic physical layout, part older grid street pattern with a fault line to more recent curvilinear street development. Curvilinear layouts became favored by modern developers as a means of selling a visually more varied location to prospective buyers. But, this is a global phenomenon, not one confined to the United States.

Even in zoning legislation, municipal governments in America have drawn on European models, particularly upon the British act of 1909, which prescribed ways to plan cities and to draw up building codes. Zoning restricts the kinds and uses of structures that may be built in particular areas of a city and has been a feature of American urban settlements since the 1920s.

23

Transportation/Communication

Before the twentieth century, European society—in both its heartland and along its frontiers—shared with the tribal societies of West Africa and North America a profoundly decentralized character. Even though elites of various kinds were aware of their kind elsewhere, most Europeans were farmers and craftsmen (as in tribal societies) who lived throughout their lives within the small compass of farmstead, craft shop, and village. Like North American and African tribesmen, most colonists lived in rural areas or villages, and their lives were primarily shaped and influenced by what went on in their families and localities, not by activities occurring in distant port cities or in the imperial capital, London. It took six weeks (on average) to cross the Atlantic. There was, therefore, a "time warp" in communications between the English and their colonists.

As among the native and African tribes they dominated, the colonists' communication and transportation systems were rudimentary. All white colonists communicated in English, as German-speaking immigrants quickly learned the language of those who dominated colonial life. Even slaves developed a language that amalgamated elements of African languages and English, and natives were sometimes educated in the language of their political and economic masters. The most basic form of communication was the mail, which moved by coastal packet boats or by inland postal riders along post roads. Not until the mid-eighteenth century did the British establish intercolonial postal service. By the same century, newsletters or journals appeared in population centers. "News" was of parts of the world far separated from the locality in which a journal was printed; local news was generally transmitted orally, face to face. Most people traveled by horse or by horse and wagon. Those able to travel for long distances either took coaches along the post roads and stayed overnight in taverns or sailed on coastal or river boats if their destination was near navigable waterways.

The typical tribesman's and colonist's world was, therefore, a localized world. His activities seldom reached much beyond his or her family, neighbors, or locality. Where he or she lived, worked, and played encased an existence with few broader referents.

Like the African slaves who had been forcibly removed from an area of Africa in which complex Islamic societies had prevailed, the English colonists' society was without a "top." The "court society" of King and nobility was three thousand miles away, and the colonies were bereft of the elites that flourished in the imperial capital. The provincial population lacked a capital city and thus had no colonial-wide cultural-social-economic-political leadership concentrated in one place and with a heightened awareness of each other as a group. In the colonies, there was no church, no army, no political leadership, no aristocracy, no profession, no group of any kind that occupied a central position at the top of a hierarchically ordered society. For, in its social arrangements, as in its spatial, political, and economic ones, British North American society was marked by its decentralized character, which was more like the African and native tribes the English colonists dominated than the European society the colonists sought to emulate.

By the early nineteenth century, various occupational groups in a politically independent United States tried to organize on a national scale. Craft unions and medical and legal associations were formed on a national, regional, state, and local basis in the 1830s, 1840s, and 1850s, falteringly so on the national level because the state of communications and transportation still made such consciousness and awareness and identity difficult to sustain on a continentwide basis. This inclination to "associate" extended far beyond occupational groups, to ethnic ones (the Irish, the Germans, and so on), to racial ones (the nonslave blacks), to reform movements (such as the pacifists, the abolitionists, the temperance advocates, the utopian socialists), but all such efforts were strongest at the local level, of varying strength at the state and regional levels, and very tentative at the national level.

American society remained very loose, fragmented, decentralized, organized into congeries of bottom-heavy federative hierarchies. Compared to the more integrated populations of Europe, America continued to lack—as had colonial society—strong central institutions. With a populace sprawled across an entire continent, it failed to produce a strong central government, church, military, professions, universities, or intellectual-scientific-cultural institutions. Washington was not London, Paris, or Madrid.

Another characteristic of the American population was its incessant geographical mobility. This was the case far more than in Europe itself, though—ironically—it was the movement of Europeans to America that initiated and partially sustained the settlement of the North American continent by white people, and westward migration constituted one way Americans (as descendants of European migrants) continued to move. Abundant and resourceful land attracted mobile Americans westward toward the frontier through the Civil War period and beyond. But, increasingly, so did water-powered mill or factory villages and commercial cities. In all these ways, geographical mobility worked against long family tenure in given communities and localities.

The American population was thinly spread on territory that became, by stages between the Revolution and the Civil War, a continent. The state of communications and transportation did not allow that population easily to organize, inform, or move itself on a national or continental basis, any more than Europeans were able to. But, what made Americans distinctive in the Western world was their linguistic uniformity as they spread over a huge continent. In contrast to the linguistic patchwork of Europe and much of the rest of the world, a lot of Asia (except for Mandarin Chinese) and Africa (except where Bantu prevailed), but like the Spanish- and Portuguese-speaking South and Middle Americans, white Americans used a common language inherited from their colonial rulers, and used it all over the North American continent. In these decades, a form of American English emerged that was codified by Noah Webster in his *Dictionary* (1828) at the elite level and involved ethnic and racial mergings at the popular level, with the popularization of many terms and expressions derived from many of Europe's languages brought to America by the non-English groups in the population.

Newspapers continued to be the most basic form of communication. There were newspapers (daily or weekly) in many local communities during these decades, and they became the means by which most people were informed about what was happening elsewhere, though letters from friends, family, and relatives received through the postal system were also a means of keeping informed. Editors of local newspapers became leading "boosters" of towns if there was any chance of their becoming cities of the future, but such journals did not feature *local* news, probably because their editors continued to believe that the news of small localities was dispersed orally, in the ordinary conversations of the area's inhabitants.

However, with the development of the mass-circulation "penny press" during the 1830s and 1840s, newspapers in the largest population centers began to include local news columns as their editors probably realized that such urban communities were too large for news to be disseminated orally and informally. With the invention of the telegraph in the 1840s, instant communication was possible, but this new device was primarily used as a source of important news or information for government agencies (especially the military in wartime), business firms, ordinary people in emergency situations, and, increasingly, as a means for supplying newspaper editors with news items. But, most Americans did not have occasion to use the telegraph in the years before the Civil War. It was not reasonable for them to communicate regularly and instantaneously with others outside of their immediate locality—and this was the basis for their overall sense of isolation from the wider world.

Similarly, the means by which Americans transported themselves or their products continued to be seriously limited in various ways. The national government's postal roads and private turnpikes provided the venue for horses and wagons and coaches that moved people singly, in families, or in groups, with taverns and inns at appropriate junctures along the way providing accommodations for such travelers. But, this means of transport was limited by season (both winter and spring created difficulties) and by length—not all localities were linked to the wider world in a network that embraced the nation. Travel by horse meant that the average distance traveled per day was only a few miles.

Canals and rivers were similarly limited by season (winter freeze-ups) and by length—many areas of the nation were not connected to a waterway of any navigable kind. Water transport was more effective as a means for transporting products than road transport, because boats could carry heavier loads and were a more durable means for moving people when boats became, with increasing frequency as the century wore on, powered by steam.

Railroads provided a markedly superior means of transporting both people and freight in the sense that they also moved by steam power, but over a "road" that was passable in all seasons. However, before the Civil War, railroad lines were not linked up into a national system, so that even rail transport did not provide a means for Americans to travel everywhere at any time at a reasonable length of time and expense (though some railroad companies built hotels at stopping points along their lines).

From the mid-nineteenth century to the Depression of the 1930s, Americans shared with Europeans an important enlargement of scale in its group and institutional life and activities. Developments in communication and transportation made possible the creation of durable nationwide organizations, with accompanying manifestations of self-awareness, identity, and loyalty. This was increasingly the case for occupational groups (such as farmers, laborers, owners and managers, doctors, lawyers, professors) and ethnic groups (such as Polish- or Italian- or Greek-Americans), as well as for various institutions (such as corporations, unions, churches, and men's and women's clubs and associations) and activities (such as recreational, associational, economic, religious, or political kinds).

Rail and then motor vehicle transportation, national magazines, telephone systems, and radio networks allowed these groups and institutions to encompass the entire nation, and not just certain localities. Even though necessarily *located* in particular places around the continent, such organizations created a national presence, with "headquarters" that interacted with their counterparts on a regional or state or local basis (or combinations of the three). This "federated" character of organizational life permeated dimension after dimension of American society during the late nineteenth and early twentieth centuries. What began as tentative, short-lived efforts before the Civil War became successful, long-term developments after the War.

Enlargement of scale was a messy, variegated process, however, and the extent to which particular groups or institutions achieved a national (or international) dimension varied enormously. Locally originated organizations coexisted with branches of nationally derived ones. But, this process of "nationalization" became quite visible with the founding of many, still-existing national organizations in the late nineteenth and early twentieth centuries.

Railroad and then motor vehicle travel made the movement of people and things possible at increasing speeds between ever-greater distances in all climates and seasons. Telephones and radio and national magazines and news services provided communications for people in all locations. The settlement of the continent—the process of westward expansion along a frontier—ended by the 1890s. The rural population, in its separate farmsteads, began to decline at steadily high rates, beginning in the 1880s, with the mechanization of agriculture. The proportion of the population engaged in agriculture shrank continuously from the 1790s onward. However, the number of farms continued to grow throughout this period, as did their size. Some of the rural population moved into the towns, which had always been service centers for farmers, the focus of community life for rural hinterlands.

In the decades between the Civil War and the Depression of the 1930s, Americans became more communally oriented, as those who lived on spatially separate farmsteads began to migrate to towns and cities, at a time when agriculture became the principal occupation of steadily fewer people in proportion to the total population. Americans still proclaimed the primacy of the individual in such matters as religious faith, civil liberties, voting, and wealth accumulation. But, growing numbers of Americans lived out their lives in the context of local communities (increasingly urban) and associations and institutions and groups (often with national dimensions). Individualism began to lose its physical, geographical, and demographic sources as Americans moved away from the rural farmsteads that had for so long kept large numbers outside of community of any kind, at least on an ongoing basis.

Since 1930, social groups, activities, and institutions have continued to be national in scope and scale, though such entities often are "federated" as well, with regional, state, and local segments. The national organization typically has an office in Washington for lobbying purposes. In recent decades, there has been an increasing incidence of American associations affiliating with other, similar national groups in international or global confederations.

Since 1930, American society has been greatly affected by the rapid development of new forms of communications and transportation. A privately owned telephone system has become a nearly universal means of communication. Until a government-mandated breakup into regional parts in the 1980s, the Bell System had gained in the middle decades of the century a nearly monopolistic control over a number of regional companies that, in turn, had absorbed the hundreds of local exchanges that had been formed in the early decades of the century.

Since the 1970s, the dizzying development of various forms of telecommunications, in particular, email on the Internet, has speeded up the ways people can make verbal, numerical, and visual computerized contact in both homes and workplaces. The Post Office Department was turned into a private, but publicly funded corporation—the U.S. Mail Service, and though regular forms of mail take days to reach their destinations, new types of assured rapid delivery systems, along with "fax" machines, have made postal communication almost as fast as other forms.

The Associated Press and United Press International remain the "wire services" for newspapers, providing instant uniformity for print journalism, whereas the telecommunications satellites allow radio and television broadcast journalists equal speed. Americans have local newspapers and radio and television stations for local and state news, national television networks and cable news channel, and one national newspaper (*USA Today*), for national news, and several others that serve as nationwide news sources for influential elites—politicians, business people, and others with power in various aspects of American life: particularly the *New York Times* and the *Washington Post*. While general-circulation magazines have declined as television networks developed in the 1950s and 1960s and cable news during the 1980s, there are a vast array of specialized periodical publications for the thousands of groups and interests Americans divide into. If a journalist or indeed any American wishes, he has easy access to governmental information of any kind not judged to be legally closed to public scrutiny, through the Freedom of Information Act.

Americans continue to share a common language, one not their own: English. This facilitates verbal intercourse throughout a huge, continental nation. But, Americans, with the development of telecommunications, have come to communicate with others everywhere in the globe since World War II. Not only do Americans share body signs, numbers, line and color, and musical notes as forms of "language" with people everywhere, but their verbal language (English)—largely because of America's midcentury hegemony and its attendant political, diplomatic, economic, and cultural penetration—has become the second language of the world. Americans thus have the means for global communication, though their persistent parochialism and assumption of superiority has often led many of them to ignore the means of access available to them.

In transportation, the airplane (propeller-driven before the 1950s; jet-engine-propulsed since) has greatly speeded up the time it takes Americans to travel to particular destinations, either within the United States or elsewhere in the world. Private airlines, large and small, move passengers and freight over air routes to and from airports built with a mixture of private and government funds—both within the United States and around the globe. Privately built motor vehicles travel over wholly government-funded road systems—national, state, and local. Since 1930, all but the poorest Americans have had their own means of transportation—automobiles. Private bus companies move Americans at fixed schedules through local, state, and national routes. Private trucking companies move a great percentage of the products made at production facilities to the retail places where they are usually sold. Since 1930, privately owned railroad corporations have continued to move people and products over their own rail lines, but competition from other nationwide forms of transportation has forced the remaining passenger rail firms to amalgamate into a government-owned service (*VIA Rail*) with a national scope, but freight lines have continued to compete with trucking firms for the shipment of products. Private (ocean) shipping firms export Americans and their products to destinations elsewhere in the world.

In all these forms of communication and transportation, there has been a mixture of public and private activity, usually, but not always, of corporate ownership and governmental regulation—as in all other aspects of American economic and social life. Americans have, since 1930, come to possess the means to communicate and travel at a very rapid rate among themselves or with others elsewhere. There has been a consequent ending of enforced physical (and psychic) isolation. As the percentage of Americans in urbanized areas has grown quickly during recent decades, so too have the mechanisms allowing them (and rural Americans as well) to move around and contact others and share information and products with a speed unimaginable in earlier times.

The Americans have shared with the Canadians, Australians, and Russians the development of a nation of continental dimensions. All have had to deal with huge, spacial settings. The Americans, Canadians, and Australians all constructed decentralized polities in liberal societies as white European migrants and their progeny settled across the usable lands of North America and Australia. The Russians, by contrast, came out of a dynastic, despotic political culture that was resilient enough to sustain its centralized supervision over the settlement of Siberia. But, from a global perspective, mass societies have emerged during the twentieth century wherever modern forms of communication and transportation have been developed. The progressive enlargement of the scale of life in America is part of a worldwide process.

24

General Economic Developments

The economic activities of the North American native tribes involved agriculture and crafts and were thus similar to the material life of most Europeans during the seventeenth and eighteenth centuries. But the tribes were also hunters; they didn't herd animals onto fixed pasturage. Native women were the farmers, planting, hoeing, and harvesting the crops. Native men were the craftsmen, but didn't include metallurgy among their skills.

Though farmers and craftsmen "possessed" their tools, and chiefs took shares and gave gifts at ceremonies, and hunters and fishermen claimed "territories," the native tribes did not have a conception of private property as something owned in perpetuity, passed on to heirs, enhanced in value, traded as a commodity. The land and what they made from it was not "theirs," but theirs to use temporarily, for as long as the land and its yield were satisfactory. The notion of a fixed, specific, ongoing possession of something was alien to them.

The black African slaves had also been farmers and craftsmen in Africa, where there were well-developed crafts in metals and where there were craft guilds of long standing, in both cases, as in Europe. In the savanna or grassland area of West Africa, black Africans had also become traders via caravans across the Sahara Desert with North Africans, Europeans around the Mediterranean, and Arabs in the Islamic world beyond. Trade gave to this part of west Africa the economic sophistication that lay back of the emergence of large states in the centuries after A.D. 600.

The Africans who were enslaved were thus capable of engaging in a wide variety of economic activity within the world of work constructed by European colonists, and did so, before the gang labor system of the plantations wrenched many of them away from the farming and craft activities that were their economic heritage.

The economic activities of the incoming European migrants contrasted sharply in some respects from those of the native population. The white immigrants from England and elsewhere wanted to improve their economic position and, as settlement moved inland from the Atlantic coast during the seventeenth and eighteenth centuries, they and their descendants found a resourceful land and waterways that could be farmed, mined, lumbered, and fished in such a way that their wealth and property and material possessions were typically increased. The Christian "work ethic" found its fullest expression on this resource-rich western frontier of European civilization and was reiterated in sermons and almanacs, sanctioning in both religious and secular phraseologies the acquisition of property and wealth through a life of industriousness, dependability, honesty, and Christian virtue. Though colonial proprietors charged nominal rent, land was variously and widely available through headrights and settlement lots and farm parcels to genuine settlers.

In sharp contrast to the native population, the English colonists developed deep-ploughing agriculture; herded livestock into pastures; and crafted metal, cloth, and wood products. The white settlers also regarded land as property, a commodity that was bought and sold and possessed and passed on to heirs. Their aim was to accumulate wealth in the form of property, whether of land, crops, crafted items, houses and buildings, or furnishings, either as producers or as traders. The expectation was that value would be enhanced, a profit made beyond costs.

The English colonists rejected efforts to reproduce feudalism or to introduce communism, and above all the other colonists in the Americas, most favored the onset of a recognizably capitalist economy. Both the French (in their seigniorial system along the St. Lawrence) and the Dutch (in their patroon system along the Hudson) had dabbled in the creation of at least quasi-feudalistic arrangements. When proprietors of Carolina colony tried to introduce something similar, it quickly became apparent that it was unworkable. When the trading companies tried to hold all property in common, the actual settlers rejected that arrangement as soon as the survival of the initial settlements was beyond question.

More powerfully than in Europe, the impulse of these transplanted Europeans to accumulate land, property, and wealth was accompanied by an urge to dominate, to control—to utilize rather than replenish the resources of the land and the water, to command labor in order to enlarge production, to own land and property and commodities in order to enhance their value (or profit), to speculate, to take risks. The land of North America and the resources on it that the English and other European migrants were able to use to such effect became a magnet for settlement, producing greatly expanded social, economic, and geographical mobility at the same time that it created a vertical spread of labor beyond anything Europe had experienced—a slave gang labor system.

But, as elsewhere in the Western world, all production, whether agricultural or craft, was manual in character, except for the grist and saw milling operations and iron furnace processing. Such crude mechanized production operated on a local basis to provide the grain and lumber and metal products needed by nearby inhabitants. By contrast, the manual labor of the farms and plantations resulted in the production of commodities that were sometimes exported to other parts of the empire and beyond. This manual labor was of many kinds, significantly more than in Europe itself—black African slaves, indentured servants, apprentices, journeymen, tenants, sharecroppers—as well as master craftsmen, farmers, and planters.

Some aspects of economic life were regional in scope. In the Northern colonies, where the growing season was relatively short and the land hilly and, except for narrow coastal plains and a few river valleys, not especially fertile, fish and lumber products found wider outlets. In the middle colonies, with a longer growing season and more prominent river valleys, significant quantities of grain and livestock were exported. Though the English wanted their colonists in the northern and middle mainland colonies to provide the empire with grain and livestock and wood and iron, these commodities were also available in Europe and, in any case, did not involve new methods of production beyond those already familiar to Europeans—milling and forging operations. So, the northern and mid-Atlantic colonists were *extensions* of a recognizably European economic world.

By contrast, in the Southern colonies, with their wide, river-packed tidewater and piedmont plains and long growing season, "staple" crops—tobacco and rice—were produced for world markets on a large scale. The discovery of commodities that could be so grown for wide markets led some of the wealthier initial settlers in the Southern colonies to buy up great tracts of land and to gather large labor forces at first consisting of white indentured servants and then, when they were not sufficient in number, of black slaves or chattels.

Like the Spanish *hacienda* and the Portuguese *fazenda*, the English colonial plantation became a huge, largely self-sufficient farm, whose labor forces produced vast quantities of commodities in wide demand: tobacco, rice, sugar, coffee, cotton, hides, gold, silver. In all cases, staple crop production dominated the economic activity of the areas it flourished in and had the effect of keeping the semitropical, tropical, and warm temperate parts of the European colonies in the Americas from diversifying economically, from duplicating western and central Europe's range and variety of economic activity.

The plantation system had originally developed in the fourteenth and early fifteenth centuries in southern Spain and Portugal and on various Mediterranean islands, in the form of sugar plantations with slave labor drawn from Africa and from eastern Europe—the Slavs (or slaves). Widely disseminated in the semitropical and tropical zones of the Americas, the plantation system was rather similar in character to the large estates that the nobility of eastern Europe developed during these same centuries, with serfs (somewhat enslaved peasants) providing the labor, in somewhat the same fashion as South Americans aboriginals were brought into debt peonage by Spanish and Portuguese landowners.

Eastern European serfdom matured during the same centuries as slavery in the Americas. Both systems depended upon forced labor, as landowners and planters sought a dependent and dependable labor force to produce on a large scale a product or products for which there was a significant market. Both systems were, especially during their maturation phase through the seventeenth and eighteenth centuries, in varying degrees harshly exploitative, as masters gained control over new forms of enslavement. The multiple estates of the Russian nobility were usually of a larger scale than the tobacco and rice and sugar and coffee and mining plantations and *haciendas* and *fazendas* of the Americas. The Russian nobility as masters were absentee landowners, a rentier class, in contrast to the usual resident planter or landowner of the Americas. Only the largest sugar planters of the West Indies, as absentee and multiple owners, approached the scale of operations that were routine among the Russian nobility.

More specifically, for the Southern English colonies, the development of staple crop agriculture created an economic zone that linked the Southern English colonists *politically* to the English empire, but *economically* to the semitropical and tropical worlds of the Spanish and Portuguese empires, and beyond them, to the great landed estates of eastern Europe. What distinguished the Southern English colonists from their Spanish and Portuguese counterparts was that their great staple crop, tobacco, could be grown profitably on both large and small farms, without a significant mechanical apparatus, whereas the profitable production of sugar, the greatest staple of Middle and South America, was dependent upon a large slave gang labor system, because the production of sugar was a large-scale operation involving substantial capital investment and combined fieldwork with grinding/filtering/boiling/curing/distilling in mill factories. This economic circumstance allowed large numbers of white settlers to operate as farmers in the southern North American mainland, whereas small white British, Spanish, and Portuguese elites managed the highly productive sugar plantations of Middle and South America.

Individually, the English and other New World colonists occupied positions along a spectrum of economic activity, from almost total self-sufficiency to an almost total dependency on goods produced by others in a market economy. In a general sense, self sufficiency declined and the market economy expanded throughout the colonial period, though this was a very messy and varied process. North America had an abundance of raw materials, and the most significant economic activity tended to involve the initial processing of these materials. By contrast, the most sophisticated craftspeople were concentrated in Europe. The prevailing pattern of trade that emerged, therefore, involved the movement of raw materials to Europe and of "finished" goods to the colonies. Economic activity in North America retained these essential characteristics until the early nineteenth century, at which time milling was expanded to involve the employment of large numbers of wage laborers in the large-scale machine production of goods other than grain and wood products.

In the broadest sense, the shift in economic activity from feudalism to modern capitalism took on various and overlapping intermediate forms. Though colonial merchants in particular were a provincial version of capitalist merchants in Europe, the large-scale agricultural and commercial organizations that merchants and planters developed were not recognizably feudalistic or fully capitalistic in a modern sense. Both merchants and planters managed enterprises that involved wage or slave labor within a political world in which the King's law prevailed, not that of sovereign landlords. This was not an economic world of self-sufficient manors, but of planters and merchants trading major cash crops and other raw materials within a market system.

Still, merchants and planters established patron-client relations with their "workers," that is, a kind of personal interaction that was quite different from the impersonal character of a modern corporation. And they did not develop machine production, another hallmark of modern capitalism. It was the millers, with their water-powered, mechanized grist and saw mills, who were crypto-industrialists. In a sense the millers, planters, and merchants were all early, premodern capitalists, who, as a group, developed in personalized settings the wage or slave labor and the machine production that together characterize modern capitalism.

The political independence of much of colonized North and South America between the 1770s and the 1820s did not in any basic way alter the continued existence of a single Atlantic economy, an economy linked by trade and capital, with a center in Europe and a periphery in the transatlantic world of both colonized and politically independent America. This Atlantic economy was defined by mercantile capitalism, which during the nineteenth century moved beyond the Americas to other parts of the world. The global reach of a European-dominated capitalist system was considerably greater in its territorial extent than the empires of the European imperial states, even though these empires grew significantly in both Asia and Africa. European merchants did not need political control to extend their trading and investing activities, and politically independent portions of the Americas became prime trading and investing locations.

Commercial capitalism expanded into industrial capitalism in the late eighteenth and early nineteenth centuries when some of those with capital invested it in mill "factories," buildings where wage laborers operated machinery that mass-produced goods sold for a significant profit in large markets. But, whereas "mills" usually had one owner, or a partnership, "factories" were usually corporations, a legal entity for a group of owner-investors liable to the limit of their investment. In this, factory owners were like those who owned railroads, canals, turnpikes, or banks: all formed corporations. But, until the late nineteenth century, most who produced products and performed services in the United States were individuals or partners. The corporation for many decades after the 1810s was an exceptional form for an economic activity to assume. Even large-scale enterprises like large plantations or intricate, complex mercantile operations were typically owned by individuals and families or partnerships.

The first factory owners were merchants who felt restricted by the Napoleonic

Wars and who were aware of early British efforts to mass-produce cloth. These mercantile-then-industrial enterprises generated economic growth in the Northeast, providing employment in both mill-factory villages and cities for women and children and immigrants and excess farmers and fisherman. Similarly, in the South, the planters stimulated economic growth as they bought more land and slaves and sometimes imported grain and livestock from elsewhere in the Union at the same time that they relied on Northern merchants to finance, store, ship, and sell their staples. And in the West, large-scale grain and livestock farmers positively affected economic development by producing foodstuffs and meat—prepared in large grain mills or meat-packing plants—for export to the industrializing and urbanizing areas of the Northeast, to the staple crop areas of the South, and to the world through foreign trade.

These large-scale regionalized enterprises continued to coexist with operators of small craft shops throughout the nation and of small cotton, grain, and livestock farms throughout the South and Midwest. Once again, the leading southern staple crop, which became cotton by the 1820s, could be profitably produced by both large and small enterprises without the necessity for a large capital investment in machinery. Smaller farmers in the South went to crossroads stores and paid for the use of the necessary machinery, the cotton gin, which separated seeds from fiber. By contrast, the great sugar and, later, coffee plantations in Middle and South America continued to be both more capital intensive, more mechanized, and more dependent on large slave labor gangs and, after slavery ended everywhere by 1888, on white southern European immigrants as wage laborers, in the case of the coffee plantations of Brazil. The mechanization of grain farming in the Midwest and the need for a large acreage for ranching activity on the Plains gradually reduced the ability of family farmers to sustain small-scale enterprises in competition with mechanized farms whose owners hired wage laborers. But economic activity in America continued to exhibit this dual character throughout the nineteenth century, which meant that there continued to be large numbers of white owners of farming and craft operations, even as large-scale plantations, factories, and mechanized farms brought the growth of capitalist enterprise and quickly accelerated slave and wage-labor work forces.

But, these regional "growth" industries did not create a "national" economy. Nor did the road, canal, and railroad corporations create a national transportation system. Nor did sporadically existing national banks or continuous, but uncoordinated state banks create a dependable, sound national currency and credit system. Economic activity remained quite fragmented and disjointed. Americans were unable to operate on a continentwide scale. Firms did not have a national scope: there was no coast-to-coast financing, production, transportation, marketing, and sale.

Complicated products with machine-made parts were most efficiently produced by the assembly line, a form of production that spread during the century from intricate mechanisms like clocks and firearms to basic commodities like shoes and clothes. But, the assembly line, or the "American way of manufacturing," was rather quickly copied in other parts of the industrializing world. Many hitherto crafted products only gradually became machine produced, sometimes part by part. Often, craft production continued alongside the onset of mass-produced machine-made products.

Only tiny groups sought alternatives to industrial capitalism during the nineteenth century: a few secular and Christian socialists who tried to build local communities based upon the common ownership of property and a few labor leaders who were either highly critical of capitalism as a system or who favored socialism on a national level. The model American was a Christian property owner. He was to *balance* humanitarian and charitable and loving religious impulses with a zest for improving his material life through the acquisition of property and the enhancement of wealth.

But, by the late nineteenth century, a tiny elite of American entrepreneurs strove to monopolize the production and sale of particular goods within a huge continental market and, in doing so, pioneered in the development and management of large-scale business organizations. Monopoly violated a key tenet of the work ethic, that secular-religious sanction for a capitalist economic life that still legitimated the focus on materialistic betterment that so animated most Americans. As self-appointed spokesman for this elite, Andrew Carnegie tried to justify extreme wealth and monopoly by invoking Social Darwinism, the popular justification for a steeply hierarchical economic-social system. Basing their views on Darwin's biological theories, advocates of Social Darwinism, such as Carnegie, asserted that life is a struggle for the survival of the fittest, and the fittest are the wealthiest, who, as Christians, must also act as public benefactors by setting up charities that benefit in a durable way the lives of everybody. Nevertheless, wealthy monopolists did not fit easily into the model of the laboring American suggested by the work ethic.

Neither did the growing number of wage laborers who worked at the machines that produced an increasing variety of products. How could such labor create opportunities for wealth, property, and leisure? As the independent farmer who owned his own farmland and the independent craftsman who owned his own shop and made his own product gave way to huge, mechanized farms (in the West) or to slave plantations and, later, sharecropper-tenant farms of great size (in the South) or to factories of all kinds everywhere there was water or steam power, how was the farm laborer or the wage earner to make a profit or gain property? This long-term development created an even greater crisis over the applicability and meaning of the work ethic than did the much shorter-lived tendency toward monopoly.

But, no one could argue that the U.S. economy was different in kind from Europe's. Industrial capitalism was an economic phenomenon that easily transcended national boundaries and was something that organized life in important ways in ever-wider areas of the globe during the nineteenth and early twentieth centuries. The United States was on the periphery of what was initially a European, especially British development, and though Americans were in the forefront of large-scale corporate enterprise and assembly-line production, all innovations involving industrial capitalism tended—in an era of ever more rapid communications and transportation—to be quickly absorbed throughout the industrialized portions of the globe.

By the turn of the century, economic activity in the United States had become the largest in the world. Having long been a debtor nation, reliant on largely British credit, especially for railroad construction, the United States became by the 1910s the world's largest creditor nation, as American investment began to seek other outlets around the globe. The United States' preeminent position was enhanced by the massive economic deterioration that Europeans experienced during World Wars I and II, and though all of the advanced industrialized areas of the world declined economically during the depression of the 1930s, after World War II economic activity in the United States was by far the largest in the world, with the United States remaining the major creditor nation, a situation that lasted until Europeans were able to rebuild their shattered economies.
swift rise to industrial preeminence can be explained by a combination of factors: entrepreneurs who knew how to organize on a continental basis, a resourceful land, a people still imbued with a religiously and secularly based work ethic, and a government that assisted in the creation of national banking and transportation systems and that "protected" both domestic production from the vagaries of the world market through high tariff duties and American commerce globally through its diplomacy—all making possible the production and sale of goods and services on a national—and increasingly, international—scale as well.

The basic structure of the economy in the United States has remained stable since the 1920s, in certain senses, with large corporations sharing the market with many small firms in the machine production of many consumer products. However, after World War II the development of "franchising" has combined large corporate structures with small local outlets, as national units provide products and services for locally organized and managed units.

When the stock market crashed at the end of the 1920s from inflated stock values, the unsoundness of the economy as a whole became apparent. Corporations were overcapitalized, their stock inflated in value. Generally low wages depressed purchasing power at the same time that corporations expanded production. Mass unemployment and rapidly declining wages and profits and prices followed. The economy within the United States functioned badly, as all the indexes that declined rapidly around 1930 failed to revive until the wartime production of World War II restored demand by bringing full employment.

The Great Depression of the 1930s was a worldwide phenomenon. Efficient globe-girdling ship and rail transportation systems as well as regional specialization in the production of goods with international markets meant that what happened in one area affected all the others. By 1930, there were structural imbalances in the world economy. There was a long-standing slump in agricultural and raw material prices, which hampered growth in nonindustrialized areas and deprived industrial areas of potential markets. The downside of the business cycle occurred in various forms in many parts of the industrialized world: bank failures, the panic selling of stock, followed by falling prices, rising unemployment, a slowing down of production, the onset of business failures, and the growth of general pessimism. In the unindustrialized parts of the world during the Depression of the 1930s, capital and labor to some extent shifted from agriculture and mining to industrial production, creating better economic balance, with industrial development resulting from low wages and cheap raw materials.

The Depression brought the highest unemployment rates ever experienced in the industrialized areas, with two-thirds of the jobless in the United States, Britain, and Germany. The unemployed lived on the margin of society, and there was a big increase in vagrancy during these years. Apathy and despair was widespread among the unemployed. The jobless typically wanted to work. For such people, nurtured on the work ethic, dependency was hard to take, and they frequently blamed themselves for an inability to find work. Within a family context, long-term joblessness tended to increase the influence of women. At the outset of the Depression in the United States, women constituted one-third of the workforce; they tended to be kept on as the Depression deepened because they were paid lower wages.

Various governments in industrialized areas of the world made efforts to get married women whose husbands worked out of the workforce, attempted to keep out foreign workers, and tried to induce the urban unemployed to move to rural areas for farm work. But, none of these efforts seriously reduced unemployment, particularly back-to-the-land inducements. Population migration patterns everywhere in the world involved movement from rural areas and towns to cities and from small to large farms.

America's World War II–induced economic hegemony was short-lived. In 1970, with 6 percent of the world's population, Americans were producing and consuming two-thirds of the world's products. But, Nixon's removal of the dollar (in its convertibility into gold at a fixed price) as the standard for the world's currencies in 1971 signaled the end, not of America's status as the world's largest economy defined in national terms, but of the obviously preeminent power Americans had exercised after they mobilized for war in the early 1940s, 30 years before. By the 1970s, the European common market and Japan (along with lesser nations on the Asian shoreline) developed as rivals and competitors of the Americans in economic terms, to the extent that the United States and Canada, and later Mexico, created a trade bloc of their own, phased in, beginning in 1988.

Of as much significance has been the emergence of multinational or global corporations that organize capital, labor, production, markets, and sales on a worldwide basis and thus do not operate within the confines of any given nation-state. The internationalization or globalization of economic activity has enormously complicated efforts of the American government to regulate, aid, protect, and develop the economic life of its own people. For, economic activity no longer confines itself within national boundaries. Business and machine technology have made the production, communication, and transport necessary for the creation of commodities that people want an activity that can be performed almost anywhere.

The development since the 1960s of foreign economic competitors with large geopolitical dimensions has occurred simultaneously with the growth of certain kinds of problems and weaknesses within the economy as it operates in the United States. One such problem is shared by all of the "older" industrialized nations and that is the *relative* decline of the industries that feature machine production and whose employees are machine operatives, as other industries that stay competitive shift to computerized production and embrace other technological innovations. The process that began with water-powered, wooden-geared mill and factory production in the early and mid-nineteenth century, and went on to employ large numbers of machine operatives, came to need fewer wage earners in an era of "high technology" and foreign competition.

The number of Americans employed in the manufacturing sector has steadily declined, especially since 1970, whereas the percentages of the working population in "services" or offices has steadily grown. The problem in the United States—as elsewhere—is what to do with those who become unemployed because firms become obsolete, declaring bankruptcy because of foreign competition or declining demand or bad management or badly trained or motivated workers.

Another problem is the long-term, relatively low level of productivity and efficiency and quality of products made by American workers. Those who produce American-made commodities have, in recent decades, seemed less well trained and educated, less motivated to create well-made products, less dedicated to the "work ethic." Americans typically show little sense of loyalty to any given firm. Collectively, they have become more influenced by consumerism than by the work ethic, more concerned to spend and to create debt than to save and invest. Corporate owners and managers are less concerned with long-term growth and stability than they are with shore-term profitability. The mania during the 1980s for corporate "takeovers" was an indication that some group and individual investors could be induced to "swarm" about, looking for quick profits, rather than sound, long-term investment, and, in the process, treating American corporations as tradable commodities.

Experiencing the highest standard of living in the world's history all alone for 30 years, Americans have not responded effectively to serious competition when it has appeared. And they expect their government—without its becoming either the manager or the owner and thus in a position of genuine control—to provide them with many economic benefits and to solve their economic problems. In terms of organization, those groups who compose the great economic interests have continued to evolve in ways apparent before 1970. In many areas of the economy—particularly in the case of those involved with an easily reproducible product or service—an oligarchy of several large corporations (often with chains, franchises, or branches) continues to dominate, but also to coexist beside many small firms whose owners continue to believe they can provide the service or product better or cheaper than the large firms.

The manufacturing sector has significantly declined as a portion of the entire workforce, as has agriculture. Farmers consist of fewer than 2 percent of those with definable occupations. A relatively new development is the growing number of those, using computer technology or serving as "consultants," who work at home (thus coming full circle by reestablishing the conjunction of workplace and living place that characterized Americans when most were farmers). There is also evidence that many in the workforce will not in the future have "careers" or sole, lifelong "principal occupations," but, given the rate of technological change, will, through retraining and further education, move from one kind of employment to another.

25

Agricultural and Extractive Activity

As the English colonies along the Atlantic coast became a continent-girdling nation between 1600 and 1850, America came to embrace the richest mix of agricultural and extractive-resource lands in the world. With its mineral-rich Appalachian and Rocky Mountain chains and its abundance of arable lands from the Atlantic coastal valleys to the central valleys and plains to the Pacific Coast valley, with its extensive forested lands through most of its eastern half, no other single political jurisdiction on earth contained within its borders such a richness of agricultural, timber, fishing, and mineral resources. The mineral resources of the Rockies and the Appalachians vie in size and variety with those of other large mountainous areas of the globe, whereas the agricultural fertility of the coastal and midcontinent valleys and plains is comparable to that of the great plains of Europe and Siberia or to that of the large river valleys of China, India, and southeast Asia.

Only Russia, which also became a continental nation during this period with the exploration and settlement of Siberia, came close to equaling the size of America's resource base—both extractive and agricultural. Within its borders lay much of the enlarged eastern end of the great European plain and its continuation through southern and western Siberia. Enclosed as well were the mineral-rich Ural Mountains and vast forested areas in the north, though Russia lacked sizable coastal waters.

During the colonial period, most farmers raised crops and livestock for their own needs, using wooden and metal hand tools and animal-driven tools, but many also focused on a particular commodity that they could sell to others and thus enter the money and market economy. Some mid-Atlantic farmers in the fertile river valleys of the area—the Delaware, the Susquehanna—attained a sufficiently large scale of operation that they exported grain and livestock abroad. In the Southern colonies, plantations and smaller farms produced such staple crops as tobacco and rice with indentured servants and then black African slave labor on so large a scale that those crops became the most valued commodities traded outside of the mainland.

After the Revolution, food and cloth production in America involved both mechanization and largely manual slave labor. As settlement went beyond the Appalachians, many migrants engaged in farming in the Ohio and Mississippi River valleys. By the 1850s, Americans learned how to farm on the treeless plains that stretched from the Mississippi to the Rockies. The large-scale, specialized grain farms of the plains that developed after 1850 made use of a great deal of machinery because of their size of operations and the relative shortage of available wage labor, just as large livestock enterprises (at first with open grazing and cattle drives and then as fenced-in ranches) employed farm wage laborers of various kinds. But, the equally specialized cotton plantations that spread across the piedmont, Gulf Plain, lower Mississippi valley, and Texas plains during the same years featured slave labor operating "gins" (or seed and fiber separators). Those who owned large-scale Southern farms sustained the slave labor system developed in the colonial period. Instead of seeking mechanization, the planters continued to rely on the manual labor of slaves for the production of the basic cloth fiber—cotton. Even after the Civil War, when planters became landowners and slaves became tenant farmers and sharecroppers, cotton production resisted mechanization. Instead, Southerners with money to invest built cotton factories in the South close to sources of supply, using Southern capital and labor. Elsewhere, wool—the other major source of cloth material—was produced on the basis of largely unmechanized sheep farming.

The sources for cloth—wool and cotton—contrasted sharply with the sources for food—grains and livestock—in the extent to which producers mechanized production. But, all these commodities became increasingly mechanized in the processes by which they were turned into usable products—that is, cloth in cotton and woolen factories, meat in meat-packing plants, grain in flour mills, and wood in sawmills. Mechanization, commercialization, and specialization all led by the 1870s to chronic overproduction and low profits for those who produced food and fiber. As steamships enlarged the volume and reach of international trade (just as steam locomotives did for domestic trade), American farmers competed with producers elsewhere in the world. All these developments brought about enlargements of scale and increasing specialization and commercialization in the agricultural sector, gradually but steadily reducing the proportion of those Americans who were farmers as well as the proportion of those in agriculture who were unspecialized family farmers.

During the course of the nineteenth century, the family farm was replaced as the basic unit of production, the basic occupation of Americans, the vocational school for the sons of the next generation. These changes had profound effects on the whole character of American life. As the family ceased to be the basis for economic life, work became separated from home and family. Independent property owners who lived on the land (or sea) typically became wage or salaried employees or partial or total owners of firms of many sizes. Fewer and fewer people owned more and more land, as increasing numbers owned only their homes or invested in enterprises owned by others as well. Economic life became less personal, familial, independent of others, and more ranging, wider in scope, increasingly corporate and commercial and impersonal in character.

Similar shifts marked fishing, lumbering, mining. In all the extractive activities, lone fishermen, loggers, and prospectors gave way to mechanized operations managed by corporations. But, whereas fishing and logging were continuous operations carried on over large forested and coastal or inland waterway regions, mining was more limited in its mountainous locales and in the durability of its veins. Coal and iron production were vital for the fueling of steam-powered mechanisms and for heavy-metal products and both ship and rail transport. These minerals were found through large areas of the mountainous parts of the continent, and their abundance was an important factor in the industrialization that occurred in the United States and other industrialized parts of the world.

Silver and gold were the rarest and thus most valuable minerals and had long been used by European, Asian, and African states as the basis for currency, a practice governments in the Americas quickly copied. As a consequence, nothing attracted Europeans around the world—as it had in Europe itself—faster than a "strike" of gold, the most valuable mineral of all. In the sixteenth and seventeenth centuries, the mines of South America produced the gold that, when exported to Spain and then circulated as currency, greatly enlarged the wealth of Spain and its dominions. After that time, all imperial and expansionist nations and empires were ever vigilant for new sources.

The "rushes" of the 1850s in the newly acquired westerly mountainous territories of the United States produced a wild melee of individual prospectors from the United States and other parts of the world. A lone, unmechanized prospector phase of mining was followed by a corporate, highly mechanized phase. These gold rushes were a great inducement for settlement in these mountainous areas, as people were quick to migrate when the possibility of sudden enrichment was put before them. This whole process was in no way unique to the United States, however. A similar sequence of development occurred in Canada, Australia, and South Africa, in all the other white settler societies with mineral-rich mountainous regions, societies whose people shared similar attitudes toward wealth and its accumulation, either slowly and steadily, or quickly and riskily.

Similarly, in farming, mechanization of production in both crops and livestock meant that, relatively speaking, steadily fewer farmers owned increasingly larger farms with machinery and farm laborers producing the agricultural products that family farms alone had once produced. Agriculture underwent the same process of mechanization, commercialization, concentration, specialization, and nationalization (in the sense that products grown or raised in one area could be sold everywhere in the nation—and beyond) that other sectors of the economy underwent. The result was that the *proportion* of small farm owners rapidly declined, while large farm owners and farm laborers, tenants, and sharecroppers increased, whereas the entire population involved in agriculture—as a share of the total population—massively hemorrhaged away after the 1880s, declining sharply decade after decade, a process whose end is not yet in sight. The appearance of an increasing percentage of machine-operating wage laborers on large, commercial farms mirrored the growing number of such persons in the other "industrial" sectors of the economy.

Farmers who supported the Populist Party in the 1890s believed that the national government should own the means of transportation and communication in order to insure fair and equitable rates in the movement of agricultural produce in a time of chronic overproduction and low prices. When worldwide production and consumption (or supply and demand) were better balanced, between the turn of the century and World War I, such demands vanished, but were replaced by the Farmers' Union's and the Farm Bureau Federation's demand for parity in the 1920s, when overproduction and low prices were again a major problem. Parity was the notion that farmers should receive the same degree of profits that those who owned other kinds of production were receiving. To assure this, farm spokesmen favored the establishment of governmental agricultural boards to buy and store "surplus" agricultural commodities in order to sustain price levels.

There were global surpluses of agricultural products throughout the 1920s, after the United States, Canada, South America, and Australia/New Zealand expanded production during World War I and Europe regained its productivity after the war. Technological improvements only added to the overproduction of those years. The introduction of synthetic goods (rayon for cotton and wool) forced other producers to cut back. Bread grains were less in demand as people ate more meat, fruits, vegetables, and dairy products. Schemes to have governments buy up excess production floundered in the 1920s.

From the 1920s onward, the number of people engaged in agriculture (in proportion to the total population) continued to hemorrhage away, as large mechanistic farms produced an ever-increasing percentage of the total agricultural production in the United States and abroad. Government programs to limit farm production and to control the amount of agricultural products sold in both the domestic and foreign markets were instituted by the federal government during the Depression of the 1930s, but so have other governments in the Western world. These government support programs have been restricted to grains and livestock and dairy and fiber production, to those commodities for which there has been a large foreign as well as domestic demand. Family farmers are still prominent in the "truck" or fruit and vegetable farming whose chief market is adjacent urban areas, but the large-scale, commercial farms of Florida and California sell produce in these same markets, and foreign imports from semitropical agricultural lands during North America's nongrowing seasons are also a significant part of the food supply. In the grain-growing and livestock-raising areas of the vast midcontinent valleys and plains, commercial farming has become overwhelmingly dominant.

Throughout the twentieth century, family and commercial farmers alike have been conservative—politically, economically, and socially—at the same time that commercial-dominated farm organizations have favored government marketing and support programs. This contradictory posture has marked the outlook of farmers everywhere in the Western world. Only in Canada have farmers supported a socialist party; only in Canada was the kind of radicalism that marked the American Populist movement of the late nineteenth century sustained well into the twentieth century. With the prosperity that returned at the turn of the century, American farmers moved away from the kind of broad reformist movement that the Populists represented and increasingly thought of themselves as a special-interest group whose adherents supported politicians who favored measures that aided the agrarian element of the population, much as industrial laborers abandoned the broadly reformist Knights of Labor for the much narrower economic focus of the American Federation of Labor. Farmers elsewhere in the West developed their own, similar kinds of "farm blocs."

From a global perspective, the white settler societies of the European frontiers have increasingly supplied the rest of the world with needed agricultural surpluses through the course of the twentieth century. The grain and livestock, if not the fruits and vegetables, of the United States, Canada, Australia, New Zealand, and Argentina—though not Siberia—help to sustain a human population that otherwise would have serious difficulty feeding itself. However, other food and beverage commodities that Western nations have not produced have continued to be major export items from many parts of the developing world to the West: coffee, tea, cocoa, various fruits and vegetables. And though some developed nations—notably Russia and the United States—have within their borders a valuable array of mineral deposits and fossil fuels and plant fiber, such nations continue to depend on the undeveloped world for much of their mineral, fuel, and cloth fiber supplies.

In a global perspective, it is important to note the dual character of American agriculture. Americans have shared with some white settler societies—Canada, New Zealand, Siberia—a preponderance of homesteaders, of family-sized farms whose kind of farming prevailed throughout their northeastern and mid-Atlantic valleys and seacoasts and the forested midcontinent valleys. But, Americans have also shared with other frontiers of Europe—South and Middle America, inland southeastern Australia, southern Africa—plantations and large-scale commercial farms with slave or wage labor in their southern and midwestern plains. It was because the southern English colonists and, later, the southern Americans developed staple crops—first tobacco and then cotton—that could be profitably grown on both family farms and on plantations that the American South became a transitional economic zone, something between tropical plantation and temperate homesteader agriculture.

There have always been both small and large operators who have engaged in agricultural and extractive activity of all kinds. Overall, small operators have given way to large ones—independent fishermen and loggers, lone mine prospectors, and family farmers have increasingly been replaced by large commercial farms (or "agribusinesses") and mining/lumbering/fishing corporations. But, through much of modern history and across much of the resource-rich areas of the world, it has also been the case that small and large operators have coexisted in various combinations. As Westerners came to dominate other parts of the world, their large-scale agricultural enterprises, in the form of plantations and ranches and extensive landed estates, were transplanted from Eastern Europe and the Mediterranean littoral to much of South and Middle America, southeastern Australia, the southern United States, southeast Asia, and to certain corridors of Africa, overlayering the small-scale farming activity of native populations. By contrast, the family farming that predominated in western and central Europe was brought by white homesteaders to the northern United States, southern Canada, much of New Zealand, and coastal southeast Australia.

What stands out about the United States is its abundant variety of large and small operators, its extensive commingling of family farms and plantations and ranches and large, mechanized farms as growers of such crops as tobacco and cotton and grains and as raisers of such livestock as beef and dairy cattle and chickens. Only in Asia, in the great river valleys of northern and central China, in Southeast Asia, in northern India, has small-scale agriculture involving masses of largely self-sufficient peasants producing food and fiber been continued throughout modern history, the kind of agricultural activity that has sustained the largest concentration of humanity in all of human history.

26

Commercial and Industrial Activity

Colonial merchants, whose trading activities were regulated by the imperial government in London, were involved in the exchange of a great array of products within and without the empire. Colonial products reached beyond local consumption if the scale and scope of production were large enough.

As had been the case in the colonial era, so too after political independence, the merchants of the Atlantic seaboard constituted an extension of the mercantile capitalist community, the first significant enlargement of the center beyond the confines of the European continent. The continued movement of American settlement westward provided this system with a steadily growing, resource-laden periphery of continental dimensions. The British mercantile community in particular understood that trade and investment opportunities were not necessarily linked to empire, as theirs became the most important presence in the development of trade and investment in the Western Hemisphere.

In the specifically American context, Europeans (but especially the British) continued to export most finished manufactured products to Americans while remaining the chief importers of the primary products (chiefly wheat and cotton) of Americans. British credit was central to the development of the transportation systems (both water and land, that is, both canal and railroad) that made this trading system grow. Barriers to an open trading system were largely removed when the British and American governments opened first the empire (1830) and then the nations themselves (low tariff policies of both governments coincided by the late 1840s) to largely unobstructed trade.

A basic shift in the nature of economic activity during the nineteenth century was the onset of industrialization, that is, the production of commodities by machines powered by sources of nonhuman energy. Industrialization constituted a new phase of capitalism, as investment was diverted from the trading and transport of commodities for which there was a widespread demand to the machine production of particular goods on a mass scale by large numbers of wage laborers who no longer handcrafted and sold these goods, but made parts of them that, when assembled, factory owners sold.

Because of a unique combination of circumstances, industrialization as a process began in Britain during the late eighteenth century. The coexistence (within a small geographical compass in a time before well-developed internal transportation and communication) of investment capital amassed by an adventurous mercantile community, of water-powered factory mills in rivers not far from the sea, of an available coal supply that was used to fuel steam engines in factory mills there and elsewhere, of clever inventors who developed machinery that vastly increased production, of overseas colonies whose inhabitants supplied needed raw materials, of a well-advanced commercial agriculture with large numbers of farmers already in the money economy as potential customers, and, as well, of a displaced agricultural labor force that was willing to become wage laborers (and potential customers) in the new factories—all together produced the conditions that resulted in the creation of industrialized zones in Britain.

Similar zones spread through parts of France, Belgium, and particular German states after the turn of the century, as similar combinations of circumstances occurred in various river valleys and mining areas of the continent—and to the same kinds of localities in the United States. The Americans quickly learned from the English by means both legal and illegal, openly and secretly, as Parliament enacted legislation barring the export of certain aspects of the industrial process. Anglo-American rivalry was soon replaced by cooperation, however, as the British ended the ban on the export of artisans and machinery by 1825, and British immigrants provided essential skills in the industrial development of mining, iron production, and textiles. Nothing more clearly reveals the emergence of the northeastern part of the United States as a transatlantic extension of the industrial world (just as American seaboard merchants had been an extension of the European mercantile community) than the creation of further industrialized zones in particular river valleys in New England and mining areas in Pennsylvania, zones that were indistinguishable in their overall character from their European counterparts.

The forerunner of the "factory" that appeared in the United States by the 1810s was the "automatic" mill developed by Oliver Evans during the 1780s. As long as water power remained the main source for mills (the other source was wind, which was more erratic and less powerful), industrial production was confined to sites at which there was a steady flow of water that could be utilized to turn wooden water-wheels or (after the mid-nineteenth century) metal turbines, which in turn moved wooden (or, later, metal) gears as well as pulleys and fabric belts. Mills continued to be places where such power-driven parts produced flour from grains, ground on millstones, and boards from logs, sawed on metal saws. These mills were either "custom mills," providing usable commodities for farmers who brought in grain or logs to be processed, or "merchant mills," whose owners bought grain and logs and sold the resulting flour and boards to those in other areas who did not produce the raw materials and had the means to buy the flour and boards.

During the late eighteenth and early nineteenth centuries, merchant capitalists bought raw materials—such as cotton or leather—and found women and men at home who would use their tools—for spinning and weaving and cobbling—to produce salable products, such as clothes and shoes. Such merchants represented a position that occupied still another niche between feudalistic and fully modern capitalistic enterprise. Like their colonial forbears and their mercantile contemporaries, their "arrangements" with those who provided household manual labor were personal, reciprocal, and varied.

The earliest factories were simply enlarged mills, the water-powered site at which some, and then all, the processes of cloth manufacture—carding, spinning, weaving, and fulling—and of metal manufacture—smelting, forging, rolling, and slitting—were performed. The process whereby these and, subsequently, many other products were turned from manual or craft-made into machine-produced items has been a complicated, sometimes gradual, sometimes overlapping one.

Oliver Evans' automatic grist mill was the model for the totally machine-made product, but many hand- or craft-made items did not suddenly or completely become a matter of factory production. A further development in the processes of industrialization came in the early nineteenth century with the introduction of "interchangeable parts," that is, mechanically produced, repetitively made parts of a given product that could be later assembled as a totality. Eli Whitney introduced the procedure to America in the production of firearms at a government-owned factory, but products with a civilian use, such as clocks, also came to be made in the same manner.

Mechanized production of all kinds usually led to a phase of intense competition, with many producers or operators competing and, in the process, providing goods and services of widely varying quality, safety, and dependability. The groups that created national enterprise were those—like Rockefeller (in oil) and Carnegie (in steel)—who understood how to organize on a continental scale; how to combine within one corporation the raw materials, production, shipping, distribution, and marketing of a good or service; how to undercut competition and move toward a monopolistic position; how to provide dependable, low-cost goods or services everywhere in the United States. These entrepreneurs transformed American industry by integrating and "nationalizing" it. They used any means at their disposal to achieve these aims, sometimes insisting on and getting unfair rebates from the railroad companies, that is, rebates larger than those given to smaller competitors.

Such industrialists were reliant on the development of a national transportation and communication system, however. Continentwide public postal and private telegraph and rail services provided the means whereby officials of such corporations made necessary communications and movement of goods involving each aspect of their nationally integrated enterprises. "Mail-order" houses—such as Sears and Roebuck and Montgomery Ward—made further use of the national postal service and sent products directly to households everywhere in the nation. Retail "chain stores"—such as the Atlantic and Pacific Tea Company—were established in many locations, distributing uniform products. These national firms competed with local and regional ones.

At first, craft unions tried—and failed—to create national organizations that would uphold their position as independent laborers. Not until the 1860s did the state of communications and transportation allow a national trade union to flourish, and, even then, it gave way to the Knights of Labor, a broad, reformist agency that was as much a social brotherhood as a union. Throughout the earliest phases of industrialization, the new wage earners had great difficulty in perceiving themselves as anything other than the independent craftsmen and farmers (or farmers' daughters, in the case of women laborers) they had been. The Knights of Labor, in its definition as a fraternal order, focused on the still-traumatic shift of those who became wage earners and who were unable to fully locate and define themselves within the context of a rapidly evolving industrial capitalism. Similarly, farmers organized the Patrons of Husbandry (or Granges) during the 1870s and 1880s. The Granges, like the Knights of Labor, emphasized fraternity.

Both groups favored producer and consumer cooperatives. Wage earners on farms or in factories, as well as craftsmen and farm owners, supported the establishment of communally owned supply centers and distribution facilities, thus *combining* individual ownership with communalistic organizations and blurring the line between private and public undertakings. So uncertain was the position of such "labor" groups during the early phases of industrialization that they were willing to compromise on one of the basic tenets of a Christian-capitalist pattern of life. Some believed that private ownership and wealth accumulation itself would have to *coexist* with communalistic arrangements.

Industrialism itself had wide ramifications for many other dimensions of American life. The unavailability of an adult male industrial labor force because of the attraction of resourceful farm, forest, and mineral lands and fishing waters meant that a high premium was placed on technological advance, with the result that Whitney's gin for the cotton staple, along with many inventions for mechanistic farming on the huge interior plains, appeared contemporaneously with patents for machinery and processes for industrial production itself. The rapid growth of mechanized production of all kinds was a powerful inducement for immigration. But, industry was tethered to water-powered sites around which grew villages until the middle decades of the century, when coal-fueled steam came rapidly into use as an industrial power source. Only then could industrial production become urban-centered—a process hastened by the introduction in the late decades of the century of hydro- and coal-fueled electrical power, which wholly freed industry from the necessity of having to be located at specially designed geographical sites.

When, in the late nineteenth century, entrepreneurs such as Carnegie and Rockefeller organized corporations on a national basis and tried to create a monopoly over the resources, purchases, production, financing, transportation, and sale of oil and steel products, the United States entered another phase of economic development. American entrepreneurial leaders developed managerial techniques and organization that advanced capitalism to a new level of complexity, but such peculiarly American contributions, as was the case earlier in the century with the introduction of the assembly line for interchangeable parts, did not remain uniquely American for long, as European industrialists and financiers quickly copied them.

Corporations created the National Association of Manufacturers and smaller firms became united in a federation of Chambers of Commerce, both of which brought owners and managers into national associations that could provide the public with positions that the "business community" favored, serving the same overall function that the AFL and the CIO later did for skilled laborers.

The power source for machine-made products changed after the 1880s: from water and steam power to electrical power, produced by water-powered turbines or, far more typically, fueled by coal. Factory or machine production could be located anywhere there was an electrical system in place. Since cities developed such systems quickly, and since they already had a pool of craft labor in shops and recent immigrants from Southern and Eastern Europe mired in poverty at ports of entry, urban centers, from the 1880s to the 1930s, for the first time, became not only commercial and cultural focal points, but major sites for industrial production. Towns tried to compete, tried to keep older, water-powered factory production going by steam and electrical power, but these smaller communities steadily lost out to the far more successful efforts of urban-based entrepreneurial groups, who had factories built and organized in ways to achieve maximum efficiency. Frederick Taylor produced highly influential studies demonstrating the salutary effects of heightened efficiency.

The consequence of such efforts was that increasing numbers of "consumer products" became mass produced in the assembly line factories of an oligarchy of large corporations that came to dominate production. These corporations produced basically the same product—household appliances and fixtures and furnishings, personal cosmetics and clothing—and developed advertising to persuade consumers to buy their products and to use their new forms of transportation (automobiles) and communication (telephones and radios and record players), even though these products and services were virtually indistinguishable from one corporation to another. Mass advertising created demand to the extent that advertisers could persuade consumers to purchase a particular product on the basis of its appeal to status, happiness, beauty, or comfort, rather than its actual superiority over its counterparts produced by other corporations.

Some products continued to be hand-crafted, as machines could not always be made that would replace older forms of craft labor, and, in these cases, the economy of scale that spawned large corporations and factories and plants was not operative. Housebuilding was (and is) a prime example, along with such service tasks as those provided by domestic labor. Indeed, the rigidity of the large corporation, its lack of responsiveness to innovative production and sales techniques meant that small firms continued to be formed even in those areas of the economy dominated by an oligarchy of large corporations.

The creation of continent-spanning corporations meant that it was at least possible for labor to attain the same scale of organization. If a particular product could be made by one corporation everywhere in the United States, those whose labor made it could also be organized everywhere in the United States. The American Federation of Labor, founded in 1886, was a national labor movement whose organizers accepted the "nationalization" of the economy and the industrial capitalism that created such an enlargement of scale. The AFL sought a place in the emergent system, for at least the skilled and still craft-oriented laborers—whether as owners or as wage earners—leaving unorganized those less skilled laborers and machine operators.

Samuel Gompers, as its long-time President, argued over many years that wage earners were an important part of industrial capitalism and deserved the best combination of hours, wages, and security that the system could afford. The laborer's best method to attain those objectives was the work stoppage or "strike," not revolution or the advocacy of reforms that would change the whole system. The major strikes throughout this period were all instances of wage laborers using that very weapon.

Socialists, supported by European immigrants already exposed to Marxist doctrines, favored state ownership of the means of production. But, labor organizations (except for the International Workers of the World) shunned a political party that would drastically alter the relationship between public and private control of the economy. The failure of the Socialist alternative during these decades reveals how supportive labor groups were of the emergent industrial capitalist system, how much they wanted to flourish within it, rather than to change its basic character.

As craft production was steadily declining, replaced by machine production, the number of laborers who were machine operators became proportionately and steadily larger. The labor movement, the AFL, continued throughout this period to restrict its membership to skilled or craft laborers, who were prominent in the construction, metal, communications, and transportation sectors and who were employed in large numbers by owners of firms. It was rare before the Depression of the 1930s for the growing number of relatively unskilled wage laborers in industries with widespread machine production to successfully organize themselves into durable unions.

Relatively unskilled laborers—drifting, transient, growing in number, without a sense of their collective identity and power—failed to perceive the advantage of supporting such large-scale organizations as unions. Not until the national government provided legal protection for union organizing under the National Labor Relations Act of 1935 did such workers successfully organize on a large scale. The Congress of Industrial Organizations organized unskilled and skilled workers industry by industry during the late 1930s, so that, for the first time, unskilled wage earners became a significant part of the union movement.

Full-time job holders were better off in the Depression-ridden 1930s than they had been before; the cost of living fell faster than wages. Everywhere in the industrialized world, large majorities of the workforce were employed throughout the decade. Those unemployed were always a minority, and for many, unemployment was a temporary condition. Industrial workers in the United States had a higher standard of living than their counterparts in Europe. Unions favored government-funded welfare programs, hoping to protect themselves against workers who would accept jobs at any price. Job security was a major priority, as there was much anxiety over the possibility of losing positions. Unions favored the seniority system, opposed work-sharing schemes, and tightened apprenticeship rules. Within the leading industrialized nations, German unions were the most radical and politicized, more than the pragmatic British unions and far more than the weak and divided French unions.

After World War II, labor unions in the United States joined together in one large national organization (the AFL-CIO) in 1955, but the great growth in the locally oriented "service sector" and the large increases of management-defined office occupations has meant that the portion of the population organized into unions has steadily declined from the 1940s onward.

The labor union movement, so significantly aided by government to organize legitimately in the crisis of the Depression during the 1930s, has, since 1970, failed to move significantly out of its traditional areas of strength in the manufacturing sector, and large segments of the service and professional and managerial aspects of the economy remained unorganized (at least by unions). Union organizations involve a progressively smaller segment of the total population, though government (at all levels) and public employees have been successfully organized since the steady growth of government bureaucracy, beginning in the 1930s.

27

Public and Private Sectors

In both the colonial and the national periods, government policies relating to economic activity, if viewed broadly, reveal the nature of the long-term relationships between political and economic or public and private power. The policies that the British imperial and the American national governments developed were always forged with an awareness of a wider context, as westerners everywhere in the world constructed a mixture of public and private elements in their economic life. A brief overview of economic policymaking reveals what the place of the government in the economy has been, at least in broad outline.

One question that the English imperial government and, later, the American government continuously dealt with was what the government's basic, overall relationship to the economic system should be. During the seventeenth and eighteenth centuries, the British imperial government, as did the others with new world empires, tried to create a trading unit based upon mercantilist principles. The Spaniards, Portuguese, Dutch, French, and English all tried to use their colonies in the Americas and elsewhere to supply them with a variety of products that could not be produced at home and to sell whatever surplus accrued to those who lived in other parts of Europe, all the while maintaining a favorable balance of exports over imports, thereby increasing the wealth of the empire. At times, these imperial governments subsidized the production of goods that were marketable in Europe and prohibited the production of other goods in the colonies that would compete with those produced in the homelands of Europe.

England's series of "Navigation Acts" were typical of this kind of governmental policymaking. They fostered, through government subsidy, the production in the colonies of hitherto scarce commodities deemed desirable for the empire, and most products moved freely, without duty, within the empire on the empire's own ships, all with the objective of increasing the empire's overall wealth and economic independence or self-sufficiency.

Mercantilism was economic imperialism in the same way that protectionism later became economic nationalism. Both were efforts to fit and confine economic activity within political boundaries, whether of an imperial or a national kind. Both were at particular times and places at least partially successful, but neither could ever be wholly so in the sense that, unless the governments involved were to outlaw all economic activity with areas outside of the empire or the nation, such activity could never be made coterminous with these political entities. No imperial or national government ever came close to so confining economic activity within its borders, but the governments of all empires and nations became involved in great debates over protectionism. The industrialization that spread through parts of Europe and North America during the nineteenth century underscored what the growth of commerce had already brought to the foreground of government policymaking: Should governments foster economic independence and maturity through protective devices or should they allow the economy to grow unrestricted from "foreign" competition?

After independence was achieved, the new American government soon became embroiled in the same debate that characterized the economic policymaking of other governments where economic activity was reaching complex levels of commercialization and industrialization. Should the national government protect domestic industry and foster the creation of a mature, independent national economy or should that government allow the economy to develop in a context of unrestricted trade in an openly competitive international setting? The Constitution did not provide the new American government the authority, and national politicians lacked the consensus, to build a truly national economy. Clear constitutional authority extended only to the regulation of interstate and foreign commerce and to the imposition of tariff duties.

The Federalists under Alexander Hamilton's early leadership advocated policies that would promote economic nationalism—especially the protection of domestic industry that would come from high tariff duties. By contrast, the Jeffersonian Republicans opposed such protection as being detrimental to American consumers and exporters. However, there wasn't sufficient support in Congress for high duties, until after the collapse of the first party system. The tariff acts of 1816, 1820, 1824, 1828, and 1832 were increasingly protective, passed in free-for-all votes by partyless Congresses.

The anti-Jacksonian Democrat coalition that became the Whig Party during the 1830s rallied round the "American system," propounded chiefly by Henry Clay. This was another program of economic nationalism whose essence was once again the protection of industries that were emerging within the United States so that Americans would not have to rely on foreign production for goods they wanted. Jacksonian Democrats came to favor low tariffs so that Americans could buy goods of the highest quality at the lowest price, whatever their place of origin. During the 1840s and 1850s, the major parties were deeply divided over the desirability of creating an American economy that was self-contained in a manner similar to the mercantilist policy of the European empires of the seventeenth and eighteenth centuries. As the Jacksonian Democrats were usually in control of the Presidency or the Congress, or both, tariff duties tended to be low during these years.

From the Civil War until the Depression of the 1930s, the two major parties were continuously divided in their official positions over the tariff. The Republicans usually argued that the tariff should be protective, with high duties on foreign imported goods, to ensure that there would be "American" industries to produce commodities and services that Americans wanted without their having to rely on foreign imports. The Republicans thus favored the kind of economic nationalism advocated by their predecessors, the Whigs, during the 1830s, 1840s, and 1850s. Democrats typically insisted that a low tariff schedule would ensure that American customers would have the widest possible choice in the price and the quality of the goods they bought. The result was continued gyrations in the level of protection that the national government provided the economy within its borders. During periods of Republican ascendancy, the tariff was protective; during the Democratic interludes, duties were lowered.

Protectionism was jettisoned during the Depression of the 1930s through the Reciprocity Trade Agreement, a policy that has been continued after World War II by the General Agreement on Tariffs and Trade and, in the 1990s, by the World Trade Organization. In a spirit of bipartisanship, both parties have usually allowed the President wide authority to lower tariff duties with other nations if such action in his view benefits American commerce. Growing "free trade" blocs in Europe (within the European Union) and North America (the North American Free Trade Agreement between Canada, Mexico, and the United States) have further opened trade beyond the confines of particular nation-states. With the increasingly transnational character of economic activity, old divisions over protectionism have declined in importance, though groups of laborers and firms in particular industries that are in decline occasionally rekindle the old debate, arguing that government should "protect" domestic industry from foreign competition.

However, since the Depression of the 1930s and World War II in the 1940s, basic government policy has not focused on whether the United States's economy should be protected or should be open to international trade, as was the case before that time. Instead, economic nationalism has become economic internationalism, as Presidencies and Congresses try to protect and advance American commerce elsewhere in a world that, since World War II, has become increasingly interdependent, and whose economy has become increasingly impervious to the efforts of those national governments, typically in the underdeveloped parts of the world, that have sought protection of the kind that Americans and other industrialized nations usually sought while in the act of industrializing during the nineteenth and early twentieth centuries.

* * *

As industrialization spread through various parts of the United States during the nineteenth and twentieth centuries, other basic questions arose as to what the relationship of the government to the economy within the borders of the United States should be: How large should economic firms be allowed to become in a privately owned and presumably competitive economy? And what should the relative strength of laborers and owners and managers be in an industrial capitalist economy in which ownership and labor were becoming increasingly separated? These were questions that were also debated by governments throughout the industrialized world, not just in the United States.

European governments—in particular the Germans, the French, and the British—responded to significant enlargements in the size of industrial firms by regulating, but not prohibiting, corporations that dominated the making of particular products or services. Only in the United States, among the early industrializing nations, was there a consensus that no firm should be allowed to attain a monopoly position. The efforts of certain industrialists to create national monopolies were not allowed to become a feature of American industrial life, as the government passed legislation—the Anti-Trust Act (1887) and the Interstate Commerce Act (1890)—making it illegal to monopolize any good or service, legislation that has, since its enactment, always received wide support in principle.

During the 1900s and 1910s, Progressive reformers emerged as politicians who accepted large, more efficient, better-managed corporations, but who sought to enlarge the authority of government to regulate them and prevent them from becoming monopolistic. Progressively oriented Presidents and Congressmen and jurists were able to enact some legislation or adjudicate some cases, trust-busting court rulings and railroad rate regulation the most notable of such political actions. The conservative politicians who dominated in the 1920s favored trade associations, groups of corporations, and firms manufacturing a particular product who shared information on sales, purchases, shipments, production, and prices in order to plan and create greater stability on costs, prices, markets, employment, and wages. The New Deal briefly experimented with national industrial planning during the height of the Depression in the early 1930s, with the enactment of the National Industrial Recovery Act. Firms dealing with particular products or services were compelled by law (rather than voluntarily associate) to do many of the same things that the trade associations had done during the 1920s. Since the early 1930s, prevailing government policy has been to leave oligarchical-sized corporations in place, but to also protect the existence of small firms through regulations imposed by the Small Business Administration, created in wartime during the 1940s, and to be ever vigilant, through adjudication, to evidence of monopoly.

As for the question of the relative power of labor and management and owners, all of the governments of the industrializing nations debated this question, and many governments in both Europe and its white settler societies overseas acted before the American government had developed a basic labor/management policy.

At the turn of the century, the national and state governments and the courts usually sided with owners in labor/management disputes, which meant that the political system had not accepted labor union leader Samuel Gompers' definition of the place of wage labor in industrial capitalism (that wage laborers are part of the industrial system and should seek ever-improved working conditions through negotiations, and, if they failed, through work stoppages), just as that same political system did not wholly accept industrial leader Andrew Carnegie's justification of extreme concentrations of economic power in monopolistic enterprise (that such extreme wealth should be allowed, but should be used in ways chosen by its holders for the benefit of society). Jurists and politicians believed that *both* monopolistic corporations and monopolistic trade unions were "in restraint of trade," illegal entities if judged to be in control of prices or labor.

The Progressive reformers believed that their efforts to strengthen industrial regulation (through trust-busting and transportation regulation and the prohibition of child labor) produced a more balanced system of countervailing power between laborers and owners/managers. By the 1920s, corporations and small firms with wage earners favored "open shop" associations in which no laborers were compelled to join unions. Some favored aggressive union-busting activities, such as the making of contracts that forced workers to agree to remain un-unionized, the employment of labor spies, the exchange of black lists, and the resorting to intimidation and coercion. Other firms introduced "welfare capitalism" or "industrial democracy" by creating company unions, bonuses, pensions, health programs, and recreational activity.

Responding to the crisis of the Great Depression in the 1930s, Roosevelt's New Deal did not change the structure of the economy. But, it did alter the relative power of the major groupings within the economy. The National Labor Relations Act of 1935 gave all workers the right to bargain through their own unions and prohibited employers from interfering with union activity. A National Labor Relations Board supervised certification elections of unions and issued cease-and-desist orders against unfair management practices. The Fair Labor Standards Act of 1938 set maximum hours and minimum wages for producers of goods in interstate commerce. The New Deal, under the crisis of the Great Depression, provided the legal mechanisms for the achievement of long-term goals for labor.

* * *

Another question that industrialization underscored was focused on an older phenomenon of capitalism: the economic cycle: How much responsibility should government assume over the growth and contraction of the economic activity that occurred within the nation's or empire's boundaries? This question was debated by governments wherever capitalism flourished. Before the cataclysm of the Depression during the 1930s, all levels of the American political system acted in very limited ways to interfere with the cycle of growth and contraction, as did governments elsewhere in the industrializing world. No level of government in this many-tiered federal system acted in ways to ameliorate the human suffering that resulted from a recession or depression. The relationship of government to the economy, in fact, moved away from the paternalism that was a feature of the seventeenth and eighteenth centuries toward a laissez-faire position, especially in the explosive phases of early industrialization. There were economic downturns in 1819–1922, 1837–1843, 1857–1859, 1873–1877, and 1893–1897. All had a distinctive mix of causes: low prices for imports, speculation, inflation, low prices for domestic goods, overproduction. At no point did any level of government in the federal system develop policies to deal with any of these contractions during the course of the nineteenth century.

The national government continued to remain apart from the economic cycle in the decades between the Civil War and the Depression of the 1930s, even as European governments in the most industrialized areas began to regulate the economic system and to provide security against its contractions. President Cleveland did nothing about the depression of the mid-1890s except to remain steadfastly loyal to a monetary policy based upon the gold standard. The recession of 1907 did result in the Wilson administration's reform of the banking system in 1913, after the recession had revealed weakness in the old banking system created during the Civil War, in 1862. In the 1920s, the government's new Federal Reserve System allowed stock purchase "on margin," which had the effect of increasing speculation, which led to the crash of the stock market in 1929, and to the Depression beyond. During the Depression and the world war that followed, Roosevelt's New Deal created national welfare funds and unemployment and old age insurance, enacted financial and banking regulation, and embarked on a fiscal (or revenue and expenditure) policy that created employment, increased incomes, and thus stimulated demand.

Since World War II, the greatest change in the national government's role in the economy is that it has been active as a stabilizer in the economic cycle, using its spending and taxation (or fiscal) and monetary (or Federal Reserve) policies to act as a countervailing force in the expansion and contraction of economic activity. In periods of economic recession, the national government increased spending on the economic infrastructure to offset rising unemployment. Governments (national, state, and local) continue to have a great effect on the economy through their fiscal and regulatory policies, as does the national government alone through its monetary policies. But, as governments do not own or control the economy, their policies cannot banish economic cycles, especially with increasing global interconnectedness, and there has been both prolonged stagflation or recession and prolonged expansion as the administrations since 1970 have applied various kinds of fiscal and monetary policies.

* * *

This brief overview of the American government's economic policies reveals a basic pattern: namely, that the relationship of governments and economic activity in America has always been mixed. There has been neither a government-owned economy nor an economy that governments have failed to regulate. American politicians have divided—as have politicians all over the westernized world—over whether to protect economic development within the United States from "foreign" competition or to allow Americans to compete openly with others, over whether to try to confine and protect economic activity within American borders or to allow it to flow through a borderless economic world. American politicians have also debated—again, like those elsewhere, wherever industrialization has flourished—how regulated large-sized corporations should be and what the relative balance in power between labor and management/capital/owners should be. Americans forged their own responses to these questions, but always in the knowledge that there was a larger, Western context in which economic policy was being formulated.

The socialist alternative—that of government or public ownership of the economy—was never seriously considered by most politicians, at either the state or national level, though such a view had some impact at the municipal level. The reason for this political indifference to the socialist alternative has been that public ownership, beyond the local level, has lacked popular support. Americans have been slower, more conservative, less intrusive, about their economic policymaking than Europeans, Australasians, or Canadians—more content to allow an industrial capitalist system to mature without the control or interference of, though always with the steadfast protection and encouragement of, government.

The question of how much the American government's economic policies actually fostered the growth of the economy within its borders is a murky one. There does not seem to be a clear relationship between the creation and maintenance of government institutions or programs and economic growth or contraction. The economic cycle has not coincided with the existence of protective tariffs, national banking systems, or publicly financed national transportation systems—all of which have existed only sporadically since 1789. Even the conscious use of fiscal and monetary policy to assure growth—a feature of economic policy since the 1930s—has not in fact always produced that result.

In most of the westernized and industrialized world, the public (or governmental) and private (or economic) spheres have been related, but each has retained its own existence, and though governments have tried to shape and direct economic activity, they have never been able to guarantee a desired result. This is the irresolvable dilemma of governments that don't publicly own the economy within their territories. Even in those polities where Communist governments assumed authority during the twentieth century and where "command" economies were directed by government officials, even where, in short, there was public ownership of the economy, governments were not able to guarantee results, if only because such economies were linked to a wider economic world through trade.

PART III

AMERICAN SOCIETY

All human societies have been hierarchical in nature. All have featured social classes, status, rank. These hierarchical arrangements either reflect the way power has been exerted by particular groups and individuals or mirror the positions in society that those who occupy various roles and occupations have been accorded. The society that Americans developed has been dominated by the white European migrants and their progeny and was, in its earlier phases, a somewhat altered borderland version of a traditional and then a modern European society. The other Americans that the white Europeans dominated were out of a mixture of tribal, traditional, and modern societies. Both the native Americans and black Americans, before contact with the Europeans, belonged to tribal societies, though the native population outside of the area claimed by Americans developed a complex society, as did those blacks from west Africa who had lived in large Islamic-dominated states. By contrast, the oriental Americans who emigrated during the nineteenth and twentieth centuries came out of a traditional society, whereas twentieth-century Hispanic or Latino migrants left a society that is a mixture of traditional and modern.

Tribal societies—whether nomadic or agricultural—have been small, largely self-contained, with social relations based upon kinship and village communities. There has been no state organization, no clear central authority, no far-reaching social hierarchy. Customs and rituals have prescribed the rights and obligations of each group within the society. Both the native tribes and black Africans who became Americans originated in societies of this description.

By contrast, the later oriental Asian immigrants came out of a traditional society. The hallmarks of a traditional society are a state organization, a pervasive hierarchical structure, a peasant majority with a small middle class, with families and castes and clans determining status, and a high density of population in both rural areas and large cities. Mature traditional societies throughout Asia and Africa—in China, Japan, India, Persia, the Islamic states of southwest Asia, and northern Africa—were marked by hierarchical arrangements that included hereditary monarchs, aristocracies, castes, and slaves.

During the seventeenth and eighteenth centuries, European society did not differ in kind from those it would come to dominate over the five centuries after 1500. It too was traditional. It too featured the inherited status of a king, a nobility, and lower classes, even exhibiting forms of slavery in its extremities, in Iberia, the Mediterranean, the Balkans. The chief characteristics of modern society are geographical and social mobility, a fluidity within the social structure, low birth and death rates, and an urbanized population. Europe was not modern, nor were its colonial offshoots, except in one significant respect: the English colonists, at least, did not attract an aristocratic elite and quickly became both socially and geographically mobile, with wealth, not inherited status, the chief arbiter of status, thus displaying early evidence of modernity, the earliest anywhere in the world. But the English migrants joined with their Portuguese and Spanish counterparts to enlarge and reinforce the caste system so characteristic of traditional societies by introducing a slave system far more comprehensive than had existed in the European society that they had left behind.

So, the early American society that the English colonists created, while in many ways simply a frontier of a larger European society, was distinctively modern in several senses and emphatically traditional in another. This strange duality continued until the late twentieth century. As Europe modernized, as it gradually displaced inherited status with mobility and fluidity, the Americans led the way, presenting themselves as a harbinger of modernity to the rest of European civilization. But, at the same time, they could not hide their caste system, inhabited by both the native and black African population, through slavery and segregation, displacement and reservation. During the twentieth century, as white Americans tried to dissolve their caste system by moving toward the ending of segregation and as Europeans tried to diminish the importance of inherited status by restricting the power of monarchies and nobilities, the West became modernized, insinuating modern ways of living along with its political and economic penetration of the mature traditional societies of Asia, Africa, and South and Middle America.

Though American society constituted a significant variation on European society with a strange mixture of progressive (no inherited status) and retrogressive (racial castes) features, the fact remains that Americans from their colonial beginnings belonged to a Western society of global dimensions, one that provided a norm for social behavior, social values, for what constituted proper rank and status. It didn't matter whether one were in Europe or along its frontiers, in its white settler societies, in the United States, British North America, South Africa, or Australia and New Zealand: one's sense of class, of proper behavior for one's class, one's likely membership in a large and growing and varied middle class, one's relationship to family and kin and to an increasing number of social institutions—schools, hospitals, jails, orphanages, insane asylums, poor houses—one's leisure time activities—all were shaped by one's membership in a white society that encircled the globe and dominated others everywhere it spread.

Even so, the frontiers of Europe—the white settler societies—were distinctive as a group in three senses. In all three, the variations that Americans displayed in their society were later mirrored in the other European frontiers. First, there was a relative crudity to their institutions and their inhabitants' social behavior, at least in their frontier, newly settled phase. But, this was something that didn't last long. Of much greater importance was the persistent social mobility that emerged in societies without inherited status, without an aristocracy. As significant and durable as a distinction was the presence of nonwhite races. Whereas Europeans could express their racism from afar, in an all-white Europe, as an element of their domination of others, their migrants abroad had to forge replicas of Europe in territories already inhabited by the other races themselves. This gave settler society racism its edge and led to the creation of a racial caste system based in the Americas on the enslavement of black Africans and in all the settler societies on the displacement of the indigenous population into various kinds of reservations where they were to be civilized if possible, warred upon if necessary. Transplanted Europeans, in the homelands of the nonwhite races, enlarged the racism and slavery of Europe into comprehensive castes, not the nuanced, hierarchical castes of traditional (Asian) Indian society, but, by contrast to Europe, a caste nonetheless.

So, though Americans have identified with an "American society," the fact is that in most senses, they were part of a larger society, a European society, and in more particular senses, part of the white settler society that emerged at the frontiers of an expansionist, domineering civilization. "American society" was a kind of fiction that Americans created to extend their sense of distinctiveness to dimensions beyond their political identity and reflects the power of their nationalism.

28

Social Structure

North American native tribal society was characterized by its rigidity of function, position, and status: women were the child-rearers, nurturers, and farmers; men hunted, engaged in political and diplomatic activity, fought wars, and led religious observances. In the nomadic hunting and agricultural tribes, chiefs emerged from significant families and were chosen for their physical, moral, and intellectual strength as much as by heredity. Ordinary families often made sharecropping arrangements with chiefs (as their protectors). But chiefs often gave gifts to tribesmen at ritualistic or ceremonial occasions. Various social and religious rituals marked the seasons and the cycle of life for individuals within the tribes, bands, and families.

Similarly, the black African slaves were forced to leave tribal societies in West Africa that were typically small in scale, communal in nature, and oriented around family, kin, and village. The least complex units were the hunting and fishing bands. Women raised food; men hunted. Kinship groups constituted households, with the senior men serving as heads of these households. Such groups lived in fixed, not seasonal villages, where heads of households constituted village councils. Within these villages, inhabitants were divided into a number of age-based groups. Village councils in turn interacted with tribal chiefs. Such West African societies had developed slavery by 1500, but slaves were war captives, became a part of family households, and were often later freed. These tribal societies—especially those located in the savanna (or grassland) area of west Africa—had often become part of large-scale west African states, but had sustained their localized character, even as parts of larger political federations.

The English migrants who dominated the society that the native and black African tribesmen also inhabited were European provincials, people who believed that they had transposed European civilization to a frontier. British North America was a vast, thinly settled extension of England. The colonial population developed a pattern of life that replicated England's wherever possible, but that differed where desirable.

European society in the seventeenth and eighteenth centuries was *more* hierarchical than African and North American tribal societies because it was larger in scale, and at least the elite groups in European social hierarchies had a self-awareness that involved far more people and far greater territories than was the case with kin, band, or tribe. But the belief that hierarchy was natural to any society was as strong in Europe as it had been in Africa or in North America before colonization. One's inherited status was central to the functioning of society on all three continents.

In Europe, the population was divided into social orders (in Latin *status*, in German *Stände*, in French *état*), with heredity, not wealth, the main criterion for determining which estate any family belonged to. The nobility were descendants of the medieval knighthood and established in these centuries legal rights to land ownership, usually had political jurisdiction over those lands, fulfilled a military function that withered away with the growth of standing armies, and were themselves stratified into greater and lesser ranks. The upper nobility enjoyed vast wealth and landholdings protected by entail, exercised enormous power as patrons, and in states such as Louis XIV's France, Peter the Great's Russia, and Frederick the Great's Prussia, they were organized for services to the state in formal, systematic ways. The burgher estate, contained within self-governing cities, was also vertically divided into patricians, freemen, and propertyless plebs. In all the great cities of Europe, a wealthy commercial and professional class grew alongside the artisans and the urban poor. The peasants were divided into an enserfed majority and a minority who were free or were emerging from serfdom. A prosperous stratum of yeoman and gentleman farmers developed at the expense of peasants who were driven from the land.

The English colonists sustained the hierarchical character of English and European society. The household, the state, and society—the public and private realms—were not distinct and separate. Political and social and economic life were meshed, inextricably linked. Over all loomed patriarchy, dependency, patronage. It was a society still marked by personal relationships of an inherited, unequal kind.

But, the widespread availability of land and property in North America made wealth a significantly greater determinant of social class, status, and position in the colonies of the Americas than in the heartland of Europe, where the basis for wealth accumulation for most people was much more limited during the seventeenth and eighteenth centuries. In Europe, aristocracies and merchants dominated agriculture and commerce through the ownership of land and shipping. Class and wealth were conjoined with inherited status in the form of monarchs and aristocracies whose social identity lay in "court societies" that constituted the fixed apex of European society, an apex to which aspiring merchants and large-scale agriculturists sought admission through the granting of titles, something denied similarly aspiring colonists in America.

The English colonists were bereft of aristocracies and monarchies and thus lacked a social structure largely based upon inherited status. By contrast, there were titled Spaniards and Portuguese, though not French or Dutch, among the elites who dominated rival New World empires. But, in all of these empires, wealth became the basis of an individual's position in the colonial population. And in North America, among the English colonists, the widespread ownership of resourceful land, the relative scarcity of craft labor, and the comparative ease of entering commerce in a land abundant in valuable commodities—all resulted in an incidence of social mobility, of movement from one stratum of society to another, far beyond what was the case in Europe or in the status-bound native American society. The English colonists became unique in the world during the seventeenth and eighteenth centuries in their relatively porous class divisions, in the relative ease with which individuals, through skill, timing, and good fortune could alter their social status, up or down.

Though the English colonists did not replicate the rigidity of either Europe's or the natives' social structure, they added a new caste at the bottom of their own, more fluid and open society—black African slavery. The enslavement of the black Africans as well as the domination of the North American native population, meant that the English, French, Portuguese, and Spanish colonists created a triracial society, in sharp contrast to the European heartland.

The gang labor system of the coffee, sugar, rice, and some tobacco plantations of South, Middle, and southern North America meant that the slaves housed in quarters on the plantations could recreate the communally oriented "village" life of their African homeland. Tribes lost their identities and linguistic purity was obliterated in the melding that both the slave trade and the plantation system produced. These slave communities developed their own means of communicating through "Gullah," or pidgin English, an amalgam of English and African languages, and constructed their own society, with its own hierarchy, with domestic service, crafts, and field labor mirroring the hierarchical nature of white colonial society.

By contrast, the serfs of eastern Europe, while physically immobilized in a slavelike relationship to the Russian nobility, lived in their customary villages and, like peasants everywhere, constituted their own local society. Through service and craft labor in addition to the basic agricultural activity, the serfs inhabited a society that was communal and not very hierarchical in nature. Land was periodically repatriated among the families of the village, so that none became too rich or too poor. The nobility were absentee landlords, a rentier class, who lived far away.

England's practice of not confining emigration to its colonies to its own inhabitants resulted in a unique ethnic variety in the English colonies, as the Spanish, French, and Dutch all barred emigration from elsewhere. Only the English conquered the territories of the other European powers—first the Dutch and later the French—and then incorporated those populations in an ever-growing British colonial empire. Only the English welcomed settlers from elsewhere—such as the Scots-Irish and the Germans—and allowed them to become incorporated in the larger English population.

This was the beginning of a multiethnic population, a new ingathering of rather well-defined, geographically separated European groups, which would later rival the movements of ancient tribes whose migrations produced, through inbreeding, the modern English, French, Spanish, Italians, and Germans. In a similar way, the West African tribes whose members were enslaved and sold in the Americas became, through inbreeding as well, a new amalgam of American blacks. Through yet another instance of inbreeding, the Spanish and Portuguese colonists produced a new kind of racial mixture—gradations of white to colored, the result of various mixings of native Americans, black Africans, and white European colonists. This was in sharp contrast to the professed beliefs of the English colonists who publicly opposed racial amalgamation, but who nonetheless created a mulatto group through the unacknowledged sexual exploitation of their female slaves.

Though lacking the rigidity of Europe's or the natives' social structure, the British colonial population sustained the Europeans' belief that society is naturally hierarchical—that it has a "better" sort, a "middling" sort, and a "meaner" sort. A person's dress, house, means of transportation, manner, and speech all indicated status and class. If a person dressed in the latest European fashion, lived in a house designed after the latest architectural style in Britain, lived in a house large enough for rooms that served particular functions and with furnishings that were used for particular purposes, dined at a table and ate with a variety of utensils, owned his own carriage and horses, exhibited a refined manner, had his own library, and spoke correct English—that person was of the elite.

What people wore defined their social position, in Europe and in the colonies, and every provincial government tried to keep class lines clear with the enactment of sumptuary laws, dictating what people could wear in accordance with their position in society, even though there was no aristocracy and therefore no obvious social divisions. But, the bulk of the population did not pay attention to fashion, only the upwardly mobile. Most colonists made their own clothes in plain styles that existed everywhere among Europeans, built their own houses without reference to architectural styles, lived in houses with only a few rooms used for many purposes, ate with bowls and spoons from common pots, used horses for farm work and basic transportation, didn't own a library, and often weren't literate enough to read anything beyond a newspaper or a pamphlet.

The most exalted position in the colonies was occupied by the planters and the merchants who constituted in terms of both occupation and wealth a nonhereditary aristocracy, an elite that dominated provincial culture, politics, and economy, as well as society—a seamless domination sustained by admiration and emulation (though of an ambivalent nature) of the rest of the population. It was commonly believed that agricultural and commercial pursuits could, if a person were able and worked hard, lead one to attain the position of a merchant or a planter, groups who thus served as social models for everyone else in the population.

However, envy could turn to jealousy, emulation to rejection, and rising social aspirations could be transformed into frustration over one's meager lot and into anger toward a small group with such enormous power and wealth. The deference that usually sustained planter-merchant political office-holding and social-religious-cultural prominence could become rebellion or antagonism in a variety of forms. Overall, such ambivalence upheld social hierarchy and order more than it undermined it. The accessibility of wealth was the basis for the reality and—equally important—the dream of upward mobility, so that a hierarchically arranged population cohered, secure in the belief that the aim of an individual's life in society was to improve one's lot, rather than to make everyone else like you.

The planter/merchant elite of English colonial society modeled itself after what were presumed to be the mother country's counterparts, the English merchants and country gentry. Just as colonial merchants perceived themselves as provincial versions of the great mercantile houses of England, so too did the colonial planters believe they were New World counterparts of the gentry, with the gentry's estate agents as the planters' overseers and the gentry's tenants as the planters' slaves.

In reality, the merchants did fit into a larger European or British commercial context, but the planters' wider world was that of the Spanish and Portuguese planters and miners. The plantation was like the *hacienda* and the *fazenda*, not the smaller English country estate. The planters were at the apex of a society that had more in common with the large landowners of Spanish and Portuguese colonial society or of eastern Europe than with English society. Plantation owners throughout the Americas dominated an agricultural or mining enclave in every sense, acting paternalistically in a semifeudal setting within which all elements had rights and obligations, within which everyone related in a personal way, but within which crops and minerals were part of a commercial capitalistic world involving the trade of staples over huge distances.

By contrast, the nobility of eastern Europe were absentee landlords, often for several scattered estates, with residences in Moscow and military and other governmental service owed the Tsar. The size of their land holdings was typically far larger than that of a mainland North American colonial British planter, even larger than a South American *hacienda* or *fazenda*. The only scale of operation in the American colonies—North, South, or Middle—that came close to those of the Russian nobility were those of the absentee planters of the Caribbean Islands.

The hierarchy in the British mainland colonies that began with the merchants and the planters continued, in descending order, with the professions (ministers, doctors, lawyers), to the middling elements (craftsmen and tradesmen and farmers), down through a succession of laborers—farm laborers, journeymen, apprentices, household servants, indentured persons, general laborers. Hierarchy was a deeply ingrained social principle and extended beyond occupations to politics (office-holders had a special, divinely sanctioned status), social groups (there were such deviant and dependent groups as orphans, the insane, criminals, and paupers who were either private or public "wards" of the population), religion (status was conferred by seating arrangements in the churches and rank was signified by such positions as minister, vestry, and deacon), and family (the family unit was patriarchal and authoritarian in nature). At the bottom of the white hierarchy were the poor, who begged, were occasionally placed in the homes of prominent colonists, or received aid through charities or poor relief administered by various kinds of local governments (modeled after the English Poor Law).

Though thoroughly hierarchical in their social arrangements, the English colonists conspicuously lacked structure in another sense, and in this, they were unlike their European ancestors and contemporaries. Lacking the formal instruction that England's Inns of Court and Scotland's medical schools provided for legal and medical practitioners across the Atlantic, those colonists who acted as doctors and lawyers were individuals who at most received a modicum of training as apprentices in the offices of those who had been trained in a European manner. Instead of the English medical divisions into physicians (doctor), surgeons (mister), and apothecaries (druggist), in the colonies the doctor performed all three functions. Instead of the English legal divisions into barristers and solicitors, in the colonies the lawyer performed all legal functions. This meant that colonial society, in its upper reaches, lacked the professionalization and specialization that characterized British life during the seventeenth and eighteenth centuries. In the colonies, a single individual could be a landowner or a planter or a merchant, but also a lawyer or a doctor; that is, he was "versatile amateur." (Such individuals, at the apex of colonial society, were thus involved in a great array of activities, but lacked the training and expertise of those who performed similar functions in England.)

But, who, exactly, was *in* colonial society? By creating racial castes, the white English colonists developed a society that was considerably smaller than the population who lived within English colonial boundaries. Certainly no English colonist regarded the black slaves (who lived in their midst) and the native tribes (who were increasingly displaced as settlement moved inland) as members of "their" society. Even the status of non-English white colonists was unclear before the naturalization law of the 1740s, and such groups were expected to communicate publicly in the English language and thus undergo a kind of cultural assimilation.

* * *

The American Revolution created a new polity, but not a new society. English colonists became Americans and continued to dominate society in what became the United States and to define who was an American. Of the white settler societies that transplanted Europeans founded from the sixteenth through the nineteenth centuries, politically independent Americans continued to constitute a distinctive triracial, multiethnic population. The Spanish and Portuguese colonists, politically independent by the 1820s, remained a racially mixed society, with fine gradations from pure white to blends of white and native or white and black. British North America, after 1763, and Dutch and, after 1795, British South Africa became dual white ethnic, dual racial societies, with the British overlaying earlier French and Dutch populations, occupying the land with native North American and African tribes.

Later, from the 1820s to the 1850s, British colonists settled in Australia and New Zealand, which became uniethnic (purely British), biracial (white immigrant/native tribal) societies. After allowing open emigration with respect to their North American colonies during the seventeenth and eighteenth centuries, the British favored a more restrictive policy after the American Revolution with respect to South Africa, Australia, and New Zealand. Immigration was the result of either renewed legislation allowing convicts the choice of exile (to Australia) or of idealistic groups who sought, with quite limited results, to entice settlement from a cross-section of English society in an effort to replicate England overseas (at various times in Australia, New Zealand, and South Africa). Only with the allure of valuable mineral deposits did significant numbers of emigrants from Britain flow into these colonies. In this wider context, only Americans were *both* multiethnic and triracial.

White Americans so completely dominated American society that the native tribes and the African slaves became partially acculturated into the white American version of European society. Societies that had flourished in precontact North America and Africa faded away as transplanted white Europeans created a somewhat altered transatlantic extension of Western society, a society that left no space for the flourishing of nonwhite societies in its midst.

The Southern slave system, like the other forced labor system of this time—serfdom—became less harshly exploitative, more paternalistic, even as it became more capitalistic. Planters and landowners throughout the Americas and eastern Europe became defensive during the course of the nineteenth century, as unforced or free labor became increasingly industrialized, that is, transformed into wage labor in a system of mechanized production. Slowly, forced labor began to seem antiquated, unnecessary, and defenders of slavery and serfdom emphasized what to them was its essentially paternalistic aspect. It was contrasted favorably with the new wage labor system, which was portrayed as harshly exploitative and impersonal.

Except for the successful slave revolt in Haiti in 1804, planters and landowners outside of the United States—in Middle and South America, in eastern Europe—all acquiesced to the ending of their forced labor systems as governmental authorities constructed peaceful and legal ways of ending the practice. Masters in all these parts of the world cooperated with the authorities, gaining the best terms for emancipation that they could manage, as forced labor was legally ended by action from above, not by popular violence. In the Americas, everywhere but in the southern United States, slavery was demographically dependent upon continued importations from Africa through the slave trade, and wherever this trade was prohibited, the legal ending of slavery soon followed. Only in the United States was the slave population growing, even long after the slave trade was ended in 1808, which meant that slaves in the American system had a better material life than their counterparts elsewhere. Only in the United States did the planter class seek to preserve slavery in the face of large-scale opposition. Only in the United States did the political leadership divide so deeply that Southerners decided to secede from the union and create a new nation dedicated to the preservation of the institution that made it a distinctive region.

The American Civil War, because slavery was ended during the course of the war, produced at least the appearance of an important change in the character of American society: the ending of the caste system as applied to Afro-Americans. But this change was of a temporary character in that, after a brief idealistic experiment with racial equality during the "reconstruction" period that followed the War, white Americans soon segregated black Americans, recreating the caste that had presumably been ended during the Civil War.

Afro-American slaves reacted to slavery as it spread inland from its original tidewater setting by accommodating and resisting, as non-British white European immigrants did, but in the context of a paternalistic, preindustrial system that gradually gave way to modern notions of capitalism, as planter ideals shifted from a feudal-like concern for personal arrangements and mutual obligations and responsibilities to a focus on the efficient, impersonal plantation-factory. The growth elsewhere in the Union of industrial capitalist ways of operating affected the newer, more inland planters, so that, by the time of the Civil War, the American plantation and slave system had greatly altered in character from its colonial origins.

It was within this shifting context that the slaves on each plantation developed their own community and way of life. In response to the overwhelming authority of the planter and his manager or overseer, slaves constructed stereotypes, each projecting an image of how the slaves wanted whites to perceive them. These stereotypes were a survival mechanism, as were all the ways of accommodating to a system of total coercion, one based on slave patrols and the requirement that all traveling slaves have passes. But, the slaves also resisted by committing arson, feigning illness, damaging property, running away, and occasionally launching rebellions. Slavery in the South always involved white anxiety, because the system was basically one of labor control and represented the most flagrant contradiction to the American ideal of freedom.

Slaves on each plantation formed a community with its own hierarchy: the "field hands," who worked in the cotton and rice and sugar fields; the craftsmen, who performed the skilled tasks that brought a large measure of self-sufficiency to the plantation; the domestic servants, who formed a kind of slave aristocracy, directly serving the planter and his family. This bottom-heavy social hierarchy differed in shape from that of the whites, but both featured the ideal of a hierarchy of unequal persons. Culturally, the slaves occupied a twilight zone, a world neither African nor white, but partaking of both. The ingathering of black African tribesmen had already created a common language. During the decades from the Revolution to the Civil War, the slaves developed a culture of dance, music, folklore, and religious observance that was distinctively their own and that was usually practiced out of the sight of whites.

The paradoxical position of the slaves as an element of the population was that physically they were clearly "in" American society, most of them living around those who constituted one of that society's most powerful elites. But, socially, they were not "Americans," not part of a white man's community, but rather a separate caste, as well defined as any (Asian) Indian caste.

The nonslave black population in the Northern states had perhaps the most heightened sense of self-consciousness of any social group in America. Their cohesion was born of adversity. Only in New England could they vote during the decades before the Civil War. There were many legal restrictions placed on their status as nonslave inhabitants, and, in 1857, the Supreme Court ruled that the "free" Negro had never been regarded as a citizen in the United States and therefore could not be then either. In response to the widespread segregation and racism and to the shadowy position they occupied between citizen and slave, the "free" Negroes of the North met at annual conferences to review their plight and to issue critical statements about the racism that was evident among white Americans. These nonslave blacks generally competed with Irish immigrants for jobs such as domestic servants, and the two groups developed a lasting mutual enmity. Some free Negroes became black abolitionists who usually worked apart from white abolitionists groups, demonstrating that segregation of the races even overrode the common goal of emancipating the slaves.

The native American population shared the experience of being a separate caste, but the tribes were geographically separated from white society. Moving ever west as a result of treaties in which they relinquished their territories, native tribes—even agricultural ones—became nomadic, literally unsettled. Under such conditions, native life and culture disintegrated. The tribes both accommodated and resisted efforts by the white population to "civilize" them.

Some tribes were responsive to government-sponsored efforts, financially supported after 1819 by the "civilization" fund, to educate native children at missionary schools and to introduce to natives the agricultural practices of white society. The "civilized" tribes in the South, before their forced removal in the 1830s, had even developed staple crop agriculture to the point of having a black slave labor force. But many tribes were divided over the desirability of ceding territory or of adopting white culture, and flashpoints of racial hostility fairly steadily erupted into war along the frontiers throughout the entire period from the Revolution to the Civil War. Like black slaves, the native population entered a cultural twilight zone, neither inheritors of a vibrant civilization, nor successful emulators of another that had overwhelmed them.

American society not only contained racial castes. It also became, sporadically, more ethnically varied in its white European population. The inclusion of numerous poor Irish immigrants (especially during periods of depression, particularly during the 1840s and 1850s) among those who emigrated from a peaceful Europe after 1815 because of political and religious repression or economic-social ambition caused native Americans to examine who "Americans" were. Just as the British learned how to colonize on the basis of their experience with the Irish during the sixteenth century, so too did white Americans learn how to define what being "American" meant as they responded to a great influx of Irish immigrants in the mid-nineteenth century.

True "Americans" were not poor, not Catholic, but were well-settled scions of migrants from the "Nordic" peoples of Northern Europe—the English, Welsh, Scottish, German, Dutch, and Scandinavian offspring of the Teutonic or Germanic tribes whose "American" descendants represented the finest ethnic blending of Europeans. Nativists in the 1840s and 1850s founded the American Party, which advocated a long tutelage period for immigrants and delays before the bestowal of citizenship and the right to vote and to hold office.

Nativism was counterpoised with another ideal: America the asylum for the oppressed and depressed, for those yearning for economic prosperity or political or religious freedom. In this view, America was indeed the land of opportunity, the place where there was a new beginning for a corrupt and aging civilization, a new ingathering of European "tribes" that would result in an assimilative society within which the best ideals of Europe would be firmly implanted. Americans were also receptive to the labor such immigrants could provide in a relatively labor-scarce republic. Immigrants became initially propertyless wage earners in factories, foundries, mills, construction projects, and domestic service, providing much of the labor needed in an economically and geographically expanding nation at a time when notably increasing amounts of labor involved processes of mechanization.

The existence of groups of recent immigrants raised the question of precisely who was an "American," who was in the national community defined as a social entity. The Irish and German migrants became U.S. citizens several years after their arrival, yet they were still perceived to be social "outsiders," not fully American. For the Germans, the barrier was a linguistic one, and when Catholic, a religious one. For the Irish, the barrier was both a religious one and an economic one—the typical Irish migrant was poor and remained relatively so. By contrast, German immigrants typically had a trade or a profession and the means to move inland and settle on resource-rich land. Irish immigrants were poverty-stricken and lacked the capacity to move beyond their ports of entry. German settlers created their own inland communities and rural neighborhoods. Irish settlers clustered into ghettoes and created slums in the largest East Coast cities and became unskilled laborers in an alien urban world: domestic servants, dock workers, construction workers of all kinds.

These two major sources of non-British immigrants reacted to their initial experiences in a British-dominated social setting by both accommodating to and resisting the dominant patterns of life, much as the black African slaves did within slavery. The Irish and German newcomers of the 1840s and 1850s attempted to succeed in the usual ways, by accumulating wealth, possessions, and property, but they also tried to sustain their old, non-British way of life by organizing their own newspapers, theaters, and mutual aid societies, through which they provided each other information, entertainment, and aid in emergencies. The Irish and the Germans also tended—as highly self-conscious minorities—to act together politically, favoring one or the other of the major parties. The Jeffersonian Republicans appealed to the Irish around 1800, in response to Federalist legislation restricting immigration and the activity of aliens during the undeclared war with France. The Jacksonian Democrats were also successful in enlisting the support of the Irish in their urban ghettoes during the 1830s, 1840s, and 1850s. Nativists who organized the American Party eventually supported the Republicans by the mid-1850s. The Germans, less densely situated, were less susceptible to the establishment of a unified political affiliation.

This process of accommodation and resistance was beneficial to the immigrants in that it made the painful and satisfying adjustment to a new social reality more bearable. But, the process also produced a nativist reaction among an impatient and anxious native-born white population, who, while proclaiming America as an asylum for the oppressed and dispossessed and poor, nonetheless wanted immigrants whose way of life diverged from the dominant American way to hurry up and become Americanized. The very existence of the immigrants, therefore, sharpened and clarified the question of American identity, as did the presence of slaves, "free" Negroes, and native tribes. American society contained both racial castes and a white ethnic hierarchy, within which old-stock, white, European Americans were dominant and, in their domination, determined who was and who was not American.

The Revolution did not change in any major way the character of society in what became the United States. The new republic did not contain "Americans" who were significantly different from what the British colonists had been. What the Revolution did leave as a legacy was an ideology whose range could extend far beyond political life. How did liberty and equality—the most basic of those ideals—manifest themselves in the economic, social, and cultural-intellectual dimensions of life?

A republican polity contained property-owning voters who deferentially elected citizens who could serve in a disinterested way to further a discernible public interest. When American political culture was enlarged to include all white men, and not just propertied ones, the enlargement was attributable to the combination of an already-large electorate and a competitive party system whose politicians sought as voters growing numbers of propertyless wage-earning white men in cities, factories, foundries, and construction. By the 1830s, all native-born white men (except criminals and the insane) shared forms of political and legal equality—certain liberties and the right to vote, to be members of political parties, to hold public office, and therefore to decide who their paid jurists, administrators, and legislators would be. To be a politician became a career, a job. These developments produced the earliest form of political democracy in the Western world. Republicanism was thereby transmogrified into democracy. This momentous political development interacted with an equally significant development in American society.

In the early nineteenth century the deeply held belief that society was naturally hierarchical was challenged in a basic way, a challenge that was uniquely American. One of the most distinctive features of American society was that large numbers within it came to support a view that was in opposition to the orthodox position that society is naturally hierarchical. "Egalitarianism" was the increasingly popular notion that white men—the dominant element in the American population, but a large element nonetheless—were inherently equal in the sense they were born without artificial and inherited rank, that there were not fixed classes, no better sort, middling sort, poorer sort, that—as the Declaration of Independence stated—"all men are created equal." This attitude differed from the prevailing beliefs of Europeans and made America, for interested European observers, a fascinating, advanced form of European civilization, located on its western frontier or periphery.

Just as political democracy changed republicanism, so too did social egalitarianism. A republican society had at its core a public interest that all could contribute to in a disinterested fashion through the exercise of civic virtue. A republican society replaced an inherited hierarchy with a natural one: elites were marked by virtue, not fixed status. An egalitarian society went further. All were to pursue their *own* interest—to be happy and healthy, to amass wealth, to develop a talent, to be comfortable and secure, to improve one's occupation and social status. There was no public interest or civic virtue. There was no elite in control of society. Everyone should have the right to hold office, not just a political elite; everyone should be able to be a preacher, not just trained ministers; everyone's work should be respected, not just those in trade or commerce; everyone should share the same social titles, and not be separated out as commoners and gentlemen and gentlewomen; everyone should wear the same dress, and not be separated by class-based fashions. In at least these aspects, there was a genuinely democratizing tendency in the social arrangements and behavior of Americans during the decades between the 1830s and the Civil War. Society ran itself; when everyone pursued his or her self-interest, society was better off than it was under the control of an elite in an hierarchical structure. This was social laissez-faire.

But, this egalitarian *attitude* also clashed with persisting social reality. There was still, in America, a hierarchical social system, albeit one more fluid, changeable, and mobile than Europe's, more obviously based on wealth, which continued to be relatively more easily attainable than in Europe. The great paradox of social egalitarianism was that, because it was based on the unbridled pursuit of each person's material self-interest, it was bound to sustain the very social hierarchy that it sought to tear down. Because people inherently differed in their capacity to amass wealth, such a society naturally fostered a new social hierarchy based upon wealth rather than on fixed, inherited status, but a hierarchy as vast in the gulf that separated the lowest (poorest) from the highest (richest) as the one it replaced. Social mobility and opportunity emphatically did not mean social equality. For example, dress and house style were signs of social status, and American elites continued to copy fashion in both dress and architecture from England and France. But, the nature of what men and women of various social levels actually wore and built varied less in style than had been the case during the seventeenth and eighteenth centuries: aspiring Americans copied building styles found in architectural handbooks, divided their homes into rooms and furnishings each of which had a particular function, ate with a variety of utensils on a variety of dishware, bought fashionable clothes that they wore on special occasions, and owned their own horses and wagons, if not carriages.

American society abounded in paradox; not only did egalitarian attitudes coexist with social hierarchy, but freedom overlay slavery, political equality coincided with social and economic inequality, the belief in classlessness was shared with the reality of not only class, but caste, and abolition and antislavery movements arose in a population thoroughly imbued with racism. At the same time white Americans proclaimed that their new republic was a laboratory for the testing of the best European ideals and that America was in the vanguard of freedom, they developed the slave labor system that had originated in the colonial period into the most comprehensive form of slavery in human history, while making the cotton staple the most valuable export commodity in the American economy.

Industrialization and its attendant commercialization and specialization created a profusion of new occupations and, in the process, America lost much of the versatility that had characterized an earlier colonial life. An unstructured provincial society gave way to one not much different from Europe's in the schooling, training, specialization, regulation, licensing, and certification it increasingly required of those who would claim to pursue an "occupation."

Industrialization profoundly affected the old class structure wherever it occurred, whether in Europe or in its frontiers abroad. A new concept of class based upon varied economic criteria was profoundly different from the concept of a fixed social order based upon birth and legal privilege. In Europe, during the nineteenth century, the old rural distinction between nobles and peasants receded in importance as the new urban distinction between the middle classes and the working classes emerged. Both the middle and working classes developed internal hierarchies, just as nobles and peasants had earlier. Professionals felt superior to traders and shopkeepers, just as supervisors in factories thought they were above unskilled machine operatives. Wage laborers became an important element of employment in both farm and factory, and domestic labor became a source of work in middle-class homes. Though America was without Europe's peasants and nobles, industrialization had a similar impact on the occupational and class structure of American society.

In one sense, American society stood apart from Europe. As America's mercantile and agricultural wealth shifted into industrialization, those with the most private power and wealth tended to abandon public office. The planter-merchant "aristocracy" of the colonial and early national periods combined public and private eminence. A deferential polity regularly elected them to public office and they—as regularly—accepted it as a public obligation. But, those who derived their power and wealth from the processes of industrialization tended increasingly, after the 1820s, to refrain from holding elective office, deferring to the careerist politicians who came to dominate the second and third party systems. These politicians shared with the economic elite the same values and priorities. Indeed, the elite stood as models for careerists of all kinds.

As before, the elite's very existence was an indication that all could hope that, through talent and fortunate circumstances, they could become wealthy as well. That social reality was far from this dream did not lead ambitious Americans to turn from either the dream or the reality. It was this widespread ambition for success, wealth, power, and fame that sustained peace and order in a society with a meager police force. Ambition was also a great deterrent to violent change in a steeply hierarchical social structure, a great depressant to those who might otherwise seek revolutionary means of achieving a more satisfying life for themselves. For, there was enough mobility, sufficient examples of lives ending far more comfortably and securely than they started, for ordinary white men to proclaim their egalitarian sentiments, at the same time that they sought to get ahead of those around them—usually in a peaceful, legitimate manner.

The planters continued to form an elite in the slave states, as production of the cotton staple crop spread inland to the Mississippi River, along the Gulf Coast, and beyond—to the Texas Plain. But, power based upon the patriarchy of tidewater planters—power that was premodern in its local, personal qualities, in its web of duties and obligations and responsibilities—slowly gave way to the power of the inland, entrepreneurial, smaller-scaled, upwardly mobile, capitalistically oriented planters, who often became office-holders. When the "newer" planters themselves developed operations on the scale of their colonial forebears, they were still characterized by more impersonal, organized, capitalistic ways of living, though they were much less apt to be office-holders. In other words, the Southern elite became, in the years after 1815, more modern, more like elites elsewhere in America.

Those with the most power and influence in the Southern region of the United States continued to serve as models, continued to dominate all facets of Southern life (except for the political, which—as elsewhere—was left to aspiring emulators, to careerists whose outlook and values differed not at all from those in the highest echelon). The planters acted as a self-conscious elite, aware of sharing a common style of life involving certain schools, forms of hospitality and leisure, and architectural settings.

Elsewhere in the Union, as merchants gradually shared power and wealth with industrialists, a Northern elite evolved a similar pattern, a common denominator of educational, social, and domestic experiences. Once again, this was an elite, serving as a model, whose style of living found many emulators. The Northern upper class, like the Southern one, typically eschewed active political careers, deferring to those basically like-minded individuals desirous of the power and status that political office typically conferred.

Federalists and Jeffersonian Republicans and, later, Whigs and Jacksonian Democrats did not substantially differ in their social background—the former set of parties' leaders drawing from the merchant-planter elite established during the colonial era, the latter set from aspiring careerists. In the nation as a whole, throughout this period, the top 5 to 10 percent owned half or more of the wealth. The American upper class owed its legitimacy (and safety) to a widely shared consensus that wealth was the rightful determinant of one's position in society. Political arrangements were symbiotically related to social reality: the Constitution contained many features that balanced and checked and limited political or public power, but did not, with the exception of the rather vague clause granting Congress the power to regulate interstate and foreign commerce, exhibit a comparable involvement with economic or private power.

Those in the professions occupied a position somewhere between the elite and those below. Doctors and lawyers gradually became more organized, with the American Medical Association and the American Bar Association founded during the 1840s, and training became more elaborate and grounded in the study that law schools and medical schools provided. Most clergymen continued to be educated in church-affiliated colleges, but some evangelically oriented sects did not require their preachers to have degrees, which had the effect of calling into question the status of clergymen as professionals. Teachers commonly lacked special training of any kind and careers were typically short, though "normal" (or teacher training) schools were introduced in several states during this period.

The "middling" elements of the American population continued to be characterized by a mobility unknown in Europe. Some farmers and craftsmen became planters, owners of large, mechanized grain and livestock farms, merchants, or industrialists. There is no evidence that the nouveau riche acted or perceived reality any differently than those already rich. They certainly did not remain notably sympathetic to those who remained as they had been—farmers and craftsmen. In other words, the experience of having been both a middling and upper-class person did not predispose one toward having a large, embracive view of the problems and concerns of those who were left behind. What became clear by the 1830s was that those who perceived themselves to be "middle class" in status engaged in nonmanual labor. This element of the population began to exhibit a particular life-style, to engage in certain kinds of social and cultural activities, to work in particular kinds of settings (stores and offices), and to live in distinguishable residential areas.

Other farmers and craftsmen became wage earners on farms or in larger craft shops owned by master craftsmen-cum-merchants. Mobility could be downward as well as upward. The anxiety of formerly independent craftsmen but newly created wage earners took on various forms in the decades before the Civil War. Such craftsmen formed unions—on local, state, and national levels—whose leaders expressed the concerns of formerly independent laborers whose skills had been essential to the functioning of a preindustrial economy. These unions were troubled by the growing gap between the wealthiest and the poorest Americans in an increasingly industrial setting. They supported the development of public education, the legal requirement that wage earners be paid their rightful wages in hard currency, an end to imprisonment for debt, and favored work stoppages or strikes if wage earners believed they were being paid unfairly low wages or were being required to work unfairly long hours.

For a brief time, these unions supported their own political party—the Workingman's Party—or factions of the major parties (the "Locofoco" wing of the Democratic Party in the 1830s) that were in agreement with their principles. At first, such craftsmen-turned-wage earners were unsure of their new identity: Were they to act as if they were independent, property-owning laborers, as before? If not, who were they and what were their rights and their obligations? Like the new middle class, workingmen began to cluster in their own neighborhoods and engage in their own forms of social and cultural and leisure-time activity.

Farmers who lost a similar kind of status failed to produce an organized reaction—at least before the Civil War—largely because, whereas craftsmen labored in groups, farmers who owned small farms labored alone or with very little additional labor. The same forms of communication and transportation that worked to limit the organizational efforts of craftsmen had a far greater isolating effect on farmers who lived and worked on widely dispersed farmsteads.

Those who were deviant, dependent members of the population occupied an ill-defined position, outside the normal categories of society. They were not "outsiders" in an ethnic or racial sense, but they constituted groups that the dominant elements of American society managed and cared for. Though they were still recipients of private charitable aid, prisoners, the insane, paupers, and orphans were also placed in institutions designed for them (by the 1830s). These institutions were organized in such a way that the deviant groups would learn through isolation and discipline how to become a functioning member of the society that had incarcerated them. The physical, social model for these institutions—prisons, asylums, orphanages, and poorhouses—was the plantation or the factory. The efficiency, impersonality, and organization of industrial capitalism became the basis for other, social institutional arrangements as well.

* * *

Within the context of European civilization American society in the decades after the Civil War continued to be distinctive in the looseness of its class system, in the incidence of its geographical and social-economic mobility, and in its greatly varied ethnic and racial composition. European society remained more structured and static, less mobile and racially/ethnically varied. The European class system lacked the blurring that an overlay of many ethnic and racial groups brought to American notions of class. But, within Europe, class was perceived somewhat differently in particular polities. Germans believed there was a definite, cohesive working class that clearly differed from a business class. The British commonly spoke of the working classes, suggesting a more nuanced sense of social strata. But, for Europeans generally "class" included a sense of culture and education, as well as occupation. In America, one's "class" was difficult to define, especially before the imposition of an income tax (during World War I and thereafter), a tax that graded and classified an individual's wealth, which everyone agreed was the most significant basis for class affiliation. But, "class" also became confused to some extent with ethnic and racial identity as well. The American social hierarchy, unlike Europe's, was connected to wealth and ethnicity and race.

But, European society and its variant, American society, also became more alike between the mid-nineteenth century and the Depression of the 1930s. Many of the developments in American society that occurred during these years mirrored those occurring in European society. Changes in transportation and communication made people all over the westernized world aware of what kind of a society existed elsewhere. But, as Europeans moved to limit the authority and power of monarchs and nobilities, thus making wealth, as in America, increasingly the arbiter of social rank and status, the Americans failed to end their caste system as the native population continued to be displaced and incarcerated on reservations and as freed blacks became segregated throughout American society.

Indeed, Americans refined racism by establishing an ethnic hierarchy that placed old-stock white Americans above new immigrants from Southern and Eastern Europe as well as continuing with an older form of racial superiority, this time with respect to Oriental immigrants from Asia. Old-stock Americans shared this more refined Anglo-Saxon racism with the British, and it became important for these dominant Americans to establish a genealogical pedigree, to be able to trace their European origins to Britain. But the British proclaimed their racial superiority over nonwhite natives in the lands the British colonized in Asia and Africa, not over other European ethnic groups, who remained geographically separate from Britain itself. By contrast, American society was characterized by its multiethnic white population, so that Anglo-Saxon racism, in the American context, turned in on itself. In a society largely without an empire and colonies, old-stock Americans created a new category of "others," of strangers in their midst, strangers who needed to be tutored in order to become real Americans.

The new constitutional guarantees of political, legal, and social equality for blacks were gradually dismantled by Southern state governments and by state and national court rulings. By the 1890s, devices and interpretations barred blacks from voting, from holding office, and from sharing the same social sphere or facilities as whites. Recalcitrant blacks were harassed by secret societies, such as the Ku Klux Klan, or were lynched by ordinary white citizens as punishment for alleged misbehavior.

After the Civil War, most black freedmen remained in the South as sharecroppers and tenants on the cotton farms of large landowners (former planters) or moved west as homesteaders or cattle drivers, thus ending black society on plantations, which had been, in its hierarchical character, a microcosm of white society. As tenants, sharecroppers, homesteaders, and cattle drivers, most blacks also no longer experienced the kind of setting that was conducive to the communalism of tribal African society. However, some blacks migrated as groups and founded "black towns." And, after the turn of the century, growing numbers migrated to the North in search of economic opportunity. Upon arrival, these voluntary black migrants tended—as did immigrants from abroad—to cluster into sections of Northern cities, sections that became known as slums, as racism and the segregation that was its consequence severely limited economic opportunity. In the slums, blacks were able to reassert the communal orientation of the old plantation by using their segregated neighborhoods as places in which family and kin were central.

During the postslavery era, white Americans came to share with white South Africans and white New Zealanders a system of segregation based upon a belief in white supremacy. Among the white settler societies of transplanted Europeans, American and South African and New Zealand whites all faced significant black populations, whether as involuntary migrants or as natives. In the decades after the beginning of white settlement, white New Zealanders and Maoris cooperated, fought, and then separated, though the dominant whites granted full citizenship and political rights to the natives. White South Africans, after independence in 1905, moved the native black population to "homelands" (as white Americans had done with the native population in North America) and segregated the "coloreds" (mixed white, black, and Oriental, as in South and Middle America), bringing to that segregation after World War II the legal and comprehensive character that white Americans had earlier brought to it in the late nineteenth century. During the course of the twentieth century, the white South Africans devised a system of controlling the movements of coloreds and blacks so that they could provide a pool of cheap and serviceable labor to do menial tasks for a privileged white minority. In the United States, there were too many whites for them all to have a privileged and protected economic status and there were too many blacks for them to do all of the menial jobs. Wherever transplanted Europeans confronted large numbers of nonwhite natives, by the late nineteenth century they moved to separate them (into reservations) or to segregate them, if allowed to live among the white population.

Native American tribes fought against white settlers who moved and settled on their hunting grounds in the Great Plains after the Civil War. The U.S. government established a series of forts to protect white (and black) settlers in this area, and there were quite frequent small wars between the U.S. Army and particular Plains tribes during the 1860s and 1870s. The government's overall policy was to continue to make treaties in order to remove and confine the tribes to "reservation" lands, which were invariably the least desirable lands from the standpoint of white settlers.

But, by the 1880s, there was a shift in emphasis to a policy of providing private land allotments, agricultural education, and citizenship for individual native families, with the intended effect of breaking up the tribes that had been placed on common reservation land. This policy of "Americanizing" and civilizing native tribes was deemed sufficiently successful that the native population as a whole was given citizenship by an act of the national government in 1924.

In the 1850s, American governmental and commercial contacts were made with China at about the same time that emigration from China to North America began. White Americans and the Chinese discovered each other simultaneously. The Chinese immigrants left behind one of the great traditional societies in the world. Chinese society emphasized group effort and group welfare. There was a mistrust of individualism and a dependence upon clearly stated and sanctioned rules for behavior. This hierarchical society was patriarchal and male-dominated. The primary institution was the family, and, within it, the oldest member ruled. Education was highly respected. It was believed that age and learning provided the wisdom essential to the smooth functioning of society, and the old and wise were expected to set a good example for others. The Chinese were the most densely populated society on earth, having developed over many centuries an intensive form of agriculture that sustained such density.

But the Chinese immigrants, like many of the European immigrants of the nineteenth century, didn't attempt to continue farming when they arrived in North America. Rather, after attempting to participate in the gold rushes of the 1850s, they became laborers of the kind that accompanied the onset of industrialization, being particularly conspicuous in the construction of the continental rail lines during the 1860s. A racist reaction led by the 1880s to legislation at the state level, legislation that restricted admission of Orientals thereafter. Orientals already in American society tended to cluster into particular, segregated urban neighborhoods, "Chinatowns."

These developments involving blacks, natives, and Orientals occurred in a context of continued racism on the part of white Americans everywhere in the Union—and by Europeans. White Americans continued to share with white populations elsewhere the ethnocentric belief that only white people were civilized, that all other races were inferior. A refinement of such racism was the articulation of the belief that Anglo-Saxon peoples of the world were in the vanguard of civilization. A corollary of British imperialism, Anglo-Saxon racism was a theoretical basis for prejudice against the influx of immigrants from Eastern and Southern Europe around the turn of the century. Leaving areas of Europe dominated by Slavic and Greco-Roman peoples, such immigrants flocked to the United States for the usual mixture of economic poverty and religious or political persecution, but advocates of Anglo-Saxon superiority distinguished America's newest citizens from older elements in the population who were "Celtic" or "Teutonic" or "Nordic" in origin.

Nativism flourished anew—as it once had in response to Irish immigration, before the Civil War—and for many of the same reasons, as Slavic, Italian, and Greek immigrants were associated with poverty, crime, slums, and authoritarian, foreign-dominated Catholicism. Nativism waxed and waned according to circumstances: it was negligible in the 1860s and 1870s, when immigrant labor was a desirable element of economic growth; it was fairly prominent in the 1880s and 1890s, when the by-then large numbers of Southern and Eastern European immigrants began to appear as an alien presence and when the rather severe economic depression of the 1890s created a reaction against additional "foreign" labor; it was not very prominent during the progressive era, when many welcomed immigrants, as long as they would consent to become "Americanized"; and it was very prominent in the 1920s, when widespread disillusionment with foreign entanglements produced anxiety about immigration, led to the reviving of the Ku Klux Klan and hostility toward Catholics, Jews, and blacks, and to a series of immigration restriction acts, which limited the number of immigrants to a quota system based on an earlier census tally of "national groups" within the American population, thus favoring the then more numerous Northern and Western European descendants over Southern and Eastern European ones.

The United States continued to contain an ethnic and racial variety unknown among European nations, though, in these decades, other nations in the Americas—Canada, Brazil, Argentina—began to share the Americans' ethnic and racial variety. The process by which ancient tribes blended to produce identifiable European "peoples" (the English, the French, the Spanish, the Dutch, the Russian, and so on) was continued as "American" progeny resulted from the intermingling of, say, Scottish, English, Irish, French, German, Dutch, and Swedish settlers. What was new in the decades after the Civil War was the source of American immigrants: southern and eastern Europe were added to the northern and western parts of the continent. The Italian, Greek, Polish, Russian, and other immigrants were—like the Irish before them—non-Protestant (Catholic, Orthodox, or Judaic) and overwhelmingly poor, whether their reason for emigrating was economic deprivation or political-religious persecution.

Like the German and Irish settlers before them, the newer immigrants developed their own mutual-aid societies, newspapers, theaters, and social clubs. Like the Irish, they settled in port cities or construction sites, where they worked as manual laborers or as operatives of machinery as ancient trades became increasingly mechanized. Like all earlier groups, they tried to maintain the identity of their homeland, of their original group, at the same time that they tried to assimilate, to become "Americans." Like the Irish, they settled in slums or ghettoes, became involved with crime to a disproportionate extent, and were often mired in poverty or illness. As before, they forced native-born white Americans to develop a heightened sense of their own "American-ness" and to gyrate between making efforts to welcome and assimilate the newcomers and turning away in nativist hostility.

"America" as a haven for the oppressed and deprived and as a land of economic and social opportunity and political and religious freedom coexisted with "America" as a white-Protestant-republican-capitalist bastion whose inhabitants opposed the authoritarian, Catholic, non-Celtic and non-Teutonic, socialist or communist character of the newer immigration. Restrictions on nonwhite Asian migrants were imposed in the 1880s, and, with the revulsion against the internationalism that inhered in America's involvement with World War I, nativism and the attendant suspicion of all things foreign led to an overtly restrictive policy on European emigration in the 1920s.

Though initially distinctive in its great ethnic and racial variety in the context of the Europeanized portions of the globe, the U.S. government, by these acts, nonetheless placed limits on the range of that variety. America was the setting for an ingathering of Europeans, Asians, and Africans. But, by the early twentieth century, limits were imposed on those who wanted to (or were forced to) leave various parts of the world and emigrate to America—Africa (1808), Asia (1886), Europe (1920–1924). Whenever the composition of the American population was perceived by its dominant elements as a threat to the hegemonic position of the early migrants from northern and western Europe and their progeny, efforts were made to prevent the already-polyglot character of Americans from altering further.

In the decades after the Civil War, the views white Americans shared of what constituted a proper society contained persisting mixtures of hierarchical and egalitarian features. There was still a prevailing acceptance of certain kinds of equality for native-born white men. No one denied that citizens should be equal in their liberty under the law and should have an equal right to vote for those who would govern them and act in their behalf politically. A new area of equality for adult white males was that they all shared citizenship in a nation that, after the supreme test of a fratricidal civil war, increasingly gained their loyalty, identity, and allegiance. A growing sense of nationalism interacted with a steadily more powerful national government to produce "Americans" with a distinctive sense of themselves as a people who continued to inhabit the world's most special nation-state.

Such "Americans" continued to believe that white men were not trapped in a class- and status-bound society; were not born into, lived, and died in an inherited social stratum; were in fact capable of changing their position in society through hard work, the development of talent, and the acquisition of wealth—in short, through the equality of opportunity that was open to all white men. Reflective Americans continued to find a theoretical base for such forms of equality in Christianity and in the natural rights philosophy that had been developed in Europe during the seventeenth and eighteenth centuries. But, ordinary Americans found their justification in the relative ease with which white men could gain wealth and property—and thus independence—in a resource-rich continent: at least "opportunity" was—or ought to be—equal for all responsible men, who should share the same liberties, and vote for their governors, and enjoy common membership in a great nation.

But "opportunity" also led to "hierarchy": Some men amassed more wealth, acquired more property, and exhibited more talent and intelligence than others. Talent and wealth produced social gradation as exacting as Europe's, though movement among these gradations in North America continued to produce social mobility to a degree unmatched by Europe's class-bound society. Americans continued to make the acquisition of wealth and property the precondition of liberty and independence, and, though they believed their fellow citizens (if white men) should have equal opportunity to acquire possessions, that was the only aspect of wealth acquisition that *could* be equal—certainly not the outcome.

Elites continued to copy European fashions, whether in dress or in architecture, and were the first to buy motor vehicles when they were made available at the turn of the century. But fashions that started as the property of elites became status symbols for aspiring middle-class Americans as such products became mass produced. Architectural styles were widely replicated in suburban developments; high fashion was sometimes copied in the mass-produced clothing of large clothing manufacturers; assembly-line-made automobiles were sold to ever-growing numbers of consumers.

Added to class distinctions based upon wealth were prevailing views on gender and race. In the case of blacks, racism was far stronger and more durable than egalitarianism, which was at least a strong enough force to begin to overcome the prejudice based upon gender. After the Civil War, male-dominated Americans continued to believe that women should not be citizens, should not vote or have other legal and political rights, should have their own social sphere largely confined to family and household management, and should not compete with men in the occupational world, confining themselves to certain "womanly" occupations. Women's rights leaders attempted to revive the egalitarian sentiment that had expressed itself during Reconstruction, when former black slaves were also given the right to vote through constitutional amendment. And, indeed state governments and the courts began to grant women particular legal rights. After 1900, the progressive movement favored women's rights and supported the women's reform movement generally and the franchise for women in particular, support that led to the adoption in 1920 of a constitutional amendment to that effect. The passage of that amendment revealed the extent to which Americans collectively had begun to change their belief on gender inferiority.

Also providing theoretical support for a hierarchical conception of society was Social Darwinism, the belief articulated by the English philosopher Herbert Spencer that Darwin's theory of biological evolution was applicable to human society and its social evolution. Human societies evolved and, in a process involving the "survival of the fittest"—like the process of natural selection in the biological world—some people became more civilized and successful than others. Spencer's views were popularized in the United States by Edward Fiske, as a lecturer, and by William Graham Sumner, in the academic world, but industrial entrepreneurs like Carnegie were quite familiar with them as well. "Social Darwinism" justified a hierarchical social order, indicating that it was a basic natural phenomenon that governments could do little to alter.

"Reform Darwinists," such as sociologist Frank Lester Ward and Henry Demarest Lloyd, while adhering to the evolutionary process at the basis of Darwinism, argued that humanity had evolved into rational beings who could indeed, through government action, reform and ameliorate the condition of all in society and thus extend and enlarge the process by which human life improved. Such a view informed the "progressive" outlook after 1900. William James' pragmatism and John Dewey's instrumentalism were specifically philosophical systems of thought that were also activist in the sense that both focused on ideas that "worked" or had practical applications in society. These dual intellectual constructs—Social Darwinism and Reform Darwinism/Pragmatism/Instrumentalism—provided the theoretical justification for more reflective Americans in their efforts to define what the proper society should be.

In another sense, America was like Europe. Throughout the more economically sophisticated parts of the world, there was, by the late nineteenth and early twentieth centuries, an obvious specialization of labor. Though there had long been guilds and trade unions and elaborate systems of training (apprenticeship, journeyman, master) in the traditional crafts nurtured in medieval Europe—a system carried over by European migrants into other parts of the world, there was also in the British colonies and, later, in the United States, much evidence of a lack of specialization: planters and merchants who were also lawyers or doctors; farmers who were also craftsmen; teachers or preachers who also labored in other ways; even craftsmen who combined trades.

America had an abundance of agriculturally resourceful land and thus had a labor shortage in other kinds of economic activity as long as farming as an occupation absorbed a high percentage of the population. In such a context, self-consciousness among occupational groups extended only to well-developed craft and professional groups, and the earliest trade unions and professional associations are indications of this. But, machine production and the mass of standardized products that resulted from it created its own profusion of new occupations. As industry and commerce reflected the complexities of large-scale corporations and their many dimensions—raw materials, production, financing, storing, marketing, and sale—many new tasks were developed, all of which required training of particular kinds (whether in institutes or schools or on the job). Increasingly, people were trained for an "occupation"—whether in offices, plants, or shops—and made a "career" of it.

Certain associations, such as the Grange and the Farmers' Alliances and the Knights of Labor and the National Association of Manufacturers and the Chambers of Commerce, tried to unite all "laboring" or "business" people within a common fraternal order, but, with the development of particular tasks and the need for specialized training, other associations, such as the American Federation of Labor, were organized along the lines of specialized occupations. Specialization of an extreme kind was created in the assembly-line technique developed by Henry Ford and others for the production of consumer products, a process in which workers created only a particular portion of a product and not the whole object. In whatever form specialization appeared, Americans and Europeans were alike, for specialization of occupation tended to follow industrialization wherever it occurred.

A related development of these decades—once again, shared with Europe—was the bureaucratization of American institutions. Linked closely to occupational specialization, this phenomenon involved the growth of "personnel" in the larger corporations, unions, institutions, indeed all associations with national dimensions. Organizations that grew generated their own, internal occupational structure, which proliferated because of both inside and outside pressures. The managers in such organizations developed a concern for the most efficient (or profitable, if an economic corporation) structure. Frederick Taylor became, during the 1910s, the most influential of a number of management experts who sought to define and refine "labor time" into its most useful components.

A concern for efficiency and well-defined structure permeated the thinking of corporate and institutional "progressive" managers of many kinds by the turn of the century. The "trade associations" movement encouraged by Secretary of Commerce Hoover during the 1920s was a continuing manifestation of an interest in rationalizing and making dependable and durable the economic activities of American corporations. In this sense, modern corporate capitalism and democratic government alike became impersonalized and increasingly functioned without reference to personal considerations or to the intimate contexts within which merchants and planters and even early industrialists had operated. Another side of bureaucratization was its tendency to proliferate personnel who managed the organization. Those who "produced" grew and declined in number according to the demand for the organization's product or service. But, those who managed were more likely to appear as a consequence of a ruling that the organization needed to be better or more fully managed.

Americans continued to divide themselves into classes after the Civil War, just as they had before. Far more than in Europe, America's class system was largely based upon wealth, not inherited status, and, because wealth was the primary determinant of social position, individuals could alter their status within their lifetime by acquiring more wealth. Those who inherited notable wealth already had a high status from birth. The loss of wealth, within families and across generations, also had the effect of diminishing status. There were some distinctions between "older" and "newer" forms of wealth—between a Rockefeller and a Roosevelt—but no one denied that wealth itself largely determined social status, whether ostentatiously displayed, as the newly rich tended to do, or tastefully managed, as the older wealthy families typically did.

America's rich continued to provide a social model for other Americans, whose efforts to acquire wealth and property *could* result in the comfort and display of the successful or famous upper class. Family farmers could hope to become major stockholders and officers in large corporations. As before the Civil War, Americans continued to emphasize the transcendent importance of social mobility or opportunity, thus undercutting the efforts of those who wanted to alter the hierarchical character of American society in various ways in order to foster social equality. The upper class, in providing themselves as a social model for other Americans, spurred on the social aspirations of a rather variable, changing middle class, and, as before the Civil War, served as a counterweight to any popular sentiment in favor of basic, revolutionary social change.

The *belief* that individual Americans could improve their socioeconomic status reinforced the more limited *evidence* that they did. The acquisition and sanctification of wealth and property and the social status that was based upon them were so central to the values of most Americans that whenever advocates of a radical position attacked wealth or property, their listeners or readers recoiled, as if some defining characteristic of their lives had been threatened.

As before the Civil War, the richest Americans continued to eschew political or public careers, especially at the national level, thus continuing the separation of public and private wealth and power that characterized all areas of the world where modern industrial capitalism developed during the nineteenth century. But, those elected or appointed to public office continued to share the basic ethics and goals of those with great private wealth and power, and, indeed, the "conservative" position that emerged in the decades after the Civil War was that the essential task of government was to facilitate and protect the private wealth-creating economic activities of individuals and groups of Americans.

By the mid-nineteenth century, there were various kinds of affluence that indicated when one was in an upwardly mobile position in society. If a family was able to afford an architecturally designed home; maintain its own horses and carriage or, after the turn of the century, its own motor vehicle; take a vacation at a resort; afford domestic servants; purchase the latest domestic appliances; and educate its children beyond secondary school—then that family had attained a position of affluence and success, even if not in the extremely wealthy "upper" class.

The very rich constituted a national elite during these decades, with the regional variations so notable before the Civil War giving way to the increasing standardization of life that developments in communications and transportation made possible. The elite became an industrial elite by the late nineteenth century, with commercial farmers (both southern and western) and merchants (or commercially oriented businessmen) sinking in status and influence before the entrepreneurs who organized the great national corporations—first in railroads, then in basic commodities (such as oil and steel and sugar), and then in consumer products (such as automobiles, furniture, refrigerators, and stoves).

The very rich amassed huge fortunes. They had large mansions built, with requisite domestic staffs; attended the same elite schools; vacationed in the same summer resorts; belonged to the same exclusive clubs and associations and charities; sat on the same boards of directors; dressed in the latest specially designed and hand-sewn clothing; attended the same weddings, as they intermarried; and believed that they deserved their wealth and power and status, constituting the survival of the fittest.

There was among them far greater self-awareness and knowledge of each other than there had ever been before. As a social elite, they patronized the more sophisticated forms of art (as long as it wasn't deeply critical of the existing society). They sometimes spoke out against radical reformers who sought to persuade Americans to alter their society in some fundamental way and, at other times, defended America as the land of freedom and opportunity, as indeed it had been—for them. But, they rarely entered politics themselves and appeared unperturbed that politicians were others, because they realized that those others favored the maintenance of the very system that had provided a favorable setting for the notable achievements of America's elite.

In the hierarchical class structure that stretched below this elite, the occupational explosion and rampant specialization that accompanied industrialization produced, by the late nineteenth century, a much more nuanced and variegated middle class than had existed since the early part of the century in the form of nonmanual labor. A proliferation of nonmanual, but rather low-income office and clerical workers made the continuation of any simply defined middle-class status unworkable.

The upper middle class consisted of managers and owners of small industrial and commercial firms and large mechanized farms, as well as professionals, such as doctors, lawyers, architects, engineers, accountants, bankers, insurance and real estate agents, politicians, military officers, and senior civil servants. These groups provided the managerial and professional skills that were crucial to the development of an industrial, capitalist economy, and thus to the economic and political management of modern America, even though they weren't the predominant owners of America's wealth. In corporation after corporation, the entrepreneurial founder was replaced by a group of trained managers and professionals who often increased the wealth of a less active elite. Similarly, all levels of civil servants in government were trained to assume the administrative functions of government, willingly abdicated by politicians who themselves often sought efficient, responsive, and fair service for the electorate.

This group lived in a style that indicated success, if not great wealth or fame. They illustrated the fact that the material comfort of the very rich was not restricted to them, that other Americans could partake of the status that things provided, even if on a much smaller scale.

The "middle" middle class consisted of family farmers, skilled craftsmen, managers and owners of small shops and stores, teachers, professors, clergymen, scientists, and anyone else neither particularly rich nor particularly poor. Such groups, while not especially well remunerated, gained self-esteem from the importance of their work and generally identified with those "above" them rather than those "below."

Whether there was an identifiable lower-middle class is not clear. Machine operatives were unskilled laborers, as were those who worked in varied construction projects or who were clerks in various stores and offices. There was some awareness on the part of former craftsmen who had become operators of machines in factories or assembly lines that they were no longer primary producers of hand-crafted products. But, this was an awareness of a shared past, not a class-defined present.

Other social groups retained a high level of awareness—the newer immigrant or ethnic groups from southern and eastern Europe; old racial groups, such as segregated blacks and reservation-bound native Americans: or newer racial groups, such as Hispanic immigrants, beginning significantly in the 1920s. But, this self-consciousness was ethnic and racial, not class-defined. Americans were aware of "class" on the basis of wealth, and income levels at least began to resonate in the public consciousness, especially after the passage of the constitutional amendment permitting an income tax (enacted in 1913), though the census bureau did not popularize such categories until the 1930s. Awareness of class before the Great Depression was imprecise, blurred by the constant movement among various levels. Such awareness as existed had many aspects insofar as levels of wealth and poverty could shape in many ways the material life, behavior, and appearance of every American.

The only "class" that shared the clear visibility of the very rich was the definitely poor. America's lower class failed to exhibit the usual hallmarks of the striving, status-conscious Americans: an ongoing job and a home. Whether handicapped, black freemen, native Americans who left the reservations, poor European immigrants, the unemployed during economic recessions—the poor, so those who were not generally believed, were America's failures, people who had moral defects of character, who were lazy or drunken. The poor lived in slums or in workhouses, were apt to commit crimes, become ill or spread communicable disease, and were in constant need of charity. If all Americans were good, moral, Christian-capitalist-republicans then—it was commonly believed—America, with its abundant resources and its people's increasing capacity to exploit those resources for humanity's benefit, would no longer provide a setting for poverty.

* * *

From the Depression years of the 1930s onward, American society and all the other white settler societies have become increasingly similar, and these frontiers of European society have in turn become more like the European motherland. A more unified Western society has in turn spawned westernized societies within the nonwhite traditional societies of Asia and Africa as well as racially mixed South and Middle America. Wherever a significant middle class has emerged with concomitant social and geographical mobility, westernized societies have developed within larger traditional ones.

Since the 1930s, Europeans and other white settler societies have joined Americans in believing that their society is and ought to be *both* egalitarian and hierarchical, social characteristics that are inherently in conflict with each other. Americans in particular continue to place a high value on freedom for the individual, which to them means (1) political and legal equality (though, for which *categories* of individuals has remained a matter of controversy) and (2) equal "opportunity" for each individual to develop his (or, increasingly, her) talents to the fullest extent possible without harming others and to accumulate wealth, property, status, and position to his (or, again, increasingly, her) fullest capacity.

Unlike Europeans, who haven't abolished all monarchies and nobilities even while rendering them increasingly impotent and less wealthy as groups, Americans continue to reject formally inherited status, though they have tried to sustain the family's position in society through the inheritance of wealth from one generation to another. They continue to adhere to the concept of equality for political voters, religious believers, and citizens under the law, but, in their passionate loyalty to the right of individuals and groups to own property and to accumulate wealth, assure ongoing social and economic inequality. They continue to equate freedom and democracy and capitalism with contradictory congeries of values: individualism, selfishness, and privatism, alongside the perceived need for order, community, and civility.

Since 1930, the objective of an egalitarian society has been broadened by the insistence of minorities that they be accorded various forms of equality, not only in the United States but throughout the Western world. Blacks, with sympathetic whites, developed a civil rights movement that crested in the 1950s and 1960s, as the national government, under pressure, ended segregation and discrimination in public places, in housing, in employment, and in voting. Significant numbers of women in the 1970s and 1980s have supported a feminist movement that has sought to end discrimination in employment and inequality in family life. Homosexuals have sought, by legal means, to end discrimination in employment and housing, and, through education, to change the public's attitude of hostility toward an "unnatural" form of sexuality to one of tolerance of a "natural" one.

The national government itself, through its use of a "progressive" tax system, has at times redistributed wealth and thus used the authority of government to promote a greater measure of social and economic equality. This was the case during the Depression of the 1930s and World War II, when surtaxes absorbed a great deal of the wealth of the richest Americans, but this has not been a conscious, deliberate policy of any administration or Congress since those crisis years.

Since 1930, the objective of a hierarchical society has been continuously sustained by a widespread and deep belief in the sanctity of private property; by a nearly universal desire to accumulate greater wealth and to consume more expensive, better-made, more prestigious products and services; by continued evidence of upward social mobility and the concomitant concern for class, status, and position; and by the resiliency of an antistatist and antisocialist tradition, strongly resistant toward government action that would place limits on wealth accumulation and the power it brings to its most successful practitioners. For the first time, Americans have originated significant fashion styles in architecture (the ranch-style house), in dress (sports clothes), in automobiles, and in industrial design generally, though European imports sometimes continue to be prestigious. As before, aspiring middle-class Americans seek to copy the style of living of the elite by emulating their houses and dress; by gaining admission to highly regarded universities; by taking vacations in other parts of the world; by using air travel; by investing in stocks and bonds.

The Americans continue to exhibit an ethnic and racial variety within a single nation that is unlike Europe's more nearly ethnically homogeneous states (or states whose ethnic groups are still largely geographically separate). There was comparatively little immigration to the United States during the Depression of the 1930s or during World War II, 15 years of global crisis. After the war, migrants to the United States were at first "displaced persons" ("DPs") from war-torn areas of the globe, followed by the usual mix of those seeking a better life than that produced by political and religious persecution, economic deprivation, or familial (or group) separation. Such migrants continued to arrive under the "quota" system established by the immigration acts of the 1920s, until the 1960s, when the resurgence of liberal reform resulted in the enactment of the Immigration Act of 1965, which ended quotas and established a new, nondiscriminatory system.

Since 1930, ethnic stereotypes have gradually declined in force, as the notions that the United States should be an asylum for those seeking a better life and that all ethnic groups are of equal potential has gained strength at the expense of nativist sentiments.

Since World War II, Hispanic-Americans from Mexico and the Caribbean (who were not subjected to the quota system established in the 1920s) have become the largest single group of immigrants in the United States. They have emigrated from a society that is both modern and traditional, with some areas much affected by Europe and North America and with others still in some respects beyond the reach of the modern world.

Hispanic-Americans are concentrated in Florida, the Southwest, and northern cities, and have usually been poor and have worked—legally or illegally—as migrant laborers or sought job opportunities in urban centers, or, if not, have fled to the United States as a political refuge away from oppressive governments. In contrast to all earlier phases of America's development, the chief sources of new citizens from outside the United States has been the western hemisphere itself, and not Europe or Africa.

The other fastest-growing group of immigrants since World War II has been Asian migrants. In 1882, Oriental Asians were the first group to be restricted from emigration to the United States as a consequence of racial prejudice. During World War II, Japanese-Americans, concentrated on the Pacific coast, were incarcerated in detention "camps" in the interior of the continent (even though they were U.S. citizens) for the duration of the war, because the national government concluded that the security of the United States was jeopardized by the freedom of those whose recent ancestors or who themselves had come from Japan.

But, the Immigration Act of 1965 provided equal access to Asians wishing to migrate to the United States. Since the 1960s, increasing numbers of mainly middle-class Oriental Asians and poor Filipinos as well as other Southeast Asians have come from the off-shore islands and appendages (if not from mainland China itself), seeking education, a better material life, enlarged economic security, and political freedom (in the case of those from parts of the Asian perimeter that have been subject to armed conflict or to pronouncedly dictatorial government of a rightist or leftist character).

But, the most important development concerning ethnicity in America since the 1930s is that intermarriage has reduced the ethnic identity of many North Americans and, in the same way that intertribal marriage produced over a number of centuries the modern European "peoples"—English, French, or Spanish—so too are "Americans" being produced out of intermixtures of those with English, French, Italian, German, Russian, Polish, or Spanish ancestors. This process has had the effect of reducing the importance of ethnicity, as increasing numbers of Americans trace their heritage to two, three, four, or more European groups.

So too has social and economic mobility, as many of the newer immigrant groups have joined older segments of the population in becoming "Americanized" as middle-class citizens whose ethnic identity has receded as an aspect of significance in their lives. New immigrants retain their closeness to old-world patterns, and even those who have focused on their "American-ness" have in recent decades nostalgically sought to revive that association from the vantage point of a secure socioeconomic position. The Heritage Act of 1972 recognized those ethnic longings and provided federal funds for "ethnic studies" in the schools.

As ethnic and racial groups from other parts of Europe, as well as from northern Africa and southwestern Asia (the Middle East), have moved as immigrants into the more prosperous parts of Europe since World War II—primarily to Britain and to Germany, nativist movements similar to those that had flourished earlier in America arose in the homeland of the West. The nativism so long associated with the United States has become an international phenomenon as migrations have created nativist reactions in other parts of the world. After the war, Britain and France enacted legislation governing the movement of those who have sought to emigrate to former imperial centers, but have tightened these regulations as nativist reactions to growing immigrant communities created social unrest. Germany has restricted its non-German immigrants to "guest worker," noncitizen status.

The racism of white Americans has declined since 1930, especially among the more educated elements of the population who have been influenced by anthropological and sociological study. These social sciences have gone beyond the boundaries of "Western" ethnocentrism and its assumption of white superiority to embrace cultural relativism: that no race or "people" or group of any kind is superior or inferior to any other, just different or more sophisticated or naive. Before the emergence of a mass reform movement, liberal-oriented, government-induced change came slowly, and was indeed out ahead of popular opinion: Franklin Roosevelt's Fair Employment Practices Commission and Truman's desegregation of the armed forces both fitted this description.

Since World War II, the notion of racial equality has been difficult for the relatively uneducated Americans who have lived in rural areas or towns or in cities near racial minorities to accept, as a tolerance of "others," especially those visibly different, has not been a characteristic of such people. Certainly, resistance to the civil rights movement during the 1950s and 1960s was strongest among such groups.

However, even educated Southerners generally resisted the new view of racial equality until the judicial decisions of the 1950s and the legislation of the 1960s made segregation illegal and public opinion seemed solidly and durably in support of these national governmental actions. Southern resistance to the early phases of these changes was deep and prolonged, but the civil rights movement, which rallied growing numbers of sympathetic whites and blacks, was even deeper and more prolonged as black-dominated organizations both old (the National Association for the Advancement of Colored People and the Congress of Racial Equality) and new (the Student Non-Violent Coordinating Committee and the Southern Christian Leadership Conference) joined to produce nonviolent protest—"sit-ins," "bus-ins," marches—against state laws that perpetuated a racially segregated society. Martin Luther King emerged as the most influential black leader of the century and, by his actions and his speeches, effectively articulated the goals of the civil rights movement. Non-Southern whites were responsive, as were Presidents Kennedy and Johnson and Congresses (especially in 1964 and 1965).

But, even with the official end of segregation, many blacks continued to protest their low socioeconomic position in American society, that is, the much-greater incidence among blacks of poverty, illness, ignorance, and crime. The civil rights movement, by the late 1960s, became more radical and much less peaceful, as large-scale rioting and widespread destruction of property occurred in a number of black ghettoes in major American cities, such as Detroit, Washington, and Los Angeles. Organizations such as the Black Panthers and the Minute Men came to dominate the black protest movement, with the goal of terrorizing American society through violent actions that would force the dominant institutions to change and somehow end the subservient position of blacks.

The black community itself, from the 1930s to the 1960s, was "bottom-heavy," that is, contained a hugely disproportionate segment of people in the lower socioeconomic positions. During the Depression of the 1930s, blacks were very badly off because, in addition to being segregated, they endured a great calamity during which their economic security was seriously jeopardized, with many more whites than usual seeking employment. During the war, many blacks found jobs of a war-related kind, but, after the war, these gains were not sustained, as most labor unions continued to resist integration and the acceptance of blacks as members.

Since the 1960s, with the official end of segregation and the establishment of a legal basis for equal treatment in housing and employment, the black middle class has grown rapidly, with many moving out of the old, segregated inner cities to the suburbs, in the manner of many white ethnic groups. But, the percentage of blacks living in poverty and within the confined ghettoes of America's large cities has remained relatively high. America's poor blacks engage in a high incidence of crime, are on welfare programs in large, single (female)-parent families in disproportionately high numbers, and constitute a kind of "underclass" in which prevailing middle-class values, such as honesty, sobriety, efficiency, diligence, and steady labor, are much impaired.

Changing racial attitudes, especially on the part of the more educated and influential segments of the white population, have affected relations between whites and the other racial minority groups as well—Native and Hispanic Americans and Asians, both Oriental and brown. Since 1930, Native Americans have remained the poorest of all identifiable groups in American society. In 1934, the national government reversed its long-standing policy of attempting to change natives, so that they could live interchangeably in white society. The Indian Reorganization Act returned substantial authority to the tribes themselves, including the right to own land collectively, and provided public funds to support tribally oriented educational and cultural activity. The act reflected the new view that races and cultures were naturally different and, therefore, that it was inappropriate for a dominant group to obliterate or "enculturate" a minority one.

By the late 1960s, mindful of the black civil rights movement and its subsequent radicalization, natives became organized into various associations, and some became militant by the 1970s, organizing "sit-ins" and "occupations." A more fruitful activity has been the successful lawsuits that particular tribes have brought to federal courts involving the charge that the national government has violated its ancient treaty obligations.

Militancy of another kind during the 1960s was reflected in the activities of the United Foodworkers' Union, a largely Hispanic organization whose membership consisted of the poorest of the Hispanic immigrants: the migrant agricultural laborers from Mexico. Led by Cesar Chavez, the "UFW" engaged in strikes and boycotts against the commercial agriculturalists in the American Southwest and enlisted the support of established civil rights groups. Since the 1960s, some Hispanic immigrants, as has been the case with other racial and ethnic groups, have experienced social and economic mobility, in this case in New York City and Florida.

Similarly, oriental Asian immigrants from Japan and China (Hong Kong, in particular)—that is, from some of East Asia's off-shore islands—have also exhibited a capacity for attaining enhanced status and wealth, though this has not been a notable characteristic of brown immigrants from the Philippines and Southeast Asia.

Through all of these changes, there have remained persisting, popular, white racial stereotypes of blacks, natives, Hispanics, and Asians. Like all such stereotypes, these are related to reality, that is, are overgeneralizations based upon what has sometimes been observed. Blacks are poor, dirty, violent, loud, lazy, sexually aggressive, and produce too many offspring. Natives are drunk, poor, lazy, passive, though occasionally erupt into violence. Hispanics are poor, grubby, teeming, and volatile. Asians are stand-offish, inscrutable, and either passive and lazy (brown Asians) or aggressive, abrupt, and excessively hard-working (Oriental Asians).

Since the 1930s, all of these racial and ethnic groups have become increasingly strident in their insistence that they are not outsiders, that they are "Americans" as much as old-stock American families are, even though such organized protest and reform movements have stressed the duality in their group's identity: they are not *just* Americans, but also identify with their place of origin. Only ethnic and racial intermarriage has blunted this dual sense of identity. The result is that while longevity of residence in North America for one's ancestors remains a basis for determining how "American" someone is, the newer white ethnic and the nonwhite racial groups have also come to claim an identity as Americans. Since the 1930s, for the first time, American society has come to include all who live in the United States.

In terms of occupations, Americans—as those in the other industrialized parts of the world do—continue to value specialization, which has burgeoned in the more sophisticated aspects of the economy and society—in the professions and in technically oriented jobs, and training for some positions has come to extend several years beyond whatever basic education seems appropriate. Skilled laboring jobs still require standardized training periods. And yet, specialization has not been a characteristic of another area of occupational life: the vastly enlarged "service sector" involves many kinds of employment for which specialized training is minimal.

And, in recent decades, especially since the 1960s, technologically generated occupational change has been so swift that many of the more educated Americans have come to expect that they might have several "careers" or occupations, with further education and training a sporadic activity throughout their lives.

Governments at the national and state levels have, since 1930, introduced job training and retraining programs in recognition of the ending of certain kinds of production and the emergence of new ones.

The bureaucratization of American life (as has been the case all over the "developed" world) has increased markedly since 1930. In all dimensions of American life, vast institutions exist, sometimes dominant, at other times co-existing with smaller entities, but always characterized by a form and a size that generate impersonal human relationships among the people who inhabit them, whether they be business organizations, corporations, labor unions, social organizations, political parties, governments, or educational institutions.

Since 1930, the very rich have continued to provide social models for other Americans. The most successful American is one who has used his talents to amass wealth and material comfort and luxury. The primary importance attached to wealth continues to give the very rich a fundamental legitimacy and authority in American society, only rarely challenged or questioned. Since 1930, only during the Depression, when it appeared to many that the future or desirability of capitalism itself was highly uncertain, and again during the 1960s, when the new left and the counterculture movement questioned the attainment of wealth and material possessions as a life goal, were those who owned a highly disproportionate segment of America's wealth challenged in their role as society's models. Each challenge, though vigorous and controversial, was not sustained for more than a few years.

The prevailing attitude of most Americans with respect to private wealth and property—that it is fundamentally desirable—has assured that the capitalist system—and the class structure it fosters—has continued to prevail, and attempts to institute revolutionary alternatives to that system have been correspondingly feeble.

Americans have also subscribed to a contradictory social objective, that of social service. The trauma of the Great Depression of the 1930s undermined their sense that all individuals who tried to develop their talents to the fullest would be successful. The political liberalism characteristic of the New Deal legislation of that decade laid the foundations for a welfare-capitalist state, a commingling of a humane, caring social order, protective of its unfortunate and "failed" people, with one that continued to give priority to the successful attainment of material comfort and wealth. Americans who seek careers or occupations in public or social service represent the obverse profile of those whose primary objective is to develop skills and talents that will lead to status, wealth, and success, though in practice the two social objectives intermingle in the life and work of most Americans.

This new system—"welfare capitalism"—continues (as elsewhere in the developed world) to consist of separate but closely interactive spheres of public and private, of the government and the economy, of politicians and business people. Government obtrudes into most aspects of social/economic/cultural life in a regulatory way, just as all aspects of American life are affected by the commercial/consuming nature of economic life. Politicians perceive the world in a businesslike manner and usually represent the dominant interests of a hierarchical, capitalist society, but also—because of America's democratic polity—are aware of the problems and concerns of minorities, whom they try to accommodate without fundamentally altering the social order. Likewise, business people pay obeisance to the varied interests of a polyglot population—its concerns for economic security and welfare, cultural activities, and environmental protection—but do so without jeopardizing the dominant place of business in the society—its wealth-generating and profit-amassing activities.

The American class system continues to be based upon wealth, though, since 1930, there has been more attention paid to whether the wealth is "new" or "old." Those with newer wealth are thought to be more focused on material opulence and less given to public service than those to the manor born. Americans generally still emphasize that, relative to Europeans, their society is more mobile and lacks the inherited status and the rigidity of class lines still prevalent across the Atlantic Ocean.

And yet, Americans have emulated Europeans when they have attempted to ensure that their status, position, and wealth be perpetuated—at least to the next generation—through inheritance. Reformist Presidents and legislators have tried, especially during the Depression and World War II, in the 1930s and 1940s, to redistribute wealth through inheritance and capital gains taxes and surtaxes and steeply progressive income taxes. But, whether such taxes have been raised or lowered—as in the more conservative 1950s and 1980s—one fact stands out with exceptional clarity: there continues to be a very small minority who have the talent to amass or perpetuate great concentrations of wealth.

This group has, since 1930, changed in composition, with newcomers entering with regularity, but it has also been rare for a well-established family to lose its position altogether, even during the Depression years. The very rich, the top 5 percent (in terms of overall wealth) have controlled half or more of the nation's wealth since 1930. As before, this group continues to send its children to the same schools (preparatory and "Ivy league"), live in the same neighborhoods (at the edge of metropolitan areas), attend the same social functions, belong to the same associations and clubs, and vacation at the same resorts. What is new is that America's elite exists in an internationalized context, which jet travel and telecommunications make feasible and desirable.

The upper middle class ("white collar" managerial and professional groups, both industrial and agricultural) have expanded somewhat (except in the agricultural sector) as a proportion of the total population. These groups "manage" the economy and the society and typically seek even greater wealth, status, and power or influence for their efforts. They are acutely conscious of living by society's prevailing norms and attempt to be trendsetters as to what is fashionable in terms of material furnishings, social and cultural activities, and personal and social behavior.

The middle class shares the upper middle class' aspirations, but lacks its success. These office and store and production and service employers and employees are *both* burgeoning (in the office and store and service areas) and declining (in productive facilities) in number, as the economy moves from a productive to a service and knowledge-based orientation. Machine operatives, whether industrial or agricultural, have declined in proportion to the total population—gradually in the case of industrial laborers, swiftly in the case of agricultural. The support that this group provides for the goals that the upper middle class articulates is crucial for the stability and order that characterize American life.

The lower class—the "poor"—have continued to be America's "failures," even though there has been increasing recognition in the wider population that poverty has many causes. Since 1930, various forms of welfare capitalism have benefited the poor, even as the capitalist system has produced them. Poverty was still represented as a condition of personal failure, and the shame attached to it led many to hide their ignominy and embarrassment as much as possible, even though others tended to blame the system as much as defects of character. During the 1930s, under the spur of the Depression, the federal government set up temporary welfare programs for those mired in poverty and established the Social Security program for the temporarily unemployed. During World War II, poverty became a rare condition, and many who had been marginal to the economy became active participants in it, with a concomitant change in status. After World War II, state governments continued to provide welfare payments to the poor and, beginning in the 1960s, the federal government produced additional funds and instituted a food stamps program. The larger public has continued to support public assistance programs at the same time that it demonstrated a growing concern that those on welfare and unemployment may be unwilling to work.

There is some evidence that the "work ethic" has been weakening as a factor in the work life of the general population, especially since the 1960s, when the "counterculture" questioned the importance and goodness of a work-"drugged" life. Relative to those in other parts of the developed world, Americans have also shown—especially since 1970—a notable predisposition to spend or consume, rather than to save or invest, and to make quick profits, rather than build for a long-term future, and to take speculative risks and then expect government "rescues."

Since 1980, there have been significant numbers of "homeless" poor as a result of the early release policy of halfway houses for criminals and mentally handicapped persons, as well as a consequence of the decline of certain kinds of skilled and unskilled manufacturing occupations along with the absence of significant quantities of government-assisted, low-cost housing projects and the presence of commercial and "gentrification" redevelopment manias. Since the Depression, when poverty was an experience shared or witnessed by most of the population, the poor have tended to live physically and socially separated from the middle and upper classes, in communities or cultures of poverty, with their own forms of income and consumption, and of social, family, and personal activity and behavior.

* * *

Viewed in a global context, America's social structure has been, as elsewhere, steeply hierarchical and has exhibited vast inequality. As a variant of European society, like the other white settler societies overseas, Americans created racial castes, thus establishing a "bottom" to the social hierarchy that went far below Europe's. But, it was also the case that America and the other frontiers of Europe lacked a nobility, Europe's caste at the top. Nevertheless, it is equally the case that American society was the first in the world to make wealth the leading determinant of status, to include great ethnic and racial variety, to develop an egalitarian outlook, and to experience significant social mobility. These characteristics alone make American society distinctive in important ways.

But, in order to determine how distinctive, it is necessary to examine the American social structure from wider perspectives. What we see from them is that first other white settler societies and then other industrialized societies elsewhere have become ethnically and racially mixed, that wealth has become the leading indicator of social status wherever industrial capitalism has become dominant, that the egalitarian outlook has challenged belief in a traditional social hierarchy in many industrialized areas of the world, and that social mobility has accompanied industrial capitalistic growth wherever it has occurred. American society has indeed been distinctive in important ways, but what Americans have initiated others have experienced later. These most significant social innovations were not encased in America for a long period of time.

29

The Family

The family is society at its smallest scale, and in America, as elsewhere, family life mirrored life in society in many ways. The families of the native tribes, the African slaves, and the European colonists were similarly authoritarian and paternalistic, with the father/husband playing the dominant role. In all three, the functions that men and women performed were clearly distinctive and defined by tradition. In general, male tasks were public, coercive, protective; female tasks were private (within the household), nurturing, caregiving. What separated the families of the English colonists from those they dominated was that the colonists, like their European contemporaries, were somewhat more flexible in their arrangements, less obedient to tradition. Though without a legal identity in public matters, a married women, if a widow, could take over her deceased husband's estate.

The native and African tribes were also more rigid in their observance of rituals attendant upon the various turning points in the lives of family members: birth, puberty, courtship, marriage, death. Alone among the three groups, the native tribes separated women during menstruation and birth. Both Africans and native Americans encased puberty in rituals, whereas the colonists, in the European manner, did not mark that time of life. Both marriage and death were the object of much ritual among all of these groups. For all, marriage and burial at death were sacred ceremonies. African marriages involved a "brideswealth," a payment from the groom's to the bride's family, whereas a dowry among the transplanted Europeans was a sum that a bride brought into her marriage.

Families in parts of Africa were polygamous and in many parts were extended, with various kin sharing a house or compound. The native tribes of North America were not polygamous, but some of them had communal longhouses as residences. The English colonists were deeply opposed to anything but monogamous marriages, and family homes were not usually shared with relatives, but kinship groupings sometimes clustered within particular neighborhoods. In all three groups, families were typically quite large, as there was a benefit in the added labor of children in family-run farms and craftshops. The fact that many children died of disease created an additional inducement for married men and women to have large families. Those who lived into adulthood could then provide for the security and welfare of aging parents.

In all three groups, the family, as the smallest and most important unit in society, performed many basic social functions. For English colonists, African slaves, and native tribes alike, the family was the mechanism for instructing and apprenticing the young, caring for the old and the insane and the sick, providing work for the poor and a place for criminals and slaves to labor. Outside of the coastal population centers, the colonists lacked the social institutions of a more thickly populated England—orphanages, insane asylums, hospitals, jails, poorhouses. Prominent colonial families in rural neighborhoods and villages were charged with caring for the deviant and dependent elements in the population. Families of all kinds constituted vocational institutes for training sons and others apprenticed out as farmers, craftsmen, and professionals. Such passages of life as birth and death were performed at home, in a family setting, though marriages involved church ceremonies.

The basic social group in American society, as elsewhere, was the family. In the decades after the Revolution, the family retained its essentially patriarchal character, even as other aspects of life were losing this characteristic, were becoming more modern, more impersonal, more stringently organized, more modeled on the "factory" as an ideal form of social organization. In this sense, the family was the last social unit in modern European civilization to retain its premodern character.

The father-husband was still in a position of indisputable authority. The mother-wife continued to be without legal rights. She could not own property, sign a contract or a will, testify in court, vote, or hold office. Unmarried women became teachers and earned income as manual domestic weavers and spinners of cotton cloth for merchant capitalists, or as the earliest factory workers in the cotton mills. But, middle- and upper-class women, women who were married and didn't have to work for an income outside of the home, were supposed to live up to the woman-belle ideal, the cult of domesticity: they were supposed to be pious, virtuous, nurturing. They were, like freed black slaves during the late nineteenth and two-thirds of the twentieth centuries, supposed to inhabit a separate but unequal world.

The woman's sphere was a paradoxical one: She was "up on a pedestal," idealized, made perfect, at the same time that she was denied the rights of men. She was to attend her own schools (except for the new public school systems whose founders denied that gender discrimination had any place in learning), work at her own occupations, nurture and raise the children, manage the home, serve as a watchdog over morality and culture, organize her own clubs and associations, and refrain from any inappropriate public and private behavior. Some women performed these roles well; others felt confined and anxious; a few started the women's rights movement and organized women's benevolent associations in an effort to effect change in a (for them) intolerable situation.

Children continued to receive early training at farm work or as apprentices to a trade or a profession (there was no "adolescence," as the teen years later came to be called), but, increasingly, youths left home for schooling and job training. The family began to shed its role as chief vocational institute and setting for the next generation's occupations.

Wage laborers of whatever kind worked elsewhere, as typically did tradesmen, professionals, and those who generated incomes from the increasingly complex mercantile and industrial spheres of the economy. As the family, home, and occupation became separated, the family setting became a refuge from the work setting, a place where family members could escape the pressures of a modernizing capitalist economy. In the process, the family shed other roles as well: social welfare and educational institutions, whether created by state governments or by private groups, were organized outside of the largest population centers in rural areas and towns by the 1830s, institutionalizing the care that better-off families had given in earlier times in an informal way to such groups as children, orphans, criminals, paupers, the sick, and the insane. The new public school systems and orphanages trained children away from homes and, through regimentation, tried to produce future adults who would be model members of society.

In the decades after the Revolution, the family continued to play a basic economic role: It transmitted through wills the accumulated wealth from one generation to the next, perpetuating and augmenting and diminishing social and economic equality. By such means, the family assured that there was rarely true equality of opportunity, that the wealth of white men was almost never simply a matter of individual ability. The desire to perpetuate wealth, success, eminence from one generation to the next meant that the Americans who proclaimed their allegiance to egalitarianism practiced the opposite.

From the mid-nineteenth through the early twentieth century, family life altered somewhat. The dominance of fathers/husbands was not directly challenged, but the world of wives/mothers and children changed to some extent. The position of women improved, partly through their own pressure and partly through the actions of sympathetic, liberally oriented men. Women continued to be educated in the growing public school systems and in colleges and universities, both their own and coeducational, and started to enter the professions. Increasing numbers of state governments gave women property rights and voting rights, and, finally, through a constitutional amendment in 1919, women gained the right to vote in federal elections as well. The occupational explosion that accompanied industrialization and the growth of social welfare institutions resulted in the hiring of large numbers of women to low-status clerical and sales and nursing positions, greatly extending remunerative work outside the home beyond earlier, domestic-connected occupations such as teaching and spinning/weaving machine operators in the first factories.

Older children were called adolescents, teenagers, a newly visible phase of life extending from sexual maturity to social/economic/political maturity, and child labor laws after 1900 began to restrict the basis on which adults could hire such children to work at the same time as other laws established a minimum age for leaving what became standardized elementary and secondary school systems. Orphanages became custodial institutions that cared for those children separated from their natural parents. Custodial too were the old people's homes and nursing homes that various levels of government as well as private organizations founded when many families sought to reduce their size to nuclear proportions as they moved away from agriculture and no longer needed a large family labor force. Institutionalized as well were such passages of life as birth and death, as increasing numbers of Americans were born and died under a doctor's care in a hospital and were buried under the supervision of an undertaking firm.

American family life, during the 15-year crisis produced by depression and war (1930–1945) had its traditional role shaken, if not durably altered. In the 1930s, the home became more than ever a refuge, a place of intimacy in a world of enormous uncertainty and insecurity. Many members of a household—which often was enlarged to embrace relatives and grandparents—were relied on to earn income of some kind, and the status and authority of the father/husband was thereby diminished. During World War II, many women—many of them wives and mothers—worked in war-related occupations, and many husbands and fathers enlisted in the armed services and thus were absent for extended periods. In either case, the traditional structure and function of the family were altered, at least temporarily.

But, so entrenched was traditional family life that these changes were not sustainable beyond the immediate crises that had produced them. Following World War II, until the early 1960s, fathers and husbands again assumed their accustomed positions of authority. The ideal for wives and mothers again became the "housewife," a woman who stayed at home, did not work, raised the children, and managed (what became for middle- and upper-income families) increasingly technologically sophisticated households.

Since the 1960s, American families have become more democratic with the emergence of women into the workforce and the resulting appearance of a standard two-income, middle-class family. The counterculture of the 1960s stressed the importance of group and communal living, which others have since sustained. From the 1960s onward there has been a steady growth in unmarried couples (heterosexual and homosexual) and in divorce and remarriage.

In the midst of all these developments, the family has become less authoritarian and patriarchal. Under the impetus of the feminist movement, women—especially working women—have become coequals in the raising of children, as well as in matters involving the financial, recreational, and social aspects of life. Middle-class children have often grown up with both parents working, a situation that has resulted in an increase in the importance of the children's peer group at school and at play. Schools have become more significant as shaping influences on children, especially on those whose parents are regularly absent. Youths themselves have experienced an adolescence that in recent decades has extended in some cases well into their twenties, as prolonged educational programs keep young adults in a twilight world of biological maturity coexistent with social and economic immaturity.

But, through all these changes, the family since World War II continues to be a refuge, a haven, but also the setting for the tensions between the intimate interaction of parents and children on one side and the impersonal standards of the wider society on the other side. Social institutions such as orphanages and old people's homes have in recent decades emphasized returning their inmates to the community through foster parents and home care, thus veering back toward the familial context of colonial times.

From a global perspective, family life within the dominant white population of America has never been significantly different from the larger European or Western norm. The black and native elements in the population, though in separate castes, were tutored by whites to have their family life mirror that of white society, in the case of natives through missionary and governmental activity, and in the case of the slaves through pressure from white owners. And though both the blacks and the natives were able to some extent to retain the communal nature of family life from their precontact cultures, as both groups have moved into American society, the character of their family life has not differed greatly from that of the white majority, even though black and native families often face problems stemming from a long legacy of racism and poverty. As for American whites, foreign observers have often thought that American family life has been more democratic and open. And, there probably was some loosening effect from the early onset of political democracy and social egalitarianism. But, both of these developments were restricted to white men until the twentieth century. During the seventeenth, eighteenth, and nineteenth centuries, the American family was hierarchical and patriarchal, as it was elsewhere in the Western world, and it has only been as a result of a great change in social values, the growing strength of liberalism as a social philosophy, and the emergence of the feminist and child rights movements that family life in the United States, as elsewhere in the developed world, has become more democratized.

30

Population Growth

Though the native tribes in the Americas were decimated by disease during the time of initial contact with the European colonists, their numbers gradually increased thereafter. African slaves had developed immunities to the same sorts of diseases as the Europeans had, and so their number steadily increased in all areas of the hemisphere, but especially in the English mainland colonies and, later, the United States, both because of high birth rates on the plantations and because of the regular infusions of new forced migrants from Africa in the slave trade.

The Portuguese, Spanish, and French all limited emigration to their colonies and so population increases were fairly small. Only the English encouraged emigration. Early in their colonial experience, the headright system was developed, which was a scheme for inducing people to emigrate through the granting of 50 acres of free land to anyone who would leave England or who would pay for the passage of someone else to leave. Later, the English enacted legislation that gave certain categories of criminals the option of being deported to the colonies in place of being incarcerated in England. Through emigration and by natural increase, the English colonists grew in number at an astonishingly high rate, the highest in the Western world by the eighteenth century.

The English colonists shared with other European colonists a fecundity that related both to a more adequate food supply for a population that was more typically rural than Europe's and to the absence of endemic disease of the sort that continuously occurred in the more crowded populations of Europe. But, even though more spread out as a population, the colonists experienced epidemics of contagious diseases, all imported from Europe. Their food supply was abundant by European standards, and the colonists added wild animals and plants (typically introduced to them by native tribesmen) not present in Europe.

Staples of the diet varied considerably from region to region, depending on the place of origin of the colonists: the Dutch, the Germans, the Swedes, and the French all tried to sustain the eating patterns they were used to, as did the English majority, even though there were regional variations *within* England and, thus, in the various part of the colonies that English migrants settled in. Eating in America quickly became a pastiche of European and African and native ways, depending on the group and on the location. Pigs and chickens, which could forage for food, were raised everywhere. Fish and pork were staples because they could easily be preserved by salting and smoking. By contrast, cattle were driven to market and slaughtered on the spot. Root vegetables were stored over the nongrowing season. Whatever the variations, most food was cooked all together in stews or pottages and, by modern standards, was dull and tasteless. Drink was either milk (in the northern and middle colonies) or beer or whiskey (both widely distilled) or rum (imported) or cider (from apples). Fruit was plentiful, orchards common.

After the Revolution, the American population continued to be very fast growing, relative to Europe's and even faster than the other white settler societies, a rate of growth that made America the wonder of the Western world. This was because of significant amounts of immigration, but even more, due to the continuing rural nature of much of the population (still more, proportionately, than in Europe). Rural Americans exhibited a continuing need for lots of children to labor on the nation's relatively large-scale farms. Such widely dispersed people had a notable access to fresh food and therefore failed to provide itself as a good host for communicable disease on an endemic basis (as in Europe). However, as American population centers became larger, epidemics of contagious disease became correspondingly more serious, sporadically through much of the nineteenth century, as were efforts to quarantine the affected population and to find ways to inoculate the rest of the population and to stop the spread of what came to be recognized by the late nineteenth century as disease-producing microorganisms.

In the decades after the Revolution, Americans ate and drank prodigious amounts of food and beverage by European standards, and their diets became more varied as the kinds of fresh vegetables considerably expanded. In the case of drink as well, tea and coffee—both imported—were added to whiskey, beer, and cider. As food came to be prepared in separate servings, Americans ate stupefying huge meals of fried foods, fat meats, and few and overdone vegetables. Pork and corn continued to be dietary staples for much of the population, with slaves subsisting on a particularly monotonous and unchanging offerings of these two foodstuffs. Sylvester Graham led a diet reform movement whose advocates urged Americans to eat more balanced, restrained, and unprocessed meals. The Grahamites had some effect on eating habits, but technological innovation had much more impact on the availability of what Americans ate. Popular by the 1840s, the "canning" of foods as well as its refrigeration in "iceboxes" (in urban areas at first) greatly enhanced the preservation of food and reduced Americans' reliance on produce grown in nearby areas.

From the Civil War to the Depression, the American population continued to increase at a rate greater than Europe's and that of other white settler societies. A rapid decline in the farming population was offset by a large influx of immigrants from the late nineteenth to the early twentieth century. Communicable diseases continued to produce epidemics. But, vaccines—quickly shared by health systems all over the developed world—proliferated during these years. Frozen foods (developed by Clarence Birdseye) were added to canned foods, as food production and food processing became a huge industry that underwent the same process of consolidation that marked many other areas of economic activity. Refrigeration was added to railroad cars, making possible the large-scale movement of meats and vegetables over great distances. By the early twentieth century, chemically derived preservatives added to the shelf life of many mass-produced food products. With the development of the science of nutrition, Americans gradually became more aware of healthy, balanced diets. Immigrants from many parts of Europe and Asia introduced varied menus in restaurants located wherever they settled. What Americans ate overall continued to be enormously varied in contrast to Europeans and still heavily dependent on sources from elsewhere than was the case of the more ethnically and geographically discrete Europeans, or even of the ethnically purer other white settler societies.

The American population was stable during the crisis-ridden 1930s and 1940s, with immigration at low ebb in a depressed and then a war-torn world, and with American families producing relatively few children at a time of economic hardship and wartime separations. But, throughout the developed world, from the late 1940s until the early 1960s, the generation that came of age during the war years produced a "baby boom" during a time of postwar optimism and a resurgence of traditional family values. Since the early 1960s, there has been a much slower growth rate everywhere in the West, as more emphasis has been placed on an individual's life apart from raising children, something that the feminist movement has particularly emphasized. Furthermore, immigration in recent decades—from South and Middle America and Asia, as well as Europe—has been relatively small. Americans—on average—live longer than before. As elsewhere, medicine, especially with vaccinations and antibiotics, has helped to extend life, as has improved food and water supplies. Beginning in the 1960s, there has been an increasing public awareness of the importance of physical fitness, nutrition, and health.

31

Social Behavior

The well-behaved English colonist was a good Christian, owned his own property and was a good farmer or craftsman or professional, and participated as a voter in a political system based upon representative government. These were the aims of life, and the behavior of individual colonists was measured by how well it exemplified these aims. For those who misbehaved, the churches they were members of censured them for un-Christian behavior and local or colony-level government punished them for infractions of the law. The administration of justice was heavily influenced by the way the British dealt with illegal behavior. Justices of the peace or judges and juries in courts determined the innocence or guilt of the accused. Jails were places of confinement as those charged awaited the outcome of judicial proceedings. The purpose of punishment was to evoke penitence on the part of the criminal or to serve as a warning to others not to commit the same offense. Punishment varied from stocks to whipping to hanging, depending on the severity of the crime. The African and native tribes both had simpler systems of justice, with victimless crimes not punished at all and with the families of victims given the responsibility of determining the punishment of those who committed serious crimes.

Americans, like Europeans, were concerned about proper personal and social—private and public—behavior. There were many sources for what constituted proper behavior. Models were delineated in sermons and published guides; in newspaper commentaries and magazine articles; in celebratory orations and commemorations; in prescriptive, melodramatic novels, plays, and poems; in lectures and debates. Various kinds of moral tutors urged Americans to be good Christians and good capitalists; to uphold the work ethic; to be hard working, improvable, competitive, dependable, sober, pious, peaceful, and loving. There was a built-in tension between the materialistic and spiritual components of a well-behaved American. The get-ahead, wealth- and property-accumulating, individualistic orientation of the American as a good capitalist could be combined only with difficulty with the generosity, selflessness, and communistic proclivities of the American as a good Christian. Or contrarily: the American who expressed his capitalistic identity by investing with others to create a corporation or by working for a wage with others in productive facilities larger than the craftsman's shop or a farmer's field and the American whose Christianity was focused on inner spirituality, on concern over his own salvation—such a combination of materialism and spirituality produced strain.

Americans, therefore, were guided in many ways on how to behave properly, even though the prescriptions were inconsistent and contradictory and therefore difficult to follow as guides. Aristocratic European observers thought that the behavior of Americans was—from their vantage point—characterized by its crudity, roughness, and lack of refinement. The egalitarian attitude that prevailed among native-born white men, beginning in the 1830s, tended to undermine the refinements of class-defined behavior that still prevailed in Europe, the homeland of these observers, but "class" still had meaning in America with respect to behavior: social greetings and leave-takings, visiting, proper deportment in the workplace, in public places, at home—all were shaped by class and status. As in Europe, an individual's class was revealed in his dress, grooming, hygiene, use of language, degree of civility, style of house, and means of transport.

Americans who misbehaved did so in particular places and settings, each with its own consequences. In their own homes, there was marital discord, wife beating, child abuse, drunkenness—all without legal penalty, largely because it was the Christian view that marriages were divinely sanctioned and permanent. Misbehavior in a public context involved pre- and extramarital sexual activity in houses of prostitution, drunkenness in saloons, and gambling in taverns, though such institutionalized settings existed only in the larger towns and in the early urban centers. There was not a consensus that these particular forms of misbehavior constituted crimes. However, murder everywhere, violence in public spaces, and the theft or destruction of private or public property—all were defined as criminal acts everywhere in the United States.

There is abundant evidence that Americans indulged in these more serious forms of misbehavior, but whether they did so in greater measure than contemporary Europeans is unclear. What is obvious is that Americans did not develop sufficient governmental instrumentalities (police) that could have served as a deterrent against major forms of misconduct, relying instead on moral suasion and precept as their chief means of prevention. Professional police departments developed in the largest urban centers beginning in the 1830s, as a response to rioting between immigrants and native-born Americans. Gradually, smaller communities established police forces of their own. The prison established before the Civil War was supposed to be a center of rehabilitation, as carefully disciplined inmates, it was hoped, would reenter society as reformed individuals.

The model for proper personal and social behavior continued from the Civil

War to the Depression to be the Christian-capitalist-republican. As increasing numbers of Americans lived in large communities, there were efforts of growing volume and visibility by clergymen, politicians, editors, and businessmen to articulate what was "proper" behavior in cities filled with strangers in need of civility for their various forms of social interaction and discourse. A "good" American learned not only that the aim of life should be to work steadily at becoming and remaining a Christian-capitalist-republican, but that such a person behaved properly while alone or in a social context. Guides to etiquette became steadily more common in the mid- and late nineteenth century and in the early twentieth century.

This American ideal continued to contain contradictory tendencies. Was the good Christian *necessarily* a good capitalist and republican? Was the good capitalist *necessarily* a good Christian and republican? Was the good republican *necessarily* a good capitalist and Christian? These ambiguities became heightened by the 1920s, when the emergence of the American city as the new focal point for American life provided the basis for an altered social model: the urbane sophisticate, whose pleasure-seeking life-style was somewhat at odds with the older, rural-town-based model of the industrious, sober, pious, responsible American. The prevailing social model began to shred apart, as one more manifestation of urban-rural tension, animosity, and ambivalence.

For those who misbehaved, civil and criminal law constituted the political and legal definitions of society's rules and were the basis—along with the common law—for the punishment of such behavior. States, counties, and municipalities all continued to develop law-enforcement institutions—notably police forces and jails—during these decades to apprehend, try, and, if found guilty, incarcerate or execute miscreants. Trials continued to be social morality "plays" or dramas at which those in attendance, and a much broader audience who learned of the proceedings through newspaper and, starting in the 1920s, radio accounts, all participated in a collective judgment on a person's bad behavior. The jail systems that developed in these decades lacked the curative objectives of those founded during the 1830s and 1840s. Criminals were subjected to public trials, which functioned as a warning for the rest of the population, but their incarceration in jails was a private punishment, as was the hanging and, increasingly, the electrocution of those who had committed the most serious crimes.

There were three forms of behavior that were the subject of much controversy in these years, the question being whether or not they should constitute sinful and criminal behavior: gambling, prostitution, and drinking alcoholic beverages. Those who believed that these acts were wrongful favored the enactment of laws—on the local, county, state, and national levels of government—that would make them crimes. Those who disagreed opposed such efforts. Movements in opposition to gambling, prostitution, and alcoholic drinking developed in various parts of the United States, the largest and most durable of which was the temperance crusade. Alcoholic drinking was by far the most widespread of the three practices.

In their personal and social behavior, Americans have not had as clearly and universally accepted a social model since 1930 as they did before that time. Non-Christian beliefs, as well as atheism and humanism, have become important alternatives to a "Christian" life. However, a devotion to capitalism and republicanism remains a central, defining characteristic of a virtuous American life. In a narrower sense, the social models that the urban sophisticate and the rural simpleton provided after World War I have given way since the 1950s to the health-conscious person, as awareness of fitness and nutrition has grown and the physical and mental dangers of drugs, alcohol, tobacco, and excessive eating have become more widely known.

Secular laws enacted and enforced and adjudicated by secular governments provide the rules for proper (or "legal") living, and churches—except for those formed by groups of fervent fundamentalist Christians, Jews, and Muslims—no longer constitute the main basis for a virtuous, moral life—or for proper behavior to the extent that they did before 1930. Social misbehavior continues to involve ingesting drugs, sexual promiscuity, and gambling, but in different forms than in earlier periods.

As for drugs, prohibition, which began when a constitutional amendment went into effect in 1919, failed by 1933, when the constitutional amendment was repealed and drinking alcoholic beverages again became socially acceptable behavior for a large segment of the population from the 1930s through the 1950s. But, since 1960, the danger to health that such drinking poses has become increasingly known. By the 1960s, drug ingestion (marijuana, cocaine, LSD, heroin, "crack") was favored by those Americans in the counterculture, and, during the 1970s and 1980s, wider segments of the population became involved, seeking instant enhancement of experience. Drug taking has divided the American population, however; it remains illegal and, since the 1970s, drug traffic has become a major law-enforcement problem, involving foreign sources (even governments) in various parts of the world. In the meantime, tobacco has become widely known as a health hazard, and the percentage of Americans who smoke, while still significant, has gradually declined.

Prostitution has been regulated locally since 1930, but still flourishes and involves both women and men (since homosexual activity has become more openly practiced and socially acceptable). During the 1960s and 1970s, advocates of the counterculture, some younger middle-class urbanites, and many in the homosexual community favored sexual promiscuity, at least until the AIDS epidemic broke out during the 1980s, an epidemic that has led to a growing awareness of the risk of such activity. Since the 1950s, contraception and abortion have also become divisive issues. The Catholic Church's hierarchy opposes contraception. Fundamentalist Protestants and Catholics have joined in opposition to abortion. Moderate Protestants and a majority of Americans have opposed restrictions on contraception and abortion in varying degrees and have increasingly favored safe sexual activity for pleasure, divorced from procreation.

Gambling has flourished in certain jurisdictions within the United States and has been widely practiced in clandestine and illegal contexts. Since the 1950s, lotteries have been organized and managed by many state governments as an additional source of revenue, and many Americans have legally gambled. The lure of instant wealth has been enormously attractive to a people for whom wealth accumulation has been of central concern.

Serious crimes—willful injury and murder, vandalism, theft of money and property—have slowly but steadily increased since World War II. During the depression-ridden 1930s, there was a decline, but the racial and class tensions of the generally prosperous post–World War II period have exhibited a lessening of respect for life and material possessions. Since the 1960s, when the new left agitation and the civil rights movement brought these tensions to a peak, all levels of government have enhanced and enlarged funding for law enforcement agencies. Since then, police forces have come to be trained to deal with a varied community in varied situations, as "guidance counselors" as well as protectors. The liberally oriented Supreme Court under Chief Justice Warren ruled that the police must respect all the Constitutional rights of suspects and those charged with crimes.

From a global perspective, there is nothing peculiar about the ways Americans misbehaved or about their efforts to combat such behavior. Throughout the Western world, wherever there has been a Protestant majority in a given polity, there has been a tendency to try to eradicate gambling, prostitution, and inebriation, to gain allegiance to a strictly Christian morality, whereas Catholic-dominated populations have tended to tolerate, though not openly condone, such sinful activity. As for the more serious forms of misbehavior, that is, with respect to violent crimes, Americans have displayed a notably deep-seated mistrust of external authority, especially if it seems arbitrary, and have strongly favored the right of citizens to bear arms, which has led to a distinctive tendency to indulge in the private and sometimes violent settlement of disputes or the forcible taking of property.

32

Social Reform

The tribal societies of the black African slaves and the native Americans contained no mechanism for the willful change of those societies by those discontented with them, other than through ongoing decisions made by widely representative tribal councils and occasional religious movements whose adherents preached in favor of new ways. Mirroring European society, the English colonists did not develop peaceful means for those who dissented or sought to reform their society. Editors of journals weren't social critics of the population they presumed to inform, dependent as they were on advertising of merchants and craftsmen and (if fortunate) on income as "public printers" for the colonial assemblies. Nor were clergymen social critics. Though many ministers found much to criticize about the failure of their parishioners to abide by God's laws, to be as moral as they should have been, ministers did not usually go on to be critical of the political, economic, and social arrangements by which their parishioners lived, mainly because such clergymen believed the Christian faith was in harmony with those arrangements. The work ethic gave divine sanction to an expansionist capitalist economy.

Among the colonists, criticisms and dissent were most often expressed through violence, through rebellions and mob actions. Frontiersmen who felt that colonial government did not equitably represent them on occasion rebelled against colonial authorities. But, during the seventeenth and eighteenth centuries, neither Europeans nor their colonists in the Americas had constructed mechanisms by which people could peacefully dissent from the positions taken by public authorities; there was no protection against libeling persons acting in the public domain. Dissent had to be expressed within legislatures, not without.

The prevailing attitude was that individuals in a Christian society sinned, and they always would. Society could not be reformed and cleansed of bad behavior.

Only in the 1760s, when opposition arose to British imperial policies, did dissenters begin to portray Europe itself as a corrupt society, whereas colonial society, by contrast, was a beneficial setting for virtuous living. It is in this context that dissenting theorizers created a portrait of America as the salvation of Europe, the place where the best European ideals would have the best chance of succeeding. The successful revolution that followed made dissent and reform respectable: no longer should people simply accept society as it was. They should criticize it, make it better, perfect it.

The American Revolution established a precedent for the revolutionary remaking of society, a precedent that the French Revolution established for Europe soon afterward. But the European model involved large-scale civil violence, not the generally peaceful, though embittered confrontation between rebels and loyalists that occurred during the American Revolution. Thereafter, the American revolutionary precedent meant to reform-minded Americans that they should at least try to achieve reform through peaceful means. The Constitution makers of 1787 thought they were reforming society through the institution of republican government. They thought of themselves as practical philosophes, putting into a Constitution the basis for a society that would be blessed by a government whose nature more nearly realized European ideals. The American state makers of the 1780s believed that in the new republic Americans would create a society that fulfilled Europe's highest expectations.

The group who led the rebellion against Britain from 1775 to 1783 and drafted a new constitution in 1787 were members of America's late-eighteenth-century political, economic, and social elite. For them, reform was a profoundly political act, one rightfully presided over by themselves, individuals who occupied the most elevated positions in the society of their time and who were routinely chosen to positions of leadership, out of deference, by those beneath them. Never again would the significant reform of American society occur both under the auspices of the highest elite and in such a purely political way. Henceforth, social change was initiated by discontented middle-class individuals who sustained social protest movements or by middle-class politicians who tried to use government to rid society of its imperfections. By the early nineteenth century, the elite, whose exemplar was Thomas Jefferson, withdrew from active public duty and became increasingly focused on the exercise of private power through the amassing of wealth.

Several decades after the great public reforms of the 1770s and 1780s, not everyone was satisfied with America society as it had evolved. By the 1830s, some individuals in the second and third generations after independence became dissatisfied with the gulf between American ideals and American reality. Only a tiny fraction of Americans ever became committed reformers, and those who did did so for a variety of reasons (like those who rebelled or remained loyal to Britain in the 1770s). Whether prompted by a secularly or religiously oriented conscience (focusing on failures to develop further the revolutionary ideals or on failures to sufficiently approximate Christian perfectibility), enough Americans became reformers, became convinced that they knew how to effect ameliorative change that the period of the 1830s, 1840s, and 1850s was a time of varied reform activity, and those most involved sometimes approximated an interlocking directorate of beneficial "do-gooders." These individuals were not usually politicians themselves and what they produced were social protest movements that sometimes pressured for political action, but that also tried to stir up the public itself, to nag at its conscience, to induce individuals to reform themselves and thus society too.

American reformers responded to an impulse that affected certain Europeans as well during these years. American reform movements were part of a wider, transatlantic world of reform, and cross-fertilization of varied kinds took place between American reformers and their European counterparts throughout these years. Many transatlantic movements shared similar kinds of organization and ways of protesting and of dividing and ebbing and flowing in strength and influence. Some of these movements have not ended yet. The kind of social reform that had its inception in the early nineteenth century has been a continuous feature of Western society thereafter. But, from the perspective of the Western world—of Europe and its extensions abroad—only in the United States were there so many contemporaneous reform movements that it is appropriate to refer to an era of reform. Within the wider European and transatlantic context, there was a unique connectedness between British and American reformers that was based upon a common linguistic and political heritage.

British reformers were typically religious dissenters, nonconformists who were outsiders, denied a place within the British establishment. They sought to reform British society and government and looked to the United States as a model and an example, as the hope of the world. The American Revolution had already led to the creation of a reformed government, a republic. From the perspective of British reformers, America was a projection of their dreams across the Atlantic, an experimental ground for reforms that in Europe were utopian, but that in the United States seemed possible. In Britain, such reform-minded groups as the Benthamites, the Chartists, the socialists, free thinkers, and dissenters—all shared a common attitude toward the United States, whether as utopians or as activists.

There were numerous direct connections between reformers in both countries. The evangelical revival of the early and mid-nineteenth century became an Anglo-American movement. It appeared at the same time in both places, and evangelists in both countries affected the activities of each other. As preachers became reformist agitators, they carried into the realm of reform the techniques for influencing public opinion developed in the proselytizing activities of the evangelists while they were focused on the Bible, tracts, and foreign missions. The American reformers came to excel as agitators, as much as British reformers stood out as organizers. The whole process of creating and sustaining voluntary organizations was developed during the British antislavery campaign of the late eighteenth and early nineteenth centuries.

Robert Dale Owen attempted to directly implant his version of utopian socialism in America at New Harmony and influenced other radical communitarian reformers who sought to create lasting communistic communities there. British radical reformers, as immigrants, became part of the American labor union reform movement. The homesteader or land reform crusade, spearheaded by the National Reform Association, was led by an English emigrant, George Henry Evans. The American and British peace societies were very closely aligned. They evolved common policies, experienced similar controversies between similar moderate and extremist elements, and even had a common membership, at least in the case of Elihu Burritt's League of Universal Brotherhood. Temperance was largely an Anglo-American phenomenon, and the American and British national societies were similarly close, though in this instance the Americans initiated the movement and provided most of its early leadership. This was also true of educational reform, where such American reformers as Horace Mann were influential in England as well as in the United States. The English dissenters, reformers in other contexts, opposed the establishment of public school systems, which they believed would mean the end of their own school systems, whereas the Anglicans, who saw that such a move would amount to an extension of their schools, were in a position to favor public systems. In the women's rights movement, beginning in the 1840s, but extending to the present time, British and American advocates were well aware of each other's activities, watched each other's progress, exchanged visits, labored in each other's campaigns.

During the 1830s and the 1840s in the United States, moderate reformers and reform movements—abolitionism, pacifism, labor, temperance, women's rights, social welfare—focused on one social ill, the one that seemed the most troublesome or the most certain to be corrected. Those who became active in various Christian benevolence societies were general "do-gooders," Christians whose interpretation of their religion was such that social activism seemed the most appropriate way of leading an exemplary Christian life. Extreme reformers—utopian socialists and radical Christians—offered wholly new alternate models for American society—local communities based upon the common ownership of all property, brotherhood, and love, rather than competition, private property, hatred, and class. Neither group—moderate or radical—greatly altered the character of American life, but both were indications that not everyone was satisfied with existing social arrangements and sought ways of creating a better society.

By the 1830s, there was a significant number of Americans who were profoundly disappointed that America had not become the setting for an overall perfecting of human life, just as in Europe there were others who, during the same years, dedicated themselves to at least the improvement of life there. But, the perfectibility of society was a peculiarly American emphasis, something that those who were affected by "enlightenment" thought believed should happen once the new republic was established or that those subscribing to the new

Christian theological precept of perfectionism thought should happen among fellow Christians.

These "reformers" and the movements they developed had in common their insistence that they knew how to improve and perfect America, and, to do so, they agitated and prodded and propagandized their fellow citizens, hoping to induce them into making the necessary changes. In order to achieve their aims, these reformers organized locally, regionally, and nationally—after splitting and dividing into more extreme and more conservative groupings, sometimes remaining apolitical, other times forming parties, or at least placing political pressure on various levels of government to legislate in appropriate ways.

Some of the moderate reformers sought to change the *behavior* of Americans. Many of the Christian benevolent associations sought to end vice (prostitution, gambling, and drunkenness), to keep the Sabbath holy, and to aid the indigent, the sick, and the abandoned. The temperance movement focused on the consumption of alcoholic beverages and the drunkenness that could ensue as America's major social defect. Temperance reformers persuaded individuals (and parishioners in the churches) to pledge not to drink and pressured state legislatures to ban the sale of intoxicants. Pacifists—in several national organizations—sought to banish war, with the more extreme arguing that the good Christian eschews violence of all kinds. Founders and managers of public and private insane asylums, poorhouses, orphanages, and penitentiaries attempted to construct buildings and devise rules in such a way that the relevant deviant and dependent groups would learn—through regimentation and rigorous discipline (as factory wage laborers were learning)—to behave properly, as good Christians, capitalists, Americans. Similarly, educational reformers sought to establish standardized schools and teaching, in order to educate all children (and thus the next generation) in the prevailing values and skills one needed to be successful in America. In all these ways, reform groups sought to improve the way Americans behaved.

Others sought to change a certain *institution* in America, an institution they believed was evil: slavery. The abolitionists—divided among several national organizations—believed that slavery was a fundamental violation of the precepts that should govern a Christian-capitalist population. No man should be able to own other human beings, only other forms of property. The chattel—human property—is a contradiction in terms. To be enlightened, to be good Christians, Americans must abolish slavery—now! To that end, the abolitionists propagandized, and some exerted political pressure, even forming their own party for a short time.

Still other reformers were concerned about the *inequality* that existed among Americans. No one seriously questioned racism and the caste system it created. The colonizers, the only group to propose a "final solution" to the race problem, supported schemes whereby black Americans would be allowed to emigrate to Africa. The abolitionists were generally quiet about a matter that vexed them;

they certainly never proclaimed that they knew of a way to end racism. Others began to support women's rights and urged that inequality based upon gender be ended. Women, they argued, should have the same rights and opportunities as men and not be exalted as paragons of domesticity, piety, and nurturing at the same time that they were denied a legal identity apart from their husband's. Women of wealth and leisure began to develop a feminist consciousness as the separate benevolent societies they founded aided layers of less fortunate women who they believed were the victims of a male-dominated society. Some labor union leaders probed the emergent capitalist society and found growing evidence of huge inequalities of wealth and power. Merchants and planters were being joined by industrialists in the amassing of great wealth at the same time that increasing numbers of Americans were either wage laborers—without significant property of any kind: no land, no shop, not even their own house—or, perhaps, unable to sustain an occupation of any kind. Most of these labor union leaders were far from seeking revolutionary change, arguing that universal education and guaranteed or protected and adequate wages would be sufficient to assure ordinary laboring Americans the good life. But, a few of these spokesmen openly questioned the direction and likely future of an economic system that fostered such large inequities.

Still more radical were the communitarians, those who set up their own model communities as alternatives to American society, as it was then structured. The communitarians eschewed American society altogether and followed the Puritans' example of establishing model local communities that served as settings for wholly alternate ways of living. Early socialists—like the followers of Robert Owen and Fourier—and religious sects—such as the Mormons—founded towns in which property was held in common, little societies in which peace, harmony, and cooperation were to replace competition, class, division, and strife. In these exclusivist experiments participants sought to create a better world, as separate from the larger American setting as they could manage. Most of these efforts were of short duration, as the participants failed to retain the requisite harmony and unity needed to survive in a generally hostile world.

So, America abounded with social critics in the 1830s, 1840s, and 1850s—reformers who made others aware of defects in American life and of ways to overcome them. The effects of all this criticism and attempts to bring about reform were quite varied. Such efforts brought some change. The lives of certain groups, such as children, orphans, the insane, the indigent, and criminals, were substantially altered. Those of women and slaves (until emancipation came during the Civil War) were not. Drinking alcoholic beverages was banned or restricted in some state and local jurisdictions, but such actions were far from general throughout the nation. Americans did not become discernibly more pacifistic, as the incidence of criminal violence and the warfare against the native tribes, the Mexicans, and the fratricidal conflict of 1861–1865 amply demonstrate. Nor did Americans become more equal in the economic or social dimensions of their lives, even though property-less white adult males were enfranchised during these years. Overall, the gap between what reformers perceived to be American ideals and what they observed as American reality was still wide, but at least the reformers had made their fellow citizens increasingly aware of that gap.

The reform movements that began with the revolutions in America and France in the late eighteenth century and that developed into major enterprises during the early and mid-nineteenth century were widely varying in their strength and durability, with temporal trajectories that differed markedly. These movements continued to share transatlantic connections and, indeed, transpacific connections as well, as the newer white settler societies in Australia and New Zealand matured. These connections became easier to sustain with access to steadily speedier means of transportation and communication. The abolitionist movement ended with the Civil War, but civil rights organizations that championed equal rights for a segregated black population emerged early in the new century. The women's rights movements continued until voting rights were attained in the early twentieth century and reemerged later in the century in the face of persisting gender inequality. The pacificist movement has had several reincarnations, usually at wartime, with opposition to war taking several forms: to persuade governments to remain neutral or to disarm; to become, as individuals, conscientious objectors. The temperance movement continued until the early twentieth century, successfully pressuring various levels of government in many parts of the Western world to restrict the sale of intoxicating beverages, and continues in weaker form as individuals, and occasionally, as groups, who favor abstinence.

In the much wider context of Western civilization, a reform movement such as woman's rights during its whole history reveals broad patterns that apply across the face of Europe, North America, and Australasia. Wherever liberalism flourished, industrialization spread, a middle class burgeoned, and Protestantism predominated, there women's rights advocates gained popular strength during the nineteenth and early twentieth centuries. Wherever conservatism was strong, political and religious (Catholic) authoritarianism flourished, and feudalistic and aristocratic influence remained, there women's rights movements were arrested, kept small. Because such advocates everywhere became politicized, national political contexts mattered. In Russia under Communism, forced industrialization meant that women were given equal access to work. In France and Italy, the power of Catholicism worked against the emergence of strong movements. In Germany, the continued influence of feudal and authoritarian structures blocked the movement's development. In Sweden, a leftist government provided the kind of equality fought for elsewhere.

But, wherever there were women's rights advocates, their aims became wider, from economic accessibility, to moral purity, to political and legal and then general equality. Their ideological outlook changed from an emphasis on individual freedom to gender identity, to innate differences between men and women (mirroring the shift in liberalism from its emphasis on individualism to a similar concern for collectivism and the exercise of government authority for the good of all). Their political orientation has been to ally with liberal parties who looked with favor on their cause, even if unable to act because of a lack of public support. Their social base has always been in the middle class, and it has been from a middle-class perspective that women's rights have been drawn. Within these broad patterns and from this broad context, the women's rights movement in the United States emerged as the classic movement: America was liberal, Protestant, middle class, and increasingly industrialized, and women's rights advocates appeared earlier than elsewhere. By the late nineteenth century, America's domination of the movement was unchallenged. European advocates looked to America for leadership, and all other movements were to a degree an imitation of the American one. No other movement attained the enormous scale of the American women's rights advocates.

Beginning in the mid-nineteenth century, the character of reform in the Western world began to change; it became more directly political in character, as it had been at its inception, in the late eighteenth century. The reformers *were* politicians and government officials, as they had been earlier. And reform became larger in scale, more national and international than local or regional. As the scale of life enlarged in the course of the nineteenth century so too did the organizational reach of those who would reform society. As national governments began to assume more authority, these same groups pressured those governments to act, to eradicate society's shortcomings. Only the "settlement house" movement, heir of the earlier, more religiously oriented benevolence societies, remained incontrovertibly localist in character, as Jane Addams and others set up centers for the care of the poor and troubled in city after city during the late nineteenth and early twentieth centuries. The settlement house movement was a transatlantic phenomenon, however, and there were British settlement houses as well as the American ones.

In America, in the decades after the Civil War, the "reformist" position came to be that the national government should not only develop the size and capacity to deal with economic corporations and unions organized on a continental scale, but that it was government's rightful task to regulate that activity as well, making sure that all economic interests and groups were treated equally and fairly under the law. The "radical" position that emerged (in its Socialist and Communist formulations) was that American life was fundamentally flawed and had to be reordered on the basis of the public ownership of property, something generally advocated before the Civil War only by small groups of "communitarian" reformers who founded local communities on the same basis. The enlargement of scale—from local to national—that characterized life in the United States during the course of the nineteenth century was thus perfectly mirrored in the changing scope of those Americans who advocated radical alternatives.

But, direct *popular* support for alternate forms of social arrangements did not follow the prescriptions of group and party leaders and theoreticians. Both the Knights of Labor and the Farmers' Alliances favored producer and consumer "cooperatives" as a practical solution to long-standing problems with costs and prices and supported, however ineptly, such nonprofit organizations, which provided supplies and marketed commodities for groups of farmers or laborers. And, local politicians created socialistic or publicly owned utilities as a pragmatic resolution of the problem of how best to satisfy the public need for dependable utilities (such as electricity and gas) or transportation services.

These practical solutions to vexing problems raised the question of what was "public" and what was "private": if the public through its government "owned" the gas works and the electrical company and the trolley or subway company, if a group in its entirety "owned" its own corporations (or producer-consumer cooperatives)—what, then, was rightfully "privately" owned, what should be "publicly" owned? When was a social or economic activity so obviously in a group's or the whole public's interest that decisions should be made by the group or the public, and not by private owners?

Americans never resolved these questions in a systematic way or applied their specific resolutions to their society as a whole. They were pragmatic, acting in limited contexts to problems that particular groups and communities felt needed drastic solutions. Only then were Americans galvanized into questioning whether the hierarchical, capitalistic character of their society was sufficient as a basis for the resolution of particular problems. When it came to questions of what constituted a "good" society, Americans were generally antitheoretical, tinkerers, responding pragmatically to sources of tension and dissatisfaction, ordinarily untroubled by the way American society was already constituted.

The moderate reform movements of the years between the Civil War and the Depression of the 1930s, as was the case in the years between the Revolution and the Civil War, were efforts to correct or perfect American life, not to alter its basic character. Moderate reformers, in both periods, were, with few exceptions, middle-class people who were particularly troubled by the discrepancy between American ideals and American realities, people who were convinced that they knew how to resolve America's problems.

Indeed, some of the moderate reform movements of this period were similar to or even originated in the pre–Civil War years. The Settlement House movement that flourished in particular American cities from the 1880s to the 1930s—though it actually originated in England—was quite like the benevolent reform associations that were so numerous in various localities during the antebellum era. Both kinds of organizations attempted in a variety of ways to improve the lives of those who lived in slums. The women's rights movement after the Civil War originated before the war, as did the temperance or prohibition movement, and both continued to have local and state as well as national chapters, and were still given to splintering at the national level, either on the matter of goals (in the case of the women's movement) or along lines of gender (in the case of the temperance/prohibition movement), though, by the end of the century, national "cover" organizations became easier to create and sustain.

There continued to be a transatlantic, and, with the development of Australia and New Zealand, a transpacific connection, that is, a cross-fertilization of reform ideas developed by reform-minded officials of both governments and private advocacy associations or by crusading journalists located in northern and western Europe as well in North America and in the south Pacific—wherever white Europeans dominated. These reformers tended to be experts, unlike earlier reformers, and often advocated the outlines of policies that would involve their governments in the regulation of the economy and the society long before legislators were in fact moved to act. Typically, advocates of reform would go on fact-finding tours or attend conferences in or near locations where governments had already acted. Such activity gave a transnational dimension to reform.

In some areas, Americans were in the vanguard, and others learned from them, or influences flowed in both directions, across the Atlantic or the Pacific. Americans excelled in those reform movements whose advocates sought to improve behavior or lessen gender inequality, in temperance and in women's rights. In other areas—in the municipal ownership of utilities or transport, in urban planning, in agricultural and labor cooperatives, in the legal protection of labor unions, in various forms of "social insurance"—Europeans and Australians were clearly the pioneers, Americans the neophytes.

In the late nineteenth and early twentieth centuries, American reformers tended to look to their European or Australasian counterparts for inspiration and ideas. Horace Plunkett, whose Irish Agricultural Organization Society fostered cooperatives in Ireland, became a transatlantic intermediary, influencing such American exponents as Clarence Poe, who edited the *Progressive Farmer*, and helped create the American Agricultural Organization in 1913–1915, which favored coops. Plunkett influenced President Theodore Roosevelt to appoint a Country Life Commission. David Lubin founded the International Institute of Agriculture in Rome in 1908 to study European agricultural reform. Americans who advocated "social insurance" schemes were active in the American Association for Labor Legislation, which served during the 1910s and 1920s as a clearinghouse of information on European and Australasian activity. Those who favored public housing and city planning often attended the Congress of International Housing and of the Town Planning Federation during the 1920s and, by the 1930s, set up their own Labor Housing and National Public Housing Conferences, where developments elsewhere were noted. In these ways, advocates of particular kinds of American reform absorbed ideas and techniques developed elsewhere in the westernized world. However, by the 1930s, during the Depression years and under Roosevelt's New Deal, American reformers generated their own prescriptions for change, producing legislative results in a more concentrated fashion than had been the case elsewhere. But, though foreign experts and reform-minded officials flocked to Washington to examine the New Deal as a distinctively American phenomenon, many of the New Deal reforms were heavily indebted to what particular European and Australasian governments had already enacted into legislation or were elaborations of what earlier progressive-minded federal administrations had already done.

There were also differences between the two periods, that is, before and after the Civil War, respecting moderate reforms and reformers. After the Civil War, such reform movements had a much more pronounced political orientation than the prewar movements had. "Progressivism" was a major force in American politics for much of the century's first two decades, and the "New Deal" dominated the political life of Washington for most of the Depression of the 1930s. There was no counterpart to this during the antebellum years. Reformers were more optimistic that there could be political solutions to America's problems, and, indeed, unlike their predecessors, some directed their energies toward the reform of the political process itself. Furthermore, reform movements after the Civil War sometimes became mass, or popular, movements, something wholly uncharacteristic of those that flourished in the earlier period.

Populism and Progressivism became (however briefly) direct, political manifestations of this tendency, as did the temperance-prohibition and women's suffrage movements, which were most strikingly successful as national crusades, culminating in the enactment in 1913 and 1919 of Constitutional amendments granting women the right to vote and prohibiting the sale of intoxicating beverages. Thousands of farmers supported (under Populist leadership) the nationalization of America's transportation and banking systems; thousands more farmers and laborers (in Granges, Farmers' Alliances, and Knights of Labor) supported production and consumer cooperatives, thus limiting the reach of private ownership; millions voted for candidates who supported reform of the political system (the initiative, referendum, recall) and the initiation of (national) governmental regulation of (national) corporations; millions more favored the prohibition of alcoholic beverages as a legal intoxicant. In all these ways, Americans supported the conscious reform or ameliorative change of American life.

Radical reform and reformers of the post–Civil War decades shared with their predecessors the belief that Christian-capitalist-republican America needed to be basically altered through the elimination of one its defining features: private property. Both groups heavily emphasized the communal, instead of the individualistic, aspects of American life. But, before the Civil War, radical reformers sought to establish communally oriented, harmonious, noncompetitive local settlements in which all property was owned in common. These "utopian" communities (so-called by critics, dissenters, and doubters), whether secularly or religiously oriented, were too exclusionist or particularist, too limited to small, like-minded groups to constitute easily copied models for the general population. Such groups failed to sustain the earlier large-scale efforts of the Puritans, who were so successful as local community builders that they dominated a whole region for almost two centuries.

By the post–Civil War years, radical reformers became both national and secular in their orientation. Though the leaders of the Christian "Social Gospel" movement favored moderate reform, there were no Christian (or other religious) advocates for radical reform during these years. And, except for the sporadic efforts of farmers and laborers to create and sustain producer/consumer cooperatives, no group of any kind sought to establish a noncapitalist life on a local basis. The new radicals were socialists (the successors of such "localist" socialist radicals as Robert Owen) and—a particular variant of the movement—communists. The Socialists favored public ownership of property as a democratic reform of a continuing, democratic state. The Communists—by the time of Lenin's formulation in the 1910s—favored the dictatorship of their revolutionary party as the vanguard of a mass "proletariat," when capitalism collapsed in bloody revolution as a result of its own excessive concentration of wealth and power.

Both socialism and communism were nurtured and developed in Europe, so that radical reform lacked native origins, even in its earlier Utopian socialist form. The early socialist leaders were all immigrants from Europe, though when first Eugene Debs and then Norman Thomas served as leaders of the Socialist Party from the turn of the century through the 1930s, socialism acquired a native American aspect. But, there was never a sizable intellectual community that advocated socialism from a middle-class perspective; nothing comparable to the British Fabians.

Only one radical proposal generated from within the United States became popular, not only in the United States, but in Canada, Australia, New Zealand: throughout the English-speaking world, and beyond. Henry George's argument in *Progress and Poverty* (1879)—that all landowners be taxed on their lands' unearned increment, thus preventing speculators from keeping land out of use, so that no one would pay such landowners an unfair tribute—led to the creation of clubs whose members tried to propagate his ideas and to pressure governments to create his panacea, a "single" tax.

The Socialists received millions of votes at the height of progressivism's impact on the political system, but that support rapidly declined when the crusade to save the world for democracy during World War I defined socialism as a threat to the American Christian-capitalist-republican ideal and strongly linked democracy with capitalism. After World War I, Americans typically blurred socialism and communism and perceived Leninist dictatorial Communist parties as a threat to the American way of life. The reformist impulse in general weakened in the disillusionment attendant upon the outcome of World War I. American society became more narrowly defined and less tolerant of dissent and reform of all kinds.

During the Depression, the entire American "way of life" seemed to be in crisis, and radical reformers questioned every aspect of the "system." Communists, for whom the Depression was capitalism in its final crisis, hoped for a revolution to be followed by the dictatorship of the proletariat. Socialists believed Americans would be peacefully persuaded to adopt public ownership of economic institutions and activities, while retaining a democratic political system. Leaders of popular movements proposed schemes for the redistribution of the wealth (Huey Long and Francis Townsend) or at least restrictions on the power of monetary and financial institutions (Father Coughlin). But the enormous popularity of Franklin Roosevelt and his pragmatic New Deal proposals meant that most Americans retained their faith in their "system," accepting moderate reform in order to preserve its essential features. The moderate reformers of the Depression years flocked to Washington both as elected officials and as administrators. There was a sense that American society would be cleansed of its imperfections by the reforming zeal of a national government that attempted to preserve capitalism, republicanism, and a society marked by an egalitarian spirit, at the same time as that government created an American version of the welfare capitalist state of the kind that had been forged in various polities throughout the westernized world in a more piecemeal fashion over longer periods of time.

Since World War II, such governmentally based reform has involved either extensions of the New Deal and thus to the welfare capitalist state it created or efforts to deal with new problems created by the American government or American industry: the proliferation of nuclear weaponry and environmental pollution. Minority groups have sought political/legal equality (blacks, Hispanics, natives, women, homosexuals). Other groups have agitated for a safer, cleaner world (disarmers and environmentalists). Such moderate reformers and reform movements have developed in an international or globalized context, given the recent developments in communication and transportation. This has meant that techniques developed and achievements made by one movement are widely known and sometimes copied by others, both in the United States and in other parts of the world. The American disarmament movement was clearly derivative of those in Europe. But, the black civil rights crusade influenced other such efforts both in the United States (the native, feminist, and homosexual causes) and elsewhere in the world (such as Northern Catholic Irish and the Australian native movements).

Since World War II, radical reform groups have consisted of the "old left" (Socialists and Communists), who continue to seek, whether peacefully and democratically or through violent revolution, the public ownership of property; the "new left" (the young radicals of the 1960s), who sought, with increasing violence and with far less articulation and precision, social and economic "justice;" and the "counterculture," whose adherents originally aimed for both "personal liberation" and communal authority (the sharing of all wealth and property), unwittingly of a kind similar to that of the communitarian reformers of the nineteenth century. Radical reformers have had little impact on American life, thus indicating the unwillingness of most Americans to embrace basic or revolutionary change.

But, the moderate groups have had considerable success in their efforts to improve and ameliorate the conditions of American life. Such reform has had its inception in both political and nonpolitical contexts. Sometimes the politicians and the institutions of government themselves have been the catalyst for change. Sometimes government has clearly responded to public pressure, which in turn has been generated by the efforts of reform groups. But, reformist agitation and governmental action have not always been in rhythm or synchronization. Since World War II, only in the 1960s has there been a widespread middle-class involvement with moderate reform in general, a popular base for an era of reform, similar in breadth and depth to those of the 1930s, the 1900s and 1910s, and the 1830s and 1840s. Such periods have been the occasions for the coming together of various reform efforts, to the point that a reform spirit has affected a whole generation.

Civil rights legislation was an obvious response to the efforts of those in the civil rights movement, but key Supreme Court decisions occurred in advance of the main growth of that movement. Nuclear disarmament treaties and environmental protection legislation have not directly related to pressure from disarmament and environmental groups. Reform activity and governmental action have both had their own internal dynamics, as Americans have continued to feel the tension set up between those who would keep their society the way it is and those who would self-consciously change it for the better.

PART IV

AMERICAN CULTURE

Human culture involves art, thought, religion, science, technology, education, leisure, and recreation. Black African slaves and the native American population came out of tribal cultures with traditions that were old and ritualistic: cultural activity had a specific, known, predictable, honorable place in the public, social, and religious life of the native and African tribes. Under the impact of the contact with white European migrants, both black African and native American cultures were altered, becoming a hybrid of white American and old tribal cultural ways.

In the more sophisticated, traditional cultures of the Islamic civilizations of West Africa and the Aztec/Mayan/Inca civilizations of Middle and South America, particular groups engaged in various cultural activities that, in their more complicated forms, were under the sponsorship of an elite court society. The European culture that the dominant English colonist brought to the North America frontier similarly involved cultural groups whose activities enjoyed the patronage of an elite society, an elite that in one significant respect differed from the European model: the colonial elite was not a hereditary nobility, but one based upon wealth. In traditional, as in tribal, societies, culture involved ordinary people as well, but even popular culture was typically prescribed, a matter of form and orthodoxy. In traditional, as in tribal, societies, culture was public, religious, social.

The culture of colonial America was both European and traditional, though, because it was without a court society, it lacked much of the infrastructure that sustained European culture. Americans slowly constructed that infrastructure during the nineteenth century, as Europe remained the cultural model. Both European culture and its American frontier variant became modern in the course of the nineteenth century. Modern culture involves a varied and steady effort to find new forms of cultural expression; it is far less set and prescribed than traditional culture, at all levels, and is far more apt to change its forms than was and is the case in traditional cultures. During the course of the nineteenth and twentieth centuries, Europe and its offshoots have produced a culture that, at its higher levels, has been broadened to include the middle class and not just the old elites, is increasingly secular in tone, and includes activity for its own sake and not just for some public or social purpose. By the twentieth century, when American political and economic power became unmistakable, those involved in American cultural activities have been less apt to regard Europe as an appropriate cultural model, far more apt to think American culture is at the center of Western culture.

In all of the European nations as well as in all the white settler societies on the frontiers of European civilization, there have been cultural nationalists, those who sought to produce a culture—in all its manifestations—that followed political boundaries. Their belief was that a population that had created a polity could also create a distinctive culture, different from those who lived in all the other nations in the world. In this, they were mistaken, as the cultural activities of the British, the French, the Dutch, the Spanish, the Germans, the Italians—as well as those of the Americans, Canadians, South Africans, Australians, and New Zealanders—were more Western, fitted in more significant ways into the larger context provided by European civilization than they did into national contexts.

Cultural activities have never followed political boundaries in tribal, traditional, or modern societies, nor have such activities been unique to ethnic groups either. The varied dimensions of human life that are cultural in nature have assumed their own territorial shapes, produced their own maps. Sometimes and in some places culture has manifested itself in markedly local or regional contexts—architectural styles, linguistic dialects, folklore, folk music. In other times and other places, a cultural phenomenon has grown beyond city states, nations, or even empires to embrace civilizations and beyond—Christianity, Islam, the English language, styles of dress.

After Britain's rebellious colonists established independence and many Loyalists had fled, one question that "Americans" confronted was: Would the population that had created a new political system (republicanism) in the revolutionary act of establishing a new nation also develop a distinctive culture? Americans did not consciously try to define their economic life differently from the way Europeans did. Instead, they attempted to improve upon European-derived activities, dividing over whether they should emulate England's industrialization or remain an agrarian people, oriented toward crafts and farming. They also became acutely aware with respect to their society of how much the egalitarian ideal (for white men) and the reality of social/geographical mobility and ethnic/racial variety separated American society from that of their European ancestors.

Americans tried to create an "American culture" in an effort to extend their sense of distinctiveness beyond its natural political context. But, "American culture" is a kind of fictional creation, for cultural activity in the United States, as in any nation, assumed varied local and regional and international contexts and was never encased precisely within political boundaries of any kind.

33

Religion

Basic to the culture of the groups who became Americans were their religious beliefs and practices. Religion has been one of the great, inclusive human activities, involving virtually everyone in an effort to understand the nature of life itself. The religion of the native and enslaved tribes was animistic in character, with spirits present in all material things, representing the many mysteries of life and death. Spirits representing animals and plants and inanimate objects were multiple manifestations of divine power, which it was the duty of everyone to placate and to please through various forms of ritual and sacrifice. Certain individuals in the tribes became holy men and acted as intermediaries between their fellow tribesmen and the spirits. There were many geographical spots, either in their natural state or through tribal constructions of various kinds, that became holy places. By contrast, monotheistic Islam was generally confined to the ruling elites of the empires of West Africa.

The monotheism of the European colonists throughout the Americas was in striking contrast to African and native American animism. As strikingly different was the proselytizing impulse of Christians who endeavored to convert both the black slaves and the native tribes. By contrast, Muslims allowed diversity, though they were intolerant of blasphemous behavior toward Islam itself. But, though Christians presented a united front of missionary activity in their common effort to convert the heathens, they were deeply divided into many sects, more so than the Muslims, but not nearly so varied in number as was the case among African and native American tribesmen.

The pluralism that was evident in the practice of welcoming non-English migrants to the English provinces was even more pronounced in the religious sphere. The Puritans tried to restrict immigration to those who subscribed to their religious orthodoxy by refusing to admit adherents of other sects into their towns during the seventeenth century, but the Toleration Act of 1691 undermined their efforts. Everywhere in the colonies, the Anglicans (or, in New England, their Puritan reformist wing) were "established" in the sense that tithes collected as taxes were allotted to them. However, Calvert's Maryland became a haven for Catholics, Penn's Pennsylvania and Williams's Rhode Island welcomed Christians of all descriptions, and New York's Dutch settlers retained their affiliation with the Dutch Reformed Church, as did the French settlers with Catholicism in New France after its capture. And, by the eighteenth century, the colonies swarmed with dissenting sects, such as the Presbyterians and, later, the Methodists, as well as Baptists, Lutherans, and many pietistic sects from the German states.

Sects that in Europe tended to be divided along political and geographical lines, in the colonies often spread across such artificial dividing lines and became geographically mixed. It was difficult to claim, beyond the assignation of nominal tithing fees, that the Church of England was a "state church" in the colonies the way it indisputably was in England, and as the Roman Catholic Church was in the neighboring Spanish and Portuguese empires. The Anglicans never managed to establish a hierarchy that reached from Canterbury to local colonial parishes. But, everywhere in Europe there were established state churches that operated under state laws that in varying degrees restricted the activity of dissenting sects: Protestant and Catholic states deprived each other of civil rights.

However varied the Christian churches were in the English colonies, their role as religious entities remained what it had been in Europe: Christian belief provided the colonists with their most basic perception of morality, reality, existence, and the purpose of life. Christianity was in a sense a metaphysical construct understood in some measure by all adults and inculcated into each generation anew. Ministers everywhere led believers in prayer and song, commented on God's word, and indicated whether the congregation was or was not living up to Christian prescriptions.

All of the major theological viewpoints that had developed in Christian Europe found expression among the clergy in the English colonies. A moderate, latitudinarian Anglicanism that attempted to balance reason and faith was probably the predominant outlook everywhere except in New England, where a vibrant Calvinism was fostered by the Puritans, who emphasized predestination with its bifurcation of humanity into the elect and the damned. More particular theological constructions—such as Arminianism, Antinomianism, or Deism—also gained adherents in the English colonies.

Evangelism quickly became a transatlantic phenomenon, even though its earliest manifestation was in the parish of the Reverend Jonathan Edwards in the Massachusetts Bay colony in 1738–1739, and even though Edwards wrote the most influential theological treatises on the nature of evangelism. George Whitfield and others from England became itinerant preachers who started revivals and staged huge outdoor services, in which penitent sinners underwent an experience of conversion and became convinced that, though sinners, they had been saved by God and pledged henceforth to lead a godly life. The evangelists split congregations on both sides of the Atlantic, dividing those who accepted evangelical ways from those who did not.

Similarly, outbreaks of witchcraft occurred in the English colonies, just as in England. The usual colonial setting for this widespread Christian phenomenon was, as in England, towns, close-knit communities, specifically Puritan towns, which, as covenanted religious communities, provided an appropriate setting for those seeking evidence of satanic possession.

The monotheism of all Christians was in sharp contrast to the polytheism of the black slaves from Africa and of the native American population. A core of Christian belief bound colonists everywhere in the Americas to the Europeans in the homeland in a fundamental way, whichever way the varied Christian sects situated themselves geographically on the two continents.

Increasingly, after the eighteenth century, the state-supported churches of Europe coexisted with other denominations, competing for the allegiance of professed Christians. Like the capitalist, commercialized, and industrialized economy that emerged during the nineteenth century throughout Europe and the "Europeanized" frontiers elsewhere in the world, Christianity continued to embrace a civilization, giving its adherents a meaning and a purpose for life, and an ethical code to live by. The religious pluralism of the British colonists led the Founding Fathers to institute a new relationship between religion and politics by severing all connection between church and state. The American Constitution forbade any action on the part of the national government respecting any church.

Americans stressed the "religious freedom" this confirmed, and the Anglican church (and its Puritan variant) lost its legal capacity to be favored by taxation, which was the only advantage Anglicans had enjoyed in the colonial period in any case. But, though many of the European states continued to be formally tied in various ways to particular sects—the Anglican in England; the Presbyterian in Scotland; the Lutheran in Scandinavia and the German states; the Dutch Reformed in the Netherlands; the Catholic in Spain, France, some German states, and the Italian states—the emergence and movement of other Christian denominations among European polities gradually resulted in a kind of religious variety similar to that which existed across the North American continent: Christians in many parts of Europe came to be members of a variety of denominations. Over the course of the nineteenth century, various European states ended the legal limitations that had been placed upon adherents of dissenting sects within their borders.

In the decades after the Revolution, Americans continued to be influenced by theological developments in Europe, just as their British colonial forebears had been. After the Revolution, during the late eighteenth and early and mid-nineteenth centuries, Christian theology generally emphasized humanity's capacity to play a leading role in the great drama of personal salvation and deemphasized the depravity of humans and the omnipotence of God, both of which had been central to Calvinism.

Evangelism—probably the most powerful Christian theological formulation during the nineteenth century—focused on the experience of conversion, that is, the sudden awareness of God's redeeming love and the individual's ability to earn salvation by living a proper Christian life. God was still omnipotent and humanity still depraved, but, through conversion, an individual's salvation could be gained. Evangelism continued to be a great transatlantic movement, and, though it attained a centrality to the religious life of America that it never gained in Europe, there were obvious cross-Atlantic connections, particularly between the British and the Americans, who shared both a language and the memory of a common experience in the initial development of evangelism during the revivals of the 1740s. There were great waves of revivals that continued from the 1790s to the 1840s. American evangelists explained both the unrestrained and emotional rural camp meeting and the later, more respectable, well-planned and indoor urban revival to British sympathizers.

Perfectionism was a peculiarly American variant of this new theological emphasis. Its definers and popularizers—like Charles Finney—believed that the individual as a Christian had the capacity to perfect his life, while living. Such a theological emphasis greatly enlarged the effect the individual Christian could have on American life. By perfecting themselves, Christians could lead the way toward the perfection of the society of which they were members. The missionary impulse was one means for achieving this end. It was a unifying force among the disparate Christian sects as they joined to convert and civilize the native American population. The reform impulse was another means, and various forms of Christian perfectionism and benevolence were a large element in the motivation and purpose of many self-styled reformers during the 1830s through the 1850s.

But overall, Christianity had a profoundly ambivalent relationship to American life in the decades after the Revolution. Some fervent Christians were galvanized into becoming "do-gooders," founding and joining benevolent and reformist associations. But others believed that American life—as it was—was "Christian," that Christianity accepted a racial caste system, a hierarchical social structure, and vast social and economic inequalities based upon the pursuit of talent, wealth, and property. Such Christians favored the status quo, arguing that Christian belief fostered morality and order. These ambivalent positions regarding religion and society reveal widely varying attitudes Christians adopted during these decades.

Christian variety came in another form as well: the creation of distinctively American sects. In a context of well-established religious pluralism, certain individuals propounded new variants of Christian belief and attracted adherents to new "American"-founded Christian sects, though these sects remained at the periphery of American life. Joseph Smith's Mormons, as the lost tribe of Israel, perceived America as the new Israel or promised land and themselves as God's chosen people. Sharing the communalistic orientation of other communitarian sects and movements, the Mormons embarked on an odyssey—surrounded by an unfriendly population—during the 1830s and 1840s that took them to remote frontier areas. William Miller's Adventists believed that the end of the world could be precisely calculated, and when their prediction was proved false, they quickly faded away as a movement, though Adventism in other forms continued to gain advocates.

In general, the clergy of the Christian churches remained the central intellectual source for most Americans, preaching in the churches and revival meetings scattered through rural neighborhoods, villages, towns, and urban centers all over the United States, interpreting the Christian meaning of life and existence, commenting on how well or how badly Americans lived up to Christian precepts. But, the Christian churches also linked Christianity to the nation itself. Some of the clergy believed that the American republic was God's republic, that the American way was the best way, God's way, that America was the land in which humanity would perfect itself. In this way, some ministers narrowed Christianity and placed it in the service of nationalism and a particular nation-state. In this formulation, what had defined a civilization would find its fullest expression in a particular portion of Europe's dominions.

After the Civil War, there continued to be a great array of Christian denominations and sects (as was the case in Europe as well), but Americans remained distinctive in their constitutional separation of church and state, that is, in their insistence that no religious group be accorded a special relationship to government and be supported by any kind of taxation from the general populace. And, although in Europe "tithing" ended during the nineteenth century, particular Christian denominations—Lutheran, Anglican, Catholic, Orthodox—retained their historical ties to national governments. Christianity appeared in its many guises across the face of Europe, but the geographical pattern continued to differ—at least in parts of Europe—from North America's. Whereas in the United States, Episcopalians, Lutherans, Presbyterians, Methodists, Baptists, Dutch Reform, and an array of smaller sects appeared all mixed together in particular localities, in some parts of Europe such groups tended to dominate significant geographical areas (thus explaining the tenacity with which state-supported churches retained their special linkages and favored positions).

In the United States, the existence of religious freedom and the close proximity of various religious groups continued to provide a setting in which religious experimentation flourished and in which the generation of uniquely American sects continued. During this period Mary Baker Eddy founded the Christian Scientists.

Along with their European brethren, American Christians created new theological emphases during these decades. Some clergy and others with an interest or training in theology forged a "liberal" position, which accommodated to scientific developments in biology (evolution) and Biblical studies (critical exegesis) and argued in favor of Christian belief while conceding the paramountcy of scientific knowledge and emphasizing the need for a "figurative" reading of the Bible itself. But, others constructed a "conservative" Christian theology, rejecting scientific theories and methods that in any way cast doubt on the literal truth of the Bible or basic Christian beliefs. These contrasting theological positions divided Christians all over the Christianized world, sometimes dividing particular sects and denominations.

In America, activists who opposed the "liberal" view became known by the 1910s as "fundamentalists," who militantly proclaimed the uncontaminated truth of traditional Christianity and adamantly opposed modern scientific inquiry when it questioned revealed beliefs. The fundamentalists' most notable campaign during this period was their effort in the 1920s to pressure (but usually failing to persuade) state governments to pass laws prohibiting the teaching of evolution in their public school systems.

There were other aspects of Christianity that Americans shared with Europeans. Missionary activity was both a unifying and a divisive force, as it had been before the Civil War: Christian sects sometimes joined together to convert the heathens of North America and of the other parts of the world, but at other times competed with one another in this task. But, throughout the Europeanized world, missions were at their most extensive in the years from the mid-nineteenth century through the early twentieth century, during the time when European and American colonization was at is peak in Asia and Africa. These were the decades when the racist theory was a powerful stimulant for the civilizing and Christianizing propensities of rabid Christians. In a world dominated by white, Christian civilization, it was the duty of good Christians to convert the heathen, wherever he might be.

Evangelism was also an aspect of Christianity with both a unifying and divisive impact. Evangelical revival meetings united diverse sects for a common purpose: exhorting lapsed and indifferent Christians to experience conversion and be "born again" as fervent believers. But, preachers and parishioners who subscribed to evangelical procedures still sometimes divided from other parishioners who rejected such "ways." Christian evangelism, like missionary activity, remained a vital part of Christian activity in the decades after the Civil War.

During these years, Christianity in general retained its central place as the basis for a prescribed purpose in life, for most Americans. Though proper behavior was encased in secular laws, those laws continued to be grounded in an ethical system that in turn was based on Christian belief. No secular equivalent to Christianity appeared to challenge religious authority as the ultimate source of belief about the meaning of life. Similarly, clergymen remained the most respected arbiters of ethical and spiritual problems, though they lost their authority as the dominant intellectual figures in the many local communities churches were located in across the continent. During this period, professors, teachers, editors, writers, and broadcasters rivaled the clergymen's position as disseminators of various kinds of knowledge. Still, most Americans continued to attend services or read the Bible, in both of which a Christian explanation for life was provided. And, sermons (though rivaled by editorials as well as written and spoken commentaries) continued to be a major form of critical and judgmental observation on the extent to which Americans were abiding by God's prescriptions.

As before the Civil War, Christianity played an ambivalent role in American society, used both to support the status quo and to challenge it. Some clerics and parishioners were comfortable with a Social Darwinian perception of American life, "liberal" in their acceptance of scientific theory, but "conservative" in their equal acceptance of a steeply hierarchical society, exhibiting a vast gulf between its richest and poorest members. The Reverend Henry Ward Beecher was the leading spokesman for this point of view for two decades after the Civil War.

But, other clergymen and Christian believers asserted that the central precept of Christianity was its social conscience, its humanitarian concerns, and not its rituals, dogmas, or mysticism. Christianity should suffuse all of society, not just the churches, governing social relations of all kinds—familial, industrial, as well as sectarian. Rev. Washington Gladden and Rev. Walter Rauschenbusch were the two most influential spokesmen for what became known as the "Social Gospel" movement at the turn of the century.

As before the Civil War, Christian-capitalist-republican Americans experienced tension and ambivalence. What being a good Christian meant in economic-political-social terms was not simple or clear, and Christians became both "conservative" and "liberal" in a variety of contexts. But, the Christian as a good American was a far less complicated proposition. In these years, American nationalism became infused with a sense of American superiority at a time when Social Darwinism was interpreted as implying that the white, Christian, British-American world was at the apex of civilization.

American clergymen expanded the practice of positioning American flags in their churches, and emphasized that the nation itself was like a church, as an entity favored of God—as God's nation. In these decades, American nationalism and Christian belief were more powerfully linked than at any time before or since. Whether "God's nation" should end its isolation and colonize, go to war, foster trade expansion—were all divisive questions. Far less so was the proposition that the United States was a nation "under God."

Since 1930, there have continued to be adherents of many Christian sects within the United States, blended territorially in a way that still differs—though far less so than in earlier periods—from the geographically separate locations occupied by European Christians. The historical linkages between the European states and particular churches have been attenuated, and tolerance of other sects has become well established, except in Eastern Europe, where, after World War II, until 1990, Communist-dominated governments attempted in various ways and with limited effect to replace the population's long-standing association with Christianity with a new loyalty to an officially atheistic state. But, in the United States, in recent decades, Asian and African religions—Islam, Hinduism, Buddhism—have become significant, not only as a result of migrants from those parts of the world, but because disaffected blacks and counterculture whites have been receptive to religious proselytizers (or gurus) from abroad who have sometimes established splinter or new sects vaguely linked to indigenous Asian faiths (for example: the Unification Church, Hare Krishna, and various Muslim sects, including the Bahai).

Moderate Protestant and Catholic theologians have developed a figurative view of Christian belief, that the Bible should be read as a myth or a story offered by humans who were space- and time-bound in their understanding of transcendental reality. Christians are deeply divided over this theological formulation, however, and spokespeople for those Christians who share a fundamentalist viewpoint argue for the literal truth of traditional Christian belief. The seeming decentralization of authority and clear modernization of the liturgy that came as a result of the Second Vatican Council have generally been accepted by the Catholic laity in the United States, but neither the Papacy's adherence to traditional views of the family, sex, and marriage nor the theologians' rejection of the literal truth of Bible has gained general acceptance.

Overall attendance and membership in the Christian sects was stable through the crisis of depression and war in the 1930s and early 1940s, as well as through the conformity derived from the Cold War during the later 1940s, 1950s, and early 1960s. But, the questioning and doubt that was a major source for the development of a "counterculture" in the later 1960s, and early 1970s and a "God Is Dead" movement in liberal theological circles during the 1960s led to a decline in attendance and traditional forms of belief among the putative Christian majority. Since the 1960s, there has been evidence of a resurgence in both attendance and belief, but this renewal has largely been the result of the growing appeal of Protestant evangelism, of old-fashioned revivalism. "Born-again" Christians—those experiencing conversion (one of whom, by the late 1970s, was the President himself: Jimmy Carter)—became a major force in American Christianity (as it had sporadically throughout the American past).

In recent years, it has been the evangelists and their adherents who have proselytized Christianity at home and become its missionaries abroad (as older Protestant and Catholic movements have declined in vitality). Evangelical Christians have developed broadcast stations, schools, publishing houses, and whole complexes. Their political action committees have, since the mid-1970s, exerted a significant influence on national political life, as only conservative political candidates have been supported. The Evangelical Christian resurgence has—in social and political terms—become a generally conservative force, as born-again Christians have favored a return to an older, simpler, more unambiguous Christian—and distinctively American—nation and have resisted the development of a more pluralistic society. Such Christians have been at the center of a recent effort to keep American Christian.

By contrast, moderate Protestants and Catholics have—since the 1940s—increasingly brought a social emphasis to churchgoing, which they have experienced as a tradition and a basis for their position or status in society, especially as Christian theology has come to be perceived in a figurative sense and has been generally deemphasized. Except for those Americans who are evangelical Christians or members of new, vigorous sects derived from Asian religious traditions, Americans no longer regard ministers and churches as explicators of the ultimate meaning of life. All Americans continue to respond to the rewards and punishments of secular laws (or rules), which are grounded in the Christian ethical system. The churches as an institution still matter, and ministers are regularly summoned to mark in age-old Christian and Jewish ways the "passages of life"—birth, marriage, death; suggesting that, even if moderate American Christians don't focus on Christian views of the nature of existence and reality, they have not yet yielded their sense that the church is still the appropriate institution to mark the most important points of a person's life.

Secular humanism, like Deism in the eighteenth and Unitarianism in the nineteenth centuries, has not become an alternative faith for most Americans. But, the notion of "human rights," which were enshrined in the United Nations Charter in 1945, and which are contained in varying versions of "Bills of Rights" in national and state (or provincial) constitutions in different parts of the globe, is becoming a widely subscribed-to notion. Americans still have faith that theirs is a special nation, that the idea of "America" is still distinctive and inherently superior, but such a faith has been shaken by recent developments, and the practice of connecting the Christian God to a favored United States is less often made in a context of increasingly obvious religious plurality.

If viewed in a global context, religion in America featured a novel Constitutional separation of church and state, which was a direct consequence of the early presence of many Christian sects. This religious pluralism (albeit within the circumscribed sphere of a single religion) was the context for the kind of religious ferment that led to the creation of new, American-founded sects, such as the Mormons and the Christian Scientists (which have since sought converts elsewhere in the world) and that provided popular evangelism with its most fertile setting. But, white and converted black and native Americans have shared a common religion—Christianity—with Europeans and with those in other parts of the world penetrated by Europeans. Christianity has been one of the great defining elements of Western civilization, and its sects and denominations have been basically the same, whether in America, Australia, South Africa, Canada, Brazil, or Argentina. In order to understand Christianity, the dominant religion in America, it is necessary to focus on what Americans shared as Christians with others in many other parts of the globe. To view religious activity within America in isolation, without this larger perspective, is to present a partial, skewed picture.

34

Education

Education in the tribal societies of the African slaves and the native tribes was family oriented, noninstitutional, and limited in scope to the mastery of skills that children would later utilize as adults. Parents were teachers; schools as separate facilities did not exist. In tribal Africa and North America, the oral tradition was central to the educational enterprise, as elderly storytellers or traditional singers spoke or sang proverbs, fables, folktales, legends, and myths.

During the seventeenth and eighteenth centuries, Europeans and their colonists were still traditional, in that learning was also conducted within the family context by parents. But, what made European education differ somewhat from what was offered in tribal and other traditional societies was its pluralism, that is, the coexistence of family education and formal institutions of learning, schools.

As in England, a variety of private schools were established in the colonies during the seventeenth and eighteenth centuries: individual schoolmasters, charity schools for the poor, private schools for the rich, church schools for the more exclusive sects, finishing schools for women, private academies to prepare youths for colleges and universities. Only the Puritans insisted upon a literate progeny; only they enacted legislation charging their towns with the responsibility of creating a public school, a fiat that met with much delay and indifference on the part of some towns. In effect, "public" education originated in towns dominated by a single Christian sect. The earliest schools in New England and elsewhere were usually located in an ordinary villager's house, with the teacher an untrained widow or widower with time to deal with other people's children. In any case, the whole pattern of life and the value system that gave it meaning were transmitted to children by their parents as much as by teachers in schools. Both vocational training and family prayer preceded the efforts of inculcation by those in the more formal institutions of church and school.

The colonists' colleges were usually church-affiliated and community-oriented and had as their primary aim the training of ministers who, throughout the seventeenth and eighteenth centuries, were typically the only learned men in the towns, villages, and countryside—if not in the port cities. Colonial colleges lacked the standards, intellectual sophistication, and national reach of Oxford and Cambridge or even of the Spanish universities chartered by the monarch and staffed by the church and located in various Spanish colonies. In the English colonial colleges, both students and faculty exhibited widely varied intellectual attainments, and the colleges relied upon their churches and those who lived in the immediate vicinity for financial support and for students. The failure of the colonists to create universities on a par with those in England and elsewhere in Europe or in other colonies in the Americas reveals that English provincial culture, as it appeared on the American colonial frontier, was not as sophisticated as Europe's—or Spanish America's.

Americans were exposed to formal philosophical, scientific, and medical inquiry only at the highest levels of education—and even there American standards did not approach those of the well-established European universities, such as Oxford and Cambridge. Both colleges and universities were locally oriented, not nationally as in England, and proposals for a "national" university were not taken seriously when introduced or recommended in Congress or by the Presidency from the 1790s to the 1820s. Standards of admission were loose, with college and university presidents—then, as now—spending much time and energy in fund raising, either at state legislatures or with alumni or prospective students. Both colleges and universities were institutions whose instructors were extremely concerned with discipline, given the wide discrepancies in the ages of the students. The objectives of educators at this level were not only to impart knowledge through the method of rote memorization, but to develop the moral character of the students, to make them good citizens and Christians.

Building on the precedent established by the Puritan-dominated colonies, a growing number of the new states in the decades after independence enacted legislation commanding local communities to establish and support public schools, at least at the primary level, and a few states also initiated secondary school systems. But, there was little to suggest that a public school "system" would grow out of these efforts, as state governments enacted and then sometimes repealed legislation designed to bring about uniformity, and as localities often ignored edicts meant to be statewide. The most articulate and "reformist" educators in state departments of education advocated attendance in school for all children, so that they could learn basic skills (reading, writing, arithmetic) from trained teachers and schoolbooks filled with American values, as well as become virtuous citizens, good Christians, and knowledgeable workers in an industrializing economy. But, the state of education varied widely in various parts of the Union, there still being a wide array of private schools, from charitable institutions to "finishing" schools for the elite. In general, formal schooling—at whatever level—involved the inculcation of prevailing values, discipline that created well-behaved citizens, and basic skills to produce a literate and numerate population equipped to deal with the occupational explosion that accompanied the industrialization and continued commercialization of the economy.

This was a situation that prevailed in Europe as well. Innovators such as Horace Mann were aware that national school systems had already been instituted in such Europeans polities as Prussia and France. But, in other parts of Europe, school systems were church-related; in Britain in particular, the Education Act of 1870 provided public funds for Anglican or other denominational schools that had already been established and set up new schools where there weren't any church schools. But, as in Europe, America continued to have a wide array of private primary and secondary and postsecondary schools founded and sustained by a variety of groups, both religious and secular. In the decades after the Civil War, state government continued to legislate requirements that county and local governments establish not only primary school systems, but secondary school systems as well. What began in the northeast corner of the nation, by the turn of the century, became a nationwide standard, including southern and western sections as well. What began as a reform movement became, in the late nineteenth century, a common recognition that education was a public, governmental responsibility.

In these decades as well, most states founded public universities, aided by land grants from the national government, which came as a result of the Land Grant Act of 1862. (Such national aid was the closest that the top tier of government in the American system came to playing an active role in educational development in the absence of any clear Constitutional sanction.)

But, the private schools—at all levels—continued to flourish, and many Americans continued to believe that teaching the young, like caring for the sick, was an intensely local (and private) undertaking. However, the teachers' training schools that were instituted by state governments as they established public school systems brought increasing uniformity to the way teachers were produced, and teachers themselves formed national unions. From the late nineteenth through the early twentieth centuries, mandatory public school systems at both the primary and secondary levels became standard across the United States. At the same time, graduate schools were added to American universities, modeled on European centers, particularly German ones, and professors received a uniform kind of training, similar in character to their European counterparts.

The purpose of primary and secondary schools as espoused in state departments of education and in teachers' colleges was to train youth in the basic skills of reading, writing, and arithmetic; to make them aware of their society and the world around them; and to inculcate in them the prevailing values of their community and their society. Two of these goals were already existing; the third—knowledge of society and world—was manifest in an increasing array of courses and texts introduced in the years after the Civil War. But, many young Americans left school in order to earn incomes and pursue occupations as soon as state laws allowed them to do so. They were trained "on the job"; schools did not usually function as vocational institutes. Indeed, the "progressive" education movement that began in the early twentieth century emphasized that schools should prepare students for life in general, and the experimental schools that were established in the 1920s and thereafter were as concerned about the fostering of life skills as they were in inculcating basic ones.

During these decades, the colleges and universities greatly augmented their classical curriculum, and many developed new "fields of study" and "faculty departments" into which formalized inquiry into various aspects of the human and natural worlds was increasingly divided. An elite of students were admitted to America's colleges and universities, and "higher education" became the objective of the upwardly mobile element of the population, the portion that continued to link the "educated person" with responsible and status-filled positions and occupations. More clearly than before, America's colleges and universities became the chief preservers and disseminators of the nation's cultural heritage (in the broadest sense) and the central institutions for the expansion of its knowledge, though private collectors and scholars and institutes of other kinds continued to participate in these processes.

Americans transmitted their prevailing values from one generation to another by means of their school system. This was a function teachers shared with others. Parents, clergymen, politicians, editors, writers, broadcasters (after 1920), and advertisers also emphasized at times what was proper and what was not to audiences of varying sizes. Similarly, though the schools imparted knowledge, so did newspapers, magazines, books, and (after 1920) radio networks. Furthermore, Americans learned informally from others, and relied on stories, anecdotes, tales, and gossip for information, as well as on more formal means. In short, the values of American life (what proper behavior was, what the goals of life were) and the knowledge needed for Americans to live effectively were both derived from a variety of sources, though the emergent educational system was increasingly more central to that process, rivaling an earlier dominance by parents and churches.

Since 1930, American education has—quite distinctively and notably—become a training ground for everything and everyone. The educational system has become to some extent another aspect of consumer culture, with schools and colleges and universities "supermarkets" of knowledge and students their "consumers." Education had become democratized up to its highest levels, with increasingly higher percentage of Americans staying in the system through college or university. (Some state universities don't even have admissions standards.) The prevailing view has been that the educational system should be capable of teaching or training people in anything, a view that is an outgrowth of the "progressive" educational philosophy.

By the "liberal"-dominated 1960s, even the national government found a constitutionally acceptable way of providing funding for elementary and secondary schools in the Education Act of 1965. But, since the 1970s, American education has veered back toward a renewed emphasis on basic skills and a core curriculum, in part because of studies that showed Americans did not fare as well in tests in which they were compared with those educated in some other parts of the world. Americans continue to learn and to develop skills and knowledge and information from sources other than schools—that is, through television, radio, and other forms of telecommunications, but they have relied relatively less in recent decades on such older sources as newspapers, magazines, and books.

From a global perspective, education in America mirrored broad developments in Europe, certainly in the sense that there were, from the beginning of white settlement, a great variety of formal institutions for learning, schools. What is distinctive to America is not its development of public education at the primary and secondary levels, a development it shared with various European polities, but its relatively open and accessible higher educational system. The Puritans—a religious group who dominated secular government within particular colonial jurisdictions—were the instigators in America of a universal or public school system. What started as a religious imperative became a secularized reform movement involving state departments of education. Modern, public education in America thus had religious origins.

In the wider sense of education, in the transmission of knowledge and values from one generation to the next, Americans drew on the same resources as people all over the Western world to ensure the survival of the culture. If education is examined in isolation, in America, what Americans shared with Europeans around the world is lost sight of: the emergence of varied school systems that have become the central institutions by which knowledge and values are inculcated in each new generation.

35

Thought/Science/Medicine

The philosophical outlook of the native American tribes was marked by its balance and reciprocity. The ideal for natives was to live in stasis or harmony with the environment, other people, and the "spirits." Native Americans were far more successful in achieving a harmonious relationship with their natural setting than they were with each other, however, for tribal warfare was sometimes quite a frequent occurrence. Similarly, the black African slaves shared a view of the universe that represented a unified spiritual totality. Spirit was not separate from matter. There was no duality, just complementary pairs of opposites, interdependent and necessary to each other. Africans combined thought and feeling to perceive reality.

Europeans, by contrast, separated mind from matter, the spiritual from the material. During the seventeenth and eighteenth centuries, their philosophy stressed the use of the rational faculty of the human mind in an effort to understand the material world. The philosophes were public philosophers who sought to apply rational inquiry to all dimensions of human life. The European enlightenment was a new, secular, philosophical outlook based upon human reason; one was "enlightened" to the extent that one developed the capability of employing this highest of human faculties.

With few exceptions (such as in the case of the theological writings of Jonathan Edwards), intellectually aspiring English colonists turned to European thinkers for the best theories of a theological, metaphysical, or scientific character. The most impressive colonists—like Franklin and, later, Jefferson—were valued by thoughtful Europeans for their empirical observations as naturalists. The colonies retained generally European and specifically English notions of what constituted a good government (one balanced between representative and hereditary elements; between monarch, nobility, and commons; between liberty and order), a good economy (one with property-and wealth-seeking individuals operating within a trading empire founded upon mercantilist principles), and a good society (one that is hierarchical, *but* with equal opportunity for social and geographical mobility for all well-behaved white men, *and* open to all white migrants), and a good life (one that is Christian).

After independence, Americans relied heavily on European philosophers and theorists and theologians as their source for formulations on the nature and purpose of existence and life in its varied metaphysical, material, political, social, and economic dimensions. A sense of intellectual inferiority was deeply ingrained in the American population throughout the nineteenth century, and those who attempted to reflect in a philosophical or theological way were rare individuals indeed. Americans took pride in their more practical or pragmatic orientation. The "naturalist" and the inventor had a status denied the philosopher-theologian. It is very revealing that the American Philosophical Society, led by first Benjamin Franklin and then Thomas Jefferson, was devoted to the compilation of "useful knowledge," that the Society was oriented toward the kind of activity "naturalists" and experimental scientists were interested in, rather than philosophical speculation.

The particular metaphysical formulation that had the most impact in America after the Revolution was the wholly European-derived "common sense" school developed mainly in Scotland during the late eighteenth century. Adherents argued that certain "self-evident" truths (matters of faith and belief) were beyond empirical investigation—beyond scientific truth or sensual experience. Advocates of "common sense" philosophy attempted to combine Christianity, enlightenment thought, and science in a harmonious way. Similarly, in one of the German states, the immensely influential philosopher Immanuel Kant argued that rational inquiry was enclosed by both religious and moral truths that exist beyond its reach. Kant was a major influence on the earliest professors of philosophy in American colleges and universities. This explanation of existence provided a thoroughly European philosophical justification for the political-social-economic theories that flourished in America, beginning in the late eighteenth century, particularly the "liberal" political philosophy that was the basis for the Revolution and the Constitution, a philosophy that emphasized "self-evident" natural laws and rights and liberties.

Clerical presidents of church-affiliated colleges became the chief spokesmen for the "common sense" view, and, as they were typically the instructors for the courses in "moral philosophy," the final course that those enrolled in American colleges were usually required to take, this particular philosophical viewpoint was explained to the most educated and, often, influential element of the population. But, whatever lasting effect exposure to the "common sense" school had on the educated elite, it is clear that the most literate Americans continued to receive theoretical explanations of life from their ministers. Clergymen continued—though with somewhat diminishing authority—to be the central intellectual figures in the American population as a whole. Professors at the church-related colleges and the new secular state universities rivaled clergymen as intellectual and moral tutors, but only for the small, though influential, portion of the population who enrolled in these institutions.

Whether secular or religious in origin, such intellectual tutelage was primarily oral, either through sermons or lectures, and not through books, philosophical treatises being very rare before the late nineteenth century. Only editors, through widely read daily or weekly journals or "newspapers" or monthly magazines, were in a position to disseminate philosophical speculation through print, and they rarely did so. Such essays were rare. Ordinary Americans looked to Christianity both for an explanation for the nature of life and for a justification for republican government and a "capitalist" economy. They thought of themselves as Christians and republicans and (what would later be popularly known as) capitalists—this was the essence of their intellectual identity.

Only twice between the Revolution and the Civil War did self-conscious "intellectual communities" have a notable impact on American life as a whole. Both drew heavily on European and Asian sources and in one sense served as conduits for the dissemination of philosophical formulations developed elsewhere. The political leaders of the revolutionary era were aware that they were spokesmen for the "enlightenment" theorists of Europe and (at least in part) justified the revolt against British rule and the later state-making act of drafting a constitution by reference to enlightenment ideals. This political leadership clearly perceived their statecraft to be an example of applied philosophy. Jefferson's generation of planter-merchant-lawyer-politicians were acutely conscious that the new American republic was conceived and defined according to philosophical principles. Political independence and the republic that followed were partly creations of the intellect.

The new nation was—from its inception—provided with a philosophical justification, a special reason for existing. It was to be the setting for the fruition of Europe's highest political and social ideals. These were the philosophically oriented actions of a highly public character and constituted vivid evidence that philosophy could have an impact on the common life of a population. More broadly, these state makers provided a philosophical basis for the communal aspects of American life: the nation itself was based upon a sacred covenant; public life was thus invested with a hopefully durable ethical foundation.

The second intellectual group with a significant impact on Americans was the Transcendentalists, and especially their spokesman, Ralph Waldo Emerson. The Transcendentalists were a group of reflective New Englanders who lived for a brief period in a utopian socialist community and supported a magazine while, once again, drawing on foreign sources (both Asian and European) to develop a mystical religious view. They believed human beings could directly commune with God (or the Oversoul) through quiet meditation. They emphasized the importance of each person's developing his highest potential, his fullest individuality, but failed to pay attention to the communal responsibilities of individuals. Emerson greatly popularized the transcendentalist viewpoint generally and individualism in particular, during extensive lecture tours during the 1830s through the 1860s.

The Transcendentalists provided a philosophical justification for individualism, something that was evident in various dimensions of American life: in the private accumulation of wealth and property, in the civil liberties that governments at all levels were to protect, in the citizens that adherents of liberal philosophy asserted existed as voters, in the Christians whom clerics declared had everlasting souls. Unlike Jefferson's generation's public philosophy, Transcendentalism was a private philosophical expression—but one with a public impact nonetheless. Americans found satisfaction in a philosophical justification for individual endeavors, just as they had found reassurance in the creation of a national community linked to liberal ideals.

In the decades after the Civil War, Europe generally remained the model for formalized thought and philosophy and theories and concepts and abstractions. Americans remained at the periphery of a civilization whose thought centered on the European heartland. Trained philosophers in America were usually educated in Europe until the turn of the century, when America's college and university philosophy departments—modeled after their European precursors—developed degree programs. But, the educated, cultured elite of the post–Civil War era did not cap their studies with a common course in moral philosophy, as their predecessors before the war had. As the curriculum of universities and colleges became more specialized, philosophy lost its unifying and central position at the core of advanced study. Followers of influential European philosophers, such as Kant, Hegel, and Nietzsche, were particular professors of philosophy and their students, who "specialized" in philosophy. University or college graduates as a whole were no longer exposed to a common philosophical point of view. The most standard overall metaphysical outlook was suffused with the notion that life evolved into more complex and superior forms. In this, philosophers such as the immensely influential Hegel were in agreement with scientific theorists such as Charles Darwin.

The only distinctively "American" philosophy to emerge in these decades was pragmatism, especially as espoused by William James, in its psychological and religious aspects, and by John Dewey, in its social aspects. The basic notion of pragmatism was that ideas are true to the extent that they "work," can be made operational in different aspects of human life. Whether as a basis for the functioning of the human personality, the development of human beliefs, or the operation of human society—James and Dewey gave the pragmatic outlook academic and philosophical respectability. Though academics themselves, their writings were widely sold and read, and their ideas became the most important instance in this era of professional intellectuals influencing their peers both in America and in Europe, as well as the wider American population.

However, in America during these years, intellectual constructs—ideas, theories, concepts—were usually popularized versions of the more refined and complicated ideas of academic specialists in many disciplines, not just philosophy.

Americans continued to be enormously influenced by developments in European thought, from various parts of the academic and intellectual spectrum.

Charles Darwin's view that biological forms evolve through a process of selectivity, whereby those best able to adapt to the environment survive, was applied to human society by Herbert Spencer. Spencer was a popularizer, and his "Social Darwinism" influenced American academics, such as sociologist William Graham Sumner, as well as popular lecturers and writers, such as historians John Fiske and John W. Burgess and clergyman Josiah Strong. Sumner argued that the emergence of powerful societies was a natural process, the result of tradition and custom, not governmental or public edict. Fiske, Burgess, and Strong proclaimed that America, with its British core culture, had risen to the apex of civilization.

Critics of Social Darwinism, such as Lester Frank Ward, insisted that human beings had evolved into rational creatures who could improve their situation, within its natural context, through the application of their reason, thus controlling the process of evolution by ameliorating poverty and promoting education. Though entrepreneurs such as Andrew Carnegie extolled a Social Darwinistic portrayal of the society through which entrepreneurs had emerged, social critics like Henry George, Henry Demarest Lloyd, Thorstein Veblen, and Edward Bellamy all rejected the vast inequality and extremes of wealth and poverty that acceptance of a Darwinian scenario justified.

Karl Marx's view—that human beings are driven by impersonal economic forces and that capitalistic societies would naturally evolve into a wealthy, powerful elite and an impoverished proletariat who would eventually overthrow governments that supported the interests of such elites—was popularized by Socialist and then Communist leaders in the United States from the 1870s to the Depression, leaders who were usually recent European immigrants. But, though Marx's social critique became widely known in these decades in versions of varying simplicity and complexity, defenders of the American system retained their political ascendancy through eras of both conservative (1870s–1890s and 1920s) and reformist (1890s and 1900–1918) domination. The Progressives, imbued as they were by a "pragmatic" outlook, rejected the inevitability of the Marxists' apocalyptic prognosis for capitalistic societies, arguing that ameliorative reform could save the system from its worst excesses.

Sigmund Freud's psychoanalytical theory—that human behavior is far more than just rational, that it is shaped by needs arising from the unconscious part of the mind—was similarly popularized by the 1920s, though critics questioned the theory's scientific validity.

In all three of the foregoing instances—Darwinian, Marxism, and Freudianism—perceptions of the nature of human reality were "deterministic" in character; that is, the life of humanity was determined by processes essentially beyond human control.

But, theoretical speculation in other academic disciplines, especially physics and anthropology, resulted in the development of other, indeterminate perceptions of the nature of things, if not of humanity itself. As physicists used instruments—both microscopic and telescopic—that allowed them to examine aspects of the universe in ever greater and ever smaller detail, Albert Einstein—early in the twentieth century—postulated that space, time, and mass are not absolutes, but are relative to the location and motion of the observer. Similarly, Werner Heisenberg—in the 1920s—argued that the measurement of things, and, therefore, human knowledge itself, has limits or is "uncertain" in the sense that one cannot know both the position and velocity of an object, because the very process of observation has an impact on the behavior of the object.

Such theorizing in physics was popularized and applied to far wider areas of human existence. These theories gave the sanction of science to the proposition that what is perceived depends on the position of the observer. Ideas of relativity and uncertainty justified the denial of absolute values in any sphere of life and could call into question the concepts that there were ethical standards and justifiable personal responsibility for human conduct.

Anthropologists, in the 1920s, transformed the term "culture" to embrace the entire way of living for human groups, *all* of which had cultures, and, since all things are relative, those in one culture should not impose their value judgments on those in other cultures. Among the thought patterns with broad influence on American life, deterministic modes of thought started to give way—by the 1920s—to indeterministic ones.

Americans continued to be shaped and influenced by ideas, but, instead of the intellectual communities that had been important to the development of American life before the Civil War—such as the Founding Fathers and the Transcendentalists—academic theorists and their popularizers continued to serve as justifiers and articulators of intellectual constructs that ordinary Americans could understand as explanations of the life they were experiencing.

With the introduction of subjects such as contemporary philosophy in universities and colleges throughout the Europeanized world by the early twentieth century, modern secular thought became internationalized, a matter of translated texts that have not in any important sense continued to be confined to their national origins, whether British, French, German, Italian, Russian, or American. But, since philosophy ceased being a required, culminating course for graduating seniors by the late nineteenth century, formal philosophy also ceased being the common "property" of an educated elite and became instead the focus of those majoring in a specialized academic discipline and of their professors.

By the 1930s and 1940s, contemporary philosophy bifurcated into two schools—linguistic analysis and existentialism. In recent decades, there has been no orthodoxy, no agreed-upon, overall system of secular thought. What has been essential to metaphysical speculation throughout the intellectual world, especially at academic centers, is the notion—first formulated by physicists—of the uncertainty of human knowledge and of the ultimate mystery (for humans) of the nature of reality itself. The belief that Christianity (and, more broadly, European civilization) contained within itself absolute truth—that is, that ultimate reality can be known wholly by means of Christian beliefs—has been shattered by scientific inquiry, whether the subject probed is inanimate matter or human societies. The result has been the development of relativism, the belief that no civilization or culture has a monopoly on truth, that all truth is contingent, relative, partial, and that ultimate reality is unknowable by human means, whether reality be examined by modern technology to its largest extent (through telescopes) or to its smallest extent (through microscopes).

From a global perspective, pragmatism aside, it is difficult to find a major current of thought that has originated in America, so reliant has the American intellectual community been on European philosophy. American and European thinkers have shared a transatlantic philosophical outlook. What has been distinctive is the way that Americans have applied thought: as the basis for their national community, as the basis for their individualism. It is altogether fitting that their sole contribution to philosophy has been pragmatism—the view that ideas are true to the extent that they can work, can be applied.

* * *

A distinctive aspect of Western culture, scientific inquiry in America was highly derivative of Europe's until at least the late nineteenth century. Before the development of large, modern universities in the United States, the few professors of science at the better established American colleges and universities were trained in Europe and contributed to a transatlantic world of scientific theorizing and experimentation. These professors served as disseminators of first (after the late seventeenth century) the Newtonian physical and later (after the mid-nineteenth century) the Darwinian biological systems under which the physical world operated according to certain natural laws and the biological world revealed an ever-more-complex hierarchy of living species that survived and evolved according to a process of natural selection.

Technology, or applied science, was almost wholly divorced from the work of "naturalists," who continued mainly to observe and categorize natural phenomena. The new national government did not actively promote science, except for the sponsoring of botanical and geographical expeditions and surveys to the West—that is, promote the work of the "naturalists." James Smithson, a Britisher, endowed the only national institute for scientific inquiry, in 1846.

The national government promoted the development of engineering through the activities of its Army Engineers Corps, in such areas as bridge, road, canal, and dam building. But, practically all of the technological innovations of this period came as the result of experimentation by individual inventors who responded to the needs of a labor-scarce economy and the desire for greater material comfort and ease in the home and workplace.

Some inventions transformed economic activity: Eli Whitney's cotton gin made possible the swift emergence of cotton as the leading staple crop of the South by the 1820s; the farm machinery developed by Cyrus McCormick and others in the 1840s and 1850s similarly stimulated the large-scale production of grain and livestock in the valleys, plains, and prairies of the midcontinent. Such machinery was exported or copied around the world, in other European agricultural frontier zones: in southern Siberia, in northern Argentina, in southeastern Australia. Other inventions greatly altered the character of domestic life. Between the 1830s and the 1870s, in upper-and middle-class homes technology vastly changed the domestic lives of people: their lighting (from grease and oil lamps to gas jets), their waste disposal (outhouse to indoor toilets), their water supply (well pumps to water pumps and plumbing), their cooking (wood stoves to coal stoves), their heating (fireplace to furnace), their washing (tub to washing machine), their food storage and preservation (cellars to canning jars and iceboxes), their sewing (spinning wheels and looms to sewing machines).

In the later nineteenth century, American universities and colleges followed the lead of the European scientific community in the development of "fields" of study, which became units or departments within such institutions. Students "specialized" in particular areas of subjects, and, with advanced training and degrees, augmented the number of scientists in each discipline. Professors of science founded their own national associations during the late nineteenth century, reflecting the much broader tendency for groups to become national (and international) in scope. In this way, in America as in Europe, the modern disciplines of physics, chemistry, biology, astronomy, geology, and geography were developed.

"Scientific method," the systematic testing of hypotheses (or interpretations) through the uniform ordering of all available evidence, became widely known among educated Americans in the decades after the Civil War. For this segment of the population, "scientific proof" began to rival religious revelation as a basis for knowledge. Gradually, American "scientists" ceased to be "naturalists," those who observed and classified the world around them, although they continued to rely on Europeans for the articulation of scientific theory. American science, to a considerable extent, sustained a well-established "practical" orientation.

Scientists, in America as well as in Europe during these years, used an increasing array of technological devices to probe the natural world. American scientists, more than any other group in American society (with the possible exception of the largest industrialists), self-consciously connected what they did to the global community of fellow practitioners and, in so doing, greatly reduced their national identity. Science was not an "American" activity; it was a human achievement.

"Applied science" or technology continued to be an activity involving amateur inventors, among whom the best known in these years was Thomas Edison, who, reflecting the bureaucratization and growing organizational complexity of life more broadly, created an invention "factory." The hallmark of these new professional inventors' method was still trail and error and random experimentation, however, and not the planned, systematized probings of the scientists. Emerson himself, with his assistants, invented or perfected the phonograph, the light bulb, the storage battery, the dictaphone, the mimeograph, the dynamo, electrical transmission, and the motion picture during the 1870s and 1880s. Such inventions were developed by Edison and many others into bases for the large-scale production of electrical energy and new forms of communication, both of which had profound effects on many dimensions of American life and, as copied and developed in other parts of the industrializing world, life elsewhere.

During the twentieth century, mathematics has spurred the development of another very important application of science: statistics, by means of which Americans are measured in many significant ways. Statistical degrees of wealth and poverty, or income levels, have become a major determinant of class and status. Intelligence and ignorance are routinely measured in "IQ" tests. Americans' life, health, and property are all insured on the basis of statistical "risk" categories (age, gender, and others). Americans—and others in the developed world—have used statistics to measure the size of virtually every group or community in their midst. Statistically defined "public opinion" polls serve as a major basis for determining prevailing views and beliefs and have become a leading guide for governmental or institutional or corporate planning or action.

Science has become openly linked to technology in the research and development departments of corporations, which have largely replaced the invention factories of people such as Thomas Edison, or earlier, the lone inventor. The national government has in recent decades become directly involved in scientific technology through the funding provided by the National Science Foundation, through the presence of the President's National Science Adviser, and through the weapons systems of the Defense Department and the space programs of the National Aeronautics and Space Administration.

Technology has continued to change the environment and activity of both workplaces and living spaces. The application of electrical energy has led to the development of a vast array of home appliances and has allowed industry to locate anywhere. The harnessing of light and sound waves and the swift growth of computer technology have transformed communications in the home, at work, or at any institution. In recent decades, technology has even altered old definitions of space and time. Buildings and homes built with glass walls and interior utilities (air and water and sewerage) have blurred the line between exterior and interior space and largely obliterated seasonal variations. Various forms of refrigeration in transport systems (rail, road, and air) and in homes have freed Americans and others from nearby sources of sustenance, as food and drink are preserved or canned or frozen or just kept sufficiently cool in their natural state to allow Americans to be far removed from the actual location at which the crop or livestock was matured. Time itself has become stored or repeatable through photography, film, audio tape, record, and disc—all replayable on television, radio, or individual movie or sound stages.

Since 1930, American scientists have made many practical, if not theoretical, advances, in which Europeans and many others in these most globalized of human activities have shared. In science, the discovery of nuclear fission has led to the creation of nuclear power and nuclear weaponry, and the development of rocket technology has resulted in the exploration of space. In biology, microscopic studies of smaller and smaller components of life have vastly increased our knowledge of the human body and the nature of health and disease. Similarly, physicists and chemists have used both microscope and telescope to probe the intricacies and possible human uses of inanimate matter and, in the process, have created widely used synthetic and nonbiogradable materials.

Viewed from a global perspective, science in America was, from its inception, heavily reliant on European developments. American scientists were at first naturalists, amateur observers of nature, and even after the appearance of professional scientists, Americans continued to rely on European theorizing. What has stood out has been an eagerness to find applications for science and technological inventiveness, both of which reflect the practical orientation of those who have sought to understand the nature of things in America.

* * *

In the African and native tribes, medicine was within the province of spiritual healers, shamans or "medicine men." Because tribal cultures did not separate the physical and the spiritual realms, diseases and wounds were treated through incantations and ministrations by holy men, those with the most spiritual authority.

Throughout the seventeenth, eighteenth, and much of the nineteenth centuries, English colonial and later white American physicians either trained in Europe or apprenticed with an established doctor. As in Europe, physicians in America continued to develop surgical techniques and treatment for wounds. American doctors also relied on European theories of what caused illness. Medical theory was confused and contradictory until the germ theory gained the ascendancy in the late nineteenth century. Practitioners during the seventeenth, eighteenth, and much of the nineteenth centuries could rely for cures on narcotics, stimulants, bleedings, sweatings, mercury, herbs, baths, or medicines that in minute amounts caused symptoms similar to the disease itself. The treatments physicians chose depended on whether they subscribed to a theory that focused on impurities or imbalances in bodily fluids, too much or too little heat or oxygen inhalation, debilities in the life or nervous force emanating from the brain, or imbalances in the excitability of the body caused by external stimuli. By the late nineteenth century, germ theory created a novel orthodoxy in medical theorizing, and medical researchers began to focus on the study of particular diseases.

What was distinctive to American medicine was its early emphasis on problems relating to the public health of a population still geographically spaced enough to avoid Europe's endemic state in the spread of contagious diseases. By the early nineteenth century, American urban centers were ravaged by sporadic epidemics, however, and it was there that the most concerted efforts were made to prevent epidemics through quarantines and improvements in water supplies and sewerage disposal. It was in this urban setting that the earliest public water and sewer systems were constructed, and some vaccinations were developed as a means of preventing some of the communicable diseases. By the 1870s, various municipal and state governments instituted public health boards.

As in Europe, hospitals in America were, in the colonial period, privately managed institutions, often by religious organizations, typically for the poor and orphaned. There was also a great deal of home care for those in the middling and higher segments of society. As hospitals became more common during the nineteenth century and as physicians became more organized, hospitals, of all the social welfare institutions, remained the most localized and the most resistant to governmental control. During that century, civic or municipal hospitals were created in population centers to supplement private ones, and hospitals typically provided care for all elements of a community. By contrast, the role of state governments in mental health has been very large. As asylums were built in the early nineteenth century, their managers (in both state-managed and private institutions) advocated a rigorous discipline for inmates, saw their institutions as rehabilitative, and believed that their inmates could be cured and returned to society as good members. When this did not turn out to be the case, these asylums became custodial institutions, places for the insane to be kept away from society.

Americans copied Europeans when they instituted medical schools at universities, commonly by the late nineteenth century. Instead of training abroad, those seeking an education in medicine could attend schools founded in all parts of the United States during the decades after the Civil War. As in Europe, the practice of medicine became an increasingly specialized endeavor, and Americans began to train specialists of a kind the European medical centers were already producing. At the same time, the apprenticeship system was gradually abandoned as a credible way to train for a general medical practice, even in towns and rural areas.

American researchers, teachers, and practitioners continued to rely on European medical theories, however, and medicine in America—like science in America—maintained its traditional "practical" orientation, with its concern for such aspects of the subject as public health, vaccination, and surgery. "Health boards" on the local, county, and state levels became practically universal governmental instrumentalities within the United States by the twentieth century. In other respects, medicine retained both its localized and privatized character. Hospitals were either privately (by church-affiliated or charitable groups) or municipally founded or maintained. Health care, like education generally, remained an activity under the control of many different groups in a vast array of localities across the continent. Only mental health and care for the handicapped seemed to present problems sufficiently complicated or intractable for even state governments to feel obliged to provide institutional care.

During the twentieth century, there has been a renewed emphasis on home care, somewhat of a cyclical return to the practice that prevailed in colonial times. Mental patients have been treated and released to their families or placed in halfway houses, whereas patients in hospitals are let out as soon as possible, with home recovery as the goal. In medicine, research has become an international activity, with Americans contributing to theoretical as well as practical aspects. Important developments that have been shared by medical practitioners everywhere include the discovery of antibiotics and additional vaccinations as well as the refinement of surgical techniques. Even the national government has become involved in medical research through the establishment and maintenance of the National Institutes of Health, beginning in the 1940s, and the provision of Medicare for the aged, starting in the 1960s.

Viewed from a global perspective, medicine in America has had until recently, relative to Europe, a practical orientation and, in the case of the insane, an early reformist zeal. But, much of what has occurred is best understood by reference to a wider, Western context.

36

Art/Entertainment

African and native American art was either public, religious, and ceremonial, or utilitarian and craft-oriented. Native American art was particularly spiritual in its basic function. Paintings were filled with spiritual references. Clothing, dwellings, and objects used daily were all designed in such a way that users were aware of their spiritual purpose. Ceremonial dance costumes and masks were similarly designed with spiritual significance.

African artistic activity was focused on the oral use of language for the telling of tales, proverbs, and myths; on music and dance characterized by their polyrhymthic and polycentric character; and on sculpture, particularly facial masks. African elites in west Africa accepted Islamic culture, but they did not become enslaved and transported to the Americas. As slaves, black Africans in North America entered an artistic twilight zone, developing arts that were a hybrid of remembered African elements along with absorbed fragments of English colonial art. The slaves' musical instruments, music, and dance all revealed a deep remembrance of African ways. During the long period of segregation that followed slavery, from the 1860s to the 1960s, the black population developed musical forms that, when they were taken up by the dominant white population, became the most distinctive forms of American popular music. The blues, gospel songs, ragtime, and jazz were all developed by blacks who amalgamated African and white American elements.

Like African and native American art, European art was public, ceremonial, and religious, that is, in the service of state or church, but the court societies of Europe also patronized art that pleased or honored themselves. Sophisticated European art consisted of fictional and poetic writing, theater, dance, music, painting, sculpture, and architecture. Unlike native American and African tribal societies, artists in Europe were often identifiable, their creations quite distinctive. Within each art were several, varied styles of artistic creation. This lack of ritualistic creativity, along with growing evidence of artistic individuality, meant that European art was becoming increasingly modern during the seventeenth and eighteenth centuries.

Over the course of these two centuries there was a general shift from a baroque to a classical style in all the arts, that is, from forms that emphasized excess, emotion, extravagance to forms that emphasized restraint, balance, reason. In artistic depiction, secular life became as important as religious faith. Fiction and poetry came to be written in modern languages, not mainly in Latin. Painting focused on portraits, historical scenes, landscapes, and social settings. Theater began to focus on contemporary life. Orchestral and operatic music and balletic dance emerged as art forms.

There were also the beginnings in these centuries of a "middle" art, something between the high art of a court society and popular art. The middle class came to be consumers of mass art that could be experienced at home or in public spaces built for that purpose: mass-produced prints, periodicals and novels, and musical instruments allowed large numbers of people beyond the aristocracy to experience art at home; museums, galleries, and concert halls allowed these same people to become involved with public performances and exhibitions.

English colonial art, like colonial society, was provincial in character. The western frontier of European civilization did not produce innovations in art. England's colonists were unable to replicate the high culture of Europe, sustained as it was by the patronage of a court society. Aspiring colonists scurried off to Europe to be trained and tutored, both because the colonies lacked artistic institutions—schools, institutes, associations, concert halls, theaters, lecture halls, libraries, museums, art galleries—and because colonial artists felt inferior and looked to European artists as models to be emulated. This was true of every art form. In some cases—such as classical music and professional theater—colonists often relied on traveling troupes of European musicians and actors for performances, which were usually confined to the largest population centers. In other cases—such as painting—artists with the fullest training went abroad often to England, as did both Benjamin West and John Singleton Copley, the two best-known painters in the colonial years. Some art forms—such as opera and operatic ballet—don't seem to have undergone an early transplantation to Europe's cultural frontiers. The private societies that sponsored concerts and exhibitions failed to mount these most elaborate of the performing arts.

England was the cultural heartland for its colonists. English literary culture was particularly rich and sophisticated, and English fiction, poetry, and drama circulated widely, especially since there were few publishers in the colonies. In other arts, England itself was newly awakened, as foreign painters, such as Van Dyke, and foreign composers, such as Handel, moved to England and served as models for others. But, in either case, the mother country provided the forms that the colonists either slavishly or loosely followed, whether the Georgian architectural style for designed homes and buildings, the stylings of English cabinet furniture, or paintings that were portraits of the rich and powerful and prominent or historical scenes of famous events. The artist in the seventeenth and eighteenth centuries—whether in Europe or in the colonies—recorded the society and natural world around him. He did not perceive himself to be a critic of that society, dependent as he was on the patronage of its elites.

In cultural terms, the colonists were at their most creative in the popular arts and crafts, though even here Europe provided the norm. All of the art forms that European elites had developed existed in popular versions as well, and the lines between popular and elite art were blurred and fuzzy well into the nineteenth century. The largely Protestant English colonists lacked the feast days of Catholic Europeans, as the occasions for a concentrated display of popular culture. Such artistic expressions were spread through both the religious and secular lives of these colonists. In music, there were hymns, most of which were composed in England, and folk songs anonymously developed in many regional variations; in architecture, there was the crafting by locally known carpenters, sometimes using English manuals, of furnishings and tools and ordinary houses; in dance, there was the importation of many European elite and popular dance forms popularized through the efforts of itinerant European dance masters and through the wide availability of European dance manuals.

In the decades after political independence, one great question about culture came to be: Would Americans, newly independent and politically unique, also develop an unmistakably "American" culture? Were a people who, in one revolutionary act, created a nation predisposed to develop other forms of distinctiveness? From the 1780s on, there were various cultural nationalists who claimed, hoped, and insisted that their countrymen either had or would produce a uniquely American art. Painter Charles Wilson Peale, playwright Henry Brackenridge, linguist Noah Webster, philosopher-poet-essayist Ralph Waldo Emerson—all tried to produce (or induce others to produce) forms of "American" artistic creations.

But in spite of their efforts, Americans lacked the cultural infrastructure—the organizations, museums, galleries, halls, theaters, publishing firms, and established universities—of Europe. And though a few of the largest urban centers began to provide such a context for those in cultural endeavors, unmistakably by the 1830s, most Americans, not living in these centers, usually did not directly experience these forms of creativity. Indeed, many who sought training continued to "go abroad," to Europe for formal instruction with masters or in schools and institutes (this was particularly the case for sculptors.) During the course of the eighteenth and nineteenth centuries, Europe's high culture became less the result of the patronage of a court society and more the product of institutionalized forms of training. America, on the cultural periphery, lagged behind Europe in this shift.

Americans still exhibited signs of cultural inferiority, and for decades after political independence continued to look to Europe for ideals and models of artistic forms, if not content. The *forms* of poetry, fiction, painting, sculpture, architecture, drama, dance, and music remained largely those derived from Europe, even though the *content* was sometimes specifically American. However, artistic depictions of European life remained popular in America, the novels of Sir Walter Scott being a spectacular example. In the case of some of the arts, slavish copying of European forms went on throughout the nineteenth, even into the twentieth centuries. Americans, at one time or another, imported practically every architectural style known to Europeans. In classical music, they relied until the twentieth century almost exclusively on the compositions of European masters. In painting and sculpture, every European "school" gained New World advocates. Many forms of European fiction and poetry were echoed in the writing of Americans.

Even in the matter of basic cultural outlooks or impulses, Americans followed the lead of Europeans. In Europe, artistic expression generally shifted from the late eighteenth to the early nineteenth centuries from a classical to a romantic form, from an emphasis on balance, restraint, reason to an emphasis on the irrational, the idiosyncratic, the emotions, passion, excess. Art in the United States similarly underwent this metamorphosis. But in both Europe and its cultural periphery, such a fundamental shift was uneven and differed from art to art.

The artist continued to be a peripheral figure in American life, usually dependent on several—often desperate—kinds of endeavor for survival, typically without much fame, success, or honor. Most artists did not criticize American life; they did not think of themselves as critics or dissenters, but rather as recorders, enhancers, beautifiers, ennoblers. As in Europe, so in America, artists continued to paint portraits or build homes for the rich, the powerful, the successful, and the famous.

But, some American artists succeeded in being cultural nationalists, creating American versions of European art. Paintings and sculptures of American heroes and leaders were included in the national and state capitol buildings and in parks and squares, something that evolved directly out of the European tradition of the artistic rendering of historical scenes. Landscape paintings included all the elements of European art, but in compositions whose creators believed conveyed a uniquely sublime nature, indeed, the presence of God, in America's wilderness. Greek and Roman revival architecture (or neoclassicism in domestic and public building design) became a popular form of architecture the builders of which asserted America's kinship with the ancient republics of Greece and Rome, even though slavishly following European styles in the process. Walt Whitman's poetry tried to define the essence of what was for him a new variant of humanity, the American people.

But, the themes or contents of artistic creations were often local, or at most regional, in scope and did not represent or depict all of America, but only those who lived in particular parts of it. Examples of this were James Fenimore Cooper's frontiersman or Nathaniel Hawthorne's New Englanders. Even storytelling at the most popular levels—folklore and the "tall tale"—involved stories and heroes that were local and regional in scope. Tall tales were hardly an American invention, even with the bigness of America; such tales were the basis for folklore all over the world. As folk heroes, Davy Crockett was a frontiersman and Sam Fink was a Yankee. Based on real lives and real incidents exaggerated in the retelling—either orally or in the subliterature of almanacs—such folk heroes and stories were enlargements of local and regional characteristics, not national representations. It was difficult to find matter of any kind that could be truly rendered artistically as uniquely American.

Perhaps because Americans lacked the kind of cultural "infrastructure" that Europeans had developed, lacked, that is, a mature, indigenous artistic community, there were certain maverick artists in the United States who created new forms of artistic expression that Europeans were to emulate. Walt Whitman became a well-known poet far beyond America as the creator of "free verse." Similarly, Edgar Allan Poe developed the horror tale and created the detective story, both of which were to be much emulated abroad.

The social role of artists began to change in America, as in Europe, during these years—from recorder, beautifier, enhancer, to critic and moralizer. This was a fundamental change, but it occurred slowly and quite unevenly from one art form to another. James Fenimore Cooper as a novelist also became a social critic in several novels called the "Home" series, in which he created scornful caricatures of "American" types—Dodge and Bragg—who personified greed and crudity. And certain reformers, such as Harriet Beecher Stowe, wrote melodramatic novels and plays to popularize their causes—whether temperance, abolition, or some other movement.

By the 1840s and 1850s, America's cultural inferiority was on the wane, and the popularity of art, even in its more sophisticated forms, was growing. The widespread familiarity that the poems of Longfellow (a professor at Harvard) had among the populace is a good example of this. The social utility of the more popular art forms was evident in their didacticism, their heuristic nature. Hundreds of melodramatic, sentimental, domestic, or family novels, plays, songs, and lithographic prints (especially those of Currier and Ives), often produced by obscure artists, recorded and moralized about American life, depicting the triumph of Christian virtue over sinful behavior, as well as the proper way to behave and appear. Popular art thus served a moral purpose. Many middle-class purchasers expressed their interest in artistic expression at the same time that they were edified and reminded of the good life.

After the Civil War, the belief that America *ought* to have a cultural uniqueness to match its political one waned. Europe continued to provide the model for artistic expressions of all kinds. Even though Americans still believed in the superiority of their political system, most retained a sense of cultural inferiority, a belief that America remained at the periphery of a civilization whose artistic center, as before, was Europe.

Americans further developed the cultural institutions (the "infrastructure" for art)—the schools, institutes, associations, museums, galleries, concert halls, lecture halls, theaters, publishing firms, bookstores, libraries—which in the decades after the Civil War were constructed in places beyond the few largest urban centers and, in this, Americans were mirroring what Europeans were doing in this same period. Throughout the Atlantic world, art was becoming institutionalized, with some groups of artists still heavily reliant on courts, aristocracies, and the wealthy, while other groups were supported by a large middle-class public. But, Europe remained the heartland for what to its American practitioners was still a provincial, parochial endeavor. Some forms of European high art continued to be almost wholly European importations. Private societies formed orchestras and opera companies in the largest cities in these years, but usually performed European compositions. Other art forms remained undeveloped in America many decades after political independence: there were no ballet companies, and American theaters continued to lack playwrights of stature who could produce serious drama of any consequence.

By the late nineteenth century, the major new development in European artistic life was modernism, that is, a fundamental revision of the mode or style of artistic expression in all of the major arts. In poetry, free verse greatly expanded expression beyond what was possible with rhyme. In fiction, streams of consciousness and flashbacks and flash-forwards basically altered storytelling. In music, atonality burst the bounds of classical sound. In dance, random movement went far beyond ballet steps. In painting and sculpture, color and line and shaped material depicted much more than an attempted recreation of the visual world. Architecture suddenly assumed a great variety of shapes. Modernism competed with traditional modes of artistic expression in both Europe and its cultural frontiers, and, though some artists in America embraced modernism, many more remained traditional in what they created.

The artist continued to be a peripheral figure in American life, even though he was—as with increasing numbers of others—far more apt to be in a position to receive formal training in the United States than his precursors in the antebellum years had been. This developing infrastructure also insured that artistic creations were presented, marketed, and sold in a more systematized, widespread fashion as well. And yet, the status and prestige of the artist remained notably low in America, and artists of all kinds still typically combined their artistic endeavors with other sources of income. As Americans moved out of rural areas and towns into cities during these decades, some artists abandoned their initial rural and town locations in favor of either cities or the world beyond the United States, usually in Europe, where they became expatriates. In the opinion of some artists, Americans were a people who failed to appreciate sophisticated art, and America was a land that true artists were driven from. Painters who developed the impressionist style in the late nineteenth century and novelists such as Henry James at the turn of the century and the literary expatriates of the 1920s are examples of artists who felt compelled to live and work abroad.

However, it was also the case that, though they existed on Europe's cultural periphery, American artists continued—at particular times and in particular places, but in a far more "connected" cultural world than had been the case before the Civil War—to influence their counterparts elsewhere in the Europeanized parts of the globe. The psychologically oriented novels of Henry James and the skyscraper architecture of Louis Sullivan, and far less spectacularly, the dissonant music of Charles Ives are significant instances of this cultural phenomenon. But, generally, artistic forms continued to be derived from European culture in painting (realism, impressionism cubism, surrealism), fiction (realism, naturalism, stream-of-consciousness), music (romanticism, atonality, neoclassicism), architecture (a bewildering variety of styles), and theater (dramatic depictions of the problems of middle-class life).

The content of art, by contrast, became wholly domesticated. American artists depicted what existed around them, not what European tradition dictated. But, art is specific in its content, not general, and most American artists were unable or unwilling to convey what was distinctively "American" about their creations. Novels, poems, music, plays, paintings, sculpture, architecture—all were usually specifically local or regional in their references. What was distinctively and specifically "American" only rarely emerged, for example in novels about Americans abroad, so that comparisons between them and "other peoples" could be made. At a time when communication and transportation provided the means whereby people anywhere could be aware of what others were doing, cultural expression and creativity did not typically remain isolated for very long. That which American artists wrote, painted, sculpted, composed, and acted was not usually "American," but was either intensely local or regional in character or became transnational in the sense that artists outside of the United States created the same forms and sorts of content.

Artists in America continued to perform several, varied functions in American life, even though ordinarily they were not given much status or held in high esteem. Some depicted what was beautiful; for example, landscape paintings of scenes around the nation. Others conveyed what was moral; for example, melodramatic fiction (just as had been the case before the Civil War). But, others were avowedly critics and dissenters; for example, after the turn of the century, novelists such as Theodore Dreiser, Sinclair Lewis, and F. Scott Fitzgerald portrayed life in America as being filled with dilemmas and dissatisfactions. Far more than in the pre–Civil War years, artist/critics became a basic source of criticism and dissent. Alongside journalists and writers who were social critics and radical politicians, these artists directed their creativity toward depictions of what was wrong with America, how it failed to live up to its ideals.

In this period, the more sophisticated art forms were appreciated and supported through attendance or purchase by an increasingly large middle- and upper-class public whose interest in art was developed as a result of family inculcation or by the taking of courses on the arts in schools and special institutes. The "fine arts" became something appreciated by a trained and educated public. They became a cultural activity increasingly separated from popular art. Though direct government support remained negligible, those who had garnered enormous wealth as entrepreneurs, investors, managers, and organizers of the new large-scale industrial corporations often became patrons of the arts, financially supporting libraries, galleries, museums, concert and lecture halls, opera houses, and theaters. Such patrons did not favor creativity that criticized the existing social order and thus left the art produced under their auspices open to the criticism of writers (journalists; those who wrote for magazines and published books of social criticism; novelists; poets) who became critics and dissenters.

It was popular commercial culture that exhibited the most distinctively "American" forms as well as content of artistic creation. In the case of the popular song, hymns (composed by such Americans as William Billings and Lowell Mason), sentimental ballads (beginning with the songs of Stephen Foster before the Civil War), or black-influenced ragtime, blues, and jazz singing were disseminated through sheet music and as a part of various kinds of stage performances. In stage entertainment, the variety show underwent various permutations from the mid-nineteenth to the early twentieth century. Influenced by both English and French forms—French vaudeville and burlesque, the English music hall—the resulting mixtures were distinctively American. The antebellum minstrel show, with its variety of entertainment and biracial character spread all over the United States from the 1840s to the 1870s. It evolved into vaudeville in the decades after the Civil War, a new form of variety show (in spite of its French name) that, while centered in New York City, became a national phenomenon through the development of traveling "circuits" of entertainers who encompassed summer and winter resort areas, thus continuing the tradition of the traveling entertainment troupes (as individuals, groups, or whole "circuses") who, up to World War I, went on tours of towns and cities over great areas of the United States. Such entertainers disseminated anecdotes, stories, jokes, dance routines, and songs to the general population. Burlesque (again, in spite of the French reference) evolved simultaneously with vaudeville and was a variety show comprised of beautiful women and bawdy humor; it evolved into the striptease by the 1930s. Popular theater, outside of the largest cities, were dime "museums" or medicine shows, which featured curiosities and itinerant entertainers, during the mid-nineteenth century, and later became a receptacle for theatrical touring companies who featured formulaic melodrama from the mid-nineteenth century to the 1920s.

Outdoor entertainment underwent the same kind of evolution of form. Circuses—derived from English equestrian training circles—were traveling groups of performers and animals who operated on a circular stage and appeared in many parts of the continent, most notably from the 1870s to the 1920s. Amusement parks—derived from English pleasure gardens—flourished at the end of trolley lines and at rural picnic groves and shore resorts, particularly from the turn of the century until the 1920s. Carnivals—derivative of European world's fairs—became traveling congeries of amusement rides and games of chance at fairs and amusement parks, starting at the turn of the century.

From the 1860s to the 1940s, "pulp" fiction (printed on cheap paper) was an extremely effective means of making certain genres (westerns, mystery, crime, detective, adventure, science fiction) available to a mass reading public in both book and magazine form. When cinema (in the 1910s) and radio (in the 1920s) developed, first locally and then nationally (like other forms of communication, transportation, and energy or power sources), the dissemination of popular culture was greatly enhanced in the sense that particular entertainers were seen or heard performing particular acts all over the United States. By the late 1920s, popular culture had a significant national dimension when traditional entertainment programs over radio networks were heard everywhere and when movie studios linked the showing of their melodramatic films to chains of theaters that they owned in all parts of the nation. Both film-making and radio-broadcasting were international phenomena from their beginnings, however, and both were marked by crossnational influences. Neither was ever entirely encased within national boundaries. American-made films and broadcasts were shown and heard in Canada and, later, in Europe as well, just as Americans, after World War II, saw English and subtitled versions of European films.

Sometimes, well-established European popular arts were transmogrified into something distinctively American, as when Jerome Kern during the 1920s turned European light opera (or "operetta") into the musical theater (replete with story, words, and songs). But, "American" theater of all kinds—musicals, comedies, tragedies alike—remained a largely New York City phenomenon for decades, as other cities were turned into tryout centers for Broadway-bound shows. Sometimes, the subculture of a particular group became a phenomenon of local, regional, and then gradually national dimensions, as when Dixieland Jazz, which evolved out of Afro-American "blues" music, became popular among the wider population, first in New Orleans, then in St. Louis, then in Chicago, then in New York City, and, by the 1930s, in many of the urban areas of the United States.

Movies and radio—and later television—all disseminated various kinds of stories and entertainment first developed in fiction and on stage. Some were especially but not entirely American—wild western or frontier adventures—but many more were common to popular culture throughout the West—crime and detective and mystery stories, science fiction. Indeed, melodramatic and adventure stories, which featured characters and situations that were caricatures of real life—existed in many variations throughout the world. In whatever form, popular culture tended to be heavily didactic and moralistic. What Americans read and sang and danced and observed and listened to was usually melodramatic in form and moralistic in content. Popular culture usually performed the conservative function of entertaining the general population with the purpose of portraying life as it *ought* to be lived by Christian-capitalistic-republican Americans. The only exceptions to this emanated from the black subculture, whose work songs, spirituals, and blues, contained a long lament about the poverty, slavery, and segregation that Afro-Americans had endured. "Jazz" came to embody what the city meant to those who lived in it, just as early "country" music—for its adherents—encapsulated the experience of living in rural areas.

In America, art in recent decades continues to exist on several levels—with respect to both its creators and its audiences, from complexity and sophistication to popular, but the distinctions among these levels have become somewhat more blurred, with the increasing education and awareness and understanding of art that have become evident among large segments of populations everywhere in the Europeanized world, as well as with the faster and more varied means of communication through which art can be experienced by increasingly large numbers of people.

Americans have continued to express themselves largely within a European-derived artistic tradition, though the globalization of life has made artists in America more easily aware of artistic forms generated elsewhere. Since 1930, American artists have made significant contributions to the form of various European-derived arts (abstract expressionism and pop art in painting; jazz in classical music), but they have also continued to copy forms developed in Europe (stream-of-consciousness in fiction, from Joyce to Faulkner).

The last of the great European art forms—dance—appeared in America in the form of ballet and modern dance companies that have developed since the 1930s and have made America, especially New York, a great center for both classical and modern dance. Similarly, there have been playwrights of stature who have created a variety of notable drama. Since the 1960s, the development of professional regional theater in every part of America has ended New York's monopoly. Similarly, New York's post–World War II claim as the art capital of the nation has dissipated as the serious art world has burgeoned to include various regional centers. Since the 1930s, American composers have occasionally created notable symphonic, operatic, and chamber music. In recent decades, Americans have made significant contributions to every art form originally developed in Europe. But, from a wider, "Western" perspective, those contributions have varied in size from one art form to another: major in dance, painting, architecture, fiction, poetry; fairly extensive in theater; not so impressive in music and sculpture.

What is distinctive to the post-1930 decades is that increasing globalization has resulted in the creation of a transatlantic artistic community, with artists everywhere in the Europeanized world capable of copying or emulating what particular artists in particular places have developed. (Writings are often translated into English—the second language of the world—from their original language, whereas musical notes, line and color, sculpted forms, and dance steps are already universal.) First in Europe and then in America "modern" artists have sometimes become inventors of new forms within the various arts. And, though many artists have remained "traditionalists," others have radically redefined what poetry, fiction, music, painting, sculpture, dance, theater, and architecture consist of, to the point that there has not been a lasting orthodoxy. Modern artists, in observing natural and social and personal and social reality, have assumed the freedom to distill the essence of their own and everyone else's experience and to render that experience in aesthetically satisfying ways. In the process, old definitions have crumbled and forms have blended.

Modernism has continued to be a major mode of artistic endeavor among Europeans and their overseas offshoots, affecting particular art forms in both continuing and new ways. Poetry has come to lack all rhyme or rhythm. In fiction, people have sometimes been presented as thinking as they actually do (in a "stream of consciousness") and sequential time and space have been routinely shattered with "flashbacks" and "zoom-aheads." Theater has enlarged itself to depict all kinds of language and behavior and, at times, has blurred the line between actors and audience. Dance has become movement of all kinds, and not just prescribed ballet steps. Music goes beyond traditional scales and harmonies to include all sounds made by musical instruments, as well as sounds from other sources, both electronic and natural. Painting and sculpture have become configurations of line and color consisting of vastly varied materials and shapes and forms. Architecture has blurred "indoors" and "outdoors" through the widespread use of glass and climate-controlling utility systems.

This artistic revolution has changed the face of culture in the Western world and has gone on through war, depression, tyranny, and anarchy, as well as through times of peace, prosperity, and conformity. Modern artists have come to think of themselves and to be perceived by their audiences as having special insights into the conditions of life in the modern age and have believed that their art has to be free and individualistic and not bound by prescribed forms.

But, there has been a large share of the artistically aware public in both Europe and America who have not attempted to understand or appreciate contemporary art and have continued to be responsive to traditional forms and the creations of earlier artists. Institutions such as universities, museums, galleries, concert halls, and theaters have collected and preserved and studied and performed and exhibited this artistic past. The result is that classical and modern art coexist, providing artistic experiences of both traditional (and thus conserving) and avant-garde (and thus liberating) nature. Art in recent times has thus come to have a deeply conservative place in modern, "developed" populations, with institutions carefully preserving the inherited culture, the artistic creations of earlier times, for significant segments of the more educated and aware population to experience. The best art, that with the most sophisticated aesthetic value, has been preserved far beyond the time of its creation, so that a broad, culturally literate population continues to have significant aesthetic experiences from art created in an earlier time.

In this way, artistic traditions and orthodoxies continue to command respect and significance, even though the artists whose work is being preserved and continuously experienced responded to situations that no longer exist. Thus preserved, historic art, which constitutes an artistic tradition much nurtured by cultural and educational institutions, means that culturally aware Americans—and Europeans—repeatedly have aesthetic experiences that originate out of the past.

In this respect, art conserves a society's culture, making the way people appreciate art a deeply conservative experience. As American society developed and changed into its modern forms, traditional art has "frozen" aesthetic experience, keeping it what it was in the past, no matter what new social realities convey to artists now.

Modern artists—by contrast—respond to changing, current social and personal experiences. They—as were their predecessors—are judged by those who create critical analyses, which have been developed in recent decades in universities and colleges, art institutions of various kinds, newspapers, magazines, and on television and radio. The best artists—old and new—have been penetrating observers of social and personal reality, observers who have also, in the act of observing, criticized or praised society, but who—above all—are able to render their depiction with aesthetic profundity. Artists who are *just* critics are polemicists or who *just* praise society are apologists.

Some notable American artists have been mainly critical in tone in aesthetically major works: in fiction, John Steinbeck (the plight of poor people during the Depression) and James Baldwin (the suffering of black Americans); in theater, Eugene O'Neill, Tennessee Williams, and Edward Albee (the tensions inherent in family life), as well as Arthur Miller (the corrosive effects of the American emphasis on success and conformity). Others have created aesthetically successful work as celebrants of American life: in music, Aaron Copland (using jazz and folk music in exuberant tones); in architecture, Frank Lloyd Wright (blurring the line between American space and America's abundant natural setting); in theater, Thornton Wilder (praising that which is decent and durable in American life) and Neil Simon (finding humor in the perplexing situations of modern middle-class life); and in painting, Pop Art (in celebration of ordinary American life). Other American artists have produced aesthetically satisfying work that features sharp, penetrating observation, without an evident bias toward either criticism or praise: in fiction, William Faulkner (on the problems of one kind of people giving way to another), John Cheever and John Updike (on the dilemmas and complications of American middle-class life), and Saul Bellow (on the difficulties of Americans who are aware of the perplexities of modern life).

Since 1930, modern artists have sometimes achieved great fame, success, and fortune. The artist has become yet another kind of social model. That a life dedicated to the creation of aesthetically penetrating depictions of American society, depictions that can run the gamut from the highly accommodating to the highly critical, has become a socially acceptable style of living is dramatic evidence of the enhanced role artists have assumed in America in recent decades, the result of which is that sources of dissent as well as reinforcements of prevailing orthodoxies have been significantly augmented. No longer does social criticism arise from self-conscious "reformers" and self-styled social critics. Artists themselves *can* join their ranks.

Both the traditional artists, who continue to create in modes that were dominant before 1930, and the modern artists, who have sometimes exhibited extreme forms of individualism and innovation, are (ironically) encased, in both Europe and America, within an institutional framework that reflects the bureaucratization of modern life. Art schools and institutes, universities and colleges, museums, galleries, concert halls, theaters, and publishers provide a setting or context for art—training the artists; educating their public; critically assessing, evaluating, and collecting art; and acting collectively as arbiters of what the best art is.

Arts organizations in recent decades have become the basis for community rivalries, as symphony orchestras, opera companies, museums, theater and dance companies, and publishers vie for fame and honor as representatives of particular local communities. Comparisons between "American" artistic organizations and their counterparts in European nations is also made, though less frequently. A many-tiered arts or cultural community has developed in America since 1930. Those who understand and appreciate art constitute a kind of substructure for those who become trained and educated as artists, who, in turn, provide a pool of talent out of which come those who emerge as talented professionals, with careers. Out of these professionals come the best artists, who achieve fame and success and fortune.

Artists in the United States have been notable for drawing on particular facets of America's popular culture as they have written, painted, sculpted, composed, choreographed, and built. Fiction writers have employed cinematic techniques; the theater has been greatly augmented by the American "musical"; composers like Copland have drawn on folk music and jazz; choreographers such as Agnes de Mille and Jerome Robbins have drawn on popular dance steps for dances in musicals and films. Such blurring of the lines between fine and popular art is peculiarly American in its frequency and significance, and is further evidence of the inventiveness and vitality of popular culture in America, whose people have never nurtured a fine arts tradition of their own. It is also the case that the "popular" forms of art conveyance—films, radio, television—have sometimes attained the level of serious art, but they have done so more notably in the more supportive settings of Europe than in America. Governments established publicly funded radio and television in Europe and Canada long before the advent of public radio and television in the United States, where national funding began during the 1960s.

Since 1930, popular culture continued to foster morality and virtue, at least until the counterculture of the late 1960s and early 1970s, when popular entertainers began to criticize American life and to depict their society more honestly and less melodramatically and idealistically. Popular music (rock, country, blues, folk, jazz), musical/comedic/melodramatic theater, mass-produced fiction, feature films, radio and television entertainment, and, more recently, video and audio tapes and records and compact discs—all have registered the movement from an emphasis on conventional morality to one on various forms of criticism of prevailing ways. Only country music seems to have remained largely loyal to the older emphasis, and, significantly, it appeals to those elements in American society least comfortable with the ethos of the questioning and doubting that the counterculture fostered. Since the 1950s, popular culture of all kinds has been communicated to mass audiences on television, records, compact discs, and tapes. American and foreign creations commingle, as popular culture has transcended national borders everywhere in the world.

Also new since 1930 is the fact that successful popular entertainers are—like successful artists—rich and famous. Such entertainers are cultural heroes and, like artists, their lives have become a social model for others. The fact that movie actors, singers, and instrumentalists can earn fortunes and attain enormous fame is dramatic evidence of the role that popular culture has come to assume in the shaping of popular attitudes and preoccupations. American popular culture has also developed in recent decades within an increasingly globalized context, as changes in rock music, jazz, the musical theater, film, television-radio entertainment have often influenced, or been influenced by, others, elsewhere in the world.

Viewed from a global perspective, American art and entertainment appear as an offshoot of Western art, a frontier variant in which Americans shared with their European progenitors a common art and common forms of entertainment, transmitting them to a new world and altering them, even blurring them, but never beyond recognition, and never for long in isolation, as various parts of Western civilization shared a churning and evolving artistic life. Art in America has to be viewed in these larger perspectives if it is to be understood.

37

Leisure/Recreation

In the port cities and plantations of the English colonies, and, later, the young American nation, merchants and planters used as models the kind of leisure engaged in by England's mercantile and agricultural hierarchy. As in art, so in leisure: the kind of activity a person was associated with helped to define his position in society. The very rich shared particular forms of socializing—visiting, dancing, listening to music—whether in urban centers or on rural plantations.

Ordinary Americans, all the way to the later nineteenth century, socialized in taverns (rather than English pubs) and combined work and play in "bees"—barn raising, cornhusking, quilting—which were at once social, communal, and task-oriented. These were undertakings that were beyond the capability of a single family. There was nothing distinctively American about this kind of activity: ordinary people in rural settings engaged in this sort of activity everywhere in the Western world. As elsewhere, leisure was mixed with labor as rural people engaged in communal activities that combined sociability with work. As in Europe, hunting and fishing as recreation were maintained by a population whose source of meat and fish continued to be partly derived from "wild" game, even with the domestication of livestock and the commercialization of fishing. Cockfighting was a common sport involving animals, reflecting the violence and competition and speculation of all elements of male society. Horse racing became the most popular spectator sport, as Americans made sport of—and gambled on—the very animal they most depended on for farming and for transportation.

By the mid-nineteenth century, urbanized Americans became more conscious of leisure time, especially as the nonfarming population grew rapidly as a percentage of the total. Work time was clock time in factories, offices, and stores.

Vacation periods became built-in parts of union contracts. Those with wealth became more aware of the desirability and propriety of having a summer place. Certain communities developed as "resorts" or vacation places, whether by the sea, in the mountains, or near beautiful settings of any kind. Vacation and leisure time became increasingly planned in these decades, as did recreational activity.

Sports—without exception derived from European, Canadian, or native sources—became organized into leagues with rules and schedules and equipment, either as amateurs (with ordinary Americans playing) or as professionals (with trained players performing for paying spectators). Hunting and fishing and sailing became participatory sports with required skills and appropriate equipment. All three had been essential economic and social activities, but were in these years turned into leisure-time entertainment, just as horse racing turned the once-essential animal for human transportation into an object to be gambled on for its speed.

Recreation and sport and leisure-time activity all reflected the greater organization made manifest in American society generally during these years. Such activities also mirrored the growing class consciousness that became apparent with the widening gulf between the richest and the poorest Americans. Certain activities clearly became "upper class" in character (hunting with horses and hounds, polo, cotillions, balls, formal dinner parties, sailing, horse-racing stables), while others were vaguely middle class in their appeal, and still others were clearly associated with those of meager means or those in poverty.

Until the twentieth century, ordinary Americans performed the popular arts in their homes, at their social gatherings, and in their churches. They sang and danced at home around the piano in the parlor or at social events in barns, taverns, hotels, and halls; they sang hymns in their churches; they learned to read music and play instruments; they read mass-produced dime novels and bought mass-produced prints and illustrated books for their home settings. But, these forms of active participation in the popular arts have atrophied to some extent in the twentieth century as Americans have increasingly become passive recipients of popular art and entertainment by listening to the radio and records and tapes and discs for music and watching television and videotapes for entertainment of all kinds.

The arts-and-crafts movement of the turn of the century—as in Britain—represented a negative reaction to the way machine products were made, removing, as the process did, the creation of basic commodities—clothing and furnishings—from the shaping hands of craftsmen. The design of machine-made products was the creative work of particular engineers, not the artistic rendering of individual craftsmen who altered in individualistic ways basic, widely recognized forms. Industrial production severed artistic creativity from production for practically everyone involved in the process (except for design engineers), and the arts-and-crafts movement was an effort to rejoin the two. However, industrial design (for machine-made products) itself became a kind of artistic endeavor, with those involved receiving training and pursuing careers in corporations and smaller firms.

In recent decades, recreation and leisure have both been responsive to the enlargement of scale, the tendency to become organized and bureaucratized and commercialized, and the acceptance of technological developments in communication and transportation—all of which have characterized so many facets of American life, as elsewhere in the developed and westernized world.

A deep and broad sports culture (similar in character to the arts culture) has developed in America, a culture that has been greatly nurtured by school and recreational systems. A professional elite who perform as athletes in the top "leagues" of each sport achieve fame, success, and fortune that rival those of the top artists and entertainers. Similar too is the obvious role modeling that such athletes provide, especially for the young, who at least are physically capable of aspiring to play sports with the same sort of acumen and skill as their heroes display.

Those at the apex of the sports culture have come out of the ranks of the lesser professionals, who, in turn, emerge from many levels of amateur players. All levels of players attract spectators: the more professional, the larger the following. In America, as elsewhere, this highly developed sports culture has reflected the enormously important emphasis given to competition in modern societies. Sport is a peaceful form of competition, but is, to some extent, also a surrogate for legitimized forms of physical prowess and violence that war fosters. The sports culture, like the arts, is also competitive in the sense that teams represent local communities or, at times, the nation itself, and partisan spectators vocally support "their" team against teams representing "others."

Even nonathletes have become involved with a related development, linked to increasing knowledge of nutrition and physical fitness. Since the 1960s, when fitness tests showed that Americans—especially non-sports-playing ones—were ignorant of fitness and health, there has been a burgeoning fitness movement, as increasing numbers of Americans have become concerned about what constitutes good health while living a sedentary existence in a setting widely polluted and while often being bombarded by unnutritional but easily available fast or junk foods.

Leisure activities have become, like recreational ones, more organized in recent decades. Americans spend their leisure time at home playing games or being entertained electronically or going on visits and trips, with vacation times—for many—built into work-time arrangements. Travel and vacationing have become more organized, as prearranged group tours flourish and resort centers of many kinds—historical, educational, animal, amusement—offer structured settings. In local communities, various kinds of clubs and taverns and stadiums provide "live" entertainment to supplement the at-home electronic variety.

Even though vacations and travel are regular and arranged parts of a work career, Americans generally remain parochial—unaware and uninterested in foreign parts of the world. Most of their travel is confined to the United States. For most, holidays are prearranged days off from work and are thus without much celebratory content.

Not only is work and leisure time prearranged clock time, with both divorced from the ebb and flow of the seasons, but even the great celebrations that dotted the calendars of pre-twentieth century people everywhere in the world—Europeanized and Christianized or not—have been largely drained of their special character and meaning. A day off from work during which one can relax or indulge in favorite leisure-time activities is vastly different in meaning from a holiday focused on some transcendant purpose, whether religious or civil. One of the most significant means for sustaining community identity—local and national—has atrophied, replaced by "rest days." Holidays have also been replaced periodically by the conventions or special meetings that bind the myriads of national and regional associations of all kinds together, as allegiance to local communities has given way to group identities.

The weekend has remained the most common leisure time, a product of labor contracts and work arrangements developed during decades of growing union activity. But, since the 1960s and the invention of ever more sophisticated technology, work time has become more varied and staggered, especially with the renewed growth of "home work" that telecommunications makes possible.

Americans have displayed an increasingly consumer orientation in recent decades, and, in this, they appear to be in the vanguard of the developed and westernized world. The work ethic has seemed less in evidence, especially since the 1960s and the questioning by those in the counterculture of lives marked by a "work-aholic" orientation. Americans, relative to other developed parts of the world—in Asia and in Europe—save less and spend and borrow more.

Leisure-time activities remain a fairly accurate indication of class, with the very rich, the middle class, the working class, and the poor all, to some extent, favoring different forms of vacationing, entertainment, games, recreation, and social activity (such as visiting, dancing or singing, and dining). For all the awareness that Americans share in a technologically linked setting of culture, recreation, and leisure, they choose to a considerable extent varied forms of those activities on the basis of class.

Viewed in a global perspective, leisure and recreation in America has mirrored developments in a much wider Western world, developments that need to be seen in that wider context. Nothing of significance in sport, recreation, and leisure has ever been peculiarly or solely American.

PART V

AMERICAN COMMUNITIES AND IDENTITIES

The people who have thought of themselves as Americans have inhabited a hierarchy of communities, as humans in general have since the beginnings of civilization. The national community was the largest in this hierarchy, but membership in it was always shared with membership in smaller communities contained within it. Enslaved black African migrants came from an area whose people had experienced life both in permanent villages and within a sucession of empires whose elites were Islamic in their affiliations. North American native bands inhabited seasonal (though a minority lived in permanent) villages and belonged to tribes with hunting and fishing territories, tribes that sometimes joined in times of crisis into larger confederacies.

So, when the English colonists established towns and cities within provinces that formed regions within the British Empire, and when Americans, after political independence, developed other towns and cities and created states within regions of a new nation, both were doing what others commonly did. The English empire was relatively more decentralized than those of its rivals. During the colonial period, the community that was most important was the local one, with provincial, regional, and imperial ones in a descending order of significance. Similarly, during the late eighteenth and much of the nineteenth centuries, in what became the large continent-girdling American republic, towns and cities were primary; states, regions, and the nation were correspondingly less so. Again, the larger the community, the smaller its importance.

The premodern world everywhere was profoundly local in its focus and dimensions. Most people lived out their lives within a short compass, interacting with the local community, little affected by life in larger and more distant ones. Empires existed throughout the ancient and medieval worlds, binding people in lots of localized settings over large segments of the globe under imperial rule, sometimes with significant authority emanating from distant capitals. But the people so bound together, affected as their daily lives were by imperial governance, *remained* localized, largely confined to narrow horizons, largely unaware of developments in the larger world.

Only with marked increases in the speed of both transportation and communication systems have these narrow horizons broadened for ordinary people. Only during the course of the late nineteenth and the twentieth centuries have global, national, regional, and state-level communities become clearly as important to individuals in all the developed areas of the world as local ones. Only over the last two centuries have the conditions emerged that produced the mass societies of the twentieth century, wherein individuals feel deeply connected to patterns of life that have national, continental, and global dimensions.

These changes have affected Europe as well as all of the white settler societies on the frontiers of European civilization, not just Americans. Canadians, South Africans, Australians, and New Zealanders have all experienced a decentralized federation of communities, the same persistent provincialism and regionalism and weak nationalism, with national unity a product of those same relatively recent conditions that have made mass societies possible in all the developed areas of the world.

Like others around the world, Americans have lived in communities that have had varied boundaries or territories, depending upon which aspect of community life is being observed. Political boundaries have been the most rigid and precise, whereas economic, social, and cultural ones have been porous, variable, murky, even unclear. Human communities have been protean in their shape, changing in size for each dimension of their inhabitants' lives.

This has been as much the case with the communities that black African, Oriental Asian, Hispanic, and European immigrants came out of as it has been for the communities these groups, as Americans, created.

* * *

Like people everywhere, Americans have identified with a number of groups beyond being inhabitants of a hierarchy of communities—town or city or state or region or nation. These groups are as fundamental as communities, and, indeed, by the mid-twentieth century, have come to be regarded as "communities" themselves. In infinite combinations, each American has had an identity with respect to family (child, parent, grandparent, childless adult), age (youth, early adulthood, middle adulthood, old age), gender (male or female), sexuality (heterosexual, bisexual, homosexual), class (upper, middle, lower, or colored caste), occupation, religion, language, ethnicity, and race, all of which have defined what sort of a person he or she is as much as a political affiliation has.

The people who, among many other forms of identification, have identified themselves as Americans have become nationalistic, that is, have developed a sense of loyalty to the American nation. American nationalism differed in its origins from western European nationalism in that it was created all at once during a revolutionary act, rather than having emerged in stages over a long period of time. In this, the Americans were a model for many other colonists around the world who subsequently revolted against European (and occasionally Asian) imperial political rule. As the European nation-state system spread all over the globe amidst the ruins of failed empires, many new national groups followed the American practice and created their own nationalism.

Americans have also identified with their subnational levels of community, with their regions, states, and localities. Regional identification lacks a political dimension, unless a region is defined as a particular group of states, and is thus vague and ill-focused (except for during the Civil War, when regions took on a specific political definition). Identification with states, counties, cities, or towns was stronger than national loyalty until at least the late nineteenth century, but these forms of subnational identity, these "localisms," lacked the emotional, psychological, symbolic force of nationalism, especially after the nation's importance became obvious. Identification with states, counties, cities, and towns typically took the form of celebrations at special anniversaries of the political founding of these communities.

What those who identified with all these levels of communities shared was a *political* definition for their communities. Both nationalism and these various forms of localism were political phenomena. It was governments that fostered identity with these communities; it was governments that sponsored celebrations, created symbols; it was governments that defined the communities' political borders. The United States, dozens of states, hundreds of counties and cities, and thousands of towns all assumed a political shape, belying the much more complicated and varied nonpolitical definitions that these communities assumed when economic, social, or cultural activities are being considered.

In all of this, Americans have been like people elsewhere in the world, where it has commonly been the case that community identification has had a political cast. National political groups like the Americans have shared with ethnic groups everywhere the *belief* that they constitute the kind of group that deserves the ultimate allegiance of its members, one that proclaims a common history, a common culture, a common homeland, common rules. Of all the human groups that individuals belong to, only a few have evoked a kind of passionate involvement, a psychological or emotional bond, something worth defending, even dying for. Politically defined communities are one of those human groups. Others are familial, ethnic, religious, linguistic, or racial in character. By contrast, identities based upon age, gender, sexuality, occupation, and class have not stimulated in their members this type of profound attachment.

Politically defined communities—whether nations, regions, states, counties, cities, or towns—share a strong proclivity to claim a distinctiveness and unity that goes beyond their purely political foundation, to embrace the economic, social, and cultural dimensions of life. Once again, the Americans are not unique. Even so, American "exceptionalism" has been particularly strong. The widely shared claim that America is a special place, the place where the world's most influential civilization will achieve its idealized form, has fostered a peculiar kind of American parochialism, an ignorance of the rest of humanity, that gives great force to assertions of economic, social, and cultural distinctiveness. In a time of increasing global interconnectedness, such assertions seem ever more strident and inaccurate, but reveal the depth to which those who have identified themselves as Americans have gone to defend an American way in all aspects of life in the United States.

38

The Changing Nature of Community

Americans have exhibited dual tendencies toward individualism and communalism, as have all human groups. Certainly the American as an individual has had an exalted place in American life. The protection of his liberty and the furtherance of his welfare have been among the main purposes of government—at all levels. Individual wealth seeking and wealth accumulation have been accorded a legitimacy equaled by few other activities. Most property has been owned by individuals, whether singly, in partnerships, or in groups. Individuals vote for those seeking political office. The Christian churches focus on individuals as children of God, with souls. Those Americans who engaged in agriculture typically sought autonomous farmsteads with farmland around them, eschewing settlement in communities altogether. And, many of those who lived in communities often moved, if not very far, at least fairly often.

And yet, Americans have also exhibited a contradictory communal orientation as well. The Puritan towns and, later, the nation itself were founded with covenants—solemn agreements—that inhabitants of these villages and the republic itself would endeavor to uphold the highest communal ideals. Americans have often lived by agreements less formal or durable. Migrants, moving across the Plains and Rocky Mountains formed caravans, and squatters and miners both created claims clubs—all indications of a communal orientation, even if for limited periods. Other Americans have developed associations of many kinds—on every level: local, county, state, regional, and national. Every "cause," every activity has expressed itself in some associational context. Growing numbers of Americans lived in settled communities during the nineteenth century, as the proportion of the population who lived in rural areas and farms steadily declined. Since the late nineteenth century, the interplay between individualistic and communalistic impulses characteristic of Americans—as with all "peoples" or human groups—has become skewed toward an emphasis on community at a time when the enlarged scope and scale in the organization of life has produced what are commonly called "mass societies."

* * *

During the seventeenth, eighteenth, and well into the nineteenth centuries, "community" for Americans, as for the westernized world, meant a place with political, physical, geographical, economic, social, and cultural dimensions, all of which differed in size, but all of which were locational, that is, could be located on a map, given cartographical definition. In contrast to the communities of the seminomadic native American tribes, but in common with African tribal villages, such communities were meant by their inhabitants to be permanent, without a time frame, and were given, through surveying, definite political boundaries, though other dimensions of community life were without such precise territorial definitions. Such communities were all named, either informally by their inhabitants or formally by the appropriate level of government, and, though they shared patterns of life with other communities of similar sized dimensions, all were unique as well in the particular circumstances of their inhabitants' lives. "Place" communities were everything from rural neighborhoods to cross-road clusters to hamlets to villages to towns to cities to states to regions to the American nation itself. Everyone lived in a hierarchy of communities, usually harmoniously, capable of moving vertically from one level to the next or laterally from one kind of community to another of the same kind, all without public regulation, except for movements that went beyond the nation itself, which were subject, through customs services, to governmental supervision.

It was an extreme propensity to move geographically that led Americans to shift and extend their definition of community so that, by the mid-nineteenth century, it even covered the groups of Americans who moved so relentlessly across the landscape of the North American continent. When, during the 1830s, 1840s, 1850s, and 1860s, Americans formed wagon trains so that groups could move on trails across the plains and mountains to particular destinations in the trans-Mississippi west, or when farmers as "squatters" moved into the Mississippi Valley during the 1840s and 1850s ahead of surveying and effectively operating government and formed farmers' claims clubs (which determined a squatter's territory), or when mining prospectors moved to the Rocky Mountains during the 1850s and 1860s out in front of functioning territorial governments and also formed claims clubs (which determined the extent of a prospector's stake)—all were forming temporary communities when they drew up constitutions or rules, appointed law-making and law enforcement officials, and meted out punishment for those who did not abide by the rules. Community came to apply to settings that were meant to be temporary, with a limited lifeline. In this peculiarly American sense of community, definition has returned to that given to it by the native American tribes, with their nomadic agricultural settlements.

As the scope and scale of life in America progressively enlarged with the speeding up of communications and transportation during the late nineteenth and throughout the twentieth centuries, the definition of community for Americans shifted yet again. In the mass society of an increasingly urbanized population, Americans have, like others throughout the westernized world, extended their sense of community to include particular groups and institutions within their impersonal urbanized settings. Americans have perceived themselves as being members of statistical, economic, social, ethnic, racial, gender, and sexual "communities." Every kind of group has been defined as a "community"—less durable and less stationary than place communities, but, like them, sharing a common identity of some kind. There, for example, are German, Italian, Polish, or Irish Americans; African, Hispanic, Native, or Oriental Americans; Islamic, Jewish, Christian, or Humanist Americans; high-, medium-, and low-income Americans; young, middle-aged, and old Americans; heterosexual, bisexual, and homosexual Americans; Americans in shopping centers and malls, in commercial complexes, in workplaces and play places.

As life has become increasingly organized on a large scale, with national and global dimensions, Americans have found a sense of "community" in all the ways they have grouped themselves, not just in place communities, which have become increasingly less particularized and distinctive as a basis for group identity. Community, in short, has come to apply less to the totality of life for a people living in a certain location, more to particular aspects of life that people living in many different locations share and identify with. Americans, like others, have applied the term "community" to all of their significant forms of identity, linguistically at least, breaking down the barriers that used to separate locational communities from other forms of group association.

39

Rural Areas and Small Local Communities

The most common local setting for the English colonists differed from that of the groups the colonists dominated. The African slaves were from long-lasting villages; the native American tribes lived in seasonal villages; like some Europeans, the typical colonist lived on a farmstead in a rural setting and on occasion went into a village to engage in particular activities. The colonists were far more apt to live outside of a town than in it. Farmsteads varied greatly in size, but on average were notably larger than in Europe. The largest were the plantations, which were cryptocommunities, replete with chapels, craft shops, transportation facilities, slave quarters (or "workers' housing"), and, in the center of it all, the planter's house and operations center. The plantation was the earliest version of a company town, owned and built, not by a corporation, but by a single owner.

The rural population was dispersed, in open rural neighborhoods, but was in need of community life. The colonial towns that were founded often served one main purpose—whether religious (the Puritans and several other small sects), economic (crossroads hamlets, mill villages), political (county or colonial capitals), or military (garrisons and forts). Some towns were dual-purpose communities, however—for example, county seats that were also market centers—and none could exist serving *only* one purpose.

Towns were hierarchical in that they grew at widely differing rates. They varied in size from crossroad hamlets, with small clusters of houses or even single buildings with a public function, to villages that served in some fashion the rural area around them, to substantial towns, which were service centers for a substantial hinterland. The shape that a community assumed for townsdwellers depended upon the dimension of their lives they were experiencing at a given time. The physical space that a hamlet or a village occupied differed from the political territory it covered, which in turn varied from the economic world that a townsman occupied as a craftsman, farmer, tradesman, or professional. A town's society could differ from the physical, political, or economic shape of the community if there were outsiders, transients, slaves, natives—anyone who insiders felt were foreigners or did not belong, even though residents. Cultural identifications could divide political and physical boundaries as school districts and religious parishes emerged within a town.

After the Revolution, Americans founded a variety of towns. The most common was the agricultural service center, but there were also special-interest towns whose inhabitants focused on fishing, lumbering, mining, and milling. Water-powered mills became the centers of machine production with wage laborers, and thus some towns became the first industrial centers. There were also carefully planned company towns founded in these decades: industrial villages built all at once, with housing and stores as well as productive facilities. Some groups of Easterners left en masse and founded towns, often given the same name, farther west. Other groups, religious and ethnic immigrants from Europe, went west and founded their own towns. Radical reform groups of both a religious or a secular character founded what they hoped would be model local communities, purged of competition and class and division, sustained by the communal ownership of property and the harmony and love that would ensue.

As in Europe, this bevy of hamlets, villages, and towns usually did not include either very rich or very poor inhabitants and did not have practitioners of the more rarefied or sophisticated trades and professions. The larger the town, the wider the array of commercial and professional services it offered for a correspondingly larger hinterland. Because of exceptionally high mobility rates, only a core or "persister" population found an attachment, identity, or loyalty to a given community—town or city. Many more transients were inhabitants of a community for a relatively short time, seeking economic and social opportunity elsewhere, though often not very far away.

Inland towns and cities also had a group of "businessmen" (the term was invented during the 1830s) who were successful in attracting settlers, investors, and firms, and in building commercial and industrial buildings and transportation facilities. Such "booster" businessmen blurred the public and private realms, making the growth of their community synonymous with their own enrichment as realtors, builders, bankers, merchants, and politicians. This "booster" element in the towns wanted their communities to grow, to become cities, and actively sought road, canal, and railroad connections in the conviction that direct linkages to transportation were essential to growth or campaigned for their communities to be chosen as county or state capitals in the belief that government, if functioning locally, would bring growth.

Inhabitants of both villages and cities usually lived harmoniously, cohering as communities because of a basic agreement on values and objectives, though such inhabitants sometimes exhibited stress and hostility between core populations and transients or natives and immigrants, between entrepreneurs who exploited local resources (such as lumber and livestock) and surrounding farmers who wanted such communities to be service centers for themselves.

As squatters, out ahead of organized government and the passage of legitimizing preemption legislation, some transients formed temporary communities, farmers' "claims clubs," and set up their own governments, their own methods (courts and trials and punishments) for dealing with those whose infractions of the rules made them criminals.

Other transients formed wagon trains on the westward trails, which were a form of temporary community, with requisite rules or constitutions, officers, mechanisms for dealing with those who disregarded the rules, and detailed prescriptions for travel along the trails. Some (mainly in the 1820s) were traders who went to rendezvous points (another type of temporary community) to deal with "Mountain Men," who more than anyone else in the white population reverted to a native American style of living. Others (again, mainly in the 1820s) were traders who went to northern Mexico to exchange products there during the years before the Texas war for independence (in the 1830s). Still others were mining prospectors who went to areas of the Rocky Mountains where gold (the most valuable of minerals) could be found and established both miners' "claims clubs," which, like the farmers' clubs, were temporary communities replete with rules for making strikes and staking claims and punishing wrongdoers, and mining camps, which were sometimes as short-lived as the local "rush," but which were also sometimes lasting communities.

After the Civil War, towns continued to be centers of industry dependent upon water power, and the process of mechanization, which in agriculture led to a proportionately decreasing number of farmers providing food and fiber for a fast-growing population, created, by contrast, a great demand for machine operators as ever-increasing parts of products were produced by machinery and not by handcrafting. Towns of many kinds developed in these decades: in addition to agricultural service and industrial centers, there were mining towns, cattle towns, forestry towns; there were county seats, state capitals, and military forts. There were also towns carefully planned: company towns (industrial or mining) and railroad towns (that is, towns designed by the railroad companies to attract settlers to their rights of way).

Town life was characterized by its face-to-face community involvement, something that manifested itself most strongly in ceremonies and holidays involving the cycle of life for individuals (birth, marriage, and death), Christians (Christmas and Easter), and Americans (Independence Day). Except when elites exploited a national resource (as in the mining, industrial, forestry, and livestock towns), towns tended not to have a steep hierarchy of wealth and poverty. Local government continued to operate in direct, important ways, even after 1900, when progressive reforms enlarged the role of the national government. None of those changes directly superseded the operations of county and municipal government, however. The major development in local government was that what had been private or had featured broad popular participation became professional and public, something towns shared with cities in an era in which professionalism became increasingly widespread.

Townsdwellers exhibited a kind of schizophrenia, as boosters sometimes tried to make towns into burgeoning cities at the same time that others insisted that neighborliness, loyalty, and togetherness continued to define that which distinguished a town from a city. Schizophrenic too was the lure of the city for those who wanted variety and excitement and change and opportunity, at the same time that others reeled back in horror over the sins (gambling, drinking, and prostitution) and major crimes that seemed to characterize life for these dense urban populations.

Since 1930, America's rural population has continued to decline at a rapid pace, because the number of people farming has continued to hemorrhage. By end of the twentieth century, only 2 percent of Americans listed farming as their principal occupation. Because the most common sort of American town was one that served as an agricultural service center, many towns were losing their very basis for existing. But, by 1970, this situation began to change, to reverse itself. Americans began to move back out to rural areas and towns at a faster rate than they were leaving them. Various groups of people, constituting a "back-to-the-land" movement, have migrated to the towns and the countryside for various reasons.

Some have sought to live simple, pollution-free lives, away from the crime and poverty and crowding and lack of civility and environmental contamination of urban life. Others are well-off ex-urbanites who have sought a second residence (and sometimes a second career and other activities) in the country, thus garnering what both urban and rural settings have to offer. Others commute from the countryside and villages to nearby plants and offices, which, increasingly, since World War II, have located everywhere there is good transportation and adequate managerial and labor supplies. Others have returned to their hometowns to retire or have deliberately found small communities for that purpose.

Towns continue to consist of about 15 percent of the population. They continue as well to provide appropriate settings for special activities, institutions, and purposes. There are military towns, resort towns, retirement villages, education centers, one-industry towns. Townsdwellers have tried to sustain their loyalty to older town values (such as neighborliness and loyalty) at the same time that these small communities have become an amalgam of local and nonlocal institutions, groups, and activities—stores, plants, and associations—thus creating a kind of schizophrenia: a longing for olden times as well as an acceptance of what the wider world has introduced into a once largely isolated world.

In a global context, Americans went beyond the classic peasant village, the kind of community in which farmers lived in town and worked out in their fields, to become truly rural, to live as farmers in rural settings, outside hamlets, villages, and towns, all of which, as service centers, provided needed services and community settings for such a rural population. Americans abandoned the peasant village, as did others on the frontiers of Europe and, indeed, some within Europe itself after 1600. Settlement by European migrants in new lands outside of Europe, lands where the scale of agriculture became enlarged, speeded up a process already under way in Europe itself. Because early industry in America was so dependent on water power, the earliest industrial centers in America were not cities, but villages situated where water power could be harnessed, which was a peculiarly American form of early industrial development. By contrast, early European industry was located near coal deposits and was powered by steam, allowing for a quick concentration of machine production in what soon became urban settings. Such distinctions have declined over the course of the nineteenth and twentieth centuries, however, as the element of the population engaged in farming has steadily declined and as first steam power and then electrical power has enabled industrial production in America to be freed from such a site-specific source as water power.

40

Cities

Unlike Europe, with its varied urban centers, only in coastal, seaport cities did the English colonists gather together in large numbers. Their early cities—Boston, Newport, New York, Philadelphia, Baltimore, Charleston—were commercial and cultural centers for large rural hinterlands, with economic and cultural definitions clearly on a much larger scale than their political ones. These port cities contained the greatest concentration and array of occupations, the greatest extremes of wealth and poverty, and the most sophisticated combination of economic and social activity. As these centers grew in size, early municipal corporations became representative governments for large, varied populations. The ports provided the urban setting for the merchants' power and influence, just as the plantations, as the most complex and sophisticated of rural settlements, provided the setting for the planters' power and influence.

After independence, cities everywhere—including the earlier coastal or port cities, from Boston to New Orleans—continued, as in Europe, to be centers of commerce (not industry) and of culture, dominating a large hinterland. The larger the community, the more varied the social, economic, and occupational structure or makeup, the greater the variety of classes and groups and types of occupations and associations of all kinds. The cities attracted immigrants (mainly from Ireland and Germany) and nonslave blacks, both of whom created their own neighborhoods.

Whether as transients or as persisters, many Americans, like Europeans, experienced life in the context of small communities in which everyone knew (or knew of) everyone else, though a significant and growing element in the population lived in large communities, too large for this kind of familiarity, communities that were impersonal and full of strangers, that encompassed a far steeper social hierarchy of groups both richer and poorer than was the case in smaller places. Inland cities—Chicago, St. Louis, Cincinnati, Cleveland, Buffalo, Louisville—emerged at transportation focal points, at places where there was a natural break in the movement of people and products. Such cities, like the coastal port cities of an earlier time, were commercial and cultural centers.

American urban communities grew at enormous rates between the Civil War and the Depression for several, interrelated reasons. Immigration increased markedly, especially from Southern and Eastern Europe, with migrants escaping economic destitution or dissatisfaction or religious-political-social oppression for putative New World opportunities. Large numbers of such immigrants found employment or business ventures in the large port-of-entry cities along the Atlantic coast or, later, in inland cities. Farmers sometimes moved off the land that was worked by fewer, larger, more commercialized and mechanized operators, directly into cities, seeking other means of income. Even Southern black sharecroppers and tenant farmers moved northward into urban industrial centers at a time when demand for labor was enhanced by the wartime production of the World War I years. Townsdwellers also sought the greater economic opportunities of urban communities, especially as the farm population they served hemorrhaged away and mechanized production was relocated, away from the water-powered mill village sites.

Cities provided income and employment for these groups because industry became increasingly centered in urban areas when new forms of power for the operation of machines were developed. It became technically feasible for steam power and then for electrical power to be generated anywhere, and not just from the flow of water along natural waterways. Cities already had large numbers of craftsmen whose trades became increasingly displaced by machine-made products. Cities also attracted entrepreneurs with managerial and organizational skills who successfully centralized and rationalized production, making it more efficient and less costly. Cities—by definition—were already commercial centers, with financial, marketing, and storage facilities and capacities. In other words, urban communities contained all the economic elements necessary for rapid demographic growth.

In the decades after the Civil War, cities added to their commercial and cultural functions, that of industrial production. And though inland communities that became highly urbanized continued to be those rare settlements that attracted notably capable business elites to places where waterborne commerce flourished, cities everywhere also became great rail centers, focal points of overland trade. Steamships and steam railroads made possible the continental distribution of products made at industrial plants owned by national corporations whose offices and productive facilities were both typically located in cities.

Urban communities contained a highly varied and vertical socioeconomic dimension, with ethnic and racial and income groups located in defined neighborhoods. Extreme wealth and extreme poverty coexisted alongside marked economic and social and geographical mobility. Urban centers were in a constant state of demographic and physical flux.

Politically, cities annexed suburbs as new neighborhoods were developed by real estate firms and became more carefully defined in socioeconomic terms—from the slums that grew around the commercial and industrial center to the ever-more-expensive outer "rings." However, a counter movement arose to combat the rapid political-territorial growth of cities, when sufficient numbers of suburbanites united to reject annexation proposals and thus maintained their political, if not their economic-social-cultural, independence. In this way, those in the newer, outer parts of urban areas could at least govern themselves in small, non-urban-like "communities," that is, in a context not greatly dissimilar to that which townsdwellers inhabited, even though in all other respects, suburbanites occupied a place in a great, sprawling urban community. Urban transportation—fast trains, then trolleys, then subways, then buses and cars and trucks—knitted together huge urban complexes, greatly extending the common radius of living and working places.

The cities themselves were governed in this period by political leaders (or "bosses") who greatly centralized the functioning of municipal government, retaining a "premodern" mode of personal interaction with various immigrant, ethnic, racial, and income groups, giving emphasis to informal arrangements as much as to laws and ordinances, sometimes involving themselves in seriously illegal activity, and always attempting to retain the loyalty of a political organization that won elections. Reform groups opposed such nonrational, extralegal procedures and periodically defeated these "bosses." But, both groups participated in the rapid and significant enlargement in the functions of municipal government as the city administrations grew to perform in a public capacity such services as were dealt with by police-fire-hospital-water-electricity-street-transport departments.

In a large community, filled with strangers for whom forms of civility became essential means of social discourse, city dwellers came to argue that it was imperative for public order that government provide services that used to be only private in character. Debate raged over to what extent these services should be made public and whether "bosses" who acted in the "personal" manner of public officials in much smaller communities should be chosen, or whether those pledged to govern large urban centers in a rational, efficient, honest, fair, just manner should be. "Progressive" reform at the urban level centrally involved this issue, and reform movements in a considerable number of cities succeeded in instituting city administrations that were organized in such a way that appointed, trained, expert officials had a large role to play in the governance of America's burgeoning urban communities. In this endeavor, reformers typically drew on European models, whether civil service commissions (along British lines), state supervisory commissions (after the British Local Government Board), or professional city managers (patterned on the German *Oberburgermeister*).

In their efforts to enlarge the public sector, whether through city planning or through municipal ownership, progressive city officials were much influenced by the experiences of like-minded urban reformers in Europe. The development of publicly owned utilities and transportation systems was well advanced in Britain and Germany by the turn of the century, though in France, cities were kept under the tight control of state officials, had no capacity to contract debts, and were thus precluded from experimenting in municipal ownership. Publicly owned waterworks and sewer systems brought municipal authorities into conflict with established private entrepreneurs: suppliers and disposers of water and refuse, operators of individual streetcars, street sweepers. Typically, municipal officials gradually bought out such private enterprise while constructing wholly publicly managed systems. Following the British lead, cities in the United States invested heavily in public water and sewer facilities in the late nineteenth century. Urban streets were in a wretched condition, full of garbage and manure, and it was a long-term struggle to grade and pave and clean them. In one area of public action, Americans excelled: their parks won the admiration of Europeans, and public city playgrounds were in fact an American invention.

But, the movement to institute municipal ownership of utilities and transportation was deflected and defused by those progressive reformers who created at the state level public utilities commissions with the authority to approve rates, oversee capital offerings, and set minimum standards of safety and service. By 1914, almost all states had such a commission. American municipal reformers started later than their European counterparts and faced various obstacles. Public transport systems were expensive and difficult to administer. Also, there was a double hurdle built into the American political system: not only did the reformers have to attain voter approval and the agreement of state authorities, but they had to face lawsuits in the court system launched by disgruntled private interests upset by the institution of public systems. And there was also corruption and boss rule, so endemic as to sap the energy of many municipal ownership movements.

City planning was also heavily influenced by European precedents. The redesign of cities along the lines of Haussmann's rational reconfiguration of old, mazelike Paris was a widely copied phenomenon in Europe by the time Americans became familiar with it. Daniel Burnham attempted to bring about such a reconstruction in several American cities, but succeeded only on a minor scale. In the United States, there were too many constraints for there to be true reconstructions on a grand scale. Haussmann had been given the authority in Paris during the 1850s and 1860s to buy building lots cheaply in slum areas, to set up whole new streets, to sell the new buildings at profitable prices, and to condemn more land than he needed, so that he was able to upgrade whole sections of inner Paris in a profitable manner. But in the United States, the courts upheld the property owners affected by clearance and wouldn't allow the condemnation of slum property without payment in full value. Similarly, reformers successfully pressed municipal governments to copy German and British zoning schemes by the time of World War I, but what in Europe had begun as a device to curb the speculative advantages of property interests at the edge of urban complexes in the United States became a realtor's asset, as whole areas could be developed with the attraction of being limited to a particular, known-in-advance use.

In a general sense, cities in these decades became the basis for the nationalization of "American" life, as they provided the means whereby Americans everywhere could live increasingly standardized lives. Cities have become the standard community for Americans. As elsewhere, the urbanized population generates most of the novelty in American life. Since 1930, urban centers have become, with the growth of suburbs, decentralized, attenuated demographic complexes. Suburbs are communities located toward the edge of metropolitan areas. Surburbanites have wanted a homogeneous, townlike setting with access to urban activities and institutions and have stopped the process by which central cities annexed outlying areas whose people had willingly joined a growing urban colossus. To sustain the sense that theirs is a small community, even if it is part of a huge urban complex, recent suburbanites have retained their political autonomy.

Since 1930, America's metropolises have exhibited the contradictory definitions of "communities" of all kinds. If defined politically, they are fragmented, "balkanized" bits of administrative territory. If defined physically and spatially, culturally, economically, or socially, they assume a much larger form and cohesion. Cities, in recent decades, are reverting to an older economic role as commercial and trade centers and are ceasing to be bastions of industry at a time when industrial facilities have come to be located everywhere. Since the 1960s, cities have changed in a social sense as well. America's large cities grew outward, with socioeconomic status in a fairly steady line from inner city slums, through working-class suburbs, middle- and upper-middle-class suburbs, and, finally, at the outer edge, the wealthiest suburbs.

But, since the beginning of black ghettoes and the race riots of the 1960s and the decline of the central retail districts as suburban malls arose, there has been a commercial regeneration of the central city, with the construction of multiuse complexes (offices, shops, hotels, apartments) and with the "gentrification" of older, run-down urban housing as some middle-class inhabitants have "escaped" from the suburbs to resume urban living in the fullest sense. The result of these developments is that metropolitan areas have become socially more complex, less separated into layers of neighborhoods and communities based upon particular levels of income, which in turn was based upon distance from the city's center.

Since World War II, old distinctions between towns and cities have become blurred as geographically situated communities, large and small, have become increasingly alike physically, socially, and economically. The Census Bureau has, in recent decades, had difficulty in defining different kinds of community. "Everywhere" communities are—physically—the product of developers (or "boomers") who construct vast tracts of homes as well as apartments, commercial complexes, shopping centers, "strip" shopping structures, or combinations of all of these. Such developers often draw on architectural styles that are national and international in scope and thus obliterate the older local and regional variations that give particular communities a distinctive appearance. Unlike the "boosters" of the nineteenth century, the larger "boomers" typically are unattached to the communities they so profoundly shape in a physical sense.

Cities and towns are also increasingly alike in their economic mix (with chain stores, franchises, and branch plants as apt to be located in one as in the other), in their social structure (status and position and class are defined in similar ways in both), and in their cultural life (the media make the same forms of art, recreation, and entertainment available in both). The basic, ongoing distinction between towns and cities is that small communities remain irreducibly personal—the entire community is familiar, known, experienced—and large communities are as unchangeably impersonal—the community is filled with strangers, and life is based upon a necessary civility that sometimes prevails and sometimes does not.

Townspeople continue to be relatively provincial, intolerant, and conservative, living as they do in small, still largely homogeneous communities. By contrast, city dwellers live with poor black ghettoes that contain an "underclass" of failed Americans. Urbanites also live in neighborhoods of vastly varying character—everything from physically and socially and economically decaying slums to the well-guarded and carefully zoned luxury apartments and houses of the very rich to income-graded neighborhoods based upon housing prices.

City dwellers often work in crowded offices and stores and service or production facilities and commute on crowded highways or rapid transit systems. Indeed, urban areas are usually defined by their "commuting range," just as midwestern towns were located by the distance a horse could "commute" in a day. In recent decades, governments in America's metropolises, which are quite fragmented politically, have been attempting with mixed results to deal with a high incidence of violent crime, large concentrations of people in poverty, and great increases in air and water pollution.

From a global perspective, the urbanization that has occurred is a fairly recent historical phenomenon. Over half of the world's population still live in rural areas (or in politically defined communities of under 5,000 people), largely because of the still-huge rural populations of eastern and southern Asia. What has had the most impact on the character of urban life in different parts of the world has been the relationship of urbanization in a given area to the timing of industrialization. In the undeveloped parts of the world, there has been a huge migration from the rural hinterlands of the port cities that have funneled commodities needed by those in the industrialized parts of the globe. This migration has come without sufficient industrialization, so that migrants have created shantytowns around the peripheries of the largest urban areas, while the centers have been reserved for the middle class and the elites and have remained the focal point of commercial, industrial, and cultural/social life. South and Middle American and African cities are the best examples of this process, whereas Islamic and Southern and Eastern Asian cities are more mixed in character, but still exhibit aspects of this development. By contrast, European cities achieved a great deal of their growth before industrialization appeared, and so have retained a relatively stable central city, with commercial and residential zones for commerce and the elite and middle class, with newer working-class suburbs toward their peripheries, but without shantytowns in outlying districts because industrialization proceeded in concert with urban growth. North American and Australasian cities have grown up *with* industrialization, which means that their period of greatest ascendancy involved growth outward and upward, with elites and aspiring middle-class residents seeking transportation-dependent newer settings on the outer fringe, with industry and commerce seeking locations in the central city to most efficiently draw on a mobile urban workforce, and with the poor herding into the now-cheaper inner-city neighborhoods.

41

Colonies and States

The English colonists and, later, white Americans related to communities of a higher level even more tenuously than to towns and cities. Because of what became, by the 1840s, a continental scale of settlement, Americans experienced a decentralized hierarchy of communities in a distinctive way. Most Europeans related to a center of life and influence located in their capital cities in ways quite beyond the comprehension of those who lived in the colonies and, later, the United States.

During the colonial period, the English colonists related to their province as an important level of a hierarchical polity that extended to imperial Britain. Provincial governments exercised significant power: they determined land policy, chartered municipal governments, organized militia units in wartime. So immersed were the colonists in the political life of their own provinces that it was difficult for them to organize in a transprovincial way during wartime or even during the period from 1765 to 1775, when a significant number of them resisted what they believed were tyrannical policies forged by the imperial government in London. During the Revolution, it was the provincial governments that transformed themselves into states with new constitutions and eventually drew up a frame of government for a new national government as well. Under the Articles of Confederation during the 1780s, the new states exercised far more authority than Congress in the fledgling confederacy. It was the states that sent delegates to what turned into a constitutional convention in 1787 and the states that established conventions for the ratification of the new constitution.

States, through the wide authority exercised by their governments, were a notable presence in the lives of all Americans, and constituted a far more important political community than the nation did until at least the 1930s. In the decades after the Revolution, the states developed the social institutions that cared for deviant and dependent groups in the population—students, orphans, the poor, the sick, the insane, the criminals. The states also aided—as the national government did not—economic development before the Civil War by investing public revenues in banking and transportation corporations and thus helping to ensure the survival of the mechanisms by which growth could occur.

States continued to play an important political role as "communities" and throughout the years from the Civil War to the Depression, state governmental activity remained more significant than that of the national government. The territories gained as a result of the Mexican War and the settlement with Britain during the 1840s became states in the established manner during the decades after the Civil War, and, by 1912, the American nation became a political entity with contiguous states from Mexico to Canada and from the Atlantic to the Pacific Oceans. During the years that "progressive" reform was a major aspect of political life, some reformers questioned the undemocratic means by which U.S. Senators were selected to represent the states in the national government (that is, their election by state legislatures). Advocates of reform argued in favor of the more democratic method of a direct popular vote. They prevailed by 1913, when a constitutional amendment embodying their proposal was ratified.

State governments continued to be a more important level of government in the federal system than the national government insofar as the internal governance of the American people was concerned. The states began to significantly regulate the large corporate firms that emerged after the Civil War, most notably the railroads, during the 1870s, a decade before the national government began to act tentatively in a similar fashion, when it enacted an antitrust act and established the first national regulatory agency, once again for the railroads.

Similarly, progressive reform movements developed in states before having much impact on the national government. Some states (most notably, Wisconsin and New Jersey) became "laboratories" of progressive reform clearly in advance of the time that progressivism, under Theodore Roosevelt's and Woodrow Wilson's leadership, affected domestic policy at the national level. Changes in the role of government—a widening and deepening of governmental authority over the lives of the American people—became evident at the state level first, because state governments clearly retained their primary role within the federal system until the Depression of the 1930s. Those who sought to use public power to achieve ameliorative goals naturally acted within the context of governments that were already focal points of activity.

The states are still an important part of the federal system, and many of the new national programs created since 1930 that involve funding by the national government are administered by state governments—such programs as unemployment insurance, welfare, education, and transportation. The enlargement of national political authority since 1930 has also sometimes resulted in direct governmental action through new agencies (such as housing ownership assistance, environmental control, arts and sciences funding, energy development). But, those activities and institutions that the states (or their counties or municipalities) had already developed—schools, hospitals, asylums, orphanages, poorhouses—have not been "nationalized" or made into nationwide systems. The national government has provided aid to enhance the capability of these subnational entities, but with that aid has come national standards.

In a global context, states or provinces have existed within nations and empires everywhere. What is distinctive about American states in the context of the West is the relatively greater authority their governments have exercised than has been the case in most of Europe (with the exception of loosely federated Switzerland), though not in such other white settler societies as Canada and Australia.

42

Regions

Beyond the localities that the English colonists lived in, American colonial society contained significant regional variations, a regionalism that remained an important aspect of American society into the twentieth century. Regions lacked a political definition, but significant aspects of economic and cultural life sometimes assumed regional forms. In New England, the Puritans spread their way of patterning life for as far and for as long as they could, an effort that marked society in New England throughout the colonial period and beyond. That many of the inhabitants of the area shared a covenanted life and believed that they were in a special relationship with God animated the Puritans and affected the way they built communities, worked, played, and worshipped. In the mid-Atlantic area, from the beginning, society was characterized by its heterogeneity, its varied ethnic and religious groups, its range of economic activity, its middle-class orientation, making this region an early microcosm of the modern style of life that would come to characterize American society as a whole.

In the South Atlantic area, the steeply hierarchical structure of society made the pattern of life there more akin to that of Middle and South America than to that of northern North America. Southern planters dominated society in all ways, in the manner of the large landowners of South and Middle America, who in turn mirrored the preeminence of the landowners of the Mediterranean world. All exhibited a many-faceted form of hegemony: personal, familial, kinship, local, political, economic, social, cultural. Similarly, the institution of slavery and the presence—physically within society and socially, through caste, outside society—of large numbers of black slaves meant that the Southern English colonists created a society similar to that of the Portuguese, Spanish, and French colonists of South and Middle America, but also different in the sense that it was a society in which white colonists were not only dominant, but in the majority, as many whites were farmers who raised the same staple crops as the planters.

As for regionalism before the Civil War, like the Puritans in New England, Southerners developed a distinctive way of life, shaped by the region's basically rural character, the common economic denominator of staple crop agriculture, and the existence of slavery and planters and plantations. None of this changed after the Revolution, but as the "South" (usually defined by contemporaries in these years as the "slave states") expanded westward, all the way to Texas, it became more varied geographically, economically, demographically, socially, and politically. The South varied from grain and livestock production in its northern tier to staple crop agriculture (cotton, rice, and sugar) in its southern tier, from broad coastal plains to the Southern Appalachian and Ozark foothills and mountains, from rural areas to towns to coastal and inland riverside cities, from Federalists and Jeffersonian Republicans and then Democrats and Whigs, from areas with large concentrations of slaves to areas with few slaves.

Many who lived in the slave states had a sense of belongingness to the "South," but it was a form of attachment, loyalty, and identity that was imprecise, inchoate. A growing sense that slavery was being threatened provided Southerners with a focus for their attachment to their region. After the abolitionist attack on slavery was launched in the early 1830s, the South increasingly became a "closed" region whose dominant elements forged a single orthodoxy (as the Puritans had earlier attempted to do)—a multifaceted defense of slavery. The "South" then became the source of a potent form of regionalism, so potent that loyalty to it could override one's national identity.

By the 1850s, Southern politicians had developed a unified view of the right of states to secede and of the total illegitimacy that attached to any Congressional proposal involving the limitation of slave property in the territories. Secession occurred only because large numbers of Southerners were willing to allow the defense of their "homeland" from dangers that came from elsewhere (namely, the ascendancy of Lincoln and the Northern Republicans) to supersede their loyalty to the nation as Americans.

The "West" was a movable region—a frontier that moved ever westward as lands occupied by natives were cleared by treaty. There is little evidence of a sense of attachment to *the* West on the part of those who lived under frontier conditions, largely because such people wanted the frontier stage to end as soon as possible, wanted their lives to replicate the lives of those in the settled East, with the huge distinction that their position in society would be much improved over whatever unsatisfying circumstances had propelled them to move, for the "West" as frontier was a land of migrants, the cutting edge of American settlement.

The existence of a movable frontier West until the 1850s meant that there was always additional land for settlers to gain property and wealth and resources from. In America, wealth seemed to be, along with expanding territory, itself infinitely expandable. A movable, augmentable West was a basis for economic expansion, a place of opportunity for those farther east who were in some way dissatisfied and had the means and the will to move, just as North America had attracted disgruntled, opportunistic European migrants.

The "West" was also the immediate or proximate cause of sectional antagonism, as slavery, the most divisive issue in American political life—the one that produced the breakdown of a functioning system—was primarily an issue involving the western territories. Paradoxically, the most explosive of issues detonated, not in the states, where there were slaves, but in the territories, where there were few, if any.

Regionalism was, thus, an important phenomenon, affecting some of the population very little (those in the mid-Atlantic area), some in a vague, but not vital way (those in New England and in the settled Midwest), but others with great impact, if only temporarily (those in the West as a frontier), and still others fatefully, becoming a source of loyalty and identity so potent as to override national allegiance.

In the years between the Civil War and the Depression, the "South" became a more united, powerful reality for those who lived there than it ever was before the Civil War. Paradoxically, those who lived on in the former Confederacy gave a far more precise definition to their "region" than Southerners ever could before the war. Those who lived in the reunited American states that had for four years constituted the Confederate States of America shared a common historical memory of a separate nation, defeated and politically reunited with the United States with which it had fought to obtain its independence. During these years, Southerners keenly felt their distinctiveness as a people who had known separation and defeat and whose region was distinctively a one-party area (Democratic), poverty-stricken, economically underdeveloped and ill-balanced, both rural and agricultural (cotton remained the staple crop over large areas) and, until the great Negro migration out of the South that began in the 1910s, profoundly biracial. Taken all together, these distinctions sustained and deepened a sense of regional uniqueness. Regional affiliation was an important element in the personal identity of all those who lived in the American South during these decades.

The "West" as a region lost the crisp definition it had as long as there was an easily identifiable frontier. As the edge of settlement moved westward, so did the area that those who lived there—as well as Americans elsewhere—thought of as the "West." After the Civil War, the frontier continued to exist until the 1890s. During these years, the West became a movable frontier whose direction took on swirling motions, rather than following the hitherto standard westward flow.

The plains to the west of the Mississippi River, especially those portions that were semiarid, were settled, first by ranchers, who raised and moved cattle on the open range, and then by farmers, who claimed free land under the terms of the post–Civil War land acts. The Rocky Mountains and Pacific Coast were settled by miners, who swarmed into areas where gold and other minerals were discovered. The Pacific Coast valleys were settled by farmers, who developed large-scale commercial and mechanized farms that featured fruits and vegetables, in contrast to similarly advanced Midwest farms, which were focused on grain and livestock.

But, once all areas of the American Union had been settled and it was impossible to find a "frontier" any longer, the "West" became a fixed geographical section of the United States, sometimes including all the states west of the Mississippi River, but more typically those states from the Dakotas to Texas westward to the Pacific coast. This specific, largely semiarid, widely irrigated West was settled in the late nineteenth century midst the boom-and-bust cycles of such extractive industries as mining as well as of such agricultural endeavors as livestock and grain farming. By the twentieth century, revolutionary technologies were applied to mineral ores and fossil fuels and lumber and mechanized agricultural units to create a more sustained prosperity.

Regionalism bereft of special economic and social and cultural connotations also affected New England, the mid-Atlantic, and what became known as the "Midwest" during these decades. Only in the South did regional identity and distinctiveness retain the vitality and significance that had marked the phenomenon in all parts of the Union and, earlier, in the British North American empire, since the seventeenth century. The basic reason for this was the progressive "nationalization" of American life that manifested itself in the increased speed of transportation and communication, in economic corporations with continental dimensions, in classes and groups with national cohesion and awareness, and in a national government that began to respond to this enlargement of scale by enlarging its regulative role in an increasingly national society.

Regionalism in the United States has greatly changed its character since 1930. The South—the most distinctive region before 1930—has steadily lost its distinctiveness as blacks have moved to other parts of the nation, as the Southern economy has developed a mix similar to that prevailing elsewhere, and as Southern politics has resumed a two-party character. A descendant of the South to some extent is a broadened "sun belt," which encompasses the entire Southern portion of the United States from the Atlantic to the Pacific, and which is commonly referred to as the region of greatest economic growth (with its longer growing seasons and its new industries based upon lower labor costs and less successful unions). In the same way, the Northeast or "rust-belt" (an amalgam of New England and the mid-Atlantic areas) is regarded as a region with economic problems (with its older, uncompetitive, basic industries and high labor costs).

But, regionalism as a defining feature of American life, as a level of community that Americans identify with, as something with a genuine and fundamental distinctiveness, region by region, has increasingly declined as America has become "nationalized." In recent decades, regions have typically become an administrative convenience for national governmental agencies, institutions, and organizations of all kinds, as well as for corporations—all of which divide up the United States into regional offices and districts. New England, the Mid-Atlantic, the South, the Midwest, the Plains, the Mountains, and the Pacific Coast—these are the typical divisions.

In a global context, regionalism has existed everywhere. It has been a truly universal phenomenon in all kinds of political contexts. Even well-integrated ethnic groups who have long had nations—like the English themselves—have exhibited marked regional variations in many aspects of their lives, and the earliest English colonists carried with them significant regional variations, depending upon which part of England a given area's settlers were from. Even well-established nations in Europe have had ethnic and regional minorities: the Scots and the Welsh in Britain, the Basques and the Catalans in Spain, for example. Regional divisions have divided some nations along northern/southern or eastern/western geographical lines: the southern and northern Italians, for example. Regional variations involving cultural, economic, or social activity have assumed a vast array of shapes across the globe and through the centuries, both greater as well as smaller than political entities.

The United States shared a frontier region with all the other emergent nations along the geographical periphery of an expanding European civilization. Canada, Australia, Russia, South Africa, southern Brazil, and northern Argentina—all had frontiers whose inhabitants shared certain characteristics with those of America's frontier: a tendency toward violence and lawlessness and "wildness" (though the extent of this depended upon the strength of the resident government and upon popular attitudes toward authority); the presence of large ranches and plantations alongside homesteading farmers (though the mix varied from frontier to frontier); geographical confinement within a larger inhospitable setting of a semiarid, arid, arctic, or tropical terrain; even the existence of similar kinds of heroic figures (whether cowboys, lawmen, outlaws, backwoodsmen, or bushmen). Even the mass movement of settlers to frontier regions echoed around the peripheries of an expansionist European civilization. These epic treks involved not only American pioneers moving westward, but Russian Cossaks moving eastward to Siberia, South African Boers moving northward, and Brazilian Paulistas moving westward into the Amazon basin.

But, regional divisions within established polities that are so deep that they lead to civil war are much rarer phenomena, and this kind of secessionist geographical regionalism Americans alone among westernized people around the globe have experienced. By contrast, Americans have shared their experience of fratricidal conflict with those Africans who have rejected the national territories imposed by Europeans during their imperial rule, territories that conflict with older tribal ones. African civil wars have been caused by tribal division; America's Civil War was based upon differing conceptions of what place African slaves should have in the American republic. Both were deeply regional, however.

43

Subnational Forms of Identity

Towns, cities, states, and regions—all these subnational levels of community played some part in defining who the individuals living within the United States were, just as gender, age, wealth, social group or class, ethnicity, race, occupation, religion, and political party affiliation did. Americans as individuals had myriads of personal identifications and allegiances, several of which were their "place" community affiliations.

It is difficult to ascertain what kind of identification, loyalty, and involvement those living within state borders experienced. The very name of the American nation—the United States of America—prosaic, even pedestrian as it is, is an indication that the Founding Fathers thought they were creating a nation that involved the uniting of many states. People with an ongoing residence could have a strong sense of identification with their own state, 13 of which were older than the Union itself and all of which contained their own historians and historical societies (something that happened rather quickly in the decades after the Revolution and the establishment of political independence). But, it is difficult to determine whether states in the minds of their inhabitants had definition as a "community" beyond their political existence. People lived "in" states, paid taxes to their governments, elected their officials, lived under their laws, were tried and jailed by them for committing illegal acts, were aided by social institutions established by them, worked in firms regulated or aided by them—but did these same people identify with them? States were without obvious economic, social, or cultural definitions, just the opposite of regions, which continued to exhibit such dimensions, albeit unevenly, but were without political content.

Regional attachments were more diffuse and attenuated, if only because of the difficulty of establishing precise boundaries for areas without a political definition. The Mid-Atlantic region was the most difficult for its inhabitants to feel they were a part of, perhaps because of the disparate character of the original British colonies in this part of North America. New York, Pennsylvania, and New Jersey (as well as Maryland and Delaware, if they are included)—all had very distinctive origins, all developed with distinctive mixtures of circumstances. From a later perspective, what all appear to have shared were forms of heterogeneity that the Union as a whole exhibited. In other words, the inhabitants of the Mid-Atlantic area, in their economic, religious, political, social, and ethnic variety, in their tolerance and liberality and individuality prefigured the "Union" to come. But, it is difficult to find any evidence that anyone living in these states thought of themselves as "Mid-Atlanticans."

There remained enough of an "overlay" of unity in the pattern of Puritan settlement and of the village life they initiated for people living east of the Hudson River to feel a "belongingness" to something called New England. The stereotypical "Yankee"—shrewd, calculating, "hard-headed"—was of New England origin, though as a type, the Yankee came to be associated with all of the northern and western areas of the Union.

The West as frontier was too temporary and movable for any long-term identification and as the fixed western half of the nation, the West is too varied and diffuse to have created significant regional loyalties. Only the South generated a powerful sense of identification as a region, so powerful that its inhabitants supported secession from the Union and the creation of a new nation.

With the exception of Southern regionalism, of all the different levels of community that Americans have identified with, only their nation has generated the kind of loyalty, of patriotic affiliation, of symbolic display that has become associated with the phenomenon called "nationalism." Evidence of various forms of "localism" are much more difficult to find.

44

Nationalism

In one sense, American nationalism has been unique in the Western world. Unlike the evolutionary character of nationalism in Europe, where modern nation-states grew out of dynastic kingdoms, or in the other white settler societies, where the British instituted a gradual process of decolonization, American nationalism was born all at once in the pain of revolution. But though revolutionary in character, American nationalism was also thoroughly European in the sense that it was imposed by a dominant elite, deliberately created as a means of bonding the population as a whole to the nation and to its government. This form of "civic" nationalism, involving the creation of nationalism ("from above") by the elite of the dominant ethnic group within a nation-state, became the standard form of nationalism wherever there were ethnic or racial minorities. By contrast, ethnic nationalism ("from below") involved the effort of such minorities to sustain their own identity within existing nations and then to attain political independence.

On both sides of the Atlantic during the nineteenth century, governments created public educational systems from which each generation of students would learn about their nation, devised national symbols and monuments and shrines for all citizens to behold, issued passports, operated customs services, and increasingly regulated immigration and citizenship procedures. Cultural nationalists worked to impose uniform national languages and to define uniform national cultures. Governments in America—whether federal or state—were as involved in these activities as any in Europe or in the other offshoots of Europe.

American nationalism was linked to the belief that America was the land of liberty, the crucible of Europe's finest ideals. The United States was a special nation, owed a special allegiance. But, of what kind? How would the Americans express the love they felt for their Union? Citizenship in the United States was an important, but far from exclusive, source of identity for the individuals so identified. It was a connection that rarely rivaled the ongoing demands of gender, family, local community, occupation, or church.

Its most pronounced effects were felt whenever "Americans" traveled outside of the boundaries of the United States, as both travelers and hosts found the national identity of visitors worthy of notice. In the realm of foreign relations, the "ideological" factor was thoroughly nationalistic in character. Both the notions of "manifest destiny" (that Americans were destined to spread the blessings of liberty and republican government) and "mission" (that Americans should provide an example of free government that the rest of the world should emulate) were manifestations of nationalism projected outward.

Internally, the national government as an actual institution consisted of elected politicians and chosen officials and employees operating in Washington and in various establishments—customs offices, forts, naval bases—around the nation. Until the mid-nineteenth century, this governmental presence was the only significant "national institution" in the republic. There were scarcely any other durable associations organized on a nationwide basis: no significant army or navy; no national universities; few scientific, artistic, or philosophical institutes with national memberships; few labor unions or professional associations of a national scope. In short, a "national community"—to which all Americans could belong as members of well-developed national institutions and associations—was scarcely visible. Even the national government was comparatively weak and small, and the mechanism through which it operated—the parties—lacked an agreed-upon legitimacy, at least until the 1830s. This contrasted sharply with the centralization of power and authority in elites clustered around the court societies in the capitals of western Europe.

White Americans loved the "republic" or union and expressed the power it held over them—intellectually, emotionally, symbolically—by responding to symbols that stood for their beloved nation. Americans gave definition to their nationalism through celebrations held on Independence Day, the nation's birthday, which became, by the 1820s, an annual rite of national self-justification, a form of secular worship.

But, Americans lacked the ready-made personal symbol that the kingdoms of Europe exhibited in their monarchs. In order to achieve the same effect, republican Americans made their own first President a myth-laden symbol, the embodiment of the highest republican virtues. In order to achieve this, George Washington's life, death, writings and speeches, images in paint and stone, and entombment—all had to be purified, cleansed of imperfection. Washington, in life, became a model of unblemished virtue as Father of His Country, his tomb at Mount Vernon a mecca for believers, his painted and sculpted visage full of rectitude and sobriety, his utterances encased in sentiments of the most noble kinds. It did not matter that his biographers invented a flawless life, that his visual depicters created false images of neoclassical grandeur, that his editors deleted unsavory language. What mattered was not the truth or any approximation of it, but rather that a myth-laden paragon be created as the Father of His Country, a personal symbol for the American republic.

However, not until the twentieth century were Americans able to agree on either a flag or an anthem, national symbols adopted by some European populations long before. Overall, nationalism was a fragile force in American life, something that could be overridden by most of those living in a particular region—the South—at a time that regional and national affiliations seemed to be in conflict. But, nationalism became stronger and deeper for others—those in the remaining Union—when Americans became involved with an internal crisis, the Civil War, that called into question their own viability as a people inhabiting a common nation-state. In a moment of supreme testing, American nationalism exhibited both fragility and underlying strength.

Since the Civil War, especially since the late nineteenth century, the nation has become a genuine and very visible level of community—politically, economically and socially. The "nationalization" of life is revealed by the presence of a powerful national government and its agencies, vast national corporations, huge national trade unions, and a great array of national institutions, associations, and organizations. In a social context, nothing illustrated the power of nationalism more than these deliberate creations of national or "American" groups, as if the most natural thing a group could do was to create a national version of itself. Similarly, labor unions and corporations developed national organizations in order to display what was for them a natural affiliation.

After 1900, Americans became more aware of the presence of their national government and its instrumentalities and agencies, something the sudden mobilization for World War I—civilian as well as military—made much more evident. The flag (1911) and the anthem (1933) became official national symbols, as did the public buildings (the Capitol and Executive Mansion) and monuments (Washington's and Lincoln's) in the nation's capital. The centennial celebrations in 1876 were widespread, occurring in many local communities, large and small. Independence Day festivities were an annual display of patriotism filled with tradition and ritual. Americans honored their nation as an emergent republic in a world still dominated by dynastic, monarchical states. America was still a special nation, favored by God, still destined to provide the setting for the fulfillment of humanity's noblest ideals. Born in revolution, triumphantly tested in a great civil war, the American republic was worthy of the loyalty of its citizens.

Nationalism flourished in these circumstances, especially during the crusade of World War I and its aftermath. "Americanism" was something patriots sought to define in ways that excluded those who did not fit a particularly "American" way—ethnically, racially, and politically. American nationalism came to focus on a definition of America and Americans that excluded Southern and Eastern European immigrants, blacks, natives, Asians, radical socialists and labor leaders, Catholics, and Jews. Only a true "American"—white, Northern European, old stock, Protestant—was wholly fit for full participation in a national civilization that occupied the top position within the civilized world, as a result of the survival of the fittest among the competing nation-states of the world.

Thus, nationalism both enlarged and narrowed the horizons of those who defined themselves as Americans. It helped to produce a stronger sense of national identity for a population in the midst of transcending its local confinements at the same time that it excluded from full participation those who were unable or unwilling to become an "American." In this, American nationalism was like European nationalism, in the sense that the phenomenon everywhere in the Europeanized world heightened national loyalties at the same time that it sharpened national definitions.

Concomitant with the emergence of a powerful national "community" has been the further development of American nationalism. The crisis of the 1930s brought both questioning of and renewed loyalty to the "American way." World War II was a time of great nationalistic fervor, as the nation defended itself from clear and dangerous aggressors. During the "Cold War" that followed, the Americans believed that the United States was the leader and defender of the "free world" against possible aggression from an "enslaved" Communist world.

But, in recent decades, there have been developments that have had the effect of reducing America's presumed leadership role. In 1957, the Soviet Union—not the United States—was the first nation to send a human being into space (though, in 1969, the United States regained the lead by being the first to land a human being on the moon). The second Asian war (in Vietnam, from 1965 to 1975) deeply divided Americans over the question of what the United States' proper role in the world should be. In 1972, the U.S. dollar ceased to be (in effect) the standard for international currencies. And, from 1985 to 1991, Soviet leader Gorbachev ended the Cold War, made significant disarmament agreements, and allowed Communist governments throughout eastern Europe to give way to more democratic political arrangements. The effect of these developments on Americans was to greatly complicate the American perception of the world as "free" and "enslaved," with the United States and the Soviet Union as two superpowers "leading" each side.

Public attitudes toward the established symbols of nationalism have reflected these changes in how Americans have perceived their nation and its place in the world. Loyalty and identity to America have been expressed through attitudes toward the flag, for example. During World War II, the flag was a sacred symbol befitting an American crusade against aggression. By the time of the United States' second Asian war, Americans were so divided in their allegiance, identity, and loyalty that there were flag burnings by some of those who opposed the war. But, by the 1980s, a resurgence of conservatism and nationalism led to a reemphasis on the sacred character of the flag.

In general, American nationalism has been strong since 1930, as Americans typically remain extremely parochial and ignorant of others and loyal to a nation they still believe is special and great—even though American hegemony is no longer clear, even if the way "Americans" live can now be shown to be not significantly different from the way "others" live in other parts of the world.

Since 1930, the process whereby life has become increasingly organized on a global scale has quickened, and yet Americans in general remain unaware that "American life" reflects worldwide phenomena: Americans are still notably parochial, provincial, and ignorant of life elsewhere, even with the ending of their political isolationism and the great changes in communication and transportation that have made such knowledge easier to obtain than ever before. The fact is that many aspects of life have become global in scope and are best understood from that perspective—such aspects of life as science, technology, warfare, money, business, industry, agriculture, labor, popular culture, sport, and art. Since World War II, there has been a widely shared presumption of American uniqueness and greatness that has not arisen from a broad and deep interest, curiosity, understanding, and knowledge of the rest of the world.

American "cultural nationalism" in these decades has become institutionalized. Some of America's most important institutions relentlessly focus their attention on the nation and life within its borders, as if other nations and peoples weren't important in any effort to understand human life as it is being lived or has been lived or will be lived. America's schools, colleges, universities, special institutes, museums, galleries, theaters, concert halls, lecture halls, publishers, television and radio news networks, newspapers, magazines, and journals—all proclaim that life must be understood above all in a national context, that what is most important for those human beings who live within the borders of the United States is their identity as citizens of a nation-state, as U.S. citizens, as Americans—and not their identity as human beings who, collectively, inhabit the earth, and who, in any case, all have other forms of identity beyond that of a national, political one.

Courses in schools and colleges on "American" subjects are far more emphasized and popular than others. News reports on television and radio and in newspapers and magazines and books routinely define subjects in national terms. Museums, galleries, concert halls, theaters, and publishers offer American art as distinct and different and identifiable. By contrast, accounts, studies, reports, depictions, descriptions, and renderings of foreigners, of those who aren't U.S. citizens, seem peripheral, secondary. Thus does institutionalized nationalism distort the reality of human life for those who live in the United States. In a period of American hegemony (and its aftermath) Americans, aided by their cultural institutions, have focused inward, upon themselves, presuming uniqueness and greatness. But, this is an emphasis they have shared with other national and imperial peoples who have attained power and influence at various times in human history—the Greeks, the Romans, the British, the French, the Germans, the Russians, the Chinese, the Indians. Even the presumption of uniqueness is not unique.

* * *

Americans have shared with those who inhabit other well-established nation-states a propensity to find general national characteristics, or character traits that apply to the whole citizenry. This is another instance of what is essentially a political phenomenon—nationalism—extending itself well beyond the political realm, ascribing to a politically defined population a collective personality, a common way of behaving. Both Americans, while at home or abroad, and foreigners, either observing traveling Americans and as travelers among Americans, have indulged in this kind of generalizing, as has been the case elsewhere. But, what *sort* of Americans, what element of the population have they thought they were depicting—*all* Americans, or just the dominant element in the population—"old stock" white men? Were the characteristics of Americans that they discovered consistent or contradictory, a revealing portrait or a muddled, blurred depiction that could apply to any group? And, if "Americans" exhibited certain characteristics, most of the observers did not or were unable to provide an explanation: Why? Why should a population that creates a government also all *behave* in certain distinctive ways?

Certainly the leisured European observers who appeared in abundance in the United States during the 1830s and 1840s thought they were examining people who were different. From an upper-class European's perspective the people on this western frontier of Europe's expanding civilization appeared to be distinctive, relative to the Europeans they lived among. In the estimation of these observers, American personality traits included their naturalness, generosity, curiosity, humorlessness, dullness, indifference, cruelty, violence, insecurity, sensitivity to criticism, boastfulness, and tendency to complain. American mental traits included their practicality, cleverness, shallowness, incommunicativeness, scandal mongering, conformity, need to join others, and busyness. Americans valued an egalitarian belief for white men and were hypocritically racist toward blacks and natives, were materialistic, were social climbers, had no respect for tradition, valued neither learning nor intellectual accomplishment, and exhibited in their violence a lack of respect for life itself.

In the decades after the Civil War, it is less clear whether foreign observers continued to believe that Americans retained the same mixture of national characteristics as noted before the war. What is clear is that such observers found Americans to be less deserving of special attention, which indicates that, as communications and transportation linked the hitherto locally focused population to much wider worlds, the texture of life in the Europeanized or "modernized" parts of the globe was becoming increasingly similar. In more recent decades, it is common for foreigners to think of Americans as loud and brash and full of braggadocio—that is, as sharing an exaggerated sense of the importance and uniqueness of "things American."

* * *

As in the case of many other national populations, American character traits also appeared in the realm of folklore, as real-life individuals were turned into folk heroes. Americans did so by telling tall tales about unusual lives in their subliterature—in almanacs, newspapers, magazines, cheap novels. Reality became transmogrified into folklore, as a moth turns into a butterfly. The most notable of a number of such transformations involved Davy Crockett, during the early and mid-nineteenth century. Crockett's actual adventures and exploits were exaggerated and made much larger than life in accounts appearing in farmers' almanacs during the 1830s and 1840s. Squarely in the European tradition of such larger-than-life folk heroes as Ulysses and Beowulf and Siegfried, but created through the obfuscation of space rather than through the mist of time, Crockett in folklore illustrated the physical prowess and naturalness of his countrymen, but also their crudity, violence, anti-intellectualism, chauvinism, and racism. Crockett as a folk hero illustrates both the strengths and weaknesses of the Americans' quest for suitable manifestations of their national identity. Crockett represented the dominant element of the American population only (that is, he was a white, adult male) and he remained, through all the yearnings for an American folk hero, a frontiersman, and thus a regionally specific creation.

Folk heroes, like Paul Bunyan, whose reputations were developed after the Civil War tended to be commercial constructs, the by-product of corporate images and marketing and sales. Paul Bunyan, in his contrived exploits, could easily stand for American bigness and "giantism," but he also became the "logo" of a particular lumber corporation. What had been natural in the case of Davy Crockett had become a commercial contrivance in an America increasingly dominated by corporate power and the commercialism and consumerism that accompanied it. Once folklore became a commodity to be shaped for commercial purposes, it lost its core as a "folk" creation, though even as altered into a corporate logo, it revealed something about what it was that American corporations believed their products and services ought to be represented by—what image best conveyed their essential character.

Similarly, particular kinds of frontiersmen, occupants of a wild west, became mythic figures displayed in various forms of popular culture, such as popular novels and movies and radio and television. The backwoodsman, the cowboy, the outlaw—all have represented the American as an extreme individualist in a setting of untamed nature. But, Canadians, Australians, New Zealanders, South Africans, Argentinians, and Brazilians have similarly created analogous mythic figures on all the other frontiers of Europe, for example, the Australian "bushman" (or frontiersman) and the Argentinian "gaucho" (or cowboy) There is nothing particularly American about such myth-making activity.

As have other national populations, Americans have turned episodes of their past into shared experiences that give a historical dimension to their identity.

Such events or developments as slavery and segregation, the growth of democracy, the Revolution, the Civil War, the frontier, immigration, industrial and urban growth, technological innovation, two World Wars, and the Great Depression are known by ordinary citizens—are parts of a collective consciousness—as a result of schooling and popular culture. These aspects of the common past (in recent decades, claimed by newer Americans, the progeny of immigrants who were not even present at the time the event or development occurred) are understood in simplified, but detailed versions as parts of an American's historical identity, as his "story," if not in sufficient complexity to be his "history."

Conclusion

The people who have come to identify themselves as "Americans" during the last four centuries have attained an identity that was for most of that time restricted to the English colonists and their descendants, even though growing numbers of black Africans, native tribesmen, and immigrants from other parts of Europe and Asia and South and Middle America also inhabited the territory of the United States. Only during the course of the twentieth century have these other groups insisted that they too are fully "Americans," rejecting the inferior position that the dominant Anglo-derived majority had placed them in.

When the Americans created their own nation in the violence of a revolution during the 1770s and 1780s, they took on a political identity and became nationalistic in ways that reflected the growth of nationalism in the European heartland. Like various groups of Europeans who created modern nations, and like many other groups around the world who gained their political independence as empires collapsed, Americans *extended* their political identity during the nineteenth and twentieth centuries to cover the other aspects of their lives: their culture, their economy, their society. They came to believe that all dimensions of the lives of Americans were encased within the same boundaries that defined their political life. Americans routinely began to imagine, as have other national political groups, that theirs was a distinctive national economy, culture, and society, different from those of all others.

That this was not in fact the case, that the reality of human life has been far more complicated and messy, did not deter Americans and many other national political groups from making such assertions. The power of nationalism became so strong by the late nineteenth century that one's political identity came to override the many other forms of identity that all individuals have had. It is as if the "sovereignty"—the ultimate political authority—that modern nations have claimed over their citizens' lives was interpreted by those citizens to mean that one's political identity was superior to all other forms of identity, greater in importance than one's gender, sexuality, age, occupation, class, race, ethnicity, language, and religion. As national governments attained domination during the seventeenth, eighteenth, and nineteenth centuries over more localized and older forms of association—such as labor guilds, churches parishes, feudal manors, and municipal corporations—they worked to bind their citizenries to their nations, making that linkage the supreme form of allegiance and loyalty.

But, if life in the United States is viewed from a global perspective, it can be shown that the efforts either to perceive all of life as being distinctively national or to actively organize all of life along national political lines failed even in the period during which the nation-state was at its most powerful. From the global perspective, one sees patterns of human life that are greater than or smaller than, but usually different from, the American nation, or any other nation.

In some respects, life in America deeply reflected British colonial origins as well as an ongoing Anglo-American connection, both based upon a common language and political experience. Americans communicated in English, developed a political system profoundly influenced by a nearly two-century-long colonial past, greatly benefited from the earlier English experience with industrialization as well as from English investment during America's own industrialization, and continued on a continental scale the global expansionist tendencies of their British imperial masters. From the beginning, Americans have communicated in English and this transatlantic linguistic connection has created an easy, ongoing awareness of what is occurring in each nation, making possible close cooperation between English and American organizations of various kinds, everything from reform movements to shared military commands.

In other respects, Americans shared a transhemispheric commonality with those of other colonial backgrounds in the Americas: a common experience with a native population that was displaced and dominated and with a forced migrant African population that was enslaved, but also a common experience in revolution and republicanism. Only in the Americas did the Europeans colonize entire continents. Only in the Americas were there large, subsequent independence movements that led to a massive loss of colonies in the midst of a much longer era of European imperialism. And, only in the Americas did republican government become instituted practically everywhere in an entire hemisphere. The English colonies and, later, the United States, extended beyond the North American temperate zone, into a semitropical area extending to the Gulf of Mexico. Alone among the white settler groups who moved beyond Europe, the Americans established a polity that embraced a more tropical part of the world, just as the Russians in Siberia spread into an arctic zone. As a result of settling to the south, Americans shared with the white Iberian elites of South and Middle America a plantation-dominated, staple crop economy and a hierarchical social structure that originated in the Mediterranean and was replicated throughout the tropical colonial American world. The American South became a transitional zone—tropical in its economic and social makeup; temperate in its political structures.

In still other respects, Americans were part of a larger world of white settler societies along the frontier of imperialistic Europe, sharing certain aspects of life with Siberians, Canadians, Australians, New Zealanders, South Africans, Argentinians, and Brazilians. European migrants in all these areas dominated native populations, expanded along land frontiers, and tried in various ways to replicate the version of European society that they had left behind. Americans, in common with other white settler societies, migrated to, settled on, and then developed the land they claimed in temperate zones similar to that of the European homeland, confronting with a white racist outlook native populations who were in various ways subdued and incorporated, creating multiracial societies through their invasions of the natives' lands long before the European heartland itself became multiracial through the in-migrations of former nonwhite colonial populations.

But above all else, Americans life reflected its European origins. America was on the frontier of Europe and shared many of the most important features of that expansionist civilization as it came to dominate the world in the centuries after 1500. Like Europeans, Americans have been mainly Christians, have became capitalistic, have undergone industrialization, have developed a large middle class, have produced first a representative and then a democratic political system, and, with cultural maturity, have exhibited a fondness for scientific inquiry, philosophical speculation, artistic innovation, and educational variety and experimentation.

Life in America was also divided into many regionalized and localized variations, so that there were rarely truly national forms of anything. Folklore and all of the major arts and entertainments were rife with regional variety. Economic activity was never simply national in scale and scope, exhibiting as it did many local, regional, and international territorial settings. Even the social class structure contained significant regional variations, with a planter elite and a racial slave caste confined to the pre–Civil War South.

However, the Americans did create some significant, distinctively national characteristics—at least for a while. Theirs was the first multiethnic, multiracial population in a modern nation. They were not the originators of republicanism, but theirs was the first great modern republic, and, even more importantly, it was a republic that was the first in the world to become democratized, at first (in the 1830s and 1840s) for white men, then (in the 1910s) for white women, then (in the late 1920s) for native men and women, and finally (in the 1960s) for black men and women. The earliest form of political democracy—that for white men—led in turn to the emergence of a significant new view of what constitutes a proper society: egalitarianism, the belief that society should be based upon merit, upon individual capacities and not on inherited status. Though initially applied only to white men, this belief has been progressively applied to other groups of adults, in harmony with the sporadic enlargement of the political community. Americans also developed techniques for mass production and pioneered in the organization and management of very large-scale industrial enterprise. They also occasionally created new types of art and developed a distinctive mode of thinking (pragmatism).

But, though peculiarly "American," all of these features can also be seen as variants of European and, more broadly, Western developments and are illuminated if examined in these broader perspectives. Certainly, they did not long remain uniquely American, as they became absorbed into a larger civilization.

Historians have been handmaidens of nationalism, helping their fellow citizens to see their collective past through a nationalistic prism, training them to equate their history with their nation and to feel that their political identity is of more importance than the other forms of identity that everyone has. It is now time for historians to be pied pipers of globalism, to lead those who look to them to interpret the past, away from the distortions of history organized around political identities, toward a new kind of historical understanding based upon a global perspective and focused upon humanity itself.

Just as astronauts see from space, not uniformity, but a swirling, overlayered, many-hued pattern across the face of the earth's surface, so too should historians point out, from earth but also from a global perspective, that human life has exhibited and continues to exhibit, not global uniformity, but complicated, varied patterns that go far beyond the political demarcations that mark the world's geography.

Some things have recently become truly global in the sense that they can appear instantly anywhere in the world, such as the movement of capital and various forms of telecommunication. Other things have become global in their universality: the products or services of certain multinational corporations or the operations of certain international organizations, such as the United Nations or the World Bank or the International Monetary Fund or the World Trade Organization. But, globalism is very uneven in its development. There is little evidence that labor unions are going to unite in significant ways beyond the national to the global level, and even multinational corporations have their headquarters in particular nations and often operate only in selected areas of the globe. Most social organizations continue to organize within nations, with weak or nonexistent worldwide offices. National governments still exercise most political authority, and the United Nations has very little power to affect the world's population directly. Nations still send delegations to the United Nations and each delegation has one vote, regardless of its nation's territorial or demographic size (much as the American states did during the 1780s). Adherents of particular religious beliefs are much intermingled with ongoing immigration, but there is little evidence that the established religious traditions are being transmogrified into one grand religious faith, any more than the world's races and ethnic groups, for all the migrating and intermingling of the modern world, are soon to become one grand racial or ethnic amalgam. And if the political authority of nations is being undermined from above and from below, this is likely to be a long and messy process, with the increasing presence of global and local and regional polities *coexisting* with national ones.

What a global perspective reveals, in short, is a crisscross, patch-quilt pattern, produced by human interrelationships of many kinds. In every aspect of human life—the political, the economic, the social, and the cultural—the larger the perspective taken, the broader the pattern, and the more numerous the variations around the world; the smaller the perspective, the narrower the pattern, and the fewer the variations. Whether the focus be broad or narrow, what these patterns reveal is that human life has been organized in an astonishing variety of ways and is profoundly distorted when it is examined only within political contexts.

As keepers of the past of the last political superpower on earth, American historians have a magnificent opportunity to relinquish the deeply held, but deeply distorting linkage of history with past politics by opening up the most written about of all the historical fields of study—American history—to the more complicated, but much more insightful global perspective. Then those with an "American" identity will be able to view their past as it should be viewed, as an integral part of our common human past.

Bibliographical Essay

THE NATIONAL PERSPECTIVE

The synthesis, analysis, and interpretation of life in America contained in this book are based to a considerable extent upon scholarship written from a solely U.S. perspective, scholarship that has appeared in great quantity since the 1960s. Over the years, I have tried continuously to assess that scholarship and, since the mid-1980s, have also prepared several drafts of an overall reinterpretation of U.S. history, a project that turned by the mid-1990s into this book. Like others who write synthetic works, it is often difficult for me to trace the genesis of various assertions and conclusions. However, I have always tried to be factually and interpretively accurate when drawing on the findings of the many historians whose writings my synthesis depends upon. Rather than include a very long bibliography of studies that have, over the years, in any way influenced my ongoing efforts to create an interpretative synthesis, what follows is a brief, highly selective list of those studies that I found to be noteworthy while working on the final drafts for this book.

In political history from the American perspective, Gordon Wood's *The Radicalism of the American Revolution* (New York: Knopf, 1991) considerably overstates the radicalism of the Revolution, which is examined without reference to any larger context. Wood himself admits that political democracy came as a result of the efforts of a later generation: republicanism was significantly different from democracy. The most insightful study on the emergence of the modern American state from a wholly American perspective is, I believe, Stephen Skowronek, *Building a New American State: The Expansion of National Administrative Capabilities, 1877–1920* (Cambridge, England: Cambridge University Press, 1982).

On economic history within America, I have found the work of Douglas North and Stuart Bruchey to be quite impressive, most recently Bruchey's *The Wealth of a Nation: An Economic History of the American People* (New York: Harper & Row, 1989).

As for American society viewed from an entirely American perspective, I found Stuart

Blumin, *The Emergence of the Middle Class: Social Experience in the American City* (Cambridge, England: Cambridge University Press, 1989) to contain useful definitions of class.

On immigration, John Bodnar, *The Transplanted: A History of Immigrants in Urban America* (Bloomington: Indiana University Press, 1985) was also quite useful.

On much-needed surveys of cultural history from an American perspective (usually absent from surveys of American history), I found Robert M. Crunden, *A Brief History of American Culture* (New York: Paragon House, 1994) to be useful, but Crunden is idiosyncratic in what he covers. The "cultural life" volumes in Harper & Row's New American Nation series by Louis B. Wright and Russell B. Nye, along with the same publisher's Everyday Life in America series (with Richard Balkin as general editor) all contain pertinent information on various aspects of American society and culture. Similarly, James Cullen, *The Art of Democracy: A Concise History of Popular Culture in the United States* (New York: Monthly Review Press, 1996) and M. Thomas Inge, *Concise Histories of American Popular Culture* (Westport, Conn.: Greenwood Press, 1982) contain a great deal of usable information on their particular subject. Especially good on education within an American perspective is Lawrence Cremin, *American Education* (New York: Harper & Row, 1970–1988, 3 vols.). Recent surveys of their respective subjects are: Lewis Perry, *Intellectual Life in America: A History* (Chicago: University of Chicago Press, 1984); George Marsden, *Religion and American Culture* (New York: Harcourt Brace Jovanovich, 1990); and Jon Butler, *Awash in a Sea of Faith; Christianizing the American People* (Cambridge, Mass.: Harvard University Press, 1990).

From a geographical perspective, D. W. Meinig, *The Shaping of America: A Geographical Perspective of 500 Years of History* (New Haven: Yale University Press, 1986–, 3 vols.) is useful. On the environment from an American perspective, I found Roderick Nash, *Wilderness and the American Mind* (New Haven, Conn.: Yale University Press, 1982, 3d ed.) to be indispensable. Equally impressive was Donald Worster, *The Wealth of Nature: Environmental History and the Ecological Imagination* (essays) (New York: Oxford University Press, 1993). William Cronon's *Changes in the Land: Colonists and the Ecology of New England* (New York: Norton, 1983) is superb, but his edited collection of essays based upon papers delivered at a University of California's Humanities Research Institute (Irvine campus) conference seemed too narrowly focused to be of much use: *Uncommon Ground: Toward Reinventing Nature* (New York: Norton, 1995).

Studies of American nationalism have been written without awareness of larger patterns, from Hans Kohn, *American Nationalism: An Interpretive Essay* (New York: Macmillan, 1957), to Wilbur Zelinsky, *Nation into State: Foundations of American Nationalism* (Chapel Hill: University of North Carolina Press, 1988) and John Bodnar, *Remaking America: Public Memory, Commemoration, and Patriotism in the Twentieth Century* (Princeton, N.J.: Princeton University Press, 1992) and David Waldstreicher, *In the Midst of Perpetual Fetes: The Making of American Nationalism* (Chapel Hill: University of North Carolina Press, 1997).

On American communities, Daniel J. Boorstin, *The Americans* (New York: Random House, 1958–1973, 3 vols.) remains indispensable. David Hackett Fischer, *Albion's Seed: Four British Folkways in America* (New York: Oxford University Press, 1989) probes colonial America from a transatlantic regional perspective, but subsequent volumes of a promised multivolume regional history have not appeared.

TRANSNATIONAL PERSPECTIVES

This part of the bibliographical essay refers only to those academic writings organized from a transnational perspective that stood out, that particularly influenced me as I developed this study. I examined far more material than appears here, but, as is always the case, only a portion of it was especially useful or germane:

The World

From the global perspective, the starting point is, of course, *world histories*, by which I mean, not texts, but interpretations. The two that I am most familiar with (and that are probably the best known among those written in English) are William H. McNeill's *The Rise of the West: A History of the Human Community* (Chicago: University of Chicago Press, 1963) and J. M. Roberts, *History of the World* (New York: Oxford University Press, 1976). The limitation of world histories such as these is that they are skewed toward political and economic history, ignore many aspects of social history, and, while usually quite full on high culture, don't cover popular culture.

I found the work of *cultural geographers* to be very useful in their divisions of human society into traditional, tribal, and modern, a categorization that I have broadened from their economic framework into a general one that takes account of all human activity. Especially good is Jan O. M. Broek and John M. Webb, *A Geography of Mankind* (New York: McGraw-Hill, 1968). Also useful is George F. Carter, *Man and the Land: A Cultural Geography* (New York: Holt, Rinehart & Winston, 1964).

Political scientists and *political historians* have also examined the state in a global context. The most useful of their efforts for me is the collection edited by John A. Hall, *States in History* (New York; B. Blackwell, 1986). Less so is Ali Kozancigil, editor, *The State in Global Perspective* (Paris: UNESCO, 1986) The best comparative government survey I found to be Jean Blondell, *Comparative Government: An Introduction* (New York: Philip Allen, 1990). The communist, socialist, and utopian movements are surveyed in Warren Lerner, *A History of Socialism and Communism in Modern Times* (Englewood Cliffs, N.J. Prentice-Hall, 1982) and Harry Wellington Laidler, *Socio-Economic Movements: An Historical and Comparative Survey of Socialism, Communism, Cooperation, Utopianism, and Other Systems of Reform and Reconstruction* (New York: Thomas Y. Crowell, 1968). On the process of state making from an American, but also from a larger, mainly European context, I found J. Rogers Hollingsworth, editor, *Nation and State Building in America: Comparative Historical Perspectives* (Boston: Little, Brown, 1971) a useful compendium of essays.

Economists and *economic historians* have also written from a global perspective. It is rare that they have taken the whole of the world's economy as their subject, as Iain Wallace has in his *The Global Economic System* (Boston: Unwin Hyman, 1990). Rare too are efforts to provide an overall theory for economic history as John Hicks has is his *A Theory of Economic History* (New York: Oxford University Press, 1969). Far more typical of these scholars has been their focus on the spread of industrialization or capitalism. Though there is Michel Beaud's broad-gauged *A History of Capitalism, 1500–1980* (New York: Monthly Review Press, 1983), among those who have studied the history of capitalism, the most impressive efforts have been those of Fernand Braudel,

Civilization and Capitalism, 15th–18th Centuries (New York: Harper & Row, 1981–1984, 3 vols.) and Immanuel Wallerstein, *The Modern World-System* (New York: Academic Press, 1974–1988, 3 vols.). To read Braudel is to read a master historian, one who carefully builds up a multitextured picture of a hugely important subject, but stops as commercial capitalism expands to become industrial capitalism as well. Wallerstein extends his coverage into the early industrial era. His work is a masterly synthesis of the existing scholarship and can be profitably read even if his theorizing about "world systems" is discounted as being overly schematic. Various sociologists, economists, and historians have focused on industrialization in particular. An informative introduction appears in William A. Faunce and William H. Form, editors, *Comparative Perspectives on Industrial Society* (Boston: Little, Brown, 1969). Tom Kemp's *Historical Patterns of Industrialization* (Harlow, Essex, England: Longman, 1978) is a good assessment. Also useful are Barry A. Turner, *Industrialization* (Harlow, Essex, England: Longman, 1975), and Peter Kreidte, Hans, Medick, and Jurgen Schlumbohm, *Industrialization before Industrialization: Rural Industry in the Genesis of Capitalism* (Cambridge, England: Cambridge University Press, 1981, English translation). With respect to labor, Marcel van der Linden, editor, *The Formation of Labour Movements. 1870–1914: An International Perspective* (Leiden, Netherlands: E. J. Brill, 1990) is disappointing in that the introduction does not attempt to find global patterns for all of the national movements written about by particular contributors. The Great Depression is treated in an international perspective by John Garraty in his *The Great Depression* (New York: Harcourt Brace, 1986), but Garraty confines himself to Europe and the United States and ignores other parts of the world.

Sociologists have also written on society from a global perspective, but their generalizing isn't based upon a deep involvement in the actual historical development of human society. But, their theorizing is of some utility. Those whose writings I found useful are Roland Mousnier, *Social Hierarchies: 1450 to the Present* (London: Croom Helm, 1973); William and Arline McCord, *Power and Equity: An Introduction to Social Stratification* (New York: Praeger, 1977); Malcolm Hamilton and Maria Hirszowicz, *Class and Inequity in Pre-Industrial, Capitalist, and Communist Societies* (New York: St. Martin's Press, 1987); and Robert Erikson and John H. Goldthorpe, *The Constant Flux: A Study in Class Mobility in Industrial Societies* (Oxford: Oxford University Press, 1992). On more particular aspects of social structure, Jonathan Powis' *Aristocracy* (New York: B. Blackwell, 1984) was also of use. But, there are many other aspects of the historical development of human society that have not been studied from a global perspective.

Similarly, *cultural historians* or scholars of any kind (in the arts disciplines) have rarely studied culture in any of its many dimensions from a global perspective. There is much scholarship on the theory and practice of culture in the present time, especially popular culture, but I have found nothing that deals with the historical development of culture in a global context.

An *American sociologist*, Seymour Martin Lipset, has also tried to find what is distinctively American about American life, and, in his attempt, places far too much emphasis on purportedly unchanging "American" values—equality and achievement—as the explanation for American exceptionalism (in *The First New Nation: The United States in Historical and Comparative Perspective* [New York: Basic Books, 1963]). *American historians* themselves have occasionally attempted to examine American history in wider contexts, though such efforts are notable for their rarity. C. Vann Woodward, editor, *The Comparative Approach to American History* (New York: Basic Books, 1968) is a pioneering effort to set American developments in a global context. All of the authors Woodward chose to present essays, originally created for the Voice of America, do so (except John Morton Blum), but what is apparent is how little they knew about that global context in the 1960s and how skewed their subjects for comparison are—a lot of attention is given to political and economic life, whereas there is only a very limited focus on social life and nothing at all on cultural life. The essays contain some useful information, however. Byron Shafer, editor, *Is America Different?: A New Look at American Exceptionalism* (Oxford: Clarendon Press, 1991) is a collection of Oxford conference papers on more varied aspects of American life than is the case in the Woodward volume, papers that are focused on the extent to which there have in fact been American distinctions. None of the authors makes a compelling case for American exceptionalism, including Shafer himself, who continues Lipset's practice of finding fundamental and unchanging American values (individualism, a market orientation, democracy, and populism) that he claims are so basic that they create an American pattern in every dimension of human life.

* * *

Because there are so many aspects of human life that have not been studied in depth from a global perspective, I examined many general histories of various parts of the world: Asia, Europe, Africa, South and Middle America—so that I could at least compare the pattern of life in what became the United States to that of different continents. But these histories mirror those that have been written from a global perspective in that there is a lot on political and economic history, far less on social history, and virtually nothing on cultural history.

Europe

William H. McNeill's *The Shape of European History* (New York: Oxford University Press, 1974) is a good interpretive overview of the subject. Norman Davies' *Europe: A History* (New York: Oxford University Press, 1996) is a popular, chronological narrative with lots of detail, but also with some passages that analyze aspects of European life in an insightful, synoptic way. There is also Shepard Clough, *European History in a World Perspective* (Lexington, Mass.: D.C. Heath, 1975). On more particular aspects of European history, I found the following to be quite useful. In political history: Charles Tilly, editor, *The Formation of National States in Western Europe* (Princeton: Princeton University Press, 1975) and Orlando Patterson, *Freedom in the Making of Western Culture* (New York: Basic Books, 1991). Tilly is a masterful sociologist-historian, and his introduction is an insightful summation of what is known about the whole process of state making in the western half of Europe. In economic history: Douglas North and Robert P. Thomas, *The Rise of the Western World: A New Economic History* (Cambridge, England: Cambridge University Press, 1973) and Shepherd Clough and Charles W. Cole, *Economic History of Europe* (Lexington, Mass.: D.C. Heath, 1966). On intellectual history: Roland N. Stromberg, *An Intellectual History of Modern Europe* (Englewood Cliffs, N.J.: Prentice-Hall, 1975). On cultural history: Peter Burke, *Popular Culture in Early Modern Europe* (London: Maurice Temple Smith, 1978). Burke's is a rare, and stimulating, investigation of cultural life across a civilization. There are also series on the society and culture of particular nations within Europe, especially—and most relevant for my purpose—on Britain. Penguin's *Social History of Britain* (J. H. Plumb, general editor) and Edward Arnold's *Social History of Britain* are both useful multivolume surveys. On Russia, a special part of Europe (and Asia), there are Nicholas Riasinovsky, *A History of Russia* (New York: Oxford University Press, 1969) and James Billington, *The Icon and the Axe: An Interpretive History of Russian Culture* (New York: Knopf, 1966).

Asia

Two general histories of Asia that I found quite useful are Rhoads Murphey, *A History of Asia* (New York: HarperCollins, 1992) and Colin E. Tweddell and Linda Kimball, *Introduction to the Peoples and Cultures of Asia* (Englewood Cliffs, N.J.: Prentice-Hall, 1985). Also: Woodbridge Bingham, Hilary Conroy, and Frank Ikle, *A History of Asia* (Boston: Allyn & Bacon, 1974, 2 vols.). On southwestern Asia (the Middle East), Bernard Lewis' studies were good summations: *The Arabs in History* (London: Hutchinson University Library, 1964) and *The Middle East: A Brief History* (New York: Scribner's, 1995). On the Australian subcontinent, I found both Keith Sinclair, *A History of New Zealand* (London: Penguin, 1959) and O. H. K. Spate, *Australia* (New York: Praeger, 1968) to be very useful.

Africa

Paul Bohannan and Philip Curtin, *Africa and Africans* (New York: Natural History Press, 1964) is a great book, written by masters of their field—detailed, yet interpretive, written with verve for general readers as well as for students of history, asking good questions and providing complexity, but also the patterns behind the complexity. John N. Paden and Edward W. Soja have edited a superbly informative series of essays by various authors on various aspects of African life and history in *The African Experience* (Evanston, Ill.: Northwestern University Press, 1970). A later and also far-ranging collection of essays with a more cultural focus is Molefi Asante and Kariamu Welsh, editors, *African Culture: The Rhythms of Unity* (Westport, Conn.: Greenwood Press, 1985). Also useful is Robert W. July, *Pre-Colonial Africa: An Economic and Social History* (New York: Scribner's, 1975).

Middle and South America

There is a notable richness of general academic studies focused on this part of the Americas. Good overall interpretations are Benjamin Keen and Mark Wasserman, *A Short History of Latin America* (Boston: Houghton Mifflin, 1984), Frank Tannenbaum, *Ten Keys to Latin America* (New York: Knopf, 1964), and Eric Wolf and Edward Hansen, *The Human Condition in Latin America* (New York: Oxford University Press, 1972). On economic history: Arthur Morris, *Latin America: Economic Development and Regional Differentiation* (London: Hutchinson, 1981) and Victor Bulmer-Thomas, *The Economic History of Latin America Since Independence* (Cambridge, England: Cambridge University Press, 1994). On geographical history: Peter R. Odell and David A. Preston, *Economies and Societies in Latin America: A Geographical Interpretation* (New York: Wiley, 1973). On sociocultural history: Julius Rivera, *Latin America: A Sociocultural Interpre-*

tation (New York: Irvington Publishers, 1978, revised edition) and Mariano Picon-Salas, *A Cultural History of Spanish America (From the Conquest to Independence)* (Berkeley: University of California Press, 1965 edition). On the West Indies: Philip Sherlock, *West Indian Nations: A New History* (New York: St. Martin's Press, 1973).

White Settler Societies

There is a large and growing literature on the white settler societies that developed on the frontiers or around the fringes of an expanding European civilization. The most useful writings involved comparisons of the United States, Canada, South Africa, Australia, New Zealand, southern Brazil, and northern Argentina in some sort of combination. The transplanted Europeans and their progeny are typically seen as inhabiting a frontier society (relative to the European homeland).

Walter Prescott Webb's *The Great Frontier* (Boston: Houghton Mifflin, 1952) was an early attempt to place the United States in a greater context of frontier societies. Louis Hartz (and other authors), *The Founding of New Societies* (New York: Harcourt, Brace & World, 1964), is the first of a number of multiauthored investigations of these white settler societies. Hartz and his colleagues present a static and overly simplistic view of the United States, Canada, South Africa, and Australia. Each group of settlers is purported to have taken over from a politically much more complex Europe a portion of Europe's political culture, a portion that was supposed to have confined each group of those settlers to a much narrower political life than was the case in Europe. For a richer, more varied examination: George Wolfskill and Stanley Palmer, editors, *Essays on Frontiers in World History* (College Station: Texas A&M University Press, 1983—The Walter Prescott Webb Lectures on Comparative World Frontiers). On the migrations that produced these white settler societies: Donald R. Taft and Richard Robbins, *International Migrations: The Immigrant in the Modern World* (New York: Ronald Press, 1955) and especially Stephen Castles and Mark J. Miller, *The Age of Migration: International Population Movements in the Modern World* (London: Macmillan, 1993). Walter Nugent's *Crossings: The Great Transatlantic Migrations, 1870–1914* (Bloomington: Indiana University Press, 1992) is a more in-depth treatment of these migrations, but is restricted to Europe and the Americas and excludes Australia/New Zealand and South Africa. Similarly, Michael Kraus, *The Atlantic Civilization: Eighteenth Century Origins* (American Historical Association, 1949) argues that there was a transatlantic civilization and ignores the other, non-Atlantic white settler societies. But, this has been a minority view, and much of the relevant literature takes a broader, dual-transoceanic perspective. On the biological impact of European expansion: Alfred Crosby, *Ecological Imperialism: The Biological Expansion of Europe, 900–1900* (Cambridge, England: Cambridge University Press, 1986). On more direct comparisons involving the United States and other white settler societies: Jorge Manach, *Frontiers in the Americas: A Global Perspective* (New York: Columbia Teacher's College, 1975), H. C. Allen, *Bush and Backwoods: A Comparison of the Frontier in Australia and the United States* (East Lansing: Michigan State University Press, 1959), and Howard Lamar and Leonard Thompson, editors, *The Frontier in History: North America and Southern Africa Compared* (New Haven, Conn.: Yale University Press, 1981). On comparisons not involving the United States, but that are useful as a basis for making further comparisons that do involve the United States: Carl E. Solberg, *The Prairies and the Pampas: Agrarian Policy in Canada and Argentina, 1880–1930*

(Palo Alto, Calif.: Stanford University Press, 1987), and Jeremy Adelman, *Frontier Development: Land, Labour, and Capital on the Wheatlands of Argentina and Canada, 1890–1914* (Oxford: Clarenden Press, 1994). And, on the only land frontier along the pathways of European expansion: Benson Bobrick, *East of the Sun: The Epic Conquest and Tragic History of Siberia* (New York: Poseidon Press, 1992), and W. Bruce Lincoln, *The Conquest of a Continent: Siberia and the Russians* (New York: Random House, 1994).

The Anglo-American Connection

There is a growing body of literature that compares the United States and Britain, tracing the influences that Britons and Americans had on each other, delineating the ways the original imperial connection influenced American life thereafter, and noting the gradual shift from a British to an American domination.

The pioneering general treatment of the subject is Frank Thistlethwaite, *America and the Atlantic Community: Anglo-American Aspects, 1790–1850* (New York: Harper & Row, 1963). A wider and more detailed study with various authors is based upon the Open University course in Comparative History: Britain and the United States: David Englander, editor, *Britain and America: Studies in Comparative History, 1760–1970* (New Haven, Conn.: Yale University Press, 1997). There are also studies that compare specific aspects of life among the two populations. On religion: Richard Cardwardine, *Transatlantic Revivalism: Popular Evangelism in Britain and America, 1790–1865* (Westport, Conn.: Greenwood Press, 1978). On reform: Betty Fladeland, *Men and Brothers: Anglo-American Antislavery Cooperation* (Urbana: University of Illinois Press, 1972) and Christine Bolt, *The Women's Movements in the United States and Britain from the 1790's to the 1920's* (Amherst: University of Massachusetts Press, 1993). On labor movements: Neville Kirk, *Labour and Society in Britain and the USA* (Aldershot, England: Scolar Press, 1994, 2 vols.) and Jeffrey Haydu, *Between Craft and Class: Skilled Workers and Factory Politics in the United States and Britain, 1896–1922* (Berkeley: University of California Press, 1988). On political sovereignty: Edmund S. Morgan, *Inventing the People: The Rise of Popular Sovereignty in England and America* (New York: Norton, 1988). On imperialism: Tony Smith, *The Pattern of Imperialism: The United States, Great Britain, and the Late Industrializing World Since 1815* (Cambridge, England: Cambridge University Press, 1981).

Particular Subjects in a Transnational Perspective

Historians have begun to deal with particular subjects in contexts that go well beyond national polities.

Revolution

Charles Tilly, editor, *European Revolutions, 1492–1992* (Oxford: Blackwell, 1993). This study contains a superb introduction by Tilly.

Patrice Higonnet, *Sister Republics: Origins of French and American Republicanism* (Cambridge, Mass.: Harvard University Press, 1988).

Lester D. Langley, *The Americas in the Age of Revolution, 1750–1850* (New Haven, Conn.: Yale University Press, 1996). The usefulness of this study is much diminished by its author's failure to find any larger patterns in the revolutionary activity that occurred in the Americas during these years. His findings seem buried in excessive detail.

Nationalism

There has been a rich translational scholarly literature on nationalism, among the most useful are: Boyd Shafer, *Nationalism: Myth and Reality* (New York: Harcourt, Brace & World, 1955) and *Faces of Nationalism* (New York: Harcourt, Brace & World, 1972); Benedict Anderson, *Imagined Communities: Reflections on the Origins and Spread of Nationalism* (London: Verso, 1983); Eric Hobsbawm, *Nations and Nationalism since 1780: Programme, Myth, Reality* (Cambridge, England: Cambridge University Press, 1990); and Liah Greenfield, *Nationalism: Five Roads to Modernity* (Cambridge, Mass.: Harvard University Press, 1992).

Government Policy

Ann Schola Orloff, *The Politics of Pensions: A Comparative Analysis of Britain, Canada, and the United States, 1880–1940* (Madison: University of Wisconsin Press, 1993).

Frank Dobbin, *Forging Industrial Policy: The United States, Britain, and France in the Railway Age* (Cambridge, England: Cambridge University Press, 1995). A fine study, with an important thesis.

Daniel Levine, *Poverty and Society: The Growth of the American Welfare State in International Comparison* (New Brunswick, N.J.: Rutgers University Press, 1988). The nations compared are Britain, Germany, Denmark, and the United States.

Family Life

Rosemary O'Day, *The Family and Family Relationships, 1500–1900, in England, France, and the United States of America* (London: Macmillan, 1994). The author concentrates to good effect on the affective aspects of family life, on its texture, rather than on its structure, composition, and size.

Slavery and Race

David Brion Davis, *The Problem of Slavery in Western Culture* (Ithaca, N.Y.: Cornell University Press, 1966).

Orlando Patterson, *Slavery and Social Death: A Comparative Study* (Cambridge, Mass.: Harvard University Press, 1982).

Robert W. Fogel, *Without Consent or Contract: The Rise and Fall of American Slavery* (New York: Norton, 1989). Though this book purports to be a study of American slavery, Fogel actually constructs his quite impressive study within a much wider context.

Peter Kolchin, *Unfree Labor: American Slavery and Russian Serfdom* (Cambridge, Mass.: Harvard University Press, 1987). An illuminating comparison.

Carl Degler, *Neither Black nor White: Slavery and Race Relations in Brazil and the United States* (New York: Macmillan, 1971).

George Frederickson, *White Supremacy: A Comparative Study in American and South African History* (New York: Oxford University Press, 1981).

Reform

James T. Kloppenberg, *Uncertain Victory: Social Democracy and Progressivism in European and American Thought* (New York: Oxford University Press, 1986). This was for me a disappointing study in its excessive focus on developments in philosophical thought that affected political reform. For my purposes the study is imbalanced: too much on philosophy and not enough on a direct comparison of the various progressive movements themselves. One of the most impressive transnational studies has been Daniel T. Rodgers, *Atlantic Crossings: Social Politics in a Progressive Age* (Cambridge, Mass.: Harvard University Press, 1998), which uncovers a multifaceted transatlantic progressive connection, through which ideas for reform were shared by like-minded advocates in many parts of the westernized world, from the 1880s to the 1940s.

The Woman's Movement

Richard J. Evans, *The Feminists: Women's Emancipation Movements in Europe, America, and Australia* (New York: Barnes & Noble, 1977). A very impressive analytical study, with deep understanding of overall patterns.

Donald Meyer, *Sex and Power: The Rise of Women in America, Russia, Sweden, and Italy* (Middleton, Conn.: Wesleyan University Press, 1987). Also impressive in its analytical insights, but those insights have to be ferreted out of a lot of descriptive writing.

Jane Rendall, *The Origins of Modern Feminism: Women in Britain, France, and the United States, 1780–1860* (London: Macmillan, 1985).

Cities

Stanley D. Bruun and Jack Williams, *Cities of the World: World Regional Urban Development* (New York: HarperCollins, 1993, 2d ed.). A fine analysis of global regional variations.

Index

About the Author

DAVID J. RUSSO is Professor of History at McMaster University in Hamilton, Ontario. Since the early 1970s he has tried to reconceptualize American history from an outsider's perspective. To this end has written *Keeper of Our Past: Local Historical Writing in the United States, 1820s to 1930s* (Greenwood, 1988) and *Clio Confused: Troubling Aspects of Historical Study from the Perspective of U.S. History* (Greenwood, 1995).

LaVergne, TN USA
03 March 2010
174740LV00003B/76/P
9 780275 968960